Prosody, Phonology and Phonetics

The series will publish studies in the general area of Speech Prosody with a particular (but non-exclusive) focus on the importance of phonetics and phonology in this field. The topic of speech prosody is today a far larger area of research than is often realised. The number of papers on the topic presented at large international conferences such as Interspeech and ICPhS is considerable and regularly increasing. The proposed book series would be the natural place to publish extended versions of papers presented at the Speech Prosody Conferences, in particular the papers presented in Special Sessions at the conference. This could potentially involve the publication of 3 or 4 volumes every two years ensuring a stable future for the book series. If such publications are produced fairly rapidly, they will in turn provide a strong incentive for the organisation of other special sessions at future Speech Prosody conferences.

More information about this series at http://www.springer.com/series/11951

Paula Orzechowska

Complexity in Polish Phonotactics

On Features, Weights, Rankings and Preferences

Springer

Paula Orzechowska
Collegium Heliodori Święcicki
Adam Mickiewicz University
Poznań, Poland

ISSN 2197-8700 ISSN 2197-8719 (electronic)
Prosody, Phonology and Phonetics
ISBN 978-981-13-7298-8 ISBN 978-981-13-7299-5 (eBook)
https://doi.org/10.1007/978-981-13-7299-5

Library of Congress Control Number: 2019935482

This Springer imprint is published by the registered company Springer Nature Singapore Pte Ltd.
The registered company address is: 152 Beach Road, #21-01/04 Gateway East, Singapore 189721, Singapore

Rodzicom

Preface

Truth is ever to be found in simplicity,
and not in the multiplicity
and confusion of things
(Sir Isaac Newton physicist, mathematician, astronomer, 1670–1680)

This thought of Sir Issac Newton accompanied him in his greatest discoveries in theoretical physics, optics and mathematics. Simple mechanisms underlie apparently complex phenomena, structures or even technologies. This idea has been explored across a wide range of disciplines. The design principles of systems in biology, the atomic theory in chemistry, the patterns of air density in the atmosphere or even the Kindle as an improvement upon a book—all are examples of underlying simplicity of things which at the first glance seem to defy comprehension. Also linguists have strived at simplicity by, among others, describing language with a set of ordered rules using the toolkit from mathematics and logic.

This line of thinking was introduced to me during the first years of my studies at the Faculty of English in Poznań (Adam Mickiewicz University, Poland). The study of the principles of Generative Phonology provided food for thought for my analytical brain, which—by the way—has never been particularly good at formulas but which has fancied the elegance of a logical and concise presentation of things. The first sentence of *The Sound Pattern of English* (henceforth SPE) held a promise: 'The goal of the descriptive study of a language is a construction of a grammar' (Chomsky and Halle 1968: 3). Although severe criticism has been articulated against abstractness and formal complexity in the generative tradition, the ideas of Noam Chomsky and Morris Halle (1968) cleared the way of my thinking about the English language. Much less so about my mother tongue.

As a late learner of English and other foreign languages, I could not help comparing the systems to Polish, and was even trained in doing so as part of university courses on English phonetics, phonology and syntax. The result of these considerations was the development of the idea that Polish grammar (in its broadest sense) is more complex than English, possibly richer in exceptions and less predictable than that of German, Portuguese and Latin (probably excluding the grapheme to phoneme correspondence). Particularly, the complexity at the level of the sound system attracted my attention.

Among a wide array of linguistic themes, my interests centred on the linear ordering of sounds, known as *phonotactics*. I soon realized that consonants, and their combinations (the so-called *consonant clusters*), have a great story to tell in Polish, and offer an excellent starting point for academic explorations. The idea came during a lecture of Katarzyna Dziubalska-Kołaczyk at the Faculty of English, who discussed syllable structure. If the absence of /t/ in Hawaiian delimits the set of possible syllables in the language, what an overwhelming effect must a full series of coronal affricates and fricatives have on the complexity of phonotactics in Polish? The Faculty of English provided all incentives and conditions to study phonotactics. Katarzyna's passion for phonology sparked my first steps in the field. Stimulating lectures, seminars and numerous discussions paved the way for taking up phonotactics as the theme of study in my doctoral dissertation and later academic work. At the graduate and postgraduate level, Katarzyna was my supervisor and advisor, who introduced me to the framework of Natural Linguistics. At that time, I opened up to a new perspective on the study of language and learned to think about phonological phenomena in functional terms. Our joint projects, talks and publications on phonotactics continue to inspire ideas, some of which have been captured in this book.

For years, I indulged in nurturing the conviction that I was a native speaker of a language whose phonology and phonetics 'inspire awe'. I proudly collected scientific evidence supporting the idea that clusters which I would freely produce on a daily basis were to be found in very few world languages, if any. More interestingly, they would serve as examples of tongue-twisters for foreigners. The specialist literature on the topic was also inspiring. Theoretical approaches to phonotactics aimed at explaining the 'enormous complexity of consonantal sequences' (Rochoń 2000: 1) and a 'formidable array' of 'odd-looking' (Cyran and Gussmann 1999: 219f.) and 'unusual phonotactic possibilities' (Rubach and Booij 1990: 454) in Polish. As regards sonority, clusters of all types found in Polish 'do not seem to follow this universal hierarchy' (Bethin 1992: 13). Unarguably, none of the quotes can be disputed. What remains unclear, however, is the very source of phonotactic complexity and its degree.

To take an obvious example, for over a century, phonological theory has studied phonotactics in relation to sonority, which has notoriously been proven as unable to cope with data coming from cluster-rich languages. Sonority relies on *a priori* premises about the universally favoured syllable structure and specifies conditions under which a sequence of consonants can be classified as good, well-formed or preferred. In consequence, the principle focuses on the classification of clusters (in particular, in terms of the manner of articulation categories), similarly to other phonotactic principles or models. It must be borne in mind that sonority was originally proposed for Greek and for Germanic languages, which permit (at best) up to several dozen consonant clusters at syllable or word edges. The applicability of the same well-formedness principle to phonological systems that proudly preserve hundreds of clusters becomes at least somewhat dubious.

The observation that different languages tend to be analysed by means of the same principle triggered further reflections. I realized that, first, the same measure of phonotactic well-formedness cannot be used equally successfully in the evaluation of such disproportionately diverse systems. Second, if the measure tested on a simple system is applied to a complex one, the ensuing classification of clusters does not necessarily reflect the degree of phonotactic complexity of the language, but possibly the inadequacy of the principle applied. Interestingly, these ideas have not been discussed much in the subject literature on Polish. Rather, linguists have been preoccupied with two themes of research. Some focused on demonstrating how severely Polish clusters violate the sonority principle. Another body of scholarship pursued theoretical analyses showing an expected, sonority-based profile of Polish syllables, similarly to a large bunch of phonotactically simpler languages.

The typological approach to phonotactics has set the stage for other observations, which eventually led to the writing of this book. The field of phonotactic typology is largely underdeveloped: it is difficult to pursue due to methodological inconsistencies and the absence of a uniform approach in data collection, description and analysis. Nevertheless, a handful of contributions on the topic provide ample evidence to put forward the following hypothesis: a reliable picture of phonotactic complexity can be provided only by a principle which reflects language-specific phonological properties. Driven by linguistic curiosity, I investigated such properties in consonant clusters in Slavic, Germanic and Berber languages that I had been working on. Ian Maddieson's systematic comparison of 486 languages published in the *World Atlas of Language Structures* suggests that Polish, Russian, Ukrainian, English, German and Tashlhiyt Berber have complex (i.e. long) onsets and codas. The classification into simple, average and complex syllables is insightful when differentiating CV and (C)(C)(C)V(C)(C)(C)(C) languages. However, among phonotactically complex systems, further hierarchies of complexity can be established.

My dictionary- and corpus-based investigation revealed obvious disproportionate differences in cluster inventories and cluster length between the aforementioned languages. Germanic languages feature 50–60 initial clusters, the longest of which are composed of three adjacent consonants (e.g. /spl/ in *split*, German /ʃtʁ/ in *Straße* 'street'). Polish features hundreds of initial clusters, some of which are composed of up to four consonants (e.g. /pstr/ in *pstrąg* 'trout'). In Tashlhiyt Berber, in turn, hundreds of vowelless words represented by one consonant (e.g. /f/ 'to give') or several consonants (e.g. /rkks/ 'to hide') can be found. This variation suggests that each language or language family selects different subsegmental characteristics as crucial building blocks of consonant clusters. As a consequence, phonotactic complexity in these systems must be defined in different ways and possibly by means of different well-formedness principles.

If a minority of the world's languages tolerate the (C)(C)(C)V(C)(C)(C)(C) structures, then a severe CV violation resulting in, for instance, CCCCV may be considered rare or even accidental. This argument, however, seems to be too far-fetched in the light of the data obtained from Polish. Hundreds of unusual and long clusters suggest that their presence is neither totally incidental nor very rare. Is it possible that Polish phonotactics is not as overwhelmingly complex as it has been claimed to be? There is a body of literature that advocates phonological unmarkedness of Polish clusters. Syllable structure in Polish has been demonstrated to be well-formed in terms of sonority in theoretical accounts by Christina Bethin, Edmund Gussmann, Jerzy Rubach, Marzena (Rochoń) Żygis and Edmund Cyran. With time, a battery of empirical analyses have provided growing evidence supporting the role of sonority also in the acquisition and online processing of Polish. The subject literature, however, has investigated phonetic and phonological well-formedness of Polish mainly in terms of the manner of articulation. What is the role of place and voicing features at the level of lexical statistics, perception and production of phonotactics?

Further reflections on phonotactics were sparked by Dafydd Gibbon. When I was a student at the Faculty of Linguistics and Literary Studies (Bielefeld University), Dafydd awoke my interest in mathematical models of computation. At that point of my training, I realized that formalism was particularly useful for the representation of complex systems such as Polish. Finite-state machines, rankings and hierarchies capture essential generalizations which have not been discussed in earlier analyses. With a growing emphasis placed on laboratory phonology, I understood that even the most elegant and simple generalizations are less meaningful when limited to constraints capturing phoneme adjacency. Therefore, aware of the paucity of empirical data on Polish phonotactics, I engaged in neurolinguistic methodology.

Richard Wiese and his research team at the Department of Germanic Linguistics (University of Marburg) inspired a new vein of study involving electroencephalography. Contrastive EEG experimentation demonstrated Polish speakers' lowered sensitivity to sonority compared to German speakers providing new insights into the psychological reality of the phonotactic principle in two typologically different languages. These observations, along with my previous work with Richard, finally shaped into a uniform phonotactic approach, which made it possible to answer some of my vexing questions. What is the role of subsegmental properties of consonants forming clusters? In what way are the place, manner and voicing features exploited in phonotactics? Which phonological features and their combinations constitute the *elementary particles* of Polish clusters? Like fermions and bosons in physics, phonological features form a backbone of phonotactics: they determine the structure of minimum and preferred clusters. These themes are central to the empirical chapters of the present work.

This book takes up the challenge of defining phonotactic complexity beyond the principles which have been traditionally used in the study of phonotactics. At the core of the analysis presented in Chaps. 3–5 is the understanding of the nature of consonant clusters in Polish, and the modelling of their structure at the level of the lexicon, processing and production. The analyses based on empirical data lay the foundations for a dynamic multi-dimensional model of phonotactic grammar of Polish. This model, as I will demonstrate throughout the book, can be captured by means of positional and weighted phonological features. Generally, this approach is a permutation of ideas intrinsic to (Post-) Generative and Natural Phonology, which are enriched with statistical modelling and tested in different areas of external evidence. Both inviolable constraints and graded preferences implicit in formal and functional theories serve as the theoretical underpinnings of this approach.

The major theme which accompanies the approach proposed here refers to the distinction between constraints and preferences. I will show throughout this book that both terms—although ontologically different—are complementary. Inviolable constraints specify the basic design of Polish word-initial and word-final phonotactics: statements that one can view as a backbone structure of all consonant clusters (Chap. 3). Preferences, on the other hand, account for phonotactics in other domains of language. In this contribution, they are inferred from the empirical data on online processing (Chap. 4) and spontaneous speech (Chap. 5). It is not my contention to question dominant views in phonology but to propose an alternative analysis where consonant clusters are investigated in greater detail and without making reference to approaches which are based on well-formedness conditions. I argue that a necessary point of reference consists in studying clusters at their basic level, namely in terms of phonological features.

Consonant clusters are here investigated in their full phonetic, phonological and morphological depth, acknowledging that there is a fragment of phonotactic reality that cannot be fully captured by the generalizing principles applied so far and analysing empirical data to verify the theoretical findings. This phonological enterprise requires the study of Polish phonotactics from broader theoretical and empirical perspectives, combining diverse branches of formal linguistics (phonology, morphology), corpus linguistics, psycholinguistics and statistical modelling. This contribution also brings insights into the contemporary discussion on linguistic universals and language-specific preferences.

The book is composed of seven chapters: two theoretical, three empirical, a synopsis of research results and conclusions. Chapter 1 is devoted to the synchronic description of Polish consonant clusters and the presentation of different aspects of phonotactic complexity. It discusses constraints and preferences by summarizing the most representative accounts on Polish phonotactics and morphonotactics, which date back to the 1950s. Phonotactic generalizations proposed for Polish range from descriptive statements on possible and impossible sequences via theory-oriented well-formedness conditions to mathematical models of computation. Each account provides a description of a different aspect of phonotactic complexity. Therefore, a large part of the chapter is devoted to discussing the qualitative and quantitative sources of phonotactic complexity which are related to the violation of linguistic universals (i.e. cluster length) or well-formedness constraints, frequency and morphological composition. The latter aspect is key in the description and classification of clusters throughout the book. Therefore, a distinction is made between phonotactic clusters which are found within a single morpheme and morphonotactic clusters which are generated in concatenative and non-concatenative morphology. The chapter leads to the compilation of representative cluster lists accounting for the word position in which clusters occur (word-initial vs. word-final), their morphological composition (phonotactic vs.

morphonotactic) and frequencies (types vs. tokens). These cluster inventories are used in the theoretical and empirical analyses presented in the book.

Chapter 2 presents selected theoretical approaches to the study of phonotactics which account for Polish. The chapter starts with the discussion on the notion of markedness. Next, I delineate two broad directions in the study of phonotactic markedness, namely approaches which are *based on well-formedness conditions*, and approaches which are *not based on well-formedness conditions*. The first type of approaches answer the question whether a consonant cluster is well-formed, i.e. whether it meets a priori statements on the expected good or preferred structure. Well-formedness conditions have their source in universals, phonological processes or higher-order principles (e.g. phonetic, cognitive), and make it possible to classify clusters into well-formed versus ill-formed, preferred versus dispreferred, or place them on a markedness scale mediating between the two options. A markedness-based classification of clusters is demonstrated on the example of two principles: the *Sonority Sequencing Generalization* and *Net Auditory Distance*. The second tradition of scholarship is represented by approaches which are not based on well-formedness conditions. Such approaches provide an in-depth analysis of subsegmental properties of consonants forming clusters. They identify minute phonetic and phonological properties which motivate the structure of consonant clusters, and from which overarching generalizations can follow. The main representative of this type of approaches is Government Phonology. Other approaches, in which sonority is derived from the acoustic signal, are presented only in passing.

The empirical part of the book starts with Chap. 3, where I argue for a feature-based description of phonotactics. The proposed method consists in a detailed analysis of (primarily) phonological features of consonants within clusters. The method is exploratory in that it is not based on well-formedness conditions: rather, it leads to the formulation of such heretofore unidentified conditions. The nature of this type of an analysis has been captured by the term *featuretactics*, which is rooted in a premise that phonotactic constraints and preferences are encoded in *positionally weighted phonological features*. Out of 26 phonetic and phonological parameters related to the place of articulation, manner of articulation, voicing and structural complexity, the statistical method of *Principal Component Analysis* allocates a numerical value to phonological features to indicate the role (i.e. weight) that they play in the construction of phonotactic inventories in different word positions. The analysis shows that Polish initial and final clusters make use of different features, from which markedness conditions are extrapolated.

The relative weight of phonological features in clusters also emerges in psycholinguistic experiments. Two reaction time experiments presented in Chap. 4 investigate the psycholinguistic reality of three factors: existence, well-formedness and distance in word-initial clusters and in word-final clusters. Existence distinguishes between clusters which are a part of the phonotactic inventory of Polish or which are unattested. Well-formedness is associated with the sonority profile of CC clusters, which is either sonority-violating or sonority-obeying following the hierarchy: plosive—affricate—fricative—nasal—liquid—glide. The concept of distance is represented by the proximity of places of articulation on a scale bilabial—labiodental—dental—alveolar—alveolo-palatal—palatal—velar. For each experiment, two pools of data were collected: accuracy rates and response latencies. The results show that online processing of phonotactics is affected by the place of articulation of clusters rather than sonority. Reaction times are the longest for medial place distances, and the shortest for large distances irrespective of word position. In other words, larger place contrasts are preferred as they entail the least cognitive effort. This preference supports the principle of the clarity of perception. As far as the behavioural data are concerned, accuracy is affected by sonority and existence. Additionally, the results shed light on sources of phonotactic knowledge, and conflicting forces related to place and manner features in online processing and in intuitive judgement.

The last empirical chapter is devoted to the study of initial and final consonant clusters in casual speech in native speakers of Polish. Chapter 5 places emphasis on processes which apply to consonant clusters, namely consonant or cluster deletion, consonant substitution, vowel prothesis or vowel deletion resulting in syllable merge. The analysis of spontaneous conversations requires distinguishing between target forms which reflect the pronunciation of a word in isolation, and casual speech forms which are pronounced in the continuum of speech sounds. The bifurcation into target forms and modified forms makes it possible to identify minute subsegmental properties which trigger cluster modification, on the one hand, and which determine the selection of a process type, on the other. The results of the analysis are threefold. First, initial and final phonotactics display different modification strategies related to phonological features. Cluster modification is due to lexical frequency word-initially, and to phonological features of consonants forming clusters word-finally. More specifically, stridency of C1, the quality of a vowel neighbouring on a cluster, a number of coronal consonants in a cluster and a continuant in absolute word-final position motivate cluster modification. Second, the selection of a process type is primarily related to stridency in initial clusters and continuancy in final clusters. Finally, due to its salience, initial position shows to support a greater variety and severeness of cluster modifications.

The synopsis of the research findings is given in Chap. 6. This chapter provides an overview of the ideas proposed in the book, where the notion of 'statistical weight' presented in Chap. 3 is reconciled with feature-based preferences in different sources of external evidence. Specifications of feature weight are proposed separately for initial and final clusters in the domain of lexical, cognitive and articulatory phonotactics. These specifications underlie phonotactic preferences which: (a) determine the structure of cluster types attested in Polish, (b) facilitate online processing and (c) motivate production in line with the target phonetic norm. Lexical statistics, processing and production mechanisms employed by native speakers reveal the basic and preferred structure of Polish consonant clusters. In this sense, featuretactics and feature weight open the possibility of accounting for the complexity of cluster-rich systems and of classifying typologically diverse systems. When viewed from a broader perspective, the proposed approach eventually leads to open speculation: a feature-based analysis of phonotactics can initiate research on elementary particles, which could contribute to the understanding of the human phonological component in general.

The amount of the relevant literature to be cited and the limitations resulting from space necessitated making some difficult decisions. I have curtailed the number of quoted publications to those which constitute a solid factual and methodological frame for the proposed approach. Some themes and questions recur in different chapters of the book in order to familiarize the Reader with their different treatment in contemporary phonological theory. In Chap. 1, I limited the discussion on phonotactic constraints to descriptive, theoretical and computational as other types of constraints re-emerge in some form in other parts of the book. For instance, cognitive constraints, which correspond with procedural knowledge of items existing in a language and Gestalt knowledge of what is generally considered to be well-formed, are discussed in Chap. 4 in terms of the psychological reality of existence, well-formedness and frequency in works of, among others, John Coleman, Janet Pierrehumbert, Iris Berent and Michael Vitevitch (Chap. 4, Sect. 4.2). Also, weighted constraints in the model of Bruce Hayes and Colin Wilson (2008) are mentioned in brief when proposing a new approach to weights in phonotactics (Chap. 3, Sect. 3.3.5, 3.3.6). I do not explicitly mention deep level constraints, surface phonetic constraints and morpheme structure constrains inherent in the generative tradition but discuss related issues, namely the phonotactic potential of the lexicon (Chap. 3), morphologically-motivated constrains and preferences (Chap. 3) as well as phonetically based choices of speakers (Chap. 5). In Chap. 2, I decided not to present markedness and syllable structure in Generative Phonology, Lexical Phonology and Optimality Theory as aspects of the theories relevant to the present argumentation are captured in terms of feature markedness (Chap. 3, Sects. 3.2.3, 3.3.5), morphological complexity in phonotactics (Chap. 1, Sect. 1.6.2.3) and formalization of constraints (Chap. 2, Sects. 2.4, 2.5), respectively.

Poznań, Poland Paula Orzechowska

References

Bethin, C.Y. 1992. *Polish syllables: The role of prosody in phonology and morphology.* Colombus, OH: Slavica Publishers.

Chomsky, N., and M. Halle. 1968. *The sound pattern of English.* New York: Harper and Row.

Cyran, E., and E. Gussmann. 1999. Consonantal clusters and governing relations: Polish initial consonant sequences. In *The syllable: Views and facts*, eds. H. van der Hulst, and A. N. Ritter, 219–249. Berlin: Mouton de Gruyter.

Rochoń, M. 2000. *Optimality in complexity: The case of polish consonant clusters* [Studia Grammatica 48]. Berlin: Akademie Verlag.

Rubach, J., and G. Booij. 1990. Edge of constituent effects in Polish. *Natural Language and Linguistic Theory* 8 (3): 427–463.

Acknowledgements

First and foremost, I am indebted to Katarzyna Dziubalska-Kołaczyk for providing me with inspiration and freedom in developing my ideas. Over the years, Katarzyna has cultivated my passion for phonetics and phonology, and encouraged new ideas on phonotactics. Her long-standing support in all my academic endeavours made it possible for me to write this book.

I would also like to express my gratitude to Richard Wiese for his unfailing friendship, introducing me to new areas of research in phonology, and readiness to discuss various phonological topics.

I owe a substantial part of the statistical analyses to numerous consultations with Harald Baayen. Generating random forests and heatmaps as well as analysing the psycholinguistic data in Chap. 4 in terms of the quantile regression would not have been possible without Harald's advice and generous help.

The research conducted for the purpose of this volume has been financed by a 3-year grant of the National Science Centre, Poland (No. 2015/18/E/HS2/00066) titled *The role of phonological features in phonotactics: A study on structure and learnability of consonant clusters in Slavic and Germanic languages*. I would like to thank all project members for their invaluable support, in particular Richard and Janina. Without computational expertise of Michał Jankowski, I would not have been able to analyse the data in Chap. 5. Without the technical and organizational support of Marta Nowak and Aleksandra Niewiadomska, the writing of the book would have taken much more time.

I would also like to thank other professionals, colleagues and friends who supported me in the writing process. My colleagues at the Faculty of English at Adam Mickiewicz University in Poznań offered valuable feedback on my work on numerous occasions. The book benefitted substantially from critical comments of my colleagues and friends: Marcin Kilarski, Richard Wiese, Janina Mołczanow and Dafydd Gibbon. Moreover, Andrzej Porębski and Waldemar Wołyński supported me at the mathematical–statistical level. Last but not least, Monika Lubacha cleared all storms on my writing path and provided inspiration at each stage of this creative process.

On a personal note, I would like to thank my close friends Ewa, Hans-Georg, Gosia, Peggy and Wolfgang, who supported me in the most challenging moments, and put up with my grumbling. Hafid's joy about the completion of each paragraph and chapter—every time greater than mine—constantly reminded me why I set out on this journey.

Przede wszystkim składam podziękowania rodzicom, Aldonie i Wojciechowi, za ich nieustającą miłość, wsparcie i kibicowanie na każdym zakręcie życia. To Wam, Rodzice, dedykuję tę książkę.

Contents

Abbreviations

1st	First person
2nd	Second person
3rd	Third person
acc	Accusative case
adj	Adjective
adv	Adverb
arch	Archaic
C	Consonant
CART	Classification and regression trees
Comp	Component in PCA
compar	Comparative
CV	Consonant vowel syllable
dat	Dative case
EX	Existent
Exp	Reaction time experiment
fem	Feminine
GAM	Generalized additive model
gen	Genitive case
ger	Gerund
GLM	General linear model
IF	Ill-formed
imp	Imperative
imperf	Imperfective
inf	Infinitive
instr	Instrumental case
loc	Locative case
masc	Masculine
MOA	Manner of articulation
n	Noun
NAD	Net Auditory Distance

NEX	Non-existent
NL	Natural Linguistics
nom	Nominative case
NP	Natural Phonology
O	Obstruent consonant
OCP	Obligatory Contour Principle
OT	Optimality Theory
past	Past tense
PCA	Principal component analysis
pej	Pejorative
perf	Perfective
PHB	Phonology as Human Behaviour
pl	Plural
POA	Place of articulation
PW	Phonological word
Q	Quantile
S	Sonorant consonant
sC(C)	/s/ + consonant (+ consonant) clusters
sg	Singular
SPE	The Sound Pattern of English
SSG	Sonority Sequencing Generalization
v	Verb
V	Vowel
VOI	Voicing
WF	Well-formed

Symbols

.	Syllable boundary
+	Morpheme boundary
#	Word boundary
//	Phonemic representation
[]	Phonetic realization
{ }	Orthographic form
*	Illegal or non-existent form
σ	Syllable

A Clarification on Orthography

All examples of words are provided in Polish orthography, which is to a large extent phonemic. Native consonants, digraphs and trigraphs along with corresponding IPA symbols used in the book are listed below. In this book, Polish retroflex affricates and fricatives are transcribed as /ʧ ʤ ʃ ʒ/ [symbols /tʂ dʐ ʂ ʐ/ found in the literature are given in brackets ()].

Grapheme	Phoneme
{c}	/ts/
{ć, ci}	/tɕ/
{cz}	/ʧ/ (/tʂ/)
{dz}	/ʣ/
{dż}	/ʤ/ (/dʐ/)
{dź, dzi}	/ʥ/
{h, ch}	/x/
{ł}	/w/
{ń, ni}	/ɲ/
{ś, si}	/ɕ/
{sz}	/ʃ/ (/ʂ/)
{rz, ż}	/ʒ/ (/ʐ/)
{w}	/v/
{ź, zi}	/ʑ/

List of Figures

List of Tables

Chapter 1
Sources of Phonotactic Complexity in Polish

A niechaj narodowie wżdy postronne znają, Iż Polacy nie gęsi, iż swój język mają!
[Among other nations let it always be known That the Poles are not geese, have a tongue of their own.]
(Mikołaj Rej Polish poet and prose writer, 1562 translation by Michał J. Mikoś)

1.1 Introduction

Sequences of consonants in Polish are certainly among the most remarkable ones reported in the subject literature. Their complexity is a function of several factors such as the number of constituent consonants, phonological structure or morphological composition. This chapter provides a synchronic description of restrictions that determine a linear arrangement of consonants in such clusters at syllable and word edges. Phonotactic constraints proposed for Polish range from descriptive statements on possible and impossible sequences, via theory-oriented well-formedness conditions to mathematical models of computation. Each approach operates on different linguistic units and accounts for a different fragment of phonotactics. Therefore, a substantial part of the chapter is devoted to the discussion on qualitative and quantitative factors, which lead to complexity, and their co-existence in Polish syllables and words. Whenever necessary, a distinction is made between phonotactic clusters which occur in a single morpheme, and morphonotactic clusters which are generated by morphological operations. The last part of the chapter is devoted to the presentation of large cluster inventories collected for the purpose of theoretical and empirical analyses presented in the book.

P. Orzechowska, *Complexity in Polish Phonotactics*, Prosody, Phonology and Phonetics, https://doi.org/10.1007/978-981-13-7299-5_1

1.2 Scope of Phonotactics

Patterns of sounds constitute one of the core areas of phonological study. Already in 1916, De Saussure pointed to the relevance of the study of "the sequential relations between sounds" (1916: 50). This postulate gained further support from other prominent linguists. Trubetzkoy noted that "the phonological description of a language is not only concerned with the analysis of phonemes, but also with the combinations into which the phonemes enter in forming morphemes and words" (Trubetzkoy 1969 [1939]: 36),[1] while Kaye et al. (1990) remarked that "what is now required is nothing less than a syntax of phonological expressions" (Kaye et al. 1990: 193). Therefore, patterns according to which sounds combine became one of the principal areas of phonological investigation.

The term phonotactics (from Greek *phōnê* meaning 'sound, voice', and *taktikê* meaning 'course, order, art of placing') has been used to describe the ordering of vowels and consonants in strings, particularly in syllables. It has been used to describe segments (segmental phonotactics) and their strings (sequential phonotactics). Segmental phonotactics studies the co-occurrence of phonetic features within a single segment. For instance, it specifies that Polish soft consonants must be alveolo-palatal, or that Polish back vowels must be rounded. Sequential phonotactics, in turn, focuses on the linear arrangement of sounds admissible in a language, and can be seen as the most fundamental form of the syntax of words facilitating phonological parsing. To take English as an example, phonotactics imposes constraints on the ordering of plosives and liquids in initial two-member clusters (C1C2). Sequences such as /tr dr/ are attested in English in *try* and *dry*, but their reverse ordering in /rt rd/ is outlawed. What is more, liquids which follow plosives are restricted only to the rhotic.

In contemporary dictionaries and encyclopedias, the definitions of phonotactics emphasize different aspects of this branch of phonology. In *The Encyclopedia of Language and Linguistics*, Asher (1994) provides the broadest definition of phonotactics:

> The study of the possibilities of phoneme combination in a language. (Asher 1994: 3139)

In his *Dictionary of Phonetics and Phonology*, Trask (1996) offers a more specific definition of the term:

> In a given language, the set of constraints on the possible sequences of consonant and vowel phonemes within a word, a morpheme or a syllable. (Trask 1996: 277)

In this account, reference is made to a set of rules that determine the structure of linguistic units in the domain of phonology (syllable and word) and morphology (morpheme and word). The definition of the term is further narrowed down in

[1]All the quotes from Trubetzkoy are based on *Principles of Phonology* (1969), Berkeley: University of California Press, which is the first reprint of Trubetzkoy's original work *Grundzüge der Phonologie* (1939).

Crystal (2003). From *A Dictionary of Linguistics and Phonetics*, the reader learns that:

> A term used in phonology to refer to the sequential arrangements (or tactic behaviour) of phonological units which occur in a language – what counts as a phonologically well-formed word. In English, for example, consonant sequences such as /fs/ and /spm/ do not occur initially in a word, and there are many restrictions on the possible consonant + vowel combinations which may occur, e.g. /ŋ/ occurs only after some short vowels /ɪ, æ, ʌ, ɒ/. (Crystal 2003: 352)

Crystal (2003) specifies the ordering of phonemes, in particular consonants. *A Student's Dictionary of Language and Linguistics* by Trask (1997) also focuses on adjacent consonants:

> In a particular language, the rules that determine which particular sequences of phonemes are allowed to occur in words. In English, for example, the rules allow /blæk/ and /bræk/, though only the first happens to exist, but they prohibit /bnæk/, which is not a possible word. (Trask 1997: 169)

What emerges from the last two definitions is that the combinations of consonants (or the so-called clusters) constitute the focal area in the study of phonotactics. In *The Oxford Companion to the English Language* (McArthur 1992), a cluster is defined as:

> A group of spoken or written consonants that come together at the beginning or end of a syllable, such as *br* in bring, *str* in street, *lfths* in twelfths. (McArthur 1992: 258)

Although both vowels and consonants are subject to phonotactic constraints, this contribution focuses on the combinations of consonants. In the sections to follow, I will elucidate why consonant clusters are key for a phonological description and theorizing.

1.3 Consonant System of Polish

The unit of the phoneme is germane to phonotactic models and principles, although the terms 'sounds', 'elements' and 'segments' have also been used in the subject literature, either less formally or in theory-oriented analyses (see Chap. 2, Sect. 2.5).[2] These units serve to formulate phonotactic constraints (or restrictions). Such constraints should be viewed as statements which prohibit a combination of phonemes, sounds or elements. The discussion of such co-occurrence restrictions, pursued in Sect. 1.4, necessitates a comment on the inventory of Polish consonants. In the following, I presents the system of Polish consonants viewed against a broader cross-linguistic context.

---

[2]In this book, the term *segment* is used interchangeably with phoneme, vowel and consonant.

Table 1.1 Consonant inventory of Polish

	Bilabial	Labio-dental	(Post) dental	Alveolar	Alveolo-palatal	(Post) palatal	Velar
Plosive	p b		t d			c ɟ	k g
Fricative		f v	s z	ʃ ʒ	ɕ ʑ		x
Affricate			ʦ ʣ	ʧ ʤ	ʨ ʥ		
Nasal	m		n		ɲ		ŋ
Lateral			l				
Trill/flap				r			
Glide	(w)					j	(w)

Adapted from Jassem (2003: 103)

From a typological perspective, languages can be categorized depending on the number of consonants, vowel qualities, and their proportion. *The World Atlas of Language Structures* (Dryer and Haspelmath 2013) presents a classification of a representative and geographically balanced sample of 563 languages in terms of their phoneme inventories. Maddieson (2013c) reports that while most languages display an *average* consonant inventory (22 ± 3 segments), the Polish set of consonants qualifies as *large* (≥ 34 segments).

The present analysis is largely based on the phonemic system proposed by Jassem (2003). The author stipulates 31 consonants, which are listed in Table 1.1. Polish has six affricates: dental /ʦ ʣ/, alveolar /ʧ ʤ/, and alveolo-palatal /ʨ ʥ/. The presence of three pairs of affricates in Polish is conspicuous, especially when compared with other Slavic languages. Voiced affricates, in particular the voiced coronal sibilant /ʣ/, are avoided cross-linguistically and are the least common among coronal obstruents (Żygis 2008). This gap is attested in Czech and Russian (e.g. Pompino-Marschall et al. 2017). What is more, Czech, Russian, and Ukrainian do not feature /ʨ ʥ/, which are produced in the alveolo-palatal region (Pompino-Marschall et al. 2017; Yanushevskaya and Bunčić 2015; Żygis 2008). It must be noted that alveolar affricates /ʧ ʤ/ and fricatives /ʃ ʒ/ are considered to be retroflex /tʂ dʐ ʂ ʐ/ in Hamann (2004), Padgett and Żygis (2003), Żygis (2003) and Żygis et al. (2012), who demonstrate that /tʂ dʐ ʂ ʐ/ are articulated with a more retracted root of the tongue than their alveolo-palatal counterparts. Similar place-related inconsistencies in the description of Polish concern /l/, which is dental in Jassem (2003) but alveolar in Gussmann (2007). Disregarding the status of some segments, the richness of the consonant inventory of Polish is unquestionable.

What is more, a large set of consonants, along with few vowel qualities, is indicative of a consonantal character of a language, and ensuing phonotactic complexity. Maddieson's (2013b) investigation of the consonant-vowel ratio (C/VQ) places 563 language on a five-point scale, whose extremes are occupied by low and high ratio. The most common cross-linguistic pattern involves an *average* C/VQ ratio (234 languages = 42%), where consonants outweigh vowels three or four times (C/VQ is larger than 2.75 and smaller than 4.5). Polish is subsumed under a *moderately high* group (C/VQ is larger than 4.5 and smaller than 6.5). In Jassem

(2003), 31 consonants and 6 pure vowels result in the ratio of 5:1. That is, consonants constitute 84% of the phonemic inventory of the language. This proportion can vary depending on the treatment of palatal(ized) consonants and nasal vowels (see Sect. 1.5). Generally, the prevalence of consonants in the phonemic system of Polish leads to longer consonant clusters, whose structure is regulated by co-occurrence restrictions. Although such restrictions hold for both vowels and consonant, given the scope of this book, Sect. 1.4 discusses only constraints on consonants.

1.4 Phonotactic Constraints

The formulation of phonotactic constraints can be based either on broad classes of segments or on their subsegmental properties. If reference is made to *phonemes*, as those listed in Table 1.1, the ordering can be expressed in the most general terms, for instance, /t/ cannot be followed by /l/ initially in English. On the other hand, if the formulation of phonotactic constraints refers to the subsegmental level of *elements* or *features*, constraints express a greater degree of phonetic detail. The place of articulation, manner of articulation and voicing have been used to account for the possible patterns. For instance, two rules determine the structure of C1C2V clusters in English onsets:

(a) C2 must not be represented by a voiced obstruent, or
(b) C1C2 must not share the place feature.

These constraints not only account for the structure of /tr dr/ in *try* and *dry* but also explain the emergence of /tl pw/ exclusively in borrowings: the combination of two adjacent alveolar or labial segments is illegal. It must be noted that such statements, apart from expressing adjacency relations, say little about a complex interplay of segmental properties such as labiality and coronality, let alone about their motivation. By the same token, a listing of constraints does not suffice in capturing a phonotactic grammar either. Given that C1C2 initials are expected to surface as an obstruent + sonorant sequence, and /tl dl/ obey the structure but are not attested in English, the place constraint must have taken over. The place co-occurrence restriction has been used to illustrate that some rules of phonotactics are not related solely to the manner of articulation (i.e. sonority). This fact suggests that phonotactic restrictions vary in importance, and that they are ordered with respect to each other. This issue is investigated in detail in Chap. 3, where constraints and preferences are ranked.

Three major themes evolve around the discussion on phonotactic constraints. The first theme refers to the theory-specific meaning of the term. In phonological theory, the term *constraint* has been used as a descriptive device particularly in Optimality Theory (Kager 1999; Prince and Smolensky 1993) to model the grammar or linguistic competence. In Natural Linguistics (Donegan 1985, 2002;

Donegan and Stampe 1979, 2009; Dressler 1984, 1985; Dressler et al. 1987; Kilani-Schoch 1988; Stampe 1979; Wurzel 1984), the term is replaced with *preferences*, which are explanatory statements derived from non-linguistic theories and principles. This distinction is addressed in detail in Chap. 3, where I defend a view that constraints and preferences are not mutually exclusive, and that both can be used in parallel for the purpose of the present analysis.

The second issue is related to the way in which such constraints and/or preferences should be formulated. As was demonstrated earlier, constraints can refer either to broader classes of segments (e.g. obstruents vs. sonorants), to individual segments (e.g. /t l w/) or to the subsegmental level, where distinctive features are evoked (e.g. coronality, stridency, voice). Again, the use of phonological features in the formulation of phonotactic constraints and preferences is justified in Chap. 3.

The last problem area refers to the selection of an adequate unit in the study of phonotactics, be it a syllable or a word. A linguist who less readily subscribes to a theory needs to consider the two domains. This aspect of phonotactics, along with the two other themes, are addressed in the following sections of the chapter.

1.4.1 Descriptive Constraints

Phonotactic constraints in Polish have been expressed in terms of generalizing statements and lists of (un)attested combinations of segments. Rochoń (2000) provides a rather straightforward summary of syllable constraints:

> If one hopes to find any kind of agreement among consonants constituting clusters such as identity with respect to place of articulation, continuance, nasality, etc., one must be satisfied with the fact that Polish consonant clusters only agree with respect to voicing with some exceptions, of course. (Rochoń 2000: 89)

To the contrary, Szpyra-Kozłowska (2002) discusses phonotactic constraints by listing examples of inadmissible two-member clusters (marked with an asterisk '*') in word-initial position (marked with a hashtag '#').

1. Examples of inadmissible word-initial CC (adapted from Szpyra-Kozłowska 2002: 34)

   (1.a) #j + consonant
   (1.b) #mb, #mp, #mt, #np, #nb, #nt, #nd, #nk, #ng
   (1.c) #pk, #bg, #tp, #dg, #pp, #tt, #kk, #gg, #bb

In order to avoid such a detailed presentation of the concatenative possibilities in the language, phonologists have successfully categorized inadmissible phoneme sequences by formulating more general phonotactic constraints. The first comprehensive attempt at systematizing the structure of Polish phonotactics was provided in Cyran and Gussmann (1999). The authors list phonotactic constraints at syllable edges, which—together with constraints discussed in other contributions (Bethin 1992; Cyran and Gussmann 1999; Gussmann 2007; Rubach and Booij 1990a, b; Szpyra-Kozłowska 2001)—re-emerge in 2 in the form of several generalizing statements for CC and CCC clusters. In 2, and in the following lists, examples in brackets represent clusters which either follow the constraints or which are illicit, or unattested ('*').

2. Phonotactic constraints on Polish initials

(2.a) Strictly outlawed CC involve:

- some sonorant + obstruent sequences (e.g. */jC nC/)
- some sonorant + sonorant sequences (e.g. */lr rl rw wr/)
- /m l/ preceded by a sonorant (e.g. */lm jm nl/)
- some obstruent + obstruent sequences (e.g. */pk bg/)
- two adjacent homorganic stops (e.g. */tt kk/)

(2.b) Strictly outlawed CCC involve:

- three adjacent liquid or nasal consonants, liquid + nasal + liquid or nasal + liquid + nasal
- three obstruent-only (apart from sequences involving /s/) or sonorant-only sequences
- sonorants other than /m l/ preceding sC sequences (e.g. */nst wɕɲ/)

As can be observed, the constraints in (2.a) and (2.b) are general and 'negative' in character as they specify non-existent or impossible combinations only. In fact, what has been conveyed in (2.a) specifically I rephrase in terms of positive constraints in 3.

3. Phonotactic constraints on Polish initials: reformulated

(3.a) adjacent stops must be heterorganic (e.g. /tk kp gd/ in *tkanina* 'fabric', *kpina* 'mockery', *gdy* 'when')
(3.b) in sonorant clusters, /m l/ must be followed by a sonorant (e.g. /ml mj ln/ in *mleko* 'milk', *miód* 'honey', *lnu* 'flax' (gen sg))
(3.c) only /m l/ can precede sC clusters (e.g. /mɕtɕ lɕɲ/ in *mścić* 'to avenge', *lśnić* 'to glitter')

The constraints in 2 focus on the absence of specific segments or segment classes in consonant strings, while constraints in 3 identify the prerequisites necessary for a sustainable onset structure in the language. Let me now summarize coda constraints in a manner comparable to 3. Cyran and Gussmann (1999), Gussmann (2007), Rubach and Booij (1990a, b) and Szpyra-Kozłowska (2001) seem to be more explicit about the right syllable-edge, as is shown in 4

4. Phonotactic constraints for Polish codas

(4.a) adjacent obstruents must agree in voicing (e.g. /ʃt sk pt/ in *maszt* 'mast', *wosk* 'wax', *szept* 'whisper')

(4.b) geminates must be sonorant-only (e.g. /ww nn ll/ in *mełł* 'to chew' (3rd sg past masc), *fontann* 'fountain' (gen pl), *will* 'villa' (gen pl))
(4.c) no Cj sequences (*/tj rj wj/)
(4.d) no palatal plosives or palatalized consonants (e.g. */c ɟ p^j f^j/)
(4.e) no voiced obstruents (e.g. */b ʒ ʤ/)

Note that at the skeletal level geminates occupy two segmental slots but phonetically are realized as a prolonged sonorant (for acoustic evidence see Rojczyk and Porzuczek 2014). Therefore, (4.b) can well specify simple codas, similarly to constraints on singletons in (4.d) and (4.e). These constraints follow directly from phonological rules of final devoicing and voicing assimilation (Bethin 1992; Rochoń 2000; Rubach 1984) which determine the phonological structure of consonants and clusters in Polish, and which are presented in detail in Sect. 1.5.

In this work, I shift the point of balance from 'negative' constraints which specify the impossible combinations, to what I see as 'positive' constraints and preferences. This change is not only terminological but has consequences for the representation of the phonotactic grammar and for my further phonological theorizing. 'Negative' constraints in (2.a) and (2.b) are absolute and inviolable. They generalize on the whole inventory of consonant clusters by distinguishing between possible and impossible sequences. In contrast, preferences define structure types which are favoured to varying degrees in the phonology of a language, and which span on a scale from the least to the most preferred. The importance of describing language in term of graded phenomena has been emphasized by Vennemann (1983, 1988) and Dressler (1985, 1999). More or less preferred options reflect the choices of speakers, and cognitive processes of the mind.

When viewed from a cross-linguistic perspective, the constraints on Polish onset and coda clusters in 2, 3 and 4 seem to be rather general. Compare these constraints with the requirements formulated for English and German onsets. The only sustainable CCC sequences in English are composed of /s/ followed by /p t k/ and /l r j w/ (Cruttenden 2014; Roach 2006). In German, the same pattern holds with the exception of the (pre-)initial fricative, which is realized either as post-alveolar /ʃ/ or as alveolar /s/ (Wiese 1996).

5. Constraints on CCC onsets in Germanic languages

(5.a) English

s	p t k	l	split, sclerosis
		r	spray, street, scream
		j	stew, skew
		w	squeak

(5.b) German

ʃ	p t k	l	Splint 'cotter'
		ʁ	Sprache 'language', Straße 'street'
s	p t k	l	Splattermovie 'splatter movie', Sklerose 'sclerosis'
		ʁ	Skrupel 'scruple', Streetball

In English, this constraint limits the set of all possible three-member clusters to 12 potential combinations, out of which eight are attested. Similar restrictions were formulated for English C1C2 onsets. Roach (2006) and Cruttenden (2014) posit that C2 must not be occupied by a voiced obstruent, or that C1C2 must not share the place feature, which is claimed to explain the emergence of alveolar and bilabial sequences /tl/ and /pw/ only in borrowings *Tlingit* and *pueblo*, respectively. As for German, the constraint licenses two types of fricatives in cluster-initial position but only liquids in cluster final position. Additionally, both languages feature other CCC onsets, which offend the structure in 5: /smj/ in *smew* in English and /skv/ in *Square* in German. Constraints on CCC in 5 tend to be expressed in terms of the places of articulation, manners of articulation and voicing. That is, a statement that initial CCCs in English are composed of /s/ followed by a voiceless plosive and an approximant makes reference to place, manner and voice categories in line with the IPA description of consonants. However, the constraints do not specify which phonological properties pertaining to the place and manner of articulation as well as voicing are involved.

Similar statements were made for syllable or word universals. Pulgram (1970) specifies universals for the 'section' (which roughly corresponds to the phonological word) in terms of the iteration between general categories of segments, namely vowels and consonants (e.g. sections must begin with consonants and end in vowels). At a more specific level, Greenberg's (1978) seminal work on universals uses distinctive features to define the structure of clusters cross-linguistically (e.g. a lateral is never followed by a rhotic word-initially, an unvoiced stop is never followed by a stop differing only by voice word-finally). The use of distinctive feature labels is limited to account for the phonological composition of each individual segment in a sequence, and a possible adjacency relation between such segments. The problem is whether the IPA categories suffice in formulating such constraints. What is more, not much is known about how complex the interplay of these restrictions is, and—more importantly—which constraints are favoured over others. Are constraints organized in a hierarchical order? Do constraints vary in the degree of importance?

1.4.2 Optimality Theory Constraints

The hierarchical or ranked organization of constraints is addressed in some theoretical approaches. For instance, Optimality Theory (henceforth OT, Kager 1999;

Prince and Smolensky 1993) derives rankings of constraints, which successfully account for language-specific distribution patterns and cross-linguistic variation. The constraints are meant to reflect universally preferred structures. In the sections to follow, emphasis is placed on different types of constraints, which have been proposed in the literature on the topic. OT has provided a set of constraints to account for the structure of consonant clusters. For instance, Pulleyblank (1997) proposes four syntagmatic constraints, referred to as *Identical Cluster Constraints*, which are listed in 6.

6. Identical Cluster Constraints (Pulleyblank 1997: 64)

    (6.a) VOICING: A sequence of consonants must be identical in *voicing*.
    (6.b) PLACE: A sequence of consonants must be identical in *place of articulation*.
    (6.c) CONSTITUANCY: A sequence of consonants must be identical in *continuancy*.
    (6.d) NASALITY: A sequence of consonants must be identical in *nasality*.

As can be seen, the constraints go beyond a typical spectrum of phonological properties used when listing phonotactic restrictions in 1–5. Pulleyblank (1997) explains that the function of the constraints is to ensure articulatory inertia. Preventing movement—as can be assumed—is meant to lead to minimal articulatory effort, and ease of production. Rochoń (2000) selects Polish phonotactics as a testing ground for the constraints, and observes that place, continuancy and nasality must be ranked lower than other constraints which require the preservation of sequences such as /gb kp db/ in Polish. A velar (dorsal) or dental (coronal) plosive can be followed by a bilabial (labial) plosive in *gburowaty* 'churlish', *kpić* 'to ridicule' and *dbać* 'to take care', violating the constraint in (6.b). Also, Polish features numerous plosive + fricative sequences such as /pɕ tʃ gʒ/ in *psioczyć* 'to curse', *trzy* 'three' and *grzyb* 'mushroom', which fail to conform to (6.c).

Constraints on continuancy were also posited in an OT account of Morelli (1998, 1999). Since the constraints are formulated in a theory-specific manner, let me rephrase them in 7 for the purpose of a more general presentation.

7. Structural onset constraints (Morelli 1999: 47f)

    (7.a) Tautosyllabic [−continuant] segments are disallowed.
    (7.b) Tautosyllabic [+continuant] segments are disallowed.
    (7.c) A tautosyllabic sequence containing a stop followed by any obstruent is disallowed.

(7.a) and (7.b) suggest that fricative + fricative and stop + stop sequences are prohibited to occur in the same syllable. (7.c), in turn, disallows sequences of a stop followed by a fricative or a stop. Morelli (1998, 1999) refutes the account of Pulleyblank (1997), and argues for the universality of the fricative + plosive ordering in onsets. A reordering of the constraints in 7 makes it possible to arrive at a universal ranking of obstruent clusters given in 8, where '>' means 'more preferred than'.

8. A harmonic ordering of obstruent clusters (Morelli 1999: 158)
fricative + plosive > fricative/plosive + fricative > plosive + plosive

At the theoretical level, plosive + plosive sequences violate the constraints in (7.a) and (7.c), which makes them the worst combinations. Fricative + fricative, and fricative + plosive clusters violate (7.b) and (7.c), respectively. Since both types of combinations offend one constraint, they cannot be ordered with respect to each other. The only combination in compliance with 7 is fricative + plosive.

It must be borne in mind that OT constraints have phonetic motivation. For instance, since there is an articulatory preference for stops to be released into a more sonorous segment, plosive + plosive sequences are the most marked ones. This preference is reflected in 8, where fricative + plosive and plosive + plosive sequences occupy the extremes of the hierarchy. However, at a purely descriptive level, phonotactic constraints in OT and in theory-less approaches are lists of statements on what is possible and impossible in a language, and therefore contribute very little to the understanding of forces which motivate a phonotactic grammar. This goal is pursued by functional approaches to phonology.

1.4.3 Functional Constraints

An attempt at explaining why some combinations are (not) attested in a language is provided by Phonology as Human Behaviour (henceforth PHB, Diver 1979; Tobin 1997) and Natural Phonology (henceforth NP, Donegan 1985, 2002; Donegan and Stampe 1979; Dressler 1985; Dressler et al. 1987; Stampe 1979), which answer the 'why' question. In Tobin's (1997) account, constraints represent the struggle to achieve maximum communication with minimal effort, particularly within developmental and clinical phonology. In NP, constraints are expressed in terms of preferences formulated on the basis of universal higher-order principles, such as phonetic, psychological, sociological or cognitive. In contrast to descriptive and OT constraints discussed in Sects. 1.4.1 and 1.4.2, phonotactic preferences formulated by PHB and NP offer an explanation and practical implementation.

One of the main advantages of PHB is the theory's capacity to find a motivation for the distributional patterns of sounds in the speech signal. In order to illustrate the explanatory power of PHB, let me return to the discussion on the existence of initial /tr dr/ and the absence of */tl dl/ in English. A typical phonotactic constraint would be the following: an alveolar plosive can precede a post-alveolar rhotic, but not an alveolar liquid. However, whether /t d/ can(not) be followed by either /l/ or /r/ says nothing about the actual motivation for such a distribution. Obviously, there must exist a constraint which eliminates /tl dl/ from the phonotactic inventory of English.

A functional approach of Diver (1979) and Tobin (1997) has been successful in formulating a constraint according to which the disfavouring of */tl dl/ is attributed to reusing the same articulatory muscles in the transition from the mobile gesture for /t d/ to the stable gesture for /l/. Segments /t d/ involve the violent motion of the plosive which needs to be immediately brought under control in order to initiate another gesture for /l/. Conversely, the burst release in /tr dr/ can naturally continue from the plosives into another mobile segment, which makes plosive + rhotic a preferred combination (Diver 1979: 173). This approach carries explanatory power, and has the potential of accounting for unattested clusters.

Such an explanation constitutes a response to the limitations of general linguistic theory, which is to a large extent relies on a listing of what is possible and impossible in a language and cross-linguistically. This point was originally made by Vennemann (1983), who rejected absolute statements. Vennemann (1983) argues that a theory of linguistic universals specifies what is possible and impossible in the languages of the world but "is by its very nature incapable of telling us what is unusual and what is rare" (1983: 10). This view calls for presenting linguistic phenomena in terms of graded, or preferred options, which can be deduced from external non-linguistic evidence.

As a response to Vennemann's (1983) plea, NP proposes phonotactic constraints derived from semiotic and functional principles, such as figure-and-ground and perceptibility/pronunceability. This idea is implemented in *Beats-and-binding Phonology* of Dziubalska-Kołaczyk (2002), where universal phonotactic preferences serve two functions. On the one hand, they counteract the preference for only consonant + vowel (henceforth CV) sequences. On the other hand, they determine degrees of cluster preferability (or difficulty), and counteract the formation of dysfunctional strings of consonants.

The universality of the CV combination is predictable from a preference for a non-beat (n), which is best realized by a consonant, and a beat (B), which is best realized by a vowel: the n $\rightarrow$ B binding. Dziubalska-Kołaczyk (2002) proposes statements on preferability for CCs and CCCs in word-initial, word-medial, and word-final position, which specify the contrast between consonants forming clusters and adjacent vowels. This contrast is expressed by calculating distances in terms of manners of articulation (sonority distance) between pairs of sounds. For instance, a well-formedness condition for a preferred initial CC states that a distance in sonority (sondis) should be larger for a consonant to consonant transition than for a consonant to vowel transition: sondis (C1C2) $\geq$ sondis (C1V). This optimal balance in distances between pairs of segments follows the prosodic principle of clarity of perception (for the development of the ideas see Chap. 2, Sect. 2.4.2).

1.4.4 Computational Constraints

Another type of constraints is found in the domain of computational phonology. Implicit in computational methods is the notion of defaults. Gibbon (2001) lists several types of defaults, among which syntagmatic defaults are crucial for the model advocated in this book (Chap. 3). Syntagmatic defaults, or constraints on compositionality, model phonological preferences exemplified by, for instance, the hierarchy of preferred syllable structure, or the hierarchies of sonority. A way of declarative modelling of such preferences is by means of models referred to as finite automata. In mathematical and computer science, automata are the basis of constructing larger networks of finite-state machines (Jurafsky and Martin 2009; McCulloch and Pitts 1943), which consist of initial states, final states and transitions determining possible connections and ways of moving between them. For this reason, finite machines have become important not only as a concept in computational linguistics, but also as a visual representation of elements existing in a language and a relationship between them.

There is a range of illustrations representing phonotactic constraints (for an overview see Sommerstein 1977) or discovering non-existent words (Jusek et al. 1994). One of them is a finite-state transition network, which transforms phonotactic patterns into a network structure. The network consists of a finite number of states (initial, medial and final) connected via transitions. The input at the initial state is processed along the transitions designated in the string, until it reaches the terminal state at which there are no more elements to process. More elaborate computational models extend the simple syntagmatic representation of segment combinations to multilinear models, which represent temporal constraints. For instance, the *Time Map* approach of Carson-Berndsen (1998, 2000), embedded in finite state phonology and event logic, integrates information on temporal patterns and gesture overlap, as identified in Autosegmental Phonology (Goldsmith 1990) and Articulatory Phonology (Browman and Goldstein 1986, 1989, 1992).

An illustration of a finite state network for word-final phonotactics in Polish was proposed in Orzechowska (2009). The phonotactic automata identify a structured set of constraints, which determine consonantal phonotactics of Polish words. To fulfil the ambition of exhaustivity, separate networks for final phonotactic and morphonotactic consonant clusters were proposed, which are given in Figs. 1.1 and 1.2, respectively. The models aim at providing a complete set of constraints for the right word edge for clusters compiled from a dictionary *Uniwersalny Słownik Języka Polskiego* (Universal Dictionary of Polish) by Dubisz (2006) and an *English-Polish Parallel Corpus* (Krynicki 2006). Lists of clusters used in the preparation of the networks differ from the inventories collected for the purpose of this book only in several items. Moreover, Orzechowska (2009) employs the same rules of morphological parsing as discussed in Sect. 1.6.2.3. Therefore, the networks in Figs. 1.1 and 1.2 are considered to be relatively faithful representations of the datasets listed in Tables 1.18 and 1.19.

The networks in Figs. 1.1 and 1.2 can be seen as a visualization of not only the distributional patterns of phonemes but also the general complexity of Polish final clusters. For instance, the arrangement of segments in a three-member sequence C1C2C3 can be reconstructed by following transitions from the left-most state of the network (C1), to the right-most state, where the network ends (i.e. C2 or C3 in phonotactic clusters; C2, C3 or C4 in morphonotactic clusters). The networks capture different aspects of complexity: the number of cluster types and their length. First, when viewed from the left-most edge, the initial state gives rise to 35 transitions in Fig. 1.1 and 24 transitions in Fig. 1.2. What is more, 17 consonants lead to the final state in phonotactic clusters, and 15 in morphonotactic clusters.

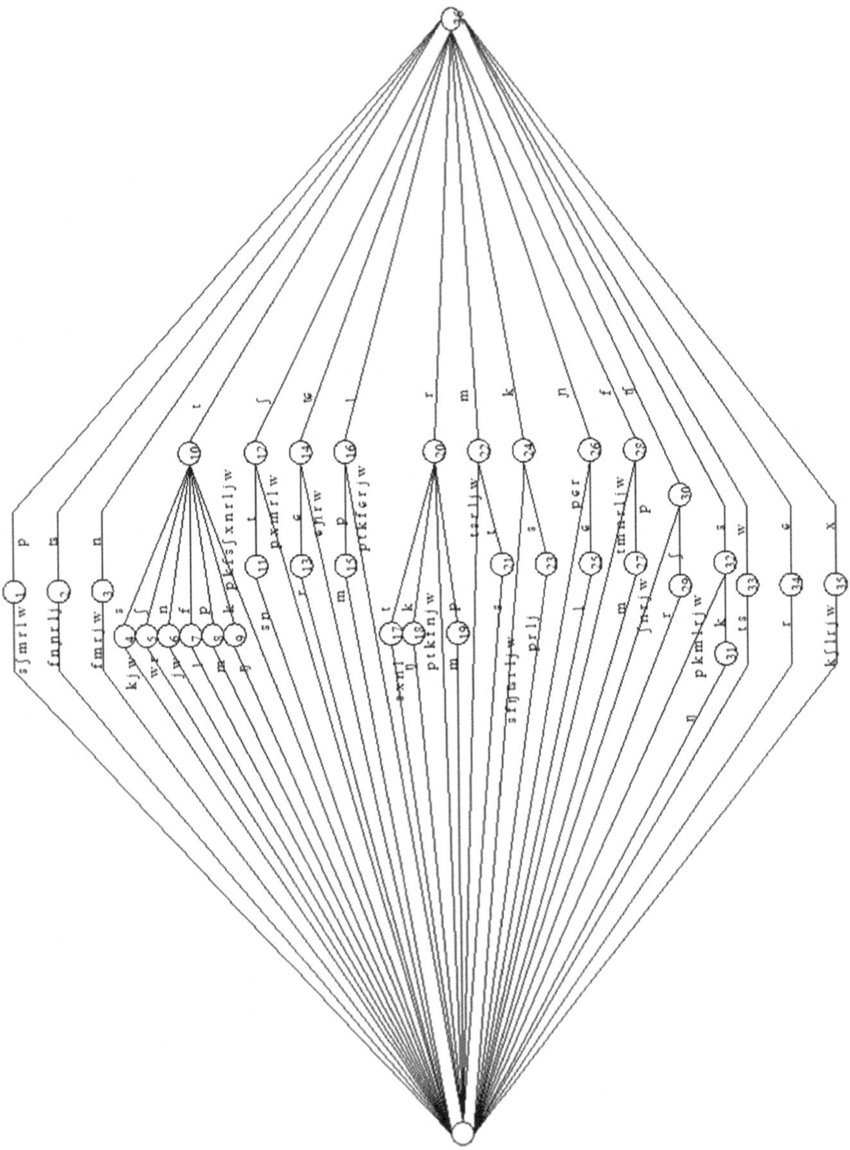

Fig. 1.1 An automaton representation of final phonotactic clusters in Polish (Orzechowska 2009: 62)

These observations show that the phonotactic set is represented by a greater variety of cluster types than the morphonotactic set. Second, the inventories differ with respect to the number of states. For instance, the longest phonotactic sequences in Fig. 1.1 involve two intervening states, e.g. 4 → 10 in /kst/, 17 → 20 in /str/,

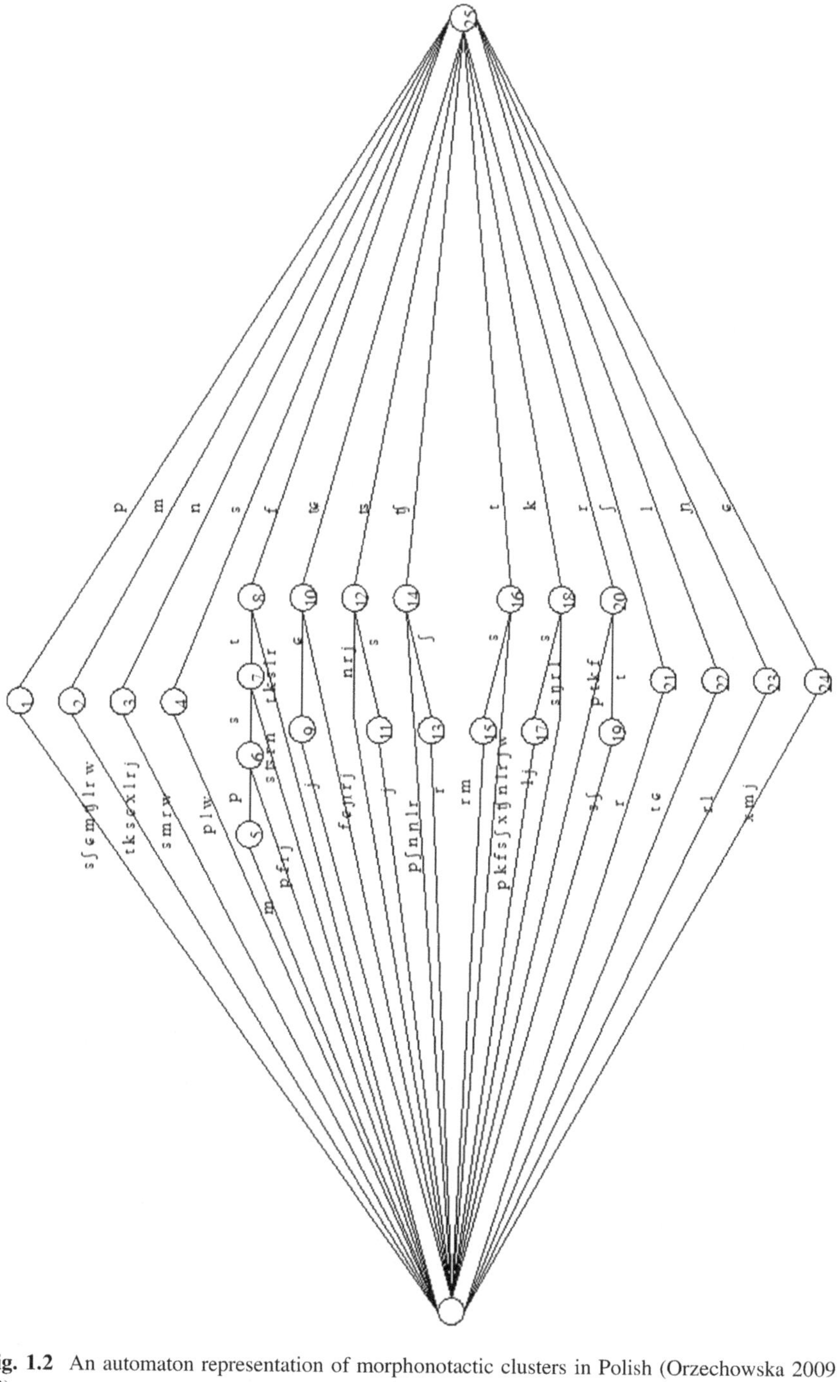

Fig. 1.2 An automaton representation of morphonotactic clusters in Polish (Orzechowska 2009: 63)

29 → 30 in /rʃʧ/. To compare with Fig. 1.2, the longest final is composed of five consonants /mpstf/, and can be reconstructed from a transition of four intervening states 5 → 6 → 7 → 8.

Apart from the number of clusters and their length, the networks illustrate types of consonants in a string. Let me illustrate this property on the example of morphonotactic clusters. Concatenative morphology yields a predictable set of sequences. The infinitive-forming morpheme {−ć} and the pronoun-forming {−ś} give rise to clusters ending in /ɕ ʨ/ as in *czyj* + *ś* 'somebody's' and *wejś* + *ć* 'to come in'. This observation suggests that the remaining 13 cluster-final segments (sonorants /m n l r ɲ/ and voiceless obstruents /p t k f s ʃ ʧ ʦ/) emerge in non-concatenative contexts. That is, non-concatenative morphology generates a wider array of sequences. Also, when one compares final consonants in both datasets, phonotactic constraints emerge. For instance, no cluster ends in /j/, which corresponds with the phonotactic constraint in (4.c) stating that no final Cj sequences are permitted in Polish (*/tj rj wj/).

As far as the pre-final segment is concerned, common manner of articulation patterns can be found in Figs. 1.1 and 1.2. First, CCs, involve two transitions, and exemplify all types of combinations of sonorants and obstruents: obstruent + obstruent (O + O), obstruent + sonorant (O + S), sonorant + sonorant (S + S) and sonorant + obstruent (S + O). The S + O pattern prevails in the morphonotactic group. It is well-depicted by the 2 → 36 transition, which yields phonotactic sequences of /n ɲ r l j/ + /ʦ/, and by the 18 → 25 transition, which results in morphonotactic combinations of /ŋ r l/ and /k/. Sequences of two sonorants and two obstruents are less common. For instance, phonotactic S + S clusters are generated by the 3 → 36 transition (i.e. /mn rn jn wn/), and morphonotactic O + O clusters are generated by the 1 → 25 transition (i.e. /sp ʃp ɕp/). Few O + S doubles such as /fn tl kr sm pɲ tw/ involve the transition from 3, 16, 20, 22, 26, 33 to the terminal state in 36 in Fig. 1.1, and 2, 3, 20, 22, 23 to the final state in 25 in Fig. 1.2. A structural constraint can be posited for CCCs and CCCCs, which end in obstruents and tend to be preceded by S + O sequences.

As regards the place of articulation features, in both networks the final /t/ follows a variety of segments. This is observable in the phonotactic group, in which /t/ is preceded by /p k f s ʃ x n r l j w/ in two-member clusters, and by S + O sequences in three-member clusters. The dental voiceless plosive /t/ is also a common final segment in sequences arising due to non-concatenative morphological operations. Such a distribution reflects Tobin's (1997) assertion that apical consonants are favoured particularly word-finally as well as Hall's (1997) and Paradis and Prunet's (1991) argumentation in favour of an unmarked status of coronals in relation to other place features.

Finite-state automata embrace phonotactic information which can be partially captured by means of matrices, which are two-dimensional expressions of phoneme co-occurrence in two-member clusters. Columns and rows correspond to the first and the second consonant in a sequence, respectively. A matrix has an advantage over an automaton in that it not only shows attested combinations but also visualizes how the phonotactic potential of a language is exploited. With a colour marking, a single matrix can be used to tease apart clusters of different morphological complexity. Tables 1.2 and 1.3 present matrices for initial and final clusters, based on the cluster lists presented in this chapter. Light grey cells mark exclusively phonotactic clusters, while dark grey cells mark exclusively morphonotactic clusters. Sequences given in yellow are shared, i.e. they can have both realizations.

The comparison of Tables 1.2 and 1.3 leads to the following observations. Morphonotactic clusters are largely predictable in word initial position. Dark grey cells cumulate where C1 is represented by /f v s z/, i.e. phonetic realizations of productive non-syllabic prefixes. Word-finally, no clear pattern for morphonotactic clusters can be posited: dark grey cells are scattered around in the matrix. As far as phonotactic clusters are concerned, they are distributed differently in initial and final positions. In Table 1.2, light grey cells accumulate in the central and right-most part at the top of the matrix. This distribution reveals a favoured pattern in initial CC clusters whereby C1, represented by a plosive, is followed by continuant (all approximants and most fricatives) and nasal consonants. The third grouping of initial phonotactic clusters embraces fricatives followed by approximant and nasal consonants. The co-occurrence of /l r j w/ with all plosives points to a preferred type of a sequence: obstruent + approximant. As regards word-final position in Table 1.3, the greatest density of light grey cells is found at the bottom of the matrix. This arrangement suggests the reverse pattern, where approximants in C1 tend to be followed by all segment with the exception of /l r j w/.

Apart from providing a complete set of phonotactic constraints by means of finite state networks, computational methods are important for another reason. A body of research has argued that they offer mechanisms to substitute for theory-laden procedural aspects of Generative Phonology (Chomsky and Halle 1968; Kean 1975) and Optimality Theory (Kager 1999; Prince and Smolensky 1993). With the developments in computational phonology, Kaplan and Kay (1994) show parallels between rewrite rules in the SPE and finite-state transducers. The authors argue for substituting the theoretical formalism with a single and simple representation, which remains intact under ever-changing theoretical pressures. In a similar fashion, Karttunen (1998) proposes to replace OT constraints with a finite-state calculus that maps underlying forms directly onto their most optimal surface realizations, and vice versa. This contribution demonstrates that generative and post-generative formalism is comparable to finite state phonology.

1.4.5 Domain of Phonotactic Generalizations

The definitions of phonotactics provided in Sect. 1.2 make reference to two units: the syllable and the word. Traditionally, constraints have been posited for the unit of the syllable (see Van der Hulst and Ritter 1999 for an overview and references), although arguments have also been put forward in favour of words (Ewen and van der Hulst 2001; Booij 1999), feet (Harris 2018) and a language-dependant domain of syllables or words (Auer 1993; Eliasson 2014). The fact that speakers can

Table 1.2 Matrix for initial phonotactic, morphonotactic and shared CC clusters

	p	b	t	d	k	g	c	ɟ	f	v	s	z	ʃ	ʒ	ɕ	ʑ	x	ts	dz	tʃ	dʒ	tɕ	dʑ	m	n	ɲ	ŋ	l	r	j	w
p			+								+		+		+		+					+			+	+		+	+	+	+
b												+		+		+												+	+	+	+
t					+				+		+		+				+			+					+	+		+	+	+	+
d		+								+				+										+	+	+		+	+	+	+
k	+		+						+		+		+		+			+				+		+	+	+		+	+	+	+
g		+		+						+		+		+		+							+	+	+	+		+	+	+	+
c																															
ɟ																															
f	+		+		+						+		+		+		+	+		+		+						+	+	+	
v		+		+		+				+		+		+		+			+						+	+		+	+	+	+
s	+		+								+		+		+		+	+		+				+				+	+	+	+
z		+		+		+				+		+		+		+							+	+	+	+		+	+	+	+
ʃ	+		+		+				+											+				+	+			+	+		+
ʒ		+		+		+				+														+		+		+	+		+
ɕ	+								+													+		+		+		+	+		
ʑ																							+					+	+		
x			+						+				+					+				+		+				+	+	+	+
ts									+															+	+			+			+
dz		+								+																					
tʃ			+		+				+								+			+		+		+							+
dʒ																					+										
tɕ	+								+															+							

(continued)

Table 1.2 (continued)

dʑ						+				+																					
m													+	+			**+**	+							+	+		+		+	+
n																															
ɲ																															
ŋ																															
l										**+**				+											**+**	**+**				+	
r			+	+						+				+					+											+	
j																															
w		**+**			+	+						+		+		+															

syllabify words in their mother tongue without any prior linguistic knowledge should at least theoretically lay the foundations for a coherent definition of the unit. However, in spite of numerous attempts, it remains unclear where syllable boundaries should be placed. Therefore, I consider the domain of a word to be adequate for the purpose of the analyses to follow.

Firstly, a word, whether phonological or lexical, has been argued to be a relatively independent linguistic unit. A word aspires to being the least problematic and controversial domain for formulating phonotactic generalizations, which for Polish has been postulated by Dziubalska-Kołaczyk (1995), Rubach (1996) and Steriade (1999). Although the latter account offers a comprehensive discussion on the advantages of syllable-based constraints, Steriade (1999) concludes that syllable-independent conditions determine segmental phonotactics: "word-edge phonotactics (…) are among the guidelines used by speakers to infer word-internal syllable divisions" (1999: 1). Surface syllabification in Polish offers evidence in support of word-edge rather than syllable-edge phonotactics (e.g. Steriade 1999; Szpyra-Kozłowska 1998, 2000). The studies on the divisions of word-medial clusters demonstrate that Polish speakers do not reject sonority violating clusters in onsets (Rubach and Booij 1990a, b).

What is more, the unit of a lexical word can accommodate morphologically-complex consonant clusters. In morphologically-rich languages, such as Polish, it is crucial to distinguish between clusters occurring within a morpheme and clusters generated by morphological operations (for a detailed exposition see Sect. 1.6.2.3).

Table 1.3 Matrix for final phonotactic, morphonotactic and shared CC clusters

	p	b	t	d	k	g	c	ɟ	f	v	s	z	ʃ	ʒ	ɕ	ʑ	x	ts	dz	tʃ	dʒ	tɕ	dʑ	m	n	ɲ	ŋ	l	r	j	j̃	w	w̃
p			+								+		+							+						+		+	+				
b																																	
t									+				+											+				+	+			+	
d																																	
k			+						+		+						+							+				+	+			+	
g																																	
c																																	
ɟ																																	
f			+		+													+				+			+			+	+				
v																																	
s	+		+		+				+															+	+							+	
z																																	
ʃ	+		+														+			+													
ʒ																																	
ɕ	+																						+	+	+			+					
ʑ																																	
x			+										+		+									+									
ts					+																												
dz																																	
tʃ	+		+																														
dʒ																																	
tɕ																																	

(continued)

Table 1.3 (contiuned)

dʑ																																	
m	+								+		+		+		+										+								
n			+						+		+		+					+		+									+				
ɲ																		+		+		+											
ŋ					+																												
l	+		+		+				+		+		+				+	+		+				+		+							
r	+		+		+				+		+		+		+		+	+		+		+		+	+	+						+	
j			+		+				+		+				+		+	+		+		+		+	+			+					
j̃															+																		
w	+		+		+				+		+		+				+			+		+		+	+			+	+				
w̃											+		+				+																

Naturally, the selection of a unit for the formulation of phonotactic constraints and the application of phonological principles has consequences for phonological theory, and the classification of clusters in terms of phonotactic well-formedness. A comprehensive discussion on the topic is provided in Rochoń (2000). The author argues that consonant clusters found at the end of the Common Slavic period largely followed the sonority principle. The only exception constituted /s/-initial and /z/-initial sequences. New onset clusters which emerged after yer deletion displayed a sonority violating pattern, by featuring a sonorant in the cluster-initial position. Phonological theory offers a solution to the problem of such clusters by incorporating the sonorant into prosodic constituents higher than the syllable.

Following Nespor and Vogel (1986) and Selkirk (1995), who propose the following hierarchy of units: syllable (σ) > foot (Ft) > prosodic word (PW), where '>' means 'larger than', Rochoń (2000) states that in a sonority-violating cluster, an initial sonorant can have different representations. The claim is illustrated on the example of the word *mgła* /mgwa/ 'fog', as shown in 9.

9. Prosodic representations of the initial sonorant /m/ (Rochoń 2000: 78)

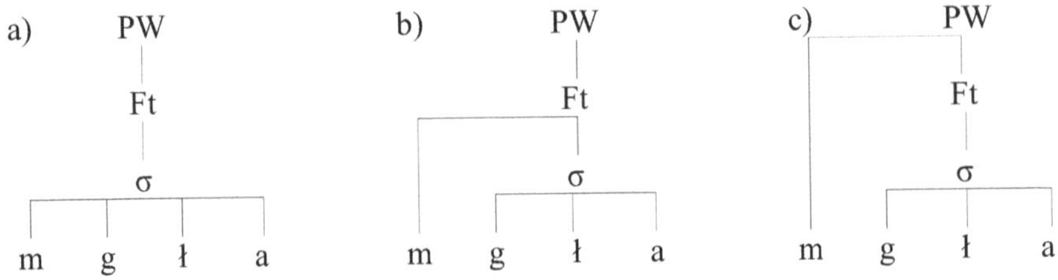

In the left-most representation, /m/ is adjoined to the syllable. In (b), the sonorant belongs to the foot where it represents the onset of the former syllable before yer deletion. In (c), /m/ is linked directly to the prosodic word. Note that the representation in (a) leads to the conclusion the syllable structure in Polish violates the universal principle of sonority (for an extended discussion see Chap. 2, Sects. 2.4.1.2 and 2.4.1.3). To the contrary, (b) and (c) ensure a well-formed syllable structure, where sonority rises gradually from the least sonorous plosive /g/ through a sonorous glide /w/ to the most sonorous vowel, and where /m/ is treated as an adjunct to the syllable. In her OT account, Rochoń (2000) argues in favour of the representation in (b) by demonstrating that Polish onsets and codas are well-formed, and that the apparent complexity is a by-product of historical prosodic changes.

1.5 Contexts Affecting Cluster Structure

Polish phonology operates on several rules which affect the properties of consonant sequences. These rules delimit a possible set of clusters, particularly in word-final position. In line with Bethin (1992), Rochoń (2000) and Rubach (1984), I discuss three contexts, which are crucial for phonotactics: final obstruent devoicing, voice assimilation, and the realization of nasal vowels.

1.5.1 Final Obstruent Devoicing and Voice Assimilation

Polish has a rule of word-final obstruent devoicing. In absolute word final position, all obstruents are pronounced as [−voice]. In 10, I provide three contexts of obstruent devoicing. (10.a) lists examples of words ending in a single consonant, which undergoes devoicing. The same rule applies to (10.b), however, devoicing extends to the preceding consonant. That is, obstruents assimilate in voicing to the following obstruent, resulting in terminal clusters such as [ɕtɕ], [ps] and [kt], rather than [ʑtɕ], [bs] and [gt]. The voicing profile of clusters is expressed by the following rule: "[i]n any given sequence of consonants, voicing is predictable from the last or rightmost consonant in the sequence" (Bethin 1992: 165). In other words, adjacent segments must exhibit agreement in voicing. The same rule applies in (10.c) in final obstruent + sonorant sequences. The structure of such clusters can be defined as [−voice] + [−voice]. This phenomenon is referred to as sonorant transparency whereby syllable-final and word-final sonorants are devoiced (for a detailed presentation see Rubach 1996; Sieczkowska et al. 2009; Strycharczuk 2012a, b).

10. Contexts of obstruent devoicing word-finally

(10.a) obstruent:
bó/g/ 'god' [buk]
gła/z/ 'stone' [gwas]
wó/ʣ/ 'chief' [vuʦ]
(10.b) obstruent + obstruent:
gwó/ʑʥ/ 'nail' [gvuɕʨ]
ko/bz/ 'bagpipe' (gen pl) [kops]
szmara/gd/ 'smaragd' [ʃmarakt]
(10.c) obstruent + sonorant:
boja/ʑɲ/ 'fear' [bojaɕɲ̊]
organi/zm/ 'organism' [organism̥]
ka/dr/ 'frame' [katr̥]

Apart from assimilation in (10.b) and (10.c), the rule applies in affixation. Prefixes /f v s z fs vz/ agree in voicing with the stem-initial segment, as I demonstrate in 11.

11. Voicing in prefixation

(11.a) voiceless + voiceless:
/sp/ *s+pisać* 'to write down' (perf)
/fkr/ *w+kroczyć* 'to slip in' (perf)
/fsx/ *ws+chodzić* 'to rise' (perf)
(11.b) voiced + voiced:
/zr/ *z+robić* 'to do' (perf)
/vj/ *w+jechać* 'to drive in' (perf)
/vzbr/ *wz+bronić* 'to prohibit' (perf)

Initial clusters found in prefixed words can thus be easily recognized from intramorphemic clusters in which no voice agreement occurs, e.g. /sw/ is *słowo* 'word'. Apart from voicing, the realization of nasal vowels generates consonant clusters of a specific type.

1.5.2 *Phonetic Realization of Nasal Vowels <ą ę>*

One of the challenges in providing a uniform phonemic classification of Polish consonants is related to nasal vowels. As noted by Bloch-Rozmej (1998: 43), <ą, ę> "display certain unique properties which distinguish them from both oral nuclei and vowel-nasal clusters". That is, the vowels have phonetically-motivated asynchronic realization, i.e. polysegmental structure (Biedrzycki 1963, 1978; Dukiewicz 1967; Dukiewicz and Sawicka 1995; Dunaj 1991; Jassem 1973; Madelska and Witaszek-Samborska 2015; Ostaszewska and Tambor 2005; Padgett 1995; Stieber 1948). Before a fricative, <ą, ę> are articulated as nasalized diphthongs /õw̃/ and /ẽw̃/. Some accounts regard the emergent sequences as combinations of the nasalized vowels and either of the nasal sonorants; /j̃/ preceding soft fricatives and /w̃/ preceding non-soft fricatives (e.g. Ostaszewska and Tambor 2005). Examples are listed in 12. In our interpretation, the glide is considered to be a part of a cluster.

12. Asynchronic articulation resulting in a vowel + glide sequence

(12.a) before hard fricatives:
labio-dental -
dental *wąs* /võw̃s/ 'moustache', *kęs* /kẽw̃s/ 'bite'
alveolar *mąż* /mõw̃ʃ/ 'husband', *węszyć* /vẽw̃ʃɪʨ/ 'to snoop'
velar *wąch* /võw̃x/ 'moustache' (pej), *w̃ęch* /vẽwx/ 'smell'

(12.b) before soft fricatives:
alveolo-palatal *kąśliwy* /kõ͠jɕlivɨ/ 'biting', *gęś* /gẽ͠jɕ/ 'goose'

In contrast, before stops and affricates, <ą, ę> are realized as a sequence of nasalized vowels /õ/ and /ẽ/ followed by a nasal homorganic with the following consonant. Compare the examples in 13:

13. Asynchronic articulation resulting in a vowel + obstruent sequence

(13.a) before plosives:
bilabial *dąb* /domp/ 'oak', *sęp* /semp/ 'vulture'
dental *prąd* /pront/ 'current', *wstręt* /fstrent/ 'abhorrence'
velar *drąg* /droŋk/ 'bar', *wdzięk* /vʥeŋk/ 'charm'

(13.b) before affricates:
dental *ksiądz* /kɕonʦ/ 'priest', *Swarzędz* /sfaʒẽnʦ/ [place name]
alveolar *oburącz* /oburonʧ/ 'with both hands', *poręcz* /porenʧ/ 'handrail'
alveolo-palatal *wziąć* /vʑoɲʨ/ 'to take', *chęć* /xeɲʨ/ 'willingness'

The contexts given in Sects. 1.5.1 and 1.5.2 are consulted when making decisions on lists of clusters for the purposes of the present studies.

1.6 Aspects of Phonotactic Complexity

In relation to phonotactics, the term *complexity* has been defined in various ways and based on different defining parameters (for a broad overview see Kretzschmar (2015) and Roussou (2017), for implementation in phonotactics see Hoole et al. (2012) and numerous references therein). Generally, complexity can be viewed in terms of markedness (see Chap. 2). I propose a division of complexity into: qualitative, quantitative and diachronic types, which are summarized in 14.

14. Aspects of phonotactic complexity

(14.a) quantitative:
violation of universals (or cluster length)
frequency
(14.b) qualitative:
violations of phonotactic principles
lack of syllabic consonants
morphological composition
(14.c) diachronic

The uniqueness of Polish is reflected in the fact that several complexity aspects can co-exist in a single cluster type. Below, I list some of the most unusual initial and final combinations. Each cluster displays one or more aspects of complexity.

15. Examples of complex clusters in Polish

(15.a) initial:
/brvj/ *brwiowy* 'eyebrow' (adj)
/drgn/ *drgnąć* 'to vibrate' (perf)
/vzbr/ *wzbronić* 'to forbid' (perf)
(15.b) final:
/psk/ *babsk* 'gorgon' (gen pl)
/ʦtf/ *ptactw* 'bird' (gen pl)
/mpstf/ *przestępstw* 'crime' (gen pl)

All the clusters are composed of three, four or five non-syllabic consonants, violate the principle of sonority, have low type and token frequencies and are the product of morphology. In order to investigate the structure of consonant clusters in detail, Sects. 1.6.1 and 1.6.2 present the qualitative and quantitative aspects of phonotactic complexity in reference to the Polish data. Since this book focuses on the synchronic analysis of phonotactics, a comprehensive discussion of the diachronic changes which led to the emergence of clusters can be found in descriptive and theoretical accounts (e.g. Bethin 2006; Długosz-Kurczabowa and Dubisz 2006; Klemensiewicz et al. 1981; Rochoń 2000; Rubach 1984; Walczak 1999).

1.6.1 Complexity Resulting from Quantitative Violations

In the vast majority of languages, syllables forming words have the prototypical consonant (C) plus vowel (V) structure (Donohue et al. 2013; Gordon 2016; Greenberg 1978; Itô 1986; Maddieson 2013a), implying that strings of adjacent consonants are universally disfavoured. A dominant view states that a longer string of consonants is more complex compared to a shorter one. This universal preference is notoriously violated in Polish. A severe violation of the CV universal can result in strings of several adjacent consonants such as (C)CCCCV or VCCCC.

A complete inventory of the phonotactic possibilities in Polish is given in Table 1.4. The first column 'Size' refers to the number of consonants forming a cluster (e.g. 2 refers to two-member clusters CC, 3 to three-member clusters CCC). For each cluster length, I provide an example of a cluster which is found in word-initial, word-medial, and word-final position. A distinction is made between three types of clusters: unmotivated clusters found within a single morpheme, morphologically-motivated clusters formed by means of adding a morpheme (affixation) or subtracting one (disfixation) (for a detailed discussion see Sect. 1.6.2.3), and clusters found across word boundaries in compounds and phrases. The presence of a morphological boundary is signalled with '+', while a word boundary is marked with '#'. The data was collected from dictionary- and corpus-based accounts of Polish phonotactics (Dziubalska-Kołaczyk et al. 2012; Marta Nowak [personal communication]; Śledziński 2013) and the author's native competence. For this reason, the collection of clusters of a given length is considered to be exhaustive.

The earliest accounts which handle the issue of cluster size date back to the mid 20th century. Bargiełówna (1950) lists initial and final clusters according to their length and morphological composition. Kuryłowicz (1952) discusses length by arguing for a bipartite structure of sequences composed of more than two consonants. The literature that followed has reported on the classification and frequency rankings of clusters collected from large resources such as dictionaries and corpora where the number of constituent consonants is a benchmark for classification (e.g. Dobrogowska 1984, 1990, 1992; Dukiewicz 1980, 1985; Dunaj 1985, 1986; Madejowa 1987, 1990, 1993; Madelska 2005; Orzechowska and Zydorowicz 2019; Sawicka 1974; Śledziński 2016; Zydorowicz and Orzechowska 2017).

The number of segments in a cluster was investigated in relation to different types of resources. Disregarding the account, two-member clusters are the most common, followed by CCC and longer sequences. For instance, Dobrogowska (1992) provides lists of word-initial and word-final clusters varying in length from CC to CCCCC in two types of resources: popular science texts and artistic prose. The frequency lists were compiled from the first and fourth volumes of the dictionary *Słownictwo Współczesnego Języka Polskiego* (Vocabulary of Modern Polish) by Kurcz et al. (1974). The results of Dobrogowska's (1992) analysis are summarized in Tables 1.5 and 1.6.

In both tables, the following terminological convention has been adopted. The length of clusters varies from two to five. The term *cluster class* stands for a broad phonotactic classification based on the manner of articulation, e.g. plosive + liquid,

Table 1.4 A complete repertoire of phonotactic possibilities in Polish

Size	Initial	Medial	Final
2	/dr/ drabina 'ladder'	/kt/ aktor 'actor'	/ʃt/ koszt 'cost'
	/ft/ w + topić 'to melt in'	/dj/ pod + jeść 'to sneak'	/ɕtɕ/ iś + ć 'to go'
	–	/jz/ trój # ząb 'trident'	–
3	/krn/ krnąbrny 'defiant'	/lbʒ/ olbrzym 'giant'	/rʃtʃ/ barszcz 'borscht'
	/spr/ s + prać 'to wash out'	/zbr/ roz + broić 'to disarm'	/jɕtɕ/ przyjś + ć 'to come'
	–	/wpr/ pół # prosta 'ray'	–
4	/pstr/ pstrąg 'trout'	/mbrj/ embrion 'embrio'	–
	/vzdw/ wz + dłużyć 'to prolong'	/skʃt/ bez + kształtny 'formless'	/rstf/ wartstw 'layer' (gen pl)
	–	/xfst/ zmartwych # wstanie 'ressurection'	–
5	/strfj/ Strwiąż [place name]	–	–
	–	/mpstf/ skąp + stwo 'miserliness'	/mpstf/ przestęp + stw 'crime' (gen pl)
	–	/ffstʃ/ przeciw + wstrząsowy 'anti-vibration'	–
6	–	–	–
	–	/ntʃzvj/ wewnątrz # związkowy 'union-internal'	–
Sandhi clusters			
7	/jstf s pr/ jest mało zabójstw # z # premedytacją 'there are few premeditated killings'		
8	/rɕtɕ s pstr/ sierść # z # pstrym wzorem 'fur of a motley pattern'		
9	/j̃ stf s krfj/ nie brakuje państw # z # krwiożerczą polityką zagraniczną 'there is no shortage of countries with bloodthirsty foreign policy'		
10	/mpstf s fstʃ/ popełnił kilka przestępstw # z # wstrząsającym skutkiem 'he committed several crimes with a harrowing effect'		
11	/mpstf f strfj/ przestępstw # w # Strwiążu 'crime (gen pl) in Strwiąż'		

Table 1.5 Word-initial cluster classes, types and tokens in scientific texts and artistic prose

Size	Scientific text						Artistic prose					
	Cluster class		Cluster type		Frequency of occurrence		Cluster class		Cluster type		Frequency of occurrence	
	No	%	No	%	No	%	No	%	No	%	No	%
2	25	36	167	59	20,601	86	24	33	164	53	18,874	88
3	31	44	100	35	3,072	13	34	47	124	40	2,473	11
4	14	20	16	6	199	1	14	20	22	7	143	1
Σ	70		283		23,872		72		310		21,490	

Adapted from Dobrogowska (1992: 57)

Table 1.6 Word-final cluster classes, types and tokens in scientific texts and artistic prose

Size	Scientific text						Artistic prose					
	Cluster class		Cluster type		Frequency of occurrence		Cluster class		Cluster type		Frequency of occurrence	
	No	%	No	%	No	%	No	%	No	%	No	%
2	14	54	80	82	3,045	96	13	52	87	79	2,920	97
3	9	34	14	14	110	3	10	40	19	17	88	3
4	2	8	3	3	27	1	1	4	3	3	5	0
5	1	4	1	1	7	0	1	4	1	1	1	0
Σ	26		98		3,189		25		110		3,014	

Adapted from Dobrogowska (1992: 58)

nasal + fricative. *Cluster type* refers to a unique combination of consonants, which is exemplified by initial /pr/ and final /ɕtɕ/. Each cluster is found in different *word types*, such as *prać* 'to wash', *praca* 'work', *prawy* 'right' (masc) and *kość* 'bone', *iść* 'to go', *puść* 'let go' (2nd sg voc). Finally, each inflected form of a word type such as *prać* (inf), *pranie* 'washing', *prał* (3rd sg past masc), *praliśmy* (1st pl past) is treated as a separate word type. Cumulative frequencies of the repetitions of such words in the corpus correspond with *word tokens* (labelled 'Frequency of occurrence'). For clarity of presentation, original percentages in Dobrogowska (1992) are here rounded to the nearest whole number.

The data show that the proportion of CCs in relation to longer clusters is the same in both resources. In both positions, CC types prevail. The number of cluster types decreases as the length of a cluster increases. Word initial position outweighs word-final position in terms of a variety of clusters. Similar differences are found when other types of resources are taken into account.

Let me compare the counts in Tables 1.5 and 1.6 with other sizeable datasets. Below, I present the data extracted from a dictionary and a corpus, reported by Zydorowicz et al. (2016). The smallest resource is represented by an 8,000-entry dictionary *Słownik Podstawowy Języka Polskiego dla Cudzoziemców* (A Basic Dictionary of Polish for Foreigners) by Bartnicka-Dąbkowska and Sinielnikoff (1999). A larger resource, a paradigm list, was created automatically on the basis of

Table 1.7 Word-initial cluster types, word types and tokens containing initial clusters

Size	Dictionary		Paradigm		Corpus		
	Cluster types	Word types	Cluster types	Word types	Cluster types	Word types	Word tokens
2	147	2,144	162	47,607	217	89,118	8,653,268
3	85	385	97	10,272	207	14,589	1,301,445
4	9	15	14	349	30	730	59,689
Σ	241	2,544	273	58,228	454	104,437	10,014,402

Adapted from Zydorowicz et al. (2016: 73ff.)

Table 1.8 Word-final cluster types, word types and tokens containing final clusters

Size	Dictionary		Paradigm		Corpus		
	Cluster types	Word types	Cluster types	Word types	Cluster types	Word types	Word tokens
2	54	565	100	2,334	142	8,874	1,524,889
3	10	34	27	82	52	244	66,238
4	–	–	8	28	9	70	18,233
5	–	–	1	2	1	5	2,706
Σ	64	599	136	2,446	204	9,193	1,612,066

Adapted from Zydorowicz et al. (2016: 73ff.)

the dictionary entries and includes 190,000 inflectional forms. The largest dataset, a corpus of raw texts of the nationwide *Rzeczpospolita* newspaper (period 2000–2001), contains 630,000 unique word forms and 48.6 million word tokens. Tables 1.7 and 1.8 present the cumulative results for the word-initial and word-final contexts, respectively.

Type frequencies reflect the structure of the lexicon, while token frequencies correspond with usage. Tables 1.7 and 1.8 demonstrate that two-member clusters are found in abundance in all the resources. That is, words which start and end with CCs not only constitute a substantial part of the Polish lexicon (types) but also are the most common in usage (tokens). The number of cluster types, words containing clusters and their repetitions decreases as cluster length increases. Generally, the difference between a mild violation of the CV universal resulting in CC, and a more severe violation leading to CCC is reflected in the frequency counts. This disproportion is systematically captured in all the resources.

The most interesting dataset for the purposes of the present discussion is the corpus. This resource reflects the actual usage frequency of words, and contains at least twice as many examples of clusters of each length as the dictionary. If I argue, without being controversial, that the corpus embraces the most exhaustive inventory of clusters, then the differences between two-member and three-member sequences are much larger than for other resources. The proportion of CC to CCC in terms of tokens equals 7:1 word-initially, and 23:1 word-finally. To compare, the proportion calculated for word types amounts to 6:1 word-initially, and 36:1 word-finally. That is, the number of CCs increases in usage.

These observations can be easily related to phonological theories which are based on frequency measures. Usage-based approaches offer insights into the dynamics of cognitive processes and language use (Bybee 2003), and make specific claims regarding the mapping between frequency and linguistic representations.

> Schemas which are organizational patterns across lexical items, gain strength from the number of different items participating – that is, by their type frequency. (Bybee 2003: 28)

Bybee (2003) states that high frequency items are accessed more quickly in contrast to low-frequency items. That is, access to infrequent structures is hindered. Viewed from this perspective, one would expect that frequency should reflect at least some degree of complexity. A favoured cluster should be more frequent, as it facilitates cognitive processing. Naturally, the key question is whether this is a valid approach. In order to provide a tentative answer to the question, let me present a lists of the most frequent word-initial and word-final clusters. Tables 1.9 and 1.10 present the 15 the most and the least frequent cluster types collected from corpora by Dobrogowska (1992).

Top frequency clusters involve /pʃ pr st vj kt/ in both scientific texts and artistic prose. In turn, the least frequent extreme is represented by different types of clusters in the two resources. This result posits the first challenge for usage-based approaches. Formulating generalizations on frequency and well-formedness can be elusive due to the fact that type and token frequencies yield conflicting results. This conflict is related to two problem areas.

Table 1.9 Token frequencies of words containing initial and final clusters: scientific texts

Scientific text								
Rank	Initial				Final			
	CC	Freq.	CCC	Freq.	CC	Freq.	CCC	Freq.
1	pʃ	3,264	ɕfj	280	ɕtɕ/ʑdʑ	766	nkt/ngd	42
2	pr	1,587	zvj	280	nts/ndz	761	ntʃ/ndʒ	22
3	st	1,248	str	188	nt/nd	418	jɕtɕ/jʑdʑ	19
4	vj	1,163	zmj	188	ɲtɕ/ɲdʑ	229	jsk/jzg	7
5	kt	769	fsp	182	st/zd	186	kst/gzd	4
6	pj	754	spr	172	kt/gd	61	stf/zdv	3
7	mj	747	skw	122	zm	55	tstf/dzdv	3
8	sp	655	zbj	109	nk/ng	52	stʃ/zdʒ	2
9	zn	499	fpw	107	sk/zg	43	jsts/jzdz	2
10	kr	426	vzr	95	mp/mb	28	rks/rgz	2
11	tr	385	fsk	73	rt/rd	25	str	1
12	tʃ	372	spʃ	70	dw	24	jgl	1
13	dr	371	fpr	67	rm	24	ndr	1
14	dl	371	kʃt	66	tʃp/dʒb	23	rɕtɕ/rʑdʑ	1
15	dv	355	dvj	61	wt/wd	22		

Adapted from Dobrogowska (1992: 70–73)

Table 1.10 Token frequencies of words containing initial and final clusters: artistic prose

Artistic prose								
Rank	Initial				Final			
	CC	Freq.	CCC	Freq.	CC	Freq.	CCC	Freq.
1	vj	1,018	str	281	nʦ/nʣ	623	jɕʨ/jʑʥ	29
2	pʃ	1,013	ɕfj	270	st/zd	519	stʃ/zdʒ	14
3	st	952	spr	202	ɕʨ/ʑʥ	399	ntʃ/ndʒ	9
4	pr	784	ɕmj	118	nt/nd	227	kst/gzd	6
5	kt	759	zmj	82	ɲʨ/ɲʥ	167	nkt/ngd	5
6	mj	746	fst	81	dw	125	jsʦ/jzʣ	5
7	sp	663	fsp	80	kt/gd	87	nʨ/ndʑ	3
8	pj	481	vzr	79	gw	66	stf/zdv	3
9	zn	443	zvj	67	sw	55	rɕʨ/rʑʥ	2
10	kr	400	dʒv	65	rt/rd	53	rst/rzd	2
11	sw	389	skr	54	mɕ/mʑ	53	nkw	2
12	mɲ	387	stʃ	54	kw	51	str	1
13	fʃ	380	skʃ	53	nk/ng	47	jnʦ/jnʣ	1
14	gw	376	ɕpj	45	tr	45	ɲɕʨ/ɲʑʥ	1
15	dr	367	spʃ	45	rw	39	jsk/jzg	1

Adapted from Dobrogowska (1992: 74–78)

First, some sequences of consonants have low type frequency but high token frequency. For instance, initial /kt/ is found in only several lexical items in Polish, namely *kto* 'who', *ktoś* 'somebody', *ktokolwiek* 'whoever', *który* 'whose' and their inflected forms in spite of the fact the cluster has high text frequency. In Tables 1.9 and 1.10, /kt/ is listed among the five most frequent initials. The same tendency is observed in usage. For instance, Madelska's (2005) corpus of spoken variants reports on 36 inflected word forms starting with /kt/ and 310 repetitions of the cluster. Also, Orzechowska and Zydorowicz (2019) report that the cluster has low logarithmic frequency in a dictionary but high logarithmic frequency in a written corpus. When trying to formulate phonological generalization based on token frequencies, sequences similar to /kt/ can tip the balance in favour of a view that Polish tolerates ill-formed clusters.

Apart from the differences between type and token frequencies, morphological productivity constitutes another problem area for usage-based phonology. Among the most frequent initials, /pʃ/ comes to the forefront. The sequence is found primarily in productive prefixes {przy−} and {przed−}, which generate a substantial portion of /pʃ/-initial nouns and verbs. Morphology also plays a role in initial /st/ and final /ɕʨ/ clusters. Both cluster types can contain a morphological boundary: /s/ signals the presence of a productive verbal prefix, while /ʨ/ is an infinitival morpheme.

Viewed from this perspective, generalizations on the complexity of phonotactics cannot be extrapolated only on the basis of frequency. Bybee's (2003) statement that frequency is a crucial factor in production, perception and grammar cannot be countered. However, it must be borne in mind that frequency is a function of various intervening properties, which have to be considered with due care.

1.6.2 Complexity Resulting from Qualitative Violations

1.6.2.1 Violations of Phonological Principles

The qualitative aspects of phonotactic complexity are associated with violations of phonological principles. An example of such a principle is the *Sonority Sequencing Generalization* (henceforth SSG, Selkirk 1984; for overviews and synopses see Cairns and Raimy 2010; Parker 2002, 2012a, b, 2017 and numerous references therein), which determines a universally preferred ordering of segments in a syllable or a word. The SSG evaluates clusters according to the sonority profile of constituent consonants before and after a vowel. Generally, a steady rise towards a vowel ensures phonotactic well-formedness. Statistically speaking, clusters composed of several consonants stand a greater chance of violating the SSG than shorter clusters. Therefore, three- and four-member sequences in Polish are likely to be classified as ill-formed.

A complex character of Polish phonotactics has been also confirmed by other phonotactic principles which reach beyond sonority. With a wider array of criteria implemented in cluster description, and more demanding well-formedness requirements, Dziubalska-Kołaczyk (2009, 2014, in press) demonstrates the complexity of Polish clusters. The author proposes an auditory model of phonotactic preferability for clusters with two and three constituents. Sequences longer than CCC are excluded from the analysis on the grounds of severe CV violations. The analysis of Polish clusters in terms of this principle is discussed in Chap. 2.

It must be noted that another pool of data suggests that Polish strives at phonotactic simplicity. A well-motivated structure of onset and coda clusters in Polish has been documented in theoretical approaches to the syllable and syllabification in Lexical Phonology, Government Phonology and (Derivational) Optimality Theory (e.g. Bethin 1992; Cyran and Gussmann 1999; Gussmann 1992, 2007; Kijak 2008; Pawelec 2012; Rochoń 2000; Rubach 1984; Rubach and Booij 1990a, b; Szpyra 1995). According to Bethin (1992: 50), the core syllable in Polish is relatively simple and is represented by CSVS, i.e. Consonant + Sonorant + Vowel + Sonorant. Theoretical accounts of Polish syllabification (e.g. Rubach and Booij 1990a, b) stress that obstruent + sonorant clusters constitute ideal onsets, which should be syllabified together (although cf. Szpyra-Kozłowska 1998, 2000). The SSG-based profile of Polish clusters was also demonstrated in Cetnarowska and Żygis (2007) who showed that sonority plays a crucial role in the phonetic syllabification of prefixed words. This statement holds when the extrasyllabic status of sonorants in initial sonorant + obstruent clusters is assumed (e.g. Gussmann 2007; Rochoń 2000; Rubach 1997; Vaux and Wolfe 2009).

Overall, Polish largely violates several principles of phonological organization. Well-formendess conditions implicit in such principles, are based on universal characteristics of consonant clusters, which tend to have a simpler obstruent + sonorant structure (Maddieson 2013a). In the sections to follow, I will demonstrate that Polish features numerous clusters which are longer than CC(C), and whose edge-most consonants are represented by sonorants, giving rise to more complex structures than commonly encountered and expected cross word languages. This aspect of complexity is related to a phonetic property of Polish sonorants, namely the lack of syllabic consonants.

1.6.2.2 Absence of Syllabic Consonants

The presence of syllabic consonants in a language results in simpler clusters. For instance, although Tashlhiyt Berber features strings of more than 30 consonants, it has a basic syllable structure: all consonants can function as vocalic peaks (among others, Boukous 1987; Dell and Elmedlaoui 1985, 2002; Ridouane 2016). In the Slavonic languages, different realizations of sonorants lead to different representations of the same sequence of segments. Scheer (2006) reports on several Slavic systems, which are known for sonority-violating clusters. Croatian, Czech, Polish, Russian and Ukrainian allow the /rv/ sequence in *rvati se*, *rvát*, *rwać*, '*rvaty*' and '*rvat*' 'tear, rip', respectively. The rhotic forms the syllable peak in Croatian and Czech (see also Dressler et al. 2015 for a discussion on Slovak), but not in Polish. What is more, Polish seems to be relatively liberal in terms of its phonotactic potential. It maintains a five-member initial cluster /strfj/ in a river and village name *Strwiąż*, for which the Ukrainian equivalent starts with a CCC sequence /str/ (*Stryvihor*), an alternative to the existing five-segment structure. Other Slavonic systems feature syllabic sonorants, leading to a bisyllabic structure of the cluster as in Russian. Compare the realization of the rhotic in Polish, Ukrainian and Russian.

(a)	Polish:	/strfj/	*Strwiąż*
(b)	Ukrainian:	/str/	*Stryvihor* versus /strʋj/ *Strvjaž*
(c)	Russian:	/strv^j/	*Strv'až*

A CCCCC cluster composed of non-syllabic consonants in (a) and (b) is complex in phonological terms; however, apparently not complex enough in Polish to alternate with a simplified pronunciation variant as in Ukrainian or Russian. The nature of these considerations is of lesser importance given the fact that /strfj/ is the only initial five-member cluster in Polish, which is found exclusively in one proper name familiar to a small population of Poles and Ukrainians. Nevertheless, the very existence of the cluster and its varied realization in other Slavic languages leads to a question: Is there a phonetic or phonological property that blocks cluster simplification in Polish? This question lies at the heart of the present volume. A possible explanation is that each language operates on an *elementary particle*, or a set of such particles, which is held responsible for the unique phonological structure of consonant clusters. As I will demonstrate in the empirical chapters of this book (Chaps. 3–5), this basic structure can be represented by *weighted* phonological features.

1.6.2.3 Intervention of Morphology

Morphological composition constitutes another factor which contributes to phonotactic complexity (for a theoretical and empirical overview see Gouskova 2018). Although the earliest observations on the interaction between phonology and morphology are found in the Kazan School of Linguistics (Baudouin de Courtenay 1895) and American structuralism (Bloomfield 1939; Harris 1942; Hockett 1950; Moulton 1947; Swadesh and Voegelin 1939), the first explicit mention of the role that morphology plays in phonotactics is due to the Prague School and the founder of morphophonology. According to Trubetzkoy (1969: 306), one of the tasks of morphophonology is to study combinatory sound changes that take place in the morphemes in morpheme combinations. For instance, in the word *decision*, the final plosive /d/ in the input verb *decide* alternates with /ʒ/ when {−ion} is suffixed. The alternating phoneme is thus a demarcation (or boundary) signal (from German *Grenzsignal*) as it signals the presence of a morphemic boundary. The idea of boundary signals has been formalized in Generative Phonology (Chomsky and Halle 1968). The theory specifies different types of boundaries as a representational device and the phonological cycle as an interpretation of the underlying representation into the surface phonetic form.

A more specific interaction between morphology and phonotactics is found in the domain of consonant clusters. The first account of Polish clusters which takes into consideration the presence of morphological boundaries dates back to 1950. Bargiełówna (1950) distinguishes between two types of clusters: intra-morphemic (i.e. occurring within a single morpheme) and inter-morphemic (i.e. occurring across morpheme boundaries). The latter type is further subdivided depending on morphological productivity. Productive morphological boundaries emerge in inflection (e.g. /pstf/ in *głup* + *stw* 'foolishness' (gen pl)), while dead morphological boundaries are lexicalized, and are thus no longer recognizable (e.g. /rɕtɕ/ in *ga* + *rść* 'handful'). Such an analysis is offered for clusters varying in length from CC to CCCCC and found in different word positions (initial, medial, final). Bargiełówna's (1950) account sparked interest in a systematic study on morphologically- complex consonant clusters.

An insightful investigation of such consonant clusters is provided in Kuryłowicz (1952), who demonstrates syntagmatic differences between *motivated* (from Polish *motywowany*) and *unmotivated* (*niemotywowany*) clusters. Combinations of consonants are motivated if they contain a morphological boundary (e.g. *w* + *stawać* 'to get up'). Kuryłowicz (1952) proposes a method of phonotactic analysis which consists in dividing CCCs into shorter constituents. In motivated clusters, this bipartite structure is determined by the presence of a productive morpheme such as {w−} in *w* + *stawać* /fstawatɕ/ 'to get up', leading to the split of a three-member cluster into C|CC. In unmotivated clusters, the splitting procedure involves identifying an existent CC. Therefore, C|CC is exemplified by /mɕtɕ/ in *mścić* 'to avenge', in which /ɕtɕ/ is a legitimate initial, while CC|C is exemplified by /krn/ in *krnąbrny* 'defiant', where /kr/ is an existing CC cluster. Note that */mɕ/ and */rn/ are not attested in Polish in word-initial position.

This line of research was further developed in Dressler and Dziubalska-Kołaczyk (2006: 252) who introduce the term *morphonotactics* to refer to "cooperative interactions between morphonotactics and phonotactics". The authors demonstrate a tightly-knit relationship between morphology and cluster size as well as phonological markedness in English, German, Italian and Polish. A distinction is made between phonologically-motivated (or *phonotactic*) clusters, which occur morpheme-internally (e.g. /ks nd mpt/ in *axe*, *band*, *tempt*), and morphologically-motivated (or *morphonotactic*) clusters, which are the product of morphological operations (e.g. *back* + *s*, *bann* + *ed*, *jump* + *ed*). The identification of morphological boundaries in English is straightforward as initial and final morphonotactic clusters emerge due to prefixation and suffixation, respectively. According to Dressler and Dziubalska-Kołaczyk (2006), Polish clusters are generated by two types of morphological operations exemplified in 16: concatenative in (16.a) and non-concatenative in (16.b) through (16.d).

16. Examples of morphologically-motivated clusters

(16.a) /vzbr/ results from prefixation: *bronić* /broɲitɕ/ 'to protect' → *wz* + *bronić* /vzbroɲitɕ/ 'to forbid' (perf)
/tw/ or /dw/ result from suffixation: *miotać* /mjotatɕ/ 'to flounce' → *miót* + *ł* /mjutw/ (3rd sg past masc)
/drgn/ emerges in the change from imperfective *drgać* /drgatɕ/ 'to vibrate' to perfective *drg* + *nąć* /drgnoɲtɕ/

(16.b) /brvj/ results from vowel ∼ zero alternation in derivation: *brew* /bref/ 'eyebrow' (n) → *brwiowy* /brvjowɨ/ 'eyebrow' (adj)

(16.c) /ltʃ/ results from the truncation of the infinitival desinence resulting in an imperative verb from: *walcz!* 'to fight' (imp sg) ← *walcz* + *yć* (inf)

(16.d) /mpstf/ results from the truncation of the final vowel indicating the neuter declension: *przestępstw* 'crime' (gen pl) ← *przestęp* + *stw* + *o* (nom sg)

In the section to follow, I present specific concatenative and non-concatenative contexts which generate morphologically-complex clusters at word edges.

Principles of Morphological Parsing

Determining the morphological complexity of clusters requires making two types of decisions. One is related to the identification of morphological boundaries. The other is concerned with the treatment of phonological phenomena which occur at morpheme boundaries.

Concatenation involves the affixation of an overt morphological marker. Word-initially, the most transparent morphological context is represented by the prefixation of {s−} and {w−}, which are phonetically realized as fricatives /f v s z fs vz/. This process entails the change of a semantic category from imperfective to perfective as in *jechać* 'to drive' → *w* + *jechać* 'to drive in', *drapać* 'to scratch' → *z* + *drapać* 'to scratch off', *krwawić* 'to bleed' (imperf) → *s* + *krwawić* 'to bleed' (perf) giving rise to clusters /vj zdr skrf/. The prefix {s−} is realized as an alveolo-palatal fricative /ɕ/ preceding /tɕ/-initial stems, as in *ś* + *cigać* 'to chaste', *ś* + *ciskać* 'to squeeze down', *ś* + *ciemniać* 'to fade out'. Initial clusters are also formed when the suffix {−nąć} is attached to a stem. /px/ in *pchać* 'to push' (imperf) changes to /pxn/ in the perfective form *pch* + *nąć*. In the formation of deverbal nouns, /n/ found in the verbal suffix {−nąć} undergoes palatalization to /ɲ/ when found in the nominal suffix {−nięcie}, resulting in a new set of morphologically-motivated clusters such as /pxɲ/ in *pch* + *nięcie* 'push' ← *pch* + *nąć* 'to push'.

A pool of clusters can be generated in non-concatenative morphology. Vowel ~ zero alternation constitutes one of typical morphonological contexts. V ~ Ø accompanies the derivation of denominal adjectives (e.g. /krfj/ *krwionośny* 'circulatory' ← /kr/ *krew* 'blood'), pluralization (e.g. /ps/ *psy* 'dog' (pl) ← /pj/ *pies* 'dog' (sg)), and declination (e.g. /mx/ *mchu* 'moss' (acc sg) ← *mech* 'moss' (nom sg)). In all the cases, the root vowel is dropped, resulting in a consonant cluster.

In word-final position, three types of morphological operations give rise to morphonotactic clusters. Polish features two suffixes which, when attached to the stem, form a final cluster. The preterit {−ł}, phonetically realized as /w/, is used to form the 3rd person singular masculine verbs. The suffix generates final clusters such as /tw dw rw sw/ in *jad* + *ł* 'to eat' (3rd sg past masc), *par* + *ł* 'to push' (3rd sg past masc), *uniós* + *ł* 'to lift' (3rd sg past masc). Similarly, the infinitival suffix {−ć}, phonetically realized as /tɕ/, yields combinations such as /ɕtɕ ɲtɕ jɕtɕ/ found in *iś* + *ć* 'to go', *wzią* + *ć* 'to take', *wejś* + *ć* 'to come in'.

Non-concatenative contexts involve the formation of imperative and genitive plural forms. In the first case, the 2nd person singular imperative form is generated by truncating the infinitival marker resulting in clusters such as /lʧ/ in *walcz* + Ø! 'fight' ← *walcz* + *yć* 'to fight', /ɕtɕ/ in *streść* + Ø ← *streśc* + *ić* 'to summarize' and /tʃ/ in *patrz* + Ø! ← *patrz* + *eć* 'to look'. Also genitive plural nouns are formed by dropping the final vowel as in /wp rʧ jsts/ in *małp* + Ø (gen pl) ← *małp* + *y* 'monkey' (nom pl), *tarcz* + Ø (gen pl) ← *tarcz* + *e* 'shield' (nom pl), *miejsc* + Ø (gen pl) ← *miejsc* + *a* 'place' (nom pl).

It must be borne in mind that some of the affixes presented above can feature as non-morphological cluster constituents. For instance, /s/ and /z/ are fully-fledged segments in morphologically simple clusters such as *sto* 'one hundred', *spać* 'to sleep' and *zło* 'evil'. Also word-finally, /tɕ/ can be found in a morpheme, e.g. in the suffix {−ość} /ɕtɕ/ which forms abstract nouns such as *wiern* + *ość* 'loyalty', *młod* + *ość* 'youth' and *mądr* + *ość* 'wisdom'.

Morphology in Relation to Other Aspects of Complexity

The impact of morphology on consonant clusters has been studied in terms of cluster size. Morphology leads to an increase in the number of consonants forming strings. I illustrate this relationship on the basis of two accounts: the earliest account by Bargiełówna (1950), and the most recent one by Zydorowicz et al. (2016). Tables 1.11 and 1.12 juxtapose the number of phonotactic (labelled 'phon') and morphonotactic (labelled 'morph') clusters in terms of cluster types, word types in which the clusters occur, and word tokens. Note that the morphological divisions in Bargiełówna (1950) account only for intra-morphemic and inter-morphemic clusters, and disregard the non-concatenative contexts.

The data show two tendencies. First, two-member clusters tend to be phonotactic. This observation holds for both cluster types and word types. Second, the propensity of a morphonotactic cluster increases with an increase in cluster size. In both word positions, cluster types which arise due to the intervention of morphology are longer than CC.

Morphological complexity in phonotactics has also been studied in relation to phonotactic markedness principles. Dressler and Dziubalska-Kołaczyk (2006) address the issue of the extent to which morphological rules offend phonotactic constraints in a language, and entail severe violations of universal phonotactic preferences proposed in phonological theory. The intervention of morphology is expected to contribute to phonotactic complexity, particularly in morphologically-rich languages.

> (…) [W]e expect, in agreement with overall morphonology, that languages approaching the ideal inflecting-fusional language type more closely (e.g. strongly inflecting languages such as Polish) will have more marked clusters (…) than languages which approach the ideal

Table 1.11 The relationship between size and morphological composition in initial clusters (A: Bargiełówna 1950; B: Zydorowicz et al. 2016)

Size	A		B				
	Cluster types		Cluster types			Word types	
	Phon	Morph	Phon	Morph	Shared	Phon	Morph
2	191	59	106	21	18	1,884	253
3	65	110	36	35	14	189	192
4 and longer	6	9	2	6	0	3	11

Table 1.12 The relationship between size and morphological composition in final clusters (A: Bargiełówna 1950; B: Zydorowicz et al. 2016)

Size	A		B				
	Cluster types		Cluster types			Word types	
	Phon	Morph	Phon	Morph	Shared	Phon	Morph
2	76	2	52	–	2	359	209
3	9	7	8	1	1	14	20
4 and longer	2	11	–	–	–	–	–

isolating language type (i.e. weakly inflecting languages such as English and less so German and Italian). (Dressler and Dziubalska-Kołaczyk 2006: 252f)

The authors note that when passing from initial CCC to CCCC in Polish, an increase in phonotactic markedness and a greater role of morphonotactics can be observed. That is, there is a tendency for Polish morphologically-motivated clusters to be longer and phonologically more complex or dispreferred (for further cross-linguistic evidence see e.g. Dressler et al. 2010; Kamandulyte 2006; Korecky-Kröll et al. 2014; Orzechowska 2012; Schadler 2006; Schwarzinger 2006).

A related question concerns the extent to which phonological rules are successful in repairing morphologically-modified clusters. This point was first raised in Dressler and Dziubalska-Kołaczyk (2006), who listed examples of strategies leading to the avoidance of morphonotactic clusters in Polish.

17. Avoidance and repair of marked clusters (based on Dressler and Dziubalska-Kołaczyk 2006: 260ff.)

(17.a) presence of empty slots in the paradigm, e.g. the genitive singular *dżdżu* 'rain' has no nominative singular form **dżdż* /ʤʤ/
(17.b) reduction in fast or sloppy speech, e.g. *wschód* 'east' → /fsx/ and /sx/
(17.c) insertion of /e/ in genitive plural to avoid a final illicit cluster, e.g. *babka* 'granny, cake' → *babek* (expected **babk* + Ø)
(17.d) insertion of /e/ in perfective forms to avoid a long initial cluster, e.g. *w + spierać* /fspj/ 'to support' (imperf) → *wesprzeć* /vespʃ/ (expected **w + sprzeć* /fspʃ/)
(17.e) a partial change of an inflectional class, e.g. *mizdrzyć się* 'to wheedle' → *mizdrz + yj się*! (imp) (expected **mizdrz się*! /stʃɕ/)
(17.f) vowel insertion in genitive plural to avoid geminates, e.g. *willa* 'villa' → *will + i* (expected **will* + Ø)

Strategies in 17 lead to the avoidance of a potential phonologically marked output. Let me now provide a detailed analysis of word-initial and word-final morphonotactic clusters along the lines proposed in 17. (18.a) presents examples of clusters generated by concatenative morphology (i.e. affixation of consonant-only morphemes). (18.b) lists examples of types resulting from non-concatenative contexts in which disfixation occurs. Generally, 18 demonstrates that the repair of morphonotactic clusters at word edges is minimal, if any.

18. Examples of phonological repair

(18.a) mild repair in prefixation:
{s−} in *ś* + *cisnąć* 'to squeeze' → /ɕtɕ/
{w−} in *w* + *padać* 'to drop in' → /fp/

(18.b) selective repair in disfixation:
rurk + *a* 'tube' (nom sg fem) → *rurek* + Ø (gen pl) (**rurk*)
torb + *a* 'bag' (nom sg fem) → *toreb* + Ø / *torb* + Ø (gen pl)
kopert + *a* 'envelope' (nom sg fem) → *kopert* + Ø (gen pl)

In (18.a), phonetic similarity between consonants forming clusters is ensured by the change of the place of articulation and voice specification of the prefix. Before /tɕ/, {s−} is realized as an alveolo-palatal /ɕ/, rather than a dental /s/. By the same token, {w−} assimilates in voicing to stem-initial consonants, and surfaces as /f/ before voiceless obstruents. The examples suggest that although phonology has the power to minimize the pressures imposed by morphology, emergent clusters continue to violate the sonority principle. What is more, the output of morphological operations is repaired selectively in non-concatenative contexts. An interesting case constitutes the genitive plural.

The nominal paradigm in Polish conflates two grammatical categories: case and number. Dąbrowska (2001) argues that among seven cases present in Polish, the genitive has no default ending. A null morpheme and {−y/−i} morphemes are found in feminine and neuter nouns. The selection of an ending is largely arbitrary, which I exemplify in (18.b). The nominative feminine ending /a/ in *kopert* + *a* 'envelope' is deleted in the genitive plural form *kopert* + Ø, resulting in word-final /rt/. However, note that similar well-formed liquid + plosive clusters are repaired in the genitive. For instance, *rurk* + *a* 'tube' is repaired in *rurek* by means of vowel insertion (**rurk* + Ø). The word *torb* + *a* 'bag' admits two variants: a more common form *toreb* + Ø /torep/, in which the final cluster is simplified to −CVC, and a rare variant *torb* + Ø /torp/, in which the cluster is preserved.

The data suggest that the phonotactic preferability of a cluster is not a motivating force for the selection of a genitive plural morpheme. If we take examples of words containing medial obstruent + obstruent or obstruent + sonorant sequences, the same irregular pattern can be observed. For instance, /fʦ tw tk ʧk/ in feminine nouns *owc* + *a* 'sheep', *miotł* + *a* 'broom', *matk* + *a* 'mother', and *paczk* + *a* 'package' are split with a vowel in the genitive plural form: *owiec* + Ø /ovjeʦ/, *mioteł* + Ø /mjotew/, *matek* + Ø /matek/ and *paczek* + Ø /paʧek/. To the contrary, *puszcz* + *a* 'wildreness' admits the final obstruent cluster /ʃʧ/ in *puszcz* + Ø, while *rózga* 'rod' has two grammatically legitimate alternatives: *rózg* + Ø /rusk/ and less common *rózeg* + Ø /ruzek/. In general, final consonant clusters in genitive plural alternate with simplified −CVC sequences, disregarding whether the clusters are well-formed or ill-formed. The extent to which this variation is systematic requires a separate study based on a large dataset, which is out of the scope of this chapter.

The observation that the effects of morphology on the phonological make-up of clusters are neutralized only to some extent is not new to phonological theory. It has been long stressed that prefixation blocks the application of some phonological rules. This aspect of Polish morphonology has been discussed in theoretical accounts in Booij and Rubach (1984), Gussmann (1980), Rubach (1984), and Szpyra (1992). Szpyra (1992) provides an overview of such rules. Although voice assimilation, surface palatalization, vowel epenthesis and stress assignment accompany affixation, a wide range of rules (e.g. vowel deletion and retraction, j-deletion, anterior palatalization) is sensitive to prefixation. The blocking of phonological rules in prefixation lends further support to the claim that morphology contributes to the complexity of phonotactics in Polish. However, apart from a general division into phonotactic and morphonotactic clusters, degrees of complexity can be specified for morphologically-motivated clusters.

Degrees of Morphonotactic Complexity

A detailed analysis of Polish morphologically-motivated clusters is proposed in Orzechowska's (2009). Since Polish is a strongly suffixing language (Dryer 2013), word-final phonotactics is expected to be particularly affected by morphology. Therefore, on the example of word-final clusters, Orzechowska (2009) establishes degrees of morphonotactic complexity in terms of (1) phonological, (2) morphophonological and (3) morphological criteria. The permutation of these properties makes it possible to establish complexity scales for morphologically-motivated clusters.

The morpho-phonological aspect of complexity is represented by morphotactic transparency (Dressler 1985). This criterion refers to a morpheme type and phonological corollaries that morphological operations bring. In general, more transparent bases and morphological markers result in more perceptible and identifiable output forms, or greater preferability. In turn, morphotactic opacity is determined on the basis of stem mutations and (allo)morph irregularity. Orzechowska's (2009) complexity continuum is summarized in Table 1.13. The column 'R' provides a ranked ordering of degrees of transparency as a function of stem and affix transparency. A darker shading indicates an increase in opacity. For each rank, an example of a word with a cluster type ('cl') is given. The coding of the grammatical information is either transparent (no shading) or opaque (light grey shading). That is, affixes are unmarked as they are overtly coded. To the contrary, a covert morphological marker in the form of a zero morpheme {−Ø} is marked. As regards the stem, Orzechowska (2009) establishes three degrees of markedness, which reflect the number of phonological changes in stem-final consonants, varying from no change (no shading) to three changes in a segment (dark grey shading).

In general, morphotactically-transparent clusters (ranked 1) are formed with the help of fully transparent morphs {−ś} and {−ć}, and involve no phonological change in the stem-final consonant. The postfix {−ś} converts interrogative

Table 1.13 Degrees of stem and affix transparency in final morphonotactic clusters

R	Cl	Word	Stem		Affix
1	jɕ	czyj+ś	j+ɕ	0	{–ś}
	ɕtɕ	paś+ć	ɕ+tɕ	0	{–ć}
2	tf	płetw+a → płetw	tf → tf	0	{–Ø}
3	nt	wind+a → wind	nd → nt	1 (voice)	{–Ø}
4	ɕp	rzeźb+a → rzeźb	ʑb → ɕp	2 (voice)	{–Ø}
5	ftɕ	sprawdz+ać →sprawdź	vdʑ → ftɕ	3 (voice, placex2)	{–Ø}

Adapted from Orzechowska (2009: 132ff.)

pronouns into affirmatives, e.g., *czyj* 'whose' → *czyj* + *ś* 'somebody's', while {−ć} is the infinitival ending in Polish, e.g., *paś* + *ś* 'to fall down'. Morphotactically-opaque clusters (ranked from 2 to 5) are the product of non-concatenative morphology and occur in imperative singular and genitive plural forms. A regards the stem, rank 2 is represented by a cluster, which is subject to no phonological changes when {−a} is truncated. The remaining ranks list examples of clusters in which two and three features are changed with respect to the basic form (i.e. nominative singular in nouns and infinitive in verbs).

Apart from morphotactic transparency, the model employs a morphological criterion in the form of the lexical cycle (Booij and Rubach 1987; Szpyra 1992; Rubach 1984). Orzechowska (2009) asserts that gradient markedness is related to the cycle at which a cluster is formed, where derivations are less marked than inflections. This ordering is implicit not only in Lexical Phonology (e.g. Halle and Mohanan 1985; Kiparsky 1982, 1985; Mohanan 1982) but also in universals (see Greenberg 1978, universal 29), and in morphological theory, especially the principles of Inflectional Morphology (for an overview see Stump 2017). According to the principles of boundedness, openness, generality, obligatoriness, and semantic abstractness (Bauer 1983; Booij 2006; Bybee 1985) derivations are less complex than inflections. The ensuing classification of morphonotactic clusters into derivational and inflectional is straightforward with the exception of indefinite pronouns. The postfix {−ś} presents a special case of a derivational morpheme (Bańko 2005). {−ś} in *kim* + *ś* /kimɕ/ attaches to *kim* (instr / loc), which is an inflected form of a pronoun *kto* 'who'. Therefore, in this word /mɕ/ is assigned the greatest degree of complexity.

I have demonstrated that the presence of a morphological boundary substantially adds to the complexity of clusters in Polish in qualitative and quantitative terms. Although the idea that phonotactic and morphonotactic clusters tend to differ in terms of length and well-formedness is not new, in this book emphasis is placed on investigating the differences between them in terms of subsegmental properties. Is there an *elementary particle* which underlies the structure of morphologically-motivated clusters? Can a single phonological feature vary in *weight* depending on the type of a cluster and prosodic position it occurs in? And if so, which features are required to form a minimum cluster and a preferred cluster? These questions are addressed in the empirical chapters of this volume.

1.7 Inventories of Phonotactic and Morphonotactic Clusters

So far, I have discussed aspects of complexity that have been discussed in the literature. The accounts differ with respect to the allocation of morphological boundaries and the treatment of phonological phenomena (see Sect. 1.5), which results in different sets of clusters. Therefore, I complied new lists of clusters based on the existing accounts, dictionaries and corpora (among others, Bargiełówna 1950; Dobrogowska 1992; Dunaj 1985, 1986; Dubisz 2006; Orzechowska 2009; Orzechowska and Wiese 2015; Rochoń 2000; Zydorowicz et al. 2016). The cluster lists presented below are not only more complete than the lists found in the literature, but are also considered to reflect a consistent and exhaustive assignment of morphological boundaries. The compiled inventories of 458 initial clusters and 169 final clusters are presented in Sects. 1.7.1 and 1.7.2. Note that different cluster types can be found in proper nouns (see Jaskuła 2010; Jaskuła and Szpyra-Kozłowska submitted). The study of such clusters can be considered for a future project.

1.7.1 Word-Initial Clusters

Inventories of initial clusters include combinations found in isolated words (e.g. /rd rt/ in *rdest* 'knotgrass', *rtęć* 'mercury'), archaic forms (e.g. /vʒd/ in *wżdy* 'but, however') as well as in some proper nouns (e.g. /vʥ fkʃ sfj/ in *Wdzydze* [place name], *wkrzański* [referring to village *Wkrzańsk*], *Swietłana* [fem name]). Phonotactics and morphonotactic clusters are listed in Tables 1.14 and 1.15, respectively. Polish also features cluster types which have both realizations. For instance, /ɕʨ ft str/ are phonotactic in *ściana* 'wall', *wtorek* 'Tuesday', *strona* 'page', but morphonotactic in *ś* + *ciąć* 'to cut (down)' (perf), *w* + *topić* 'to melt' (perf) and *s* + *tracić* 'to lose' (perf). For this reason, apart from exclusively phonotactic (N = 269), and exclusively morphonotactic (N = 122) items, the data pool contains 67 *shared* clusters (also referred to as *mixed*). Shared clusters are subsumed under both sets in Tables 1.14 and 1.15 (marked in bold type), and increase the number of all available phonotactic and morphonotactic clusters to 336 and 189, respectively. For clarity of presentation, shared clusters are additionally listed in Table 1.16.

Table 1.14 Initial phonotactic clusters (N = 336)

CC	CCC	CCCC
bj, bl, br, bw, **bz**, bʑ, bʒ, ɕf, ɕl, ɕm, ɕɲ, ɕp, ɕr, **ɕʨ**, db, dj, dl, dm, dn, **dɲ**, dr, dv, dw, ʣb, ʣv, ʥg, ʥv, dʒ, ʤʤ, **fɕ**, fj, fl, fr, **fʃ**, **ft**, **fʧ**, gb, gd, gʥ, gj, gl, gm, gn, gɲ, gr, gv, gw, gz, gʑ, gʒ, kɕ, kf, kj, kl, km, kn, kɲ, kp, kr, ks, kʃ, kt, kʨ, kʦ, kw, lj, lʒ, mj, ml, mn, mɲ, mr, mʃ, mʦ, mw, mʒ, **pɕ**, pj, pl, pn, **pɲ**, pr, **ps**, pʃ, pt, pʨ, pw, px, rd, rʣ, rj, rt, rv, rʒ, **sf**, sj, **sk**, sl, sm, **sn**, **sp**, sr, **ss**, **st**, sʦ, sw, **sx**, **ʃf**, ʃk, ʃl, ʃm, ʃn, ʃp, ʃr, ʃt, ʃʧ, ʃw, ʨf, ʨm, ʨp, tf, tj, tk, tl, tn, tɲ, tr, ts, ʦf, ʦl, ʦm, ʦn, ʦw, tʃ, ʧf, ʧk, ʧm, ʧt, ʧʨ, ʧʧ, ʧw, ʧx, tʧ, tw, tx, **vd**, vʣ, **vʥ**, **vj**, **vl**, **vn**, **vɲ**, **vr**, **vw**, **vz**, vʑ, **vʒ**, wg, wk, wz, wʑ, wʒ, xf, xj, xl, xm, xr, xʃ, xt, xʨ, xʦ, xw, **zb**, **zd**, **zg**, **zm**, **zn**, **zr**, **zv**, **zw**, **zz**, ʑʥ, ʑl, ʑr, ʒb, ʒd, ʒg, ʒl, ʒm, ʒɲ, ʒr, ʒv, ʒw	brd, brʥ, brn, brɲ, bzd, bʑʥ, bʒd, bʒm, ɕfj, ɕmj, ɕpj, dmj, drg, drj, drv, drʒ, dvj, ʥvj, dʒv, fɕʨ, fkl, **fkr**, fkʃ, **fsp**, **fst**, **fʃʧ**, grd, gvd, gvj, gʒm, kfj, kln, klɲ, klv, kmj, kpj, krj, krn, krt, kʃt, kʃʧ, lɕɲ, lgn, lgɲ, mɕʨ, mdl, mdw, mgj, mgl, mgɲ, mgw, mkn, mkɲ, mst, mʃʧ, plv, prj, psk, pʃt, pʃʧ, pxl, pxw, rvj, rʒn, rʒɲ, sfj, **skf**, **skj**, **skl**, **skn**, **skr**, **skʃ**, smr, **spj**, **spr**, **spʃ**, stj, **str**, sʦj, **stʃ**, **sxl**, sxn, sxɲ, ʃkf, ʃkj, ʃkl, ʃkr, ʃkw, ʃpj, ʃpr, ʃtr, ʃʧf, ʨfj, ʨmj, tfj, tkf, tkl, tkn, tkɲ, trf, trj, ʦfj, ʦkl, ʦkɲ, ʧkɲ, tʃn, tʃʨ, txn, txɲ, vbr, **vzn**, **vzr**, vʒd, xfj, xmj, xʃʨ, xʃʧ, **zbr**, **zdj**, **zdr**, **zgj**, zgl, **zgr**, **zgʒ**, **zmj**, **zvj**, **zvw**, ʑʥb	bʒmj, drvj, dʒvj, gʒbj, gʒmj, pstr, skfj, **skrf**, ʃtfj, tkfj, tʃmj, tʃpj, **vzdr**, ʑʥbl, ʑʥbw

Table 1.15 Initial morphonotactic clusters (N = 189)

CC	CCC	CCCC
bz, **ɕʨ**, **dɲ**, **fɕ**, fk, fp, fs, **fʃ**, **ft**, fʨ, fʦ, **fʧ**, fx, ln, lɲ, lv, mx, **pɕ**, **pɲ**, **ps**, sɕ, **sf**, **sk**, **sn**, **sp**, **ss**, sʃ, **st**, sʦ, sʧ, **sx**, **ʃf**, vb, **vd**, **vʥ**, vg, **vj**, **vl**, vm, **vn**, **vɲ**, **vr**, vv, **vw**, **vz**, **vʒ**, wb, **zb**, **zd**, zʥ, **zg**, zj, zl, **zm**, **zn**, zɲ, **zr**, **zv**, **zw**, **zz**, zʑ, zʒ	brv, ʥgn, ʥgɲ, fɕl, fɕr, **fkr**, fkw, fpj, fpl, fpr, fpʃ, fpw, fsk, **fsp**, fsʃ, **fst**, fsw, fsx, **fʃʧ**, ftr, ftʃ, ftw, fxw, krf, lvj, pwʨ, pxn, pxɲ, sfl, sfr, **skf**, **skj**, **skl**, **skn**, **skr**, sks, **skʃ**, skw, spɕ, **spj**, spl, **spr**, **spʃ**, spw, sst, stf, stl, **str**, **stʃ**, stw, stx, sxf, sxj, **sxl**, sxr, sxʃ, sxw, ʃfj, ʧkn, vbj, vdm, vdr, vgj, vgl, vgɲ, vgr, vgw, vgʒ, vmj, vvj, vzb, vzd, vzg, vzl, vzm, **vzn**, vzɲ, **vzr**, vzv, wbj, xʃt, zbj, zbl, **zbr**, zbw, zbʑ, zbʒ, **zdj**, zdm, **zdr**, zdv, zdw, zʣv, zdʒ, **zgj**, zgn, zgɲ, **zgr**, zgv, zgw, **zgʒ**, **zmj**, zmɲ, zmr, zmw, **zvj**, zvl, zvr, **zvw**, ʒgn	brvj, drgn, drgɲ, fskr, fskʃ, fspj, fstr, fstʃ, krfj, **skrf**, stfj, vzbj, vzbr, **vzdr**, vzdw, vzgl, vzmj

Table 1.16 Shared initial phonotactic and morphonotactic clusters (N = 67)

CC	CCC	CCCC
bz, ɕtɕ, dɲ, fɕ, fʃ, ft, ftʃ, pɕ, pɲ, ps, sf, sk, sn, sp, ss, st, sts, sx, ʃf, vd, vdʑ, vj, vl, vn, vɲ, vr, vw, vz, vʒ, zb, zd, zg, zm, zn, zr, zv, zw, zz	fkr, fsp, fst, fʃtʃ, skf, skj, skl, skn, skr, skʃ, spj, spr, spʃ, str, stʃ, sxl, vzn, vzr, zbr, zdj, zdr, zgj, zgr, zgʒ, zmj, zvj, zvw	skrf, vzdr

The compilation of cluster lists required making a decision on palatal consonants. While Jassem (2003) lists (post)palatal plosives /c ɟ/ in *kieł* /cew/ 'fang' and *giełda* /ɟewda/ 'stock exchange' as phonemic in Polish, Ostaszewska and Tambor (2005) regard the segments as phonetic variants [kʲ gʲ] of the corresponding velar plosives palatalized by the front vowel <−i>, as in [kʲiew] and [gʲiewda]. In this work, we adopt the interpretation of a cluster-like structure of the velar plosives followed by a glide, resulting in /kjew/ and /gjewda/.

The principles of morphological parsing adopted here are based on the description of concatenative and non-concatenative contexts given in Sect. 1.6.2.1. The morphonotactic dataset includes geminates such as /ss zz vv/ in *z* + *suwać* 'to slide', *z* + *za* 'from behind', *w* + *wozić* 'to import', which have been referred to as 'fake' geminates (Hayes 1986; Kenstowicz 1982). In phonological theory, they are represented differently than truly phonotactic geminates such as /ss zz dʒdʒ/ in *ssak* 'mammal', *zzuwać* 'to take off' (arch) and *dżdżownica* 'earth worm'. No specific stand is taken on the interpretation and underlying representation of such sequences as both types of geminates are included in the data.

The most natural phonetic context for the occurrence of geminates is intervocalic. Sequences of obstruents /ss tt kk tʃtʃ/ are found in *wyssać* 'to suck out', *motto* 'motto', *Mekka* 'Mecca' or /tʃtʃ/ in *uczczę* 'to celebrate' (1st sg future). Word-medial position also permits adjacent sonorants /nn mm rr ll jj ww/ in words such as *panna* 'miss', *wanna* 'bathtub', *ranny* 'hurt'. Occasionally, sonorant sequences are found word-finally where they tend to undergo simplification to a single prolonged consonant (Dukiewicz and Sawicka 1995: 140, 152f.), e.g. *mełł* 'to chew' (3rd sg past masc), pronounced as /mɛww/ or /mɛw/, *fontann* 'fountain' (gen pl), *mann* 'manna' (gen pl), *lass* 'lasso' (gen pl) 'lasso' and *miąższ* 'pulp'.

A summary of morphological operations which generate word-initial morphonotactic clusters is given in Table 1.17. The table lists cluster types and words in which they occur. The columns 'Morph' and 'Function' provide the spelling of an affix and its grammatical function, respectively.

The table lists all cluster types found in the dataset which are generated by non-concatenative morphological operations, and the suffixation of {−nąć} and {−nięcie}. Since prefixation is productive and leads to a large variety of clusters, only one example of a cluster is provided for each prefix.

Table 1.17 A list of morphological contexts generating word-initial morphonotactic clusters

Morph	Context	Example	Cluster	Function
Concatenative morphology				
{s−}	Prefix	kończyć 'to finish' → s + kończyć	sk	Perfective
{ś−}		ciąć 'to cut down' → ś + ciąć	ɕtɕ	
{z−}		walczyć 'to fight' → z + walczyć	zv	
{w−}		topić 'to melt down' → w + topić	ft	
{ws−}		pomóc 'to support' → ws + pomóc	fsp	
{wz−}		bogacić 'to become rich' → wz + bogacić	vzb	
{−nąć}	Suffix	drgać 'to vibrate' → drg + nąć	drgn	Perfective
		dźgać 'to jab' → dźg + nąć	ʥgn	
		pchać 'to push' → pch + nąć	pxn	
		żgać 'to sting' → żg + nąć	ʒgn	
{−nięcie}	Suffix	drgnąć 'to vibrate' → drg + nięcie	drgɲ	Deverbal noun
		dźgnąć 'to jab' → dźg + nięcie	ʥgɲ	
		pchnąć 'to push' → pch + nięcie	pxɲ	
Non-concatenative morphology				
{Ø}	V ~ Ø	brew 'eyebrow' → brwiowy	brvj	Denominal adjective
		bez 'lilac' → bzowy	bz	
		dzień 'day' → dniowy	dɲ	
		krew 'blood' → krwawy 'bloody'	krf	
		krew 'blood' → krwionośny 'circulatory'	krfj	
		len 'flax' → lniany	lɲ	
		lew 'lion' → lwi (nom sg)	lv	
		lew 'lion' → lwiemu (acc sg)	lvj	
		pies 'dog' → psi	pɕ	
		płeć 'sex' → płciowy	pwtɕ	
		szew 'stitch' → szwowy	ʃf	
		brew 'eyebrow' → brwi	brv	Plural (nom sg)
		pień 'trunk' → pnie	pɲ	
		pies 'dog' → psy	ps	
		sen 'dream' → sny	sn	
		łeb '(animal) head' → łby	wb	
		len 'flax' → lnu (dat)	ln	Change of case
		mech 'moss' → mchu (dat)	mx	
		szew 'stitch' → szwie (loc)	ʃfj	
		łeb '(animal) head' → łbie (loc)	wbj	
		chrzest 'baptism' → chrztu (dat)	xʃt	

1.7.2 Word-Final Clusters

Lists of final clusters comprise sequences found in rare forms (e.g. /nr fn nf/ in *henr* 'henry' (electrical unit), *hafn* 'hafnium' (chemical element), *tynf* [Polish silver coin] as well as technical terms (e.g. /lft stm/ in *delft* 'tin glazed pottery', *istm(us)* 'isthmus') and proper nouns (e.g. /ʦk/ in *Płock,* /j̃sk/ in *Gdańsk*, /lsk/ in *Starobielsk*). The dataset also contains clusters occurring in assimilated borrowings such as /jl jx tw xx/ in *koktajl* 'cocktail', *Rajch* [the German Empire, col], *sztetł* 'shtetl' and *szlauch* 'rubber hose' (col).

In determining word-final clusters, some phonological decisions had to be made. First, clusters can arise at the juncture of a nasal followed by a fricative. Following Jassem (1973), Dukiewicz and Sawicka (1995), Ostaszewska and Tambor (2005), nasal + fricative are phonetically realized as a sequence of a nasalized glide followed by a fricative. For instance, <n> followed by a fricative is realized as semivowels in *kunszt* /kuw̃ʃt/, *tynf* /tyw̃f/. Similarly, the anticipatory articulation for <ń> before spirants <s, ś, ź> results in /j̃/ as in the place name *Gdańsk* /gdaj̃sk/.

Exclusively phonotactic (N = 67), exclusively morphonotactic (N = 39) and mixed (N = 64) clusters are presented in Tables 1.18, 1.19 and 1.20, respectively. Mixed clusters, which can have both realizations (e.g. phonologically-motivated /ɕʨ/ in *kość* 'bone' vs. morphologically-motivated /ɕʨ/ in *iś* + *ć* 'to go'), are

Table 1.18 Final phonotactic clusters (N = 131)

CC	CCC
ɕl, ɕɲ, **ɕʨ**, fk, fl, fn, **fr**, **ft**, **fʦ**, j̃ɕ, jf, jk, jl, **jm**, jn, js, **jt**, **jʦ**, jʧ, **jx**, kl, **kr**, ks, **kt**, kx, **lf**, **lk**, **lm**, **lp**, **ls**, lʃ, **lt**, lʦ, lx, mf, **mn**, **mp**, ms, mʃ, nf, nr, ns, nʃ, **nt**, **nʦ**, **nʧ**, **ɲʨ**, ɲʦ, **ŋk**, pl, pɲ, **pr**, **ps**, pʃ, **pt**, rɕ, **rf**, **rk**, **rm**, **rn**, **rɲ**, **rp**, **rs**, **rʃ**, **rt**, **rʨ**, **rʦ**, **rʧ**, rx, **sk**, **sm**, **st**, sw, **ʃp**, **ʃt**, **ʃʧ**, ʃx, **tf**, **tl**, **tm**, **tr**, ʦk, **tw**, wf, wk, wl, **wm**, **wn**, wp, wr, ws, **w̃s**, wʃ, **w̃ʃ**, **wt**, wʨ, wʧ, wx, w̃x, xʃ, **xt**	**j̃ɕʨ**, jnt, j̃sk, jst, kst, lɕɲ, lft, **lsk**, ltr, mpl, mpr, mpt, **ntr**, **ntʃ**, ŋkr, ŋks, ŋkt, **psk**, rɕʨ, rsk, rʃt, **rʃʧ**, stm, **str**, stʃ, **wnt**, wst, w̃ʃt, w̃ʃʧ, xtr

Table 1.19 Final morphonotactic clusters (N = 103)

CC	CCC	CCCC	CCCCC
ɕl, ɕm, ɕp, **ɕʨ**, **fr**, **ft**, **fʨ**, fʦ, jɕ, **jm**, **jt**, jʨ, **jʦ**, **jx**, kf, km, **kr**, **kt**, kw, **lf**, **lk**, **lm**, lɲ, **lp**, **ls**, **lt**, lʧ, mɕ, **mn**, **mp**, **nt**, **nʦ**, **nʧ**, **ɲʨ**, ɲʧ, **ŋk**, **pr**, **ps**, **pt**, pʧ, **rf**, **rk**, **rm**, **rn**, **rɲ**, **rp**, **rs**, **rʃ**, **rt**, **rʨ**, **rʦ**, **rʧ**, rw, sf, **sk**, **sm**, sn, sp, **st**, sw, **ʃp**, **ʃt**, **ʃʧ**, **tf**, **tl**, **tm**, **tr**, tʃ, ʧp, ʧt, **tw**, **wn**, **wp**, **w̃s**, **w̃ʃ**, **wt**, xɕ, xm, **xt**	jɕʨ, **j̃ɕʨ**, jsk, jsʦ, **lsk**, mst, ntf, **ntr**, **ntʃ**, **psk**, rst, **rʃʧ**, rtf, stf, **str**, ʃtr, ʦtf, **wnt**	fstf, jstf, j̃stf, pstf, rstf	mpstf

Table 1.20 Shared final phonotactic and morphonotactic clusters (N = 64)

CC	CCC
ɕl, ɕtɕ, fr, ft, fʦ, jm, jt, jʦ, jx, kr, kt, lf, lk, lm, lp, ls, lt, mn, mp, nt, nʦqq, nʧ, ɲtɕ, ŋk, pr, ps, pt, rf, rk, rm, rn, rɲ, rp, rs, rʃ, rt, rtɕ, rʦ, rʧ, sk, sm, st, ʃp, ʃt, ʃʧ, tf, tl, tm, tr, tw, wn, wp, w̃s, w̃ʃ, wt, xt	j̃ɕtɕ, lsk, ntr, ntʃ, psk, rʃʧ, str, wnt

Table 1.21 A list of clusters with (non-)nasal realization of glides

Cluster	Phonotactic	Morphonotactic
jɕ	–	czyj + ś 'somebody's'
j̃ɕ	gęś 'goose'	–
jɕtɕ	–	przyjś + ć 'to come'
j̃ɕtɕ	pięść 'fist'	usiąś + ć 'to sit down'
jsk	–	wojsk 'army' (gen pl)
j̃sk	Gdańsk	–
jstf	–	dobrodziejstw 'benefaction' (gen pl)
j̃stf	–	państw 'country' (gen pl)
ws	aplauz 'applause'	pauz 'break' (gen pl)
w̃s	wąs 'moustache'	–
wʃ	fałsz 'falsehood'	małż 'mussel' (gen pl)
w̃ʃ	wąż 'snake'	–
wx	szlauch 'rubber hose'	–
w̃x	węch 'smell'	–
wsw	–	spełz + ł 'to crawl' (3rd sg past masc perf)
w̃sw	–	zatrząs + ł 'to shake' (3rd sg past masc perf)

included in bold type in Tables 1.18 and 1.19, and enlarge the inventories of all phonotactic and morphonotactic clusters to 131 and 103, respectively.

It must be noted that cluster types featuring nasalized glides /j̃ w̃/ can have identical counterparts in clusters containing non-nasalized glides. Table 1.21 juxtaposes final clusters which have both variants: oral /j w/ and nasal /j̃ w̃/. In the majority of cases, the variants have different motivation. For instance, in the /jɕ/ versus /j̃ɕ/ pair, the first cluster is morphologically-motivated, while the latter is found only intramorphemically. For this reason, the inventories of clusters encompass both variants as separate cluster types.

An overview of concatenative and non-concatenative morphological operations which lead to word-final morphonotactic clusters is given in Table 1.22. I list all exclusively morphonotactic cluster types (N = 39) and examples of words in which they occur. For each context, a morpheme and its grammatical function are provided.

The morphological contexts and cluster types presented in this section constitute the basis for empirical analyses to be pursued in the following chapters of the book. It must be noted that the inventory of final clusters is large, but probably not exhaustive. The formation of imperative and past verbs as well as genitive plural

Table 1.22 A list of morphological contexts generating word-final morphonotactic clusters

Morph	Context	Example	Cluster	Function
Concatenative morphology				
{−ł}	Suffix	pleść 'to blab' → plót + ł	tw	3rd singular masc past
		zmoknąć 'to get wet' → zmók + ł	kw	
		trzeć 'to rub' → tar + ł	rw	
		nieść 'to carry' → niós + ł	sw	
{−ć}	Suffix	iś + ć 'to go'	ɕtɕ	Infinitive
		przyjś + ć 'to come'	jɕtɕ	
{−ś}	Suffix	czyj 'whose' → czyj + ś	jɕ	Affirmative pronoun
		czym 'what' → czym + ś	mɕ	
		jakich 'which' → jakich + ś	xɕ	
Non-concatenative morphology				
{−Ø}	Truncation	prawodawstw + o 'legislation' → prawodawstw + Ø	fstf	Genitive plural
		flegm + a 'phlegm' → flegm + Ø	km	
		wojsk + o 'army' → wojsk + Ø	jsk	
		dobrodziejstw + o 'benefaction' → dobrodziejstw + Ø	jstf	
		państw + o 'country' → państw + Ø	j̃stf	
		miejsc + e 'place' → miejsc + Ø	jsʦ	
		strzykw + a 'sea cucumber' → strzykw + Ø	kf	
		kopalnia 'mine' → kopalń + Ø	lɲ	
		przestępstw + o 'crime' → przestępstw + Ø	mpstf	
		zemst + a 'revenge' → zemst + Ø	mst	
		klatw + a 'curse' → klątw + Ø	ntf	
		hrabstw + o 'county' → hrabstw + Ø	pstf	
		wiorst + a 'viost' → wiorst + Ø	rst	
		warstw + a 'layer' → warstw + Ø	rstf	
		nazw + a 'name' → nazw + Ø	sf	
		wysp + a 'island' → wysp + Ø	sp	
		towarzystw + o 'company' → towarzystw + Ø	stf	
		musztr + a 'drill' → musztr + Ø	ʃtr	
		taśm + a 'tape' → taśm + Ø	ɕm	
		ptactw + o 'birds' → ptactw + Ø	ʦtf	
		liczb + a 'number' → liczb + Ø	ʧp	
		poczt + a 'post office' → poczt + Ø	ʧt	
		drachma 'drachma' → drachm + Ø	xm	
		trucizn + a 'poison' → trucizn + Ø	sn	
		sprawdzić 'to check' → sprawdź!	ftɕ	Singular imperative
		wejść 'to come in' → wejdź!	jtɕ	
		walczyć 'to fight' → walcz!	lʧ	
		deptać 'to tread' → depcz!	pʧ	
		kończyć 'to finish' → kończ!	ɲʧ	
		garbić 'to stoop' → garb!	rp	
		martwić 'to worry' → martw!	rtf	
		patrzeć 'to look' → patrz!	tʃ	

nouns is likely to give rise to some more clusters, whose identification is impossible without inflecting all nouns and verbs attested in Polish. However, the inventories presented in Tables 1.18, 1.19 and 1.20 are based on dictionary- and corpus-based accounts, and are therefore considered to be sufficiently large for the purposes of the present analyses.

1.8 Conclusions

In this chapter, I have delineated key issues in the study of phonotactics as well as descriptive, theoretical and computational approaches to formulating phonotactic constraints and preferences. Such generalizations account for sequences of consonants which are (imp)possible, (un)likely, and (dis)preferred, and are particularly important in the study of Polish, whose phonotactic complexity is triggered by several factors.

At a quantitative level, complexity is represented by long strings of consonants. Adjacent non-syllabic CCCs, CCCCs and CCCCCs lead to moderate and severe violations of the CV structure, which is the basic syllable template attested across the languages of the world. At a qualitative level, complex clusters are the product of the intervention of morphology, which manifests itself in two ways. First, morphonotactic clusters tend to be longer. Second, since phonology has a limited power of repair or avoidance of structures generated by morphology, morphonotactic clusters tend to violate well-formedness principles (such as sonority). Viewed from this perspective, the "difficulty" or "abnormality" of Polish clusters is unarguable, and offers an excellent testing ground for phonological theories. As it turns out, theoretical approaches account for different aspects of phonotactic complexity depending on a linguistic unit they operate on.

On the one hand, syllable-based approaches posit that Polish onsets and codas are simple and well-motivated. As we have seen, such an assertion is possible only when an approach incorporates mechanisms which successfully account for extrasyllabic consonants. Syllable-based approaches propose rules which allocate the unsyllabified segments into higher prosodic units like the foot or phonological word. This procedure substantially limits the number of clusters which can be considered to be true onsets and codas. On the other hand, extrasyllabic consonants are easily accommodated into word-based approaches. However, when formulating phonotactic generalizations for the domain of a word, one must be able to account for clusters which results from the intervention of morphology, and which tend to be ill-formed. Morphonotactic sequences are found in abundance in Polish, and contribute to phonotactic complexity of the language.

In the light of these facts, I am interested in finding out whether, and in what way, Polish phonotactics is a well-motivated phenomenon. This point was raised by Dukiewicz and Sawicka (1995) who observed that a great variety of unusual clusters can lead to a misconception that Polish phonotactics operates on very few or no constraints whatsoever. I take this statement as a starting point for my further considerations, and verify it by collecting theoretical and empirical evidence. In Chap. 2, I analyse Polish initial and final consonant clusters in terms of the most representative theoretical approaches. In Chap. 3, I propose an alternative exploratory analysis in search of heretofore unidentified constraints and preferences, which reveal subtle phonological properties motivating the synchronic structure of Polish phonotactic and morphonotactics.

References

Asher, R.E. (ed.). 1994. *The Encyclopedia of Language and Linguistics*, vol. 6. Oxford: Pergamon Press.

Auer, P. 1993. *Is a rhythm-based typology possible? A study of the role of prosody in phonological typology* [KontRI Working Paper 21]. Konstanz: Universität Konstanz.

Bańko, M. 2005. Wykłady z polskiej fleksji. Warszawa: Państwowe Wydawnictwo Naukowe.

Bargiełówna, M. 1950. Grupy fonemów spółgłoskowych współczesnej polszczyzny kulturalnej. *Biuletyn Polskiego Towarzystwa Językoznawczego* 10: 1–25.

Bartnicka-Dąbkowska, B., and R. Sinielnikoff. 1999. *Słownik podstawowy języka polskiego dla cudzoziemców*. Kielce: Wydawnictwo Takt.

Baudouin de Courtenay, J.N. 1895. *Versuch einer Theorie Phonetischer Alternationen: Ein Capitel aus der Psychophonetik*. Strassburg: Trübner.

Bauer, L. 1983. *English word-formation*. Cambridge: Cambridge University Press.

Bethin, C.Y. 1992. *Polish syllables: The role of prosody in phonology and morphology*. Colombus, OH: Slavica Publishers.

Bethin, C.Y. 2006. *Slavic prosody: Language change and phonological theory* [Cambridge studies in linguistic, vol. 86]. Cambridge: Cambridge University Press.

Biedrzycki, L. 1963. Fonologiczna interpretacja polskich głosek nosowych. *Biuletyn Polskiego Towarzystwa Językoznawczego* 22: 24–45.

Biedrzycki, L. 1978. *Fonologia angielskich i polskich rezonantów. Porównanie samogłosek oraz spółgłosek*. Warszawa: Państwowe Wydawnictwo Naukowe.

Bloch-Rozmej, A. 1998. Contour structures in the vocalic system of Polish. In *Structure and interpretation. Studies in phonology*, ed. E. Cyran, 41–54. Lublin: Folium.

Bloomfield, L. 1939. Menomini morphophonemics. *Travaux du Cercle Linguistique de Prague* 8: 105–115. [Reprinted in: *A Leonard Bloomfield anthology*, ed. C. F. Hockett, 1970, 351–362. Bloomington: Indiana University Press.].

Booij, G. 1999. The role of the prosodic word in phonotactic generalizations. In *Studies on the phonological word*, eds. A.T. Hall, and U. Kleinhenz, 47–72. Amsterdam, Philadelphia: John Benjamins.

Booij, G. 2006. Inflection and derivation. In *Encyclopaedia of Language and Linguistics*, 2nd ed, ed. K. Brown, 654–661. Oxford: Elsevier.

Booij, G., and J. Rubach. 1984. Morphological and prosodic domains in Lexical Phonology. *Phonology* 1: 1–27.

Boukous, M. 1987. *Phonotactique et domaine prosodique en berbère*. Ph.D. diss., Paris: Université Paris 8.

Browman, C.P., and L.M. Goldstein. 1986. Towards an articulatory phonology. *Phonology Yearbook* 3: 219–252.

Browman, C.P., and L.M. Goldstein. 1989. Articulatory gestures as phonological units. *Phonology* 6: 201–251.

Browman, C.P., and L.M. Goldstein. 1992. Articulatory phonology: An overview. *Phonetica* 49 (3–4): 155–180.

Bybee, J. 1985. *Morphology. A study of the relation between meaning and form*. Amsterdam: John Benjamins.
Bybee, J. 2003. *Phonology and language use*. Cambridge: Cambridge University Press.
Cairns, C.E., and E. Raimy (eds.). 2010. *The handbook of the syllable*. Leiden: Brill.
Carson-Berndsen, J. 1998. *Time map phonology: Finite state models and event logics in speech recognition*. Dordrecht, Holland: Kluwer Academic Publishers.
Carson-Berndsen, J. 2000. Finite-state models, event logics and statistics in speech recognition. *Philosophical Transactions: Mathematical, Physical and Engineering Sciences* 358 (1769): 1255–1266.
Cetnarowska, B., and M. Żygis. 2007. Phonetic syllabification and morphological parsability: The case of prefixed words in Polish. In *Challenging tasks for psycholinguistics in the New Century*, ed. J. Arabski, 149–163. Katowice: Uniwersytet Śląski.
Chomsky, N., and M. Halle. 1968. *The Sound Pattern of English*. New York: Harper and Row.
Cruttenden, A. 2014. *Gimson's pronunciation of English*, 8th ed. London, New York: Routledge.
Crystal, D. 2003. *Dictionary of Linguistics and Phonetics*. Oxford, Malden: Blackwell.
Cyran, E., and E. Gussmann. 1999. Consonantal clusters and governing relations: Polish initial consonant sequences. In *The syllable: Views and facts*, eds. H. van der Hulst and A.N. Ritter, 219–249. Berlin: Mouton de Gruyter.
Dąbrowska, E. 2001. Learning a morphological system without a default: The Polish genitive. *Journal of Child Language* 28 (3): 545–574.
De Saussure, F. 1916. *Cours de Linguistique Générale*. Lausanne, Paris: Payot.
Dell, F., and M. Elmedlaoui. 1985. Syllabic consonants and syllabification in Imdlawn Tashlhiyt Berber. *Journal of African Languages and Linguistics* 7: 105–130.
Dell, F., and M. Elmedlaoui. 2002. *Syllables in Tashlhiyt Berber and in Moroccan Arabic*. Dordrecht: Kluwer.
Diver, W. 1979. Phonology as human behavior. In *Psycholinguistic research: Implications and applications*, eds. D. Aaronson and P. Reiber, 161–186. Hillside NJ: Lawrence Erlbaum Associates.
Długosz-Kurczabowa, K., and S. Dubisz. 2006. *Gramatyka Historyczna Języka Polskiego*. Warszawa: Wydawnictwa Uniwesytetu Warszawskiego.
Dobrogowska, K. 1984. Śródgłosowe grupy spółgłoskowe w polskich tekstach popularnonaukowych. *Polonica* 10: 15–34.
Dobrogowska, K. 1990. Word internal consonant clusters in Polish artistic prose. *Studia Phonetica Posnaniensia* 2: 43–67.
Dobrogowska, K. 1992. Word initial and word final consonant clusters in Polish popular science texts and in artistic prose. *Studia Phonetica Posnaniensia* 3: 47–121.
Donegan, P.J. 1985. *On the Natural Phonology of vowels*. New York: Garland Publishing.
Donegan, P.J. 2002. Phonological processes and phonetic rules. In *Future challenges for Natural Linguistics*, eds. K. Dziubalska-Kołaczyk and J. Weckwerth, 57–82. Muenchen: Lincom Europa.
Donegan, P.J., and D. Stampe. 1979. The study of Natural Phonology. In *Current approaches to phonological theory*, ed. D.A. Dinnsen, 126–173. Bloomington, London: Indiana University Press.
Donegan, P.J., and D. Stampe. 2009. Hypotheses of Natural Phonology. *Poznań Studies in Contemporary Linguistics* 45 (1): 1–31.
Donohue, M., R. Hetherington, J. McElvenny, and V. Dawson. 2013. *World phonotactics database*. Department of Linguistics, The Australian National University. Online access: http://phonotactics.anu.edu.au. Date of access 20.11.2017.
Dressler, W.U. 1984. Explaining Natural Phonology. *Phonology Yearbook* 1: 29–51.
Dressler, W.U. 1985. *Morphonology: The dynamics of derivation*. Ann Arbor: Karoma Publishers.
Dressler, W.U. 1999. What is natural in natural morphology (NM)? *Travaux du Cercle Linguistique de Prague* 3: 135–144.
Dressler, W.U., and K. Dziubalska-Kołaczyk. 2006. Proposing morphonotactics. *Wiener Linguistische Gazette* 73: 1–19.

Dressler, W.U., W. Mayerthaler, O. Panagl, and W.U. Wurzel. 1987. *Leitmotifs in natural morphology*. Amsterdam: John Benjamins.

Dressler, W.U., K. Dziubalska-Kołaczyk, and L. Pestal. 2010. Change and variation in morphonotactics. *Folia Linguistica Historica* 31: 51–67.

Dressler, W.U., M. Hliničanová, M. Ďurčo, K. Mörth, and K. Korecky-Kröll. 2015. Phonotactic vs. morphonotactic obstruent clusters in Slovak and German. *Italian Journal of Linguistics* 27: 45–60.

Dryer, M.S. 2013. Prefixing vs. suffixing in inflectional morphology. In *The World Atlas of Language Structures online*, eds. M. Dryer, and M. Haspelmath. Munich: Max Plank Digital Library. Online access: http://wals.info/. Accessed on 2018-03-12.

Dryer, M.S., and M. Haspelmath (eds.). 2013. *The World Atlas of Language Structures online*. Leipzig: Max Planck Institute for Evolutionary Anthropology.

Dubisz, S. (ed.). 2006. *Uniwersalny słownik języka polskiego*. Warszawa: Państwowe Wydawnictwo Naukowe.

Dukiewicz, L. 1967. *Polskie Głoski Nosowe: Analiza Akustyczna* [Instytut Podstawowych Problemów Techniki Polskiej Akademii Nauk]. Warszawa: Państwowe Wydawnictwo Naukowe.

Dukiewicz, L. 1980. Rodzaje i częstość występowania nagłosowych grup fonemów typu CC(V)-, CCC(V)- i CCCC(V)- w polskich tekstach prasowych. *Lětopis Instituta za Serbski Ludospyt* 27 (2): 142–157.

Dukiewicz, L. 1985. Nagłosowe grupy spółgłosek w polskich tekstach popularnonaukowych i prasowych. *Studia Gramatyczne* 6: 17–34.

Dukiewicz, L., and I. Sawicka. 1995. *Gramatyka współczesnego języka polskiego: Fonetyka i fonologia*. Kraków: Instytut Języka Polskiego PAN.

Dunaj, B. 1985. *Grupy spółgłoskowe współczesnej polszczyzny mówionej (w języku mieszkańców Krakowa)*. Kraków: Uniwersytet Jagielloński.

Dunaj, B. 1986. Wygłosowe grupy spółgłoskowe współczesnej polszczyzny mówionej. *Zeszyty Naukowe Uniwersytetu Jagiellońskiego. Prace Językoznawcze* 82: 103–117.

Dunaj, B. 1991. Dwa dyskusyjne problemy polskiej fonologii. In *Prace językoznawcze 19*, eds. A. Kowalska, and A. Wilkoń, 40–46. Katowice: Uniwersytet Śląski.

Dziubalska-Kołaczyk, K. 1995. *Phonology without the syllable: A study in the natural framework*. Poznań: Motivex.

Dziubalska-Kołaczyk, K. 2002. *Beats-and-binding Phonology*. Frankfurt am Main: Peter Lang.

Dziubalska-Kołaczyk, K. 2009. NP extensions: B&B phonotactics. *Poznań Studies in Contemporary Linguistics* 45 (1): 55–71.

Dziubalska-Kołaczyk, K., M. Jankowski, P. Orzechowska, D. Pietrala, P. Wierzchoń, and P. Zydorowicz. 2012. *Phonotactics and morphonotactics of Polish and English: Description, tools and applications*. Unpublished research project report. Poznań: Adam Mickiewicz University.

Dziubalska-Kołaczyk, K. 2014. Explaining phonotactics using NAD. *Language Sciences* 46 (A): 6–17.

Eliasson, S. 2014. The typology of syllable and word languages and Swedish phonological structure. In *Syllable and word languages*, eds. J. Caro Reina, and R. Szczepaniak, 43–86. Berlin, Boston: De Gruyter.

Ewen, C.J., and H. van der Hulst. 2001. *The phonological structure of words: An introduction*. Cambridge: Cambridge University Press.

Gibbon, D. 2001. Preferences as defaults in computational phonology. In *Constraints and preferences*, ed. K. Dziubalska-Kołaczyk, 143–199. Berlin: Mouton de Gruyter.

Goldsmith, J.A. 1990. *Autosegmental and metrical phonology*. Oxford: Blackwell.

Gordon, M. 2016. *Phonological typology*. Oxford: Oxford University Press.

Gouskova, M. 2018. Morphology and phonotactics. In *The Oxford research encyclopedia of linguistics*. Online publication date: Sep 2018.

Greenberg, J.H. 1978. Some generalizations concerning initial and final consonant clusters. In *Universals of human language*, eds. J.H. Greenberg, C.A. Ferguson, and E.A. Moravcsik, 243–279. Stanford. CA: Stanford University Press.
Gussmann, E. 1980. *Studies in abstract phonology*. Cambridge, MA: The MIT Press.
Gussmann, E. 1992. Resyllabification and delinking: The case of Polish voicing. *Linguistic Inquiry* 23 (1): 29–56.
Gussmann, E. 2007. *The phonology of Polish*. Oxford: Oxford University Press.
Hall, T.A. 1997. *The phonology of coronals* [Current issues in linguistic theory, vol. 149]. Amsterdam: John Benjamins.
Halle, M., and K.P. Mohanan. 1985. Segmental phonology of modern English. *Linguistic Inquiry* 16 (1): 57–116.
Hamann, S. 2004. Retroflex fricatives in Slavic languages. *Journal of the International Phonetic Association* 34: 53–67.
Harris, Z.S. 1942. Morpheme alternants in linguistic analysis. *Language* 18: 169–180. [Reprinted in: *Readings in linguistics: The development of descriptive linguistics in America since 1925*, ed. M. Joos, 1963, 109–115. New York: American Council of Learned Societies.].
Harris, J. 2018. The foot as a phonotactic domain: aw and wa in English. In *Revealing structure (lecture notes)*, eds. E. Buckley, T. Crane, and J. Good. Chicago: University of Chicago Press.
Hayes, B. 1986. Inalterability in CV phonology. *Language* 62: 321–351.
Hockett, C.F. 1950. Peiping morphophonemics. *Language* 26: 63–85. [Reprinted in: *Readings in linguistics: The development of descriptive linguistics in America since 1925*, ed. M. Joos, 1963, 315–328. New York: American Council of Learned Societies.].
Hoole, P., L. Bombien, M. Pouplier, C. Mooshammer, and B. Kühnert (eds.). 2012. *Consonant clusters and structural complexity*. Berlin: Mouton de Gruyter.
Itô, J. 1986. *Syllable theory in prosodic phonology*. Ph.D. diss., Amherst: University of Massachusetts.
Jaskuła, K. 2010. Polish place-names and word-final consonant groups: More affricates and diphthongs in Polish? *Poznań Studies in Contemporary Linguistics* 46 (4): 391–406.
Jaskuła, K., and J. Szpyra-Kozłowska. (submitted). Wychódźc, Pcim i Rzgów. Grupy spółgłoskowe w nazwach miejscowości a fonotaktyka polska.
Jassem, W. 1973. *Podstawy fonetyki akustycznej*. Warszawa: Państwowe Wydawnictwo Naukowe.
Jassem, W. 2003. Polish. *Journal of the International Phonetic Association: Illustrations of the IPA* 33 (1): 103–107.
Jurafsky, D., and J.H. Martin. 2009. *Speech and Language Processing: An introduction to natural language processing, computational linguistics and speech recognition*. New Jersey: Prentice Hall.
Jusek, A., H. Rautenstrauch, G.A. Fink, F. Kummert, G. Sagerer, J. Carson-Berndsen, and D. Gibbon. 1994. Detektion unbekannter Wörter mit Hilfe phonotaktischer Modelle. In *Mustererkennung 94, 16. DAGM-Symposium und 18. Workshop der OAGM*, eds. H. Bischof, and W.G. Kropatsch, 238–245. Wien: Springer.
Kager, R. 1999. *Optimality Theory*. Cambridge: Cambridge University Press.
Kamandulyte, L. 2006. The acquisition of morphonotactics in Lithuanian. *Wiener Linguistische Gazette* 73: 88–96.
Kaplan, R., and M. Kay. 1994. Regular models of phonological rule systems. *Computational Linguistics* 20 (3): 331–378.
Karttunen, L. 1998. On the proper treatment of optimality in computational phonology. In *Proceedings of the international workshop on finite state methods in natural language processing*, Ankara, 30 June–1 July, eds. L. Karttunen, and K. Oflazer, 1–12. Stroudsburg: Association for Computational Linguistics.
Kaye, J., J. Lowenstamm, and J.-R. Vergnaud. 1990. Constituent structure and government in phonology. *Phonology* 7 (2): 193–231.
Kean, M.L. 1975. *The theory of markedness in generative grammar*. Ph.D. diss., Massachusetts Institute of Technology.

Kenstowicz, M. 1982. Gemination and spirantization in Tigrinya. *Studies in the Linguistic Science* 12 (1): 103–122.

Kijak, A. 2008. *Polish and English consonantal clusters: A contrastive analysis within the strict CV framework*. Katowice: Wydawnictwo Uniwersytetu Śląskiego.

Kilani-Schoch, M. 1988. Discontinuity or continuity of the morphological basis in Classical Arabic and in Tunisian Arabic? *Zeitschrift für Arabische Linguistik* 19: 81–92.

Kiparsky, P. 1982. From Cyclic Phonology to Lexical Phonology. In *The structure of phonological representations*, vol. 1, eds. H. van der Hulst, and N. Smith, 131–175. Dordrecht: Foris Publications.

Kiparsky, P. 1985. Some consequences of Lexical Phonology. *Phonology Yearbook* 2: 85–138.

Klemensiewicz, Z., T. Lehr-Spławiński, and S. Urbańczyk (eds.). 1981. Gramatyka historyczna języka polskiego. 4th ed. Warszawa: Państwowe Wydawnictwo Naukowe.

Korecky-Kröll, K., W.U. Dressler, E.M. Freiberger, E. Reinisch, K. Mörth, and G. Libben. 2014. Morphonotactic and phonotactic processing in German-speaking adults. *Language Sciences* 46: 48–58.

Kretzschmar Jr., W.A. 2015. *Language and complex systems*. Cambridge: Cambridge University Press.

Krynicki, G. 2006. *Compilation, annotation and alignment of a Polish-English parallel corpus*. Ph.D. diss., Poznań: Adam Mickiewicz University.

Kurcz, I., A. Lewicki, J. Sambor, and J. Woronczak. 1974. *Słownictwo współczesnego języka polskiego*. Warszawa: Polska Akademia Nauk, Instytut Badań Literackich.

Kuryłowicz, J. 1952. Uwagi o polskich grupach spółgłoskowych. *Biuletyn Polskiego Towarzystwa Językoznawczego* XI: 54–69.

Maddieson, I. 2013a. Syllable structure. In *The World Atlas of Language Structures online*, eds. M. Dryer, and M. Haspelmath. Munich: Max Plank Digital Library. Online access: http://wals.info/. Accessed on 2017-07-21.

Maddieson, I. 2013b. Consonant-vowel ratio. In *The World Atlas of Language Structures online*, eds. M. Dryer, and M. Haspelmath. Leipzig: Max Planck Institute for Evolutionary Anthropology. Online access: http://wals.info/ . Accessed on 2017-08-20.

Maddieson, I. 2013c. Consonant inventories. In *The World Atlas of Language Structures online*, eds. M. Dryer, and M. Haspelmath. Leipzig: Max Planck Institute for Evolutionary Anthropology. Online access: http://wals.info/ . Accessed on 2018-10-16.

Madejowa, M. 1987. Współczesna polska norma językowa w zakresie wymowy samogłosek nosowych. *Studia Phonetica Posnaniensa* 1: 31–56.

Madejowa, M. 1990. Modern Polish linguistic norm with special reference to the pronunciation of consonants. *Studia Phonetica Posnaniensa* 2: 69–105.

Madejowa, M. 1993. Normative rules of Modern Polish pronunciation. *Studia Phonetica Posnaniensa* 4: 19–30.

Madelska, L. 2005. *Słownik wariantywności fonetycznej współczesnej polszczyzny*. Kraków: Collegium Collumbinum.

Madelska, L., and M. Witaszek-Samborska. 2015. *Zapis fonetyczny. Zbiór ćwiczeń*. Poznań: Wydawnictwo Naukowe Uniwersytetu im. Adama Mickiewicza.

McArthur, T. (ed.). 1992. *The Oxford Companion to the English Language*. Oxford: Oxford University Press.

McCulloch, W., and W. Pitts. 1943. A logical calculus of the ideas immanent in nervous activity. *Bulletin of Mathematical Biophysics* 5: 115–133.

Mohanan, K.P. 1982. *Lexical Phonology*. Bloomington: Indiana University Linguistic Club.

Morelli, F. 1998. Markedness relations and implicational universals in the typology of onset obstruent clusters. In *Proceedings of NELS 28*, 107–120. GLSA-Graduate Linguistic Student Association, Amherst: University of Massachusetts.

Morelli, F. 1999. *The phonotactics and phonology of obstruent clusters in Optimality Theory*. Ph. D. diss., College Park: University of Maryland.

Moulton, W.G. 1947. Juncture in modern standard German. *Language* 23: 212–226.

Nespor, M., and I. Vogel. 1986. *Prosodic phonology*. Dordrecht: Foris Publishers.

Orzechowska, P. 2009. *Morphonotactics in English and Polish. A dictionary- and corpus-based study of word-final consonant clusters*. Ph.D., diss., Poznań: Adam Mickiewicz University.

Orzechowska, P. 2012. Effects of morphology on the syllables structure. In *Monosyllables: From phonology to typology*, eds. T. Stolz, N. Nau, and C. Stroh, 93–113. Berlin: Akademie Verlag.

Orzechowska, P., and P. Zydorowicz. 2019. Frequency effects and markedness in phonotactics. *Poznań Studies in Contemporary Linguistics* 55 (1): 157–179.

Orzechowska, P., and R. Wiese. 2015. Preferences and variation in word-initial phonotactics: A multi-dimensional evaluation of German and Polish. *Folia Linguistica* 49: 439–486.

Ostaszewska, D., and J. Tambor. 2005. *Fonetyka i fonologia współczesnego języka polskiego*. Warszawa: Państwowe Wydawnictwo Naukowe.

Padgett, J. 1995. *Stricture in feature geometry* [Dissertations in linguistics]. Stanford: CSLI Publications.

Padgett, J, and M. Żygis. 2003. The evolution of sibilants in Polish and Russian. *ZAS Papers in Linguistics* 32: 155–174.

Paradis, C., and J.-F. Prunet. 1991. *The special status of coronals: Internal and external evidence*. San Diego: Academic Press.

Parker, S. 2002. *Quantifying the sonority hierarchy*. Ph.D., diss., Amherst: University of Massachusetts.

Parker, S. 2012a. Sonority distance vs. sonority dispersion—A typological survey. In *The sonority controversy*, ed. S. Parker, 101–166. Berlin: Walter de Gruyter.

Parker, S. (ed.). 2012b. *The sonority controversy*. Berlin: Walter de Gruyter.

Parker, S. 2017. Sounding out sonority. *Language and Linguistics Compass* 11 (9): 1–197.

Pawelec, P. 2012. The sonority sequencing generalization and the structure of consonant clusters with trapped sonorants in Polish. *Anglica Wratislaviensia* 50: 183–195.

Pompino-Marschall, B., E. Steriopolo, and M. Żygis. 2017. Ukrainian. *Journal of the International Phonetic Association: Illustrations of the IPA* 47: 349–357.

Prince, A., and P. Smolensky. 1993. *Optimality Theory: Constraint interaction in generative grammar*. Cambridge, MA: The MIT Press.

Pulgram, E. 1970. *Syllable, word, nexus, cursus*. The Hague: Mouton.

Pulleyblank, D. 1997. Optimality Theory and features. In *Optimality Theory: An overview*, eds. D. Archangeli, and T.D. Langendoen, 59–101. Malden, MA: Blackwell Publishers.

Ridouane, R. 2016. Leading issues in Tashlhiyt Berber phonology. *Language and Linguistics Compass* 10: 644–660.

Roach, P. 2006. *English phonetics and phonology: A practical course*. Cambridge: Cambridge University Press.

Rochoń, M. 2000. *Optimality in complexity: The case of Polish consonant clusters* [Studia grammatica 48]. Berlin: Akademie Verlag.

Rojczyk, A., and A. Porzuczek. 2014. Acoustic properties of nasal geminates in Polish. In *Crossing phonetics-phonology lines*, eds. E. Cyran, and J. Szpyra-Kozłowska, 347–364. Newcastle upon Tyne: Cambridge Scholars Publishing.

Roussou, A. 2017. Markedness, naturalness and complexity. In *The Cambridge handbook of historical syntax (Cambridge handbooks in language and linguistics)*, eds. A. Ledgeway, and I. Roberts, 360–380. Cambridge: Cambridge University Press.

Rubach, J. 1984. *Cyclic and Lexical Phonology*. Dordrecht: Foris Publications.

Rubach, J. 1996. Nonsyllabic analysis of voice assimilation in Polish. *Linguistic Inquiry* 27 (1): 69–110.

Rubach, J. 1997. Extrasyllabic consonants in Polish: Derivational Optimality Theory. In *Derivations and constraints in phonology*, ed. I. Rocca, 551–581. New York: Oxford University Press.

Rubach, J., and G. Booij. 1990a. Syllable structure assignment in Polish. *Phonology* 7: 121–158.

Rubach, J., and G. Booij. 1990b. Edge of constituent effects in Polish. *Natural Language & Linguistic Theory* 8 (3): 427–463.

Sawicka, I. 1974. *Struktura grup spółgłoskowych w językach słowiańskich*. Wrocław: Ossolineum.

Schadler, D. 2006. Morphonotaktik im Schwedischen. *Wiener Linguistische Gazette* 73: 1–19.

Scheer, T. 2006. Initial sonorant-obstruent clusters in Slavic languages, ver. 5.2. Database. Online access: http://sites.unice.fr/scheer/.

Schwarzinger, T. 2006. Morphonotaktik bei Konsonantengruppen im Portugiesischen. *Wiener Linguistische Gazette* 73: 20–46.

Selkirk, E.O. 1984. On the major class features and syllable theory. In *Language sound structure*, eds. M. Aronoff, and R.T. Oehrle, 107–136. Cambridge, MA: The MIT Press.

Selkirk, E.O. 1995. The prosodic structure of function words. In *Papers in Optimality Theory. University of Massachusetts Occasional Papers 18.*, eds. J. Beckman, L.W. Dickey, and S. Urbańczyk, 439–469. Massachusetts: University of Massachusetts.

Sieczkowska, J., B. Möbius, A. Schweitzer, M. Walsh, and G. Dogil. 2009. Voicing profile of Polish sonorants: [r] in obstruent clusters. In *Proceedings of the 10th interspeech conference*, Brighton, 6–10 Sept, 2319–2322.

Śledziński, D. 2013. Podział korpusu tekstów na sylaby—analiza polskich grup spółgłoskowych. *Kwartalnik Językoznawczy* 3 (15): 48–100.

Śledziński, D. 2016. Tworzenie reguł dla programu dzielącego tekst w języku polskim na sylaby. *Biuletyn Polskiego Towarzystwa Językoznawczego* 72: 151–161.

Sommerstein, A.H. 1977. *Theoretical linguistics 2: Modern phonology*. London: Edward Arnold.

Stampe, D. 1979. *A dissertation on Natural Phonology*. Bloomington: IULC.

Steriade, D. 1999. Alternatives to the syllabic interpretation of consonantal phonotactics. In *Item order in language and speech*, eds. O. Fujimura, B.D. Joseph, and B. Palek, 205–242. Columbus: The Karolinum Press.

Stieber, Z. 1948. Dwa problemy z polskiej fonologii. *Biuletyn Polskiego Towarzystwa Językoznawczego* 8: 56–78.

Strycharczuk, P. 2012a. Phonetics–phonology Interaction in Pre-Sonorant Voicing. Ph.D. diss., Manchester: University of Manchester.

Strycharczuk, P. 2012b. Sonorant transparency and the complexity of voicing in Polish. *Journal of Phonetics* 40 (5): 655–671.

Stump, G. 2017. Inflectional morphology. In *The Oxford research encyclopedia of linguistics*. Online publication date: Jun 2017.

Swadesh, M., and C.F. Voegelin. 1939. A problem in phonological alternation. *Language* 15, 1–10. [Reprinted in: *Readings in linguistics: The development of descriptive linguistics in America since 1925*, ed. M. Joos, 1963, 88–92. NewYork: American Council of Learned Societies.].

Szpyra, J. 1992. The phonology of Polish prefixation. In *Phonological investigations* [Linguistic and literary studies in Eastern Europe 38], eds. J Fisiak, and S. Puppel, 185–220. Amsterdam, Philadelphia: John Benjamins.

Szpyra, J. 1995. *Three tiers in Polish and English phonology*. Lublin: Wydawnictwo Uniwersytetu Marii Curie-Skłodowskiej.

Szpyra-Kozłowska, J. 1998. The sonority scale and phonetic syllabification in Polish. *Biuletyn Polskiego Towarzystwa Językoznawczego* 54: 63–82.

Szpyra-Kozłowska, J. 2000. On some misconceptions concerning phonetic syllabifications in Polish. *Folia Linguistica Anglica* 2: 159–173.

Szpyra-Kozłowska, J. 2001. Fonologia—System dźwiękowy języka. In *Współczesny język polski*, ed. J. Bartmiński, 485–502. Lublin: Wydawnictwo Uniwersytetu Marii Curie-Skłodowskiej.

Szpyra-Kozłowska, J. 2002. *Wprowadzenie do współczesnej fonologii*. Lublin: Wydawnictwo Uniwersytetu Marii Curie-Skłodowskiej.

Tobin, Y. 1997. *Phonology as Human Behaviour: Theoretical implications and clinical applications*. Durham: Duke University Press.

Trask, R.L. 1996. *Dictionary of phonetic and phonology*. London, New York: Routledge.

Trask, R.L. 1997. *A Student's Dictionary of Language and Linguistics* [Arnold student reference]. London: Hodder Education.

Trubetzkoy, N.S. 1969. *Principles of phonology*. Berkeley: University of California Press. [Reprint of: *Grundzüge der Phonologie*, 1939. Travaux du Cercle Linguistique de Prague, vol. 7].

Van der Hulst, H., and N.A. Ritter (eds.). 1999. *The syllable. Views and facts*. Berlin: Mouton de Gruyter.

Vaux, B., and Wolfe, A. 2009. The appendix. In *Contemporary views on architecture and representations in phonology* [Current studies in linguistics], eds. E. Raimy, and C.E. Cairns, 101–143. Cambridge, MA: The MIT Press.

Vennemann, T. 1983. Casuality in language change. Theories of linguistic preferences as a basis for linguistic explanations. *Folia Linguistica Historica* 6: 5–26.

Vennemann, T. 1988. *Preference laws for syllable structure and the explanation of sound change*. Berlin, New York, Amsterdam: Mouton de Gruyter.

Walczak, B. 1999. *Zarys dziejów języka polskiego*. Wrocław: Wydawictwo Uniwersytetu Wrocławskiego.

Wiese, R. 1996. *The phonology of German*. Oxford: Clarendon Press.

Wurzel, W.U. 1984. *Flexionsmorphologie und Natürlichkeit*. Berlin: Akademie-Verlag.

Yanushevskaya, I., and D. Bunčić. 2015. Russian. *Journal of the International Phonetic Association: Illustrations of the IPA* 45 (2): 221–228.

Zydorowicz, P., and P. Orzechowska. 2017. The study of Polish phonotactics: Measures of phonotactic preferability. *Studies in Polish Linguistics* 12 (2): 97–136.

Zydorowicz, P., P. Orzechowska, M. Jankowski, K. Dziubalska-Kołaczyk, P. Wierzchoń, and D. Pietrala. 2016. *Phonotactics and morphonotactics of Polish and English: Description, tools and applications*. Poznań: Wydawnictwo Naukowe UAM.

Żygis, M. 2003. Phonetic and phonological aspects of Slavic sibilant fricatives. *ZAS Papers in Linguistics* 32: 175–213.

Żygis, M. 2008. On the avoidance of voiced sibilant affricates. *ZAS Papers in Linguistics* 49: 23–45.

Żygis, M., D. Pape, and L.M.T. Jesus. 2012. (Non-)retroflex Slavic affricates and their motivation: Evidence from Czech and Polish. *Journal of the International Phonetic Association* 42: 281–329.

Chapter 2
Theoretical Approaches to Phonotactic Complexity of Polish

Essentially, all models are wrong, but some are useful.
(George Edward Box statistician, mathematician, 1976)

2.1 Introduction

This chapter presents an overview of theoretical approaches to phonotactic markedness (or complexity). Emphasis is placed on models which account for Polish consonant clusters from the synchronic perspective. The chapter introduces the term *markedness*, and discusses various definitions of the word. Two broad traditions of scholarship related to phonotactic markedness are delineated. There are approaches which (1) are *based on well-formedness conditions*, and approaches which (2) are *not based on well-formedness conditions*. The first answer the question whether a consonant cluster is well-formed or not, while the latter ask about the motivation for the existence of clusters, even if they are classified as ill-formed by the first approaches. In (1) well-formedness conditions are a priori statements which have their source in universals, phonological processes or higher-order principles (e.g. phonetic, cognitive). The analysis consists in classifying clusters into well-formed versus ill-formed, preferred versus dispreferred, or placing them on a markedness continuum mediating between the two options along the proposed criteria. The second tradition (2) consists in an in-depth analysis of subsegmental properties of consonants forming clusters as if from scratch, without positing a priori requirements on what the structure should be like. Such exploratory approaches search for minute phonetic and phonological properties which underlie the structure of consonant clusters, from which overarching generalizations can follow. These traditions account for different fragments of the phonotactic reality.

P. Orzechowska, *Complexity in Polish Phonotactics*, Prosody, Phonology and Phonetics, https://doi.org/10.1007/978-981-13-7299-5_2

2.2 Definitions of Markedness

The term *markedness* dates back to early works of Jakobson (1941) and Trubetzkoy (1969). Trubetzkoy (1969) described privative oppositions, in which one member is *mark-bearing* (from German *merkmaltragend*), while the other is *markless* (*merkmalloss*). According to this distinction, voiced and nasalized segments bear a mark, while voiceless and oral segments lack it. Since then various senses of the term have been proposed. For instance, in the generative framework (e.g. Chomsky and Halle 1968; Kean 1975) markedness is seen as an absolute category which involves two values: *marked* and *unmarked*. The theory of markedness refers to rules postulated for the "optimal, or most likely" (Kean 1975: 7) combinations of distinctive features in a segment: a likely specification is unmarked, while an unlikely specification is marked. In turn, Natural Linguistics (Donegan 1985, 2002; Donegan and Stampe 1979; Dressler 1985; Dressler et al. 1987; Kilani-Schoch 1988; Stampe 1979; Wurzel 1984) views markedness in terms of preferences, which can be captured by gradient continua between the most *preferred* and *dispreferred* linguistic options.

A large body of scholarship devoted to markedness represents different linguistic traditions and phonological theories (e.g. Andersen 2001, 2008; Battistella 1990, 1996; Calabrese 1995, 2005; Chomsky 1986; De Lacy 2002; Eckman et al. 1986; Guitart 1976; Haspelmath 2006; Hayes and Steriade 2004; Herbert 1986; Hume 2004; Kaye 1979; Moravcsik and Wirth 1986; Ludwig 2001; Roussou 2017; Tomić 1989, Wurzel 1998), although criticism has been voiced against markedness-based approaches (e.g. Gurevich 2001; Haspelmath 2006). The presentation of conflicting viewpoints on the topic is out of the scope of this chapter. In the following sections, I shall focus on a more general goal of identifying the most influential trends in the study of phonotactic markedness and different interpretations of the term, with particular reference to Polish.

A polysemous nature of the term *markedness* is discussed in Haspelmath (2006). Based on an insightful overview of the literature, Haspelmath (2006) outlines twelve *senses* of the term. The paper leads to the ultimate proposal of abandoning the concept altogether. Table 2.1 presents a compilation of the senses of markedness, which are grouped into three broad types. Marked properties or phenomena can be seen as displaying greater complexity, difficulty or divergence from normality compared to their unmarked counterparts. The column 'Proposed alternatives' summarizes Haspelmath's (2006) instructions on how to handle linguistic complexity, difficulty or abnormality without the necessity of invoking the traditional concept of markedness. The author's proposal is to substitute the term with other concepts, principles and tools available in linguistic theory, which adequately describe the same phenomena. The only exception constitutes the first sense of the term originally proposed by Trubetzkoy (1969). Since this interpretation of markedness was not widely adopted in phonology, Haspelmath (2006) does not argue against it.

A similar holistic perspective on markedness is presented in Rice (2007). The author offers a complete summary of the terms which have been associated with

Table 2.1 'Senses' of markedness

Sense	Markedness senses	Proposed alternatives
Markedness as complexity		
1	Trubetzkoyan markedness: as specification for a phonological distinction	No proposal
2	Semantic markedness: as specification for a semantic distinction	Use standard semantic concepts (hyponymy, polysemy), conversational implicatures and their conventionalization
3	Formal markedness: as overt coding	Terminological change: replace 'marked' with 'overtly coded', 'unmarked' with 'uncoded' (or 'zero-coded')
Markedness as difficulty		
4	Phonetic markedness: as phonetic difficulty	Terminological change: replace 'marked' with 'phonetic difficulty' and other system-external factors (frequency effects, regularity of sound change)
5	Markedness as morphological difficulty/dispreference/unnaturalness	Explain 'unnatural' phenomena with reference to substantive factors like type/token frequency and regularities of language change
6	Cognitive markedness: as conceptual difficulty	Explain 'conceptual difficulty' in terms of low frequency of use
Markedness as abnormality		
7	Textual markedness: as rarity in texts	Explicitly refer to the terms frequency of use, 'frequent' and 'rare'
8	Situational markedness: as rarity in the world	Irrelevant for linguistics; can be sometimes correlated with text frequency
9	Typological markedness: as typological implication or cross-linguistic rarity	Is merely a consequence of phonetic difficulty or other substantive factors
10	Distributional markedness: as restricted distribution	Terminological change: replace 'unmarked' with 'distributionally unrestricted' or 'occurs elsewhere'
11	Markedness as deviation from default parameter setting	Should be understood in terms of the 'non-default' sense of distributional markedness
12	Markedness as a multidimensional correlation	Explain solely on the basis of the first correlating dimension, i.e. frequency asymmetries

Adapted from Haspelmath (2006: 26–40)

markedness. The literature used for the compilation of the terms involves textbooks, linguistic dictionaries, encyclopedia articles, and theory-oriented phonological contributions (among others, Battistella 1990; De Lacy 2002, 2006; Greenberg 1978; Jakobson 1941; Kenstowicz 1994; Lombardi 2002; Steriade 1995; Trask 1996; Trubetzkoy 1969). Table 2.2 lists the terms representing the opposition between marked and unmarked linguistic properties and phenomena.

The left and right column of the table specify all the properties which have been used to describe the opposition between marked and unmarked, respectively. Rice

Table 2.2 Terms used to refer to markedness

Marked	Unmarked
Non-phonological criteria	
Less natural	More natural
More complex	Simpler
More specific	More general
Less common	More common
Unexpected	Expected
Not basic	Basic
Less stable	Stable
Appear in few grammars	Appear in more grammars
Later in acquisition	Earlier in acquisition
Early loss in language deficit	Late loss in language deficit
Implies unmarked feature	Implied by marked feature
Harder to articulate	Easier to articulate
Perceptually more salient	Perceptually less salient
Smaller phonetic space	Larger phonetic space
Phonological criteria	
Subject to neutralization	Result of neutralization
Unlikely to be epenthetic	Likely to be epenthetic
Trigger of assimilation	Target of assimilation
Remains in coalescence	Lost in coalescence
Retained in deletion	Lost in deletion

Adapted from Rice (2007: 80)

(2007) groups the terms into two classes: phonological and non-phonological. The characteristics subsumed under phonological criteria, also referred to as *structural markedness*, describe phonological systems. The terms listed under non-phonological criteria capture the phonetic aspects of markedness, which can be generally referred to as *natural markedness* or *frequency markedness*.

The interpretations of markedness captured in Tables 2.2 and 2.1 refer to properties and phenomena belonging to different branches of linguistics, including morphology, syntax and semantics. Markedness has also been studied in the domain of phonotactics. Two directions of research aimed at accounting for 'complexity', 'difficulty' or 'abnormality' of consonant clusters are introduced in 2.3, and discussed in Sects. 2.4 and 2.5.

2.3 Two Directions in the Study of Phonotactics

For clarity of exposition, I introduce the distinction between two types of approaches in the study of phonotactics depending on whether markedness, or well-formedness, statements are employed in the analysis or not. That is, there are approaches which are *based on well-formedness conditions*, and approaches which are not based *on well-formedness conditions*. The first answer the question whether a cluster is well-formed or not. The latter, in turn, ask about the motivation underlying the structure of clusters, even if they are classified as ill-formed. The bifurcation reflects the differences in terms of goals pursued in the study of phonotactics, and methodologies used in getting answers to the questions posed. The two-fold division is a simplified way of capturing the nature of phonotactic modelling. Approaches based on well-formedness make use of *already derived* principles, while approaches not based on well-formedness look for *new* principles.

Well-formedness conditions are a priori statements on phonotactic markedness. Such statements are derived from the structure of segments forming clusters or have their source in phonological processes or higher principles (e.g. psychological, cognitive, phonetic). More specifically, markedness conditions reflect, for instance, the need to adhere to the preferred CV structure, from syllabification strategies or from the principle of perceptual contrast, and are adequately defined at the outset of the phonotactic analysis. Approaches based on well-formedness conditions aim at answering the following question: *Do clusters follow well-formedness conditions, and possibly to what extent*? This goal is reached by measuring clusters in terms of the established set of principles. As a result, sequences of consonants are classified into those which either follow the markedness predictions (i.e. well-formed) or violate them (i.e. ill-formed). Apart from a binary division into well-formed versus ill-formed, preferred versus dispreferred, good versus bad, further granularity can be introduced by placing clusters on markedness scales, which mediate between the two extremes.

This type of an analysis is mainly represented by the *Sonority Sequencing Generalization* (Selkirk 1984). Sonority regulates the ordering of consonants in a sequence based on one or several criteria. As I will show in Sects. 2.4 and 2.5, a degree of detail plays a substantial role in the ensuing classification of clusters. First, depending on whether a sonority scale is composed of four or six classes of consonants based on the manner of articulation, clusters can be classified either as sonority-obeying or sonority-offending. Second, further differences in the classification of clusters can be observed when additional criteria are implemented in the analysis, such as the place of articulation and voicing.

Another direction in the study of phonotactics is delineated by approaches which are not based on well-formedness conditions. They provide an in-depth analysis of subsegmental properties of consonants with a view to discovering the mechanisms which underlie the phonological characteristics of clusters. The core question addressed by the approaches is the following: *What properties or principles motivate the phonological structure of clusters (even if they are classified as ill-formed)*? The nature of this type of modelling is exploratory: it offers new insights into phonetic and / or phonological properties of sequences of consonants, from which eventually overarching principles can follow. Adopting this methodology makes it possible to explain why ill-formed combinations are attested in a language.

An example of an approach which is not based on well-formedness conditions but infers them from the intrinsic properties of segments is *Government Phonology* (e.g. Charette 1990; Harris 1990, 1996; Kaye et al. 1985, 1990). The theory starts with a meticulous analysis of vowels and consonants in terms of tiny subsegmental properties, or melodic primes. Mechanisms which motivate the structure of consonant clusters are extrapolated from the complexity of segments, which is, in turn, derived from the number of constituent melodic primes. The theory shows that clusters are motivated by criteria other than the ones captured by well-formedness conditions.

Both directions of study account for different fragments of phonotactics. Approaches based on well-formedness conditions focus on what the structure of clusters *should be* like, while approaches which do not employ well-formedness conditions focus on what the structure of clusters *is* like. Measuring markedness and exploration factors that contribute to it offer a wholistic picture of consonant clusters. These directions in the study of phonotactics can apply to other phenomena in phonology, and to linguistics in general. A detailed exposition of these types of methods are discussed in Sects. 2.4 and 2.5.

2.4 Approaches Based on Well-Formedness Conditions

2.4.1 Sonority Sequencing Generalization

For over a century, the study of phonotactics has been largely monopolized by the principle of sonority (Jespersen 1904; Sievers 1881; Whitney 1865). Although sonority has been defined in both phonetic and phonological terms, the most oft-quoted definition is articulatory, and refers to "the degree of openness of the vocal apparatus during production" (Goldsmith 1990: 110), which corresponds to loudness. In a sonority scale, consonants are ordered in affinity to a vowel, where loudness increases from obstruents through sonorants to a vocalic peak. Examples of sonority scales are given in 19 (for historical overviews and detailed descriptions see Clements 1990; Cser 2000; Katamba 2009; Parker 2002, 2008, 2012b).

19. Major sonority scales

(19.a) Dell and Elmedlaoui (1985)
low vowels > high vowels > liquids > nasals > voiced fricatives > voiceless fricatives > voiced stops > voiceless stops

(19.b) Foley (1972)
vowels > glides > liquids > nasals > fricatives > oral stops

(19.c) Jespersen (1904)
voiced low vowels > voiced mid vowels > voiced high vowels > voiced /r/-sounds > voiced lateral, voiced nasals > voiced fricatives > voiced stops > voiceless stops, voiceless fricatives

(19.d) Hooper (1976)
vowels > glides > liquids > nasals > voiced continuants > voiceless continuants, voiced stops > voiceless stops

(19.e) Hogg and McCully (1987)
low vowels > mid vowels > high vowels > flaps > laterals > nasals > voiced fricatives > voiceless fricatives > voiced stops > voiceless stops

(19.f) Wiese (1988), Hall (1992)
vowels > /r/ > /l/ > nasals > obstruents

(19.g) Clements (1990)
vowels > glides > liquids > nasals > obstruents

(19.h) Goldsmith (1990)
low vowels > mid vowels > high vowels > glides > liquids > nasals > fricatives > affricates > stops

(19.i) Zec (1995)
vowels > sonorants > obstruents

(19.j) Parker (2002)
low vowels > mid vowels (except /ə/) > high vowels (except /ɨ/) > /ə/ > /ɨ/ > glides > /r/ > laterals > flaps > trills > nasals > /h/ > voiced fricatives > voiced stops and affricates/voiceless fricatives > voiceless fricatives/voiced stops and affricates > voiceless stops and affricates.

(19.k) Basbøll (2005)
non lateral non stop sonorant > consonantal sonorant > voiced obstruent > voiceless obstruent with non spread glottis > obstruent with spread glottis.

Sonority has phonological and phonetic bases. For instance, some scales have emerged from the study syllable-related processes, e.g. Dell and Elmedlaoui (1985), Zec (1995), Hall (1992). Other scales have resulted from acoustic measurements of intensity, e.g. Parker (2002). Additionally, the scales have been proposed for different languages such as Berber (Dell and Elmedlaoui 1985), German (Wiese 1988), and English (Clements 1990), although a universal scale is given in Parker (2002). As can be observed in 19, sonority has been mainly defined in terms of the manner of articulation (Clements 1990; Foley 1972; Wiese 1988; Zec 1995). Other properties used in the classification of segments such as voicing and vowel height are taken into consideration, albeit rarely (e.g. Hogg and McCully 1987; Goldsmith 1990; Jespersen 1904; Parker 2002).

The hierarchies in (19.a) through (19.k) present the ordering of segments according to their increasing sonority slope. Vennemann (1988), in turn, proposes an inverse ordering of *consonantal strength* where vowels are the weakest and plosives are the strongest. The scale in (19.l) is proposed to account for the *Syllable Contact Law* (Murray and Vennemann 1983), according to which syllable contact pairs tend to have a falling sonority profile.

(19.l) Vennemann (1988)
voiceless plosives > voiced plosives > voiceless fricatives > voiced fricatives > nasals > /l/ > /r/ > high vowels > mid vowels > low vowels

In spite of a wide array of hierarchies proposed in the subject literature, there is a coarse ordering which holds universally. Acoustic studies demonstrate that (19.a) through (19.k) follow the same general pattern: glides > liquids > nasals > obstruents. For instance, in his study on English, Spanish and Quechua, Parker (2008) observes no overlaps at the undisputed junctures between vowels versus sonorants, and sonorants versus obstruents. Similar observations are made in Jany et al. (2007). Egyptian Arabic, Hindi, Malayalam and Mongolian are shown to differ only in terms of fine contrasts between rhotics versus laterals, voiceless fricatives versus voiced stops, affricates versus stops, as well as sibilants versus other fricatives. The hierarchies are used to account for syllable structure.

The ordering of vowels and consonants in a syllable is regulated by the *Sonority Sequencing Generalization* (henceforth SSG, Selkirk 1984), which states that:

> "[i]n any syllable, there is a segment constituting a sonority peak that is preceded and/or followed by a sequence of segments with progressively decreasing sonority values" (Selkirk 1984: 116).

The principle evaluates clusters according to the sonority profile of constituent consonants before and after a vowel. A sonority rise from syllable margins towards a vowel ensures that a cluster is well-formed. For instance, initial /pr tw sm/ in *pray, twin* and *smog* are sonority-obeying, and constitute *core* clusters (Clements 1990). The reordering of consonants in a string results in *reversals* (Clements 1990), which are either unattested in English (e.g. /rp wt ms/), or which are ill-formed (e.g. /sp st sk/ in *spin, stand, skin*).

Central to this discussion is the fact that sonority has been originally proposed to account for syllabification. In fact, the SSG is an obligatory condition for syllabification, rather than just a universal prerequisite defining syllable structure. As was pinpointed by Goldsmith (1990), the implementation of the principle can vary cross-linguistically in that languages may require that the differences in sonority between neighbouring segments be of a particular degree. Sonority distances have been measured to account for the complexity of Polish phonotactics.

A body of research has demonstrated the relevance of sonority in Polish. For instance, the principle plays a role in blocking of voice assimilation (Bethin 1992; Gussmann 1992), in the selection of allomorphs (Rubach and Booij 1990a), and in syllabification (Bethin 1992; Cyran and Gussmann 1999; Gussmann 1991, 1992, 2007; Rubach and Booij 1990a, b; Szpyra 1995). However, the studies on Polish have relied on sonority scales which vary in terms of the degree of detail. The differences are found in the class of obstruents. As was shown earlier, languages such as English (Clements 1990) and German (Hall 1992; Wiese 1988) do not display sonority distinctions between plosives, affricates and fricatives. The same observation was made for Polish by Rubach and Booij (1990a, b), who propose the ordering of segments in the syllable presented in 20 '>' refers a decrease in sonority.

20. Sonority scale for Polish (Rubach and Booij 1990a, b)

vowels > glides > liquids > nasals > obstruents

The validity of this 5-point scale in syllabification was demonstrated by Cetnarowska and Żygis (2004, 2007). Other contributions have made use of more detailed scales, where consonants are allocated to 5 and 6 classes (cf. Foley 1972; Goldsmith 1990), which are presented in (21.a) and (21.b). The terms '6-point scale' and '7-point scale' refer to all segment classes, including vowels.

21. Other sonority scales used in research on Polish

(21.a) 6-point scale:
vowels > glides > liquids > nasals > fricatives > affricates and plosives
(21.b) 7-point scale:
vowels > glides > liquids > nasals > fricatives > affricates > plosives

The scales were tested on Polish in surface and automatic syllabification (among others, Bertinetto et al. 2007; Szpyra-Kozłowska 1998, 2000; Śledziński 2013, 2016, 2017; Śledziński et al. 2013) and in the classification of consonant clusters (Orzechowska and Wiese 2015; Orzechowska and Zydorowicz 2019; Pawelec 2012; Śledziński 2010; Zydorowicz and Orzechowska 2016). While most of the contributions are descriptive, empirical evidence in Szpyra-Kozłowska (1998, 2000) lends further support to the scale of Rubach and Booij (1990a, b). Other studies on syllabification in Polish involve Bigi and Klessa (2015), Klessa and Śledziński (2006) and Malisz and Wagner (2012).

It must be noted that the hierarchies in 21 make more or less fine-grained predictions as to the ordering of segments in a successfull syllable. In Sect. 2.4.1.1, I put the hierarchies to empirical testing by analysing a large inventory of Polish consonant clusters, and present additional requirements which constrain the sonority profile in Polish syllables.

2.4.1.1 Constraints on the Sonority Sequencing Generalization

In line with earlier contributions by Fudge (1969) and Halle and Vergnaud (1980), Rubach and Booij (1990b) propose a constraint that places a condition on the ordering of obstruent consonants in a sequence.

22. Obstruent Sequencing Constraint (Rubach and Booij 1990b: 431)

With obstruents there is no requirement for sonority distance.

The authors observed that the syllabification of word-medial CC clusters is regulated by the algorithm in 22. Native speakers of Polish syllabify word-internal obstruent + obstruent sequences in two ways. Clusters such as /tk/ in *matka* 'mother' are either tautosyllabic in onsets in *ma.tka* or heterosyllabic in *mat.ka*. To the contrary, sonorant-obstruent clusters such as /rt/ in *ka.rta* 'card' and /wk/ in *pa.łka* 'stick' are strictly avoided. This strategy also holds in three-member and four-member clusters. Polish speakers display a preference for onset maximization, with the exception of clusters starting with a sonorant. For instance, *kontakt*

Table 2.3 Examples of initial obstruent CC clusters

CC	Cluster	Word-initial	Syllable-initial
Plosive + affricate	pɕ	#psikać 'to sneeze'	mo.psik 'small pugdog'
Plosive + fricative	bʑ	#bzik 'craze'	ko.bziarz 'piper'
Affricate + plosive	ʧt	#cztery 'four'	po.czta 'post office'
Affricate + fricative	ʧf	#czwartek 'Thursday'	po.czwa.ra 'monster'
Fricative + plosive	st	#stać 'to stand'	pa.sta 'tooth paste'
Fricative + affricate	ɕtɕ	#ściskać 'to squeeze'	ko.ści 'bone' (pl)

'contact' is unexceptionally syllabified as *kon.takt*. The results suggest that obstruents require no sonority differential in Polish.

Rubach and Booij (1990b: 431) claim that apart from the suspension of the sonority-based sequencing in obstruents (see 22), "Polish indeed obeys the SSG". That is, onset maximization is blocked if parsing of a cluster would result in a violation of the SSG. Obviously, the condition ensures that, firstly, some tricky initial clusters are syllabified into a single syllable, and, secondly, that the sonority principle is not violated. The constraint ensures that all combinations of obstruents are admitted in onsets. A handful of CC clusters which satisfy the condition of Rubach and Booij (1990b) is exemplified in Table 2.3.

Geminate clusters are excluded from the table. As Rubach and Booij (1990b) explain, intervocalic geminates are not syllabified together which results in splitting plosive + plosive, affricate + affricate and fricative + fricative sequences into respective codas and onsets. For instance, /tt ʧʧ ss/tend to be heterosyllabified as in *brut.to* 'gross', *ucz.czony* 'honoured' and *las.so* 'lasso'.

Following the postulates of Rubach and Booij (1990b), Rochoń (2000) posits a constraint in Optimality Theory (Kager 1999; Prince and Smolenski 1993), which prohibits decreasing sonority from the edges of the syllable towards a vowel. Rochoń (2000) formalizes the constraint in the following way:

23. *Son ↘ V constraint (Rochoń 2000: 125)

No decreasing sonority from the edge of the syllable towards the peak.

The constraint in 23 is violated only if a sonorant precedes an obstruent in the onset or follows an obstruent in the coda, as in /wg mʒ tr/ in *łgać* 'to lie', *mrzonka*

Table 2.4 Onset CC clusters which display no decrease in sonority from the edge of the syllable towards the peak

CC	**Son ↘ V*
Obstruent + obstruent	✓
Obstruent + sonorant	✓
Nasal + nasal	✓
Nasal + liquid	✓
Nasal + glide	✓
Liquid + liquid	✓
Liquid + glide	✓
Glide + glide	✓

Rochoń (2000: 125)

'pipe dream', *wiatr* 'wind'. A list of CC sequences which would satisfy the constraint in 23 is tabulated in Table 2.4.

It must be noted that the constraint serves to account for the syllabification of word-medial clusters. In contrast to the SSG, the general formulation of the constraint permits plateau clusters with the same sonority level to function as well-formed onsets. However, Polish syllable onsets do not permit plateaus composed of two nasals, liquids and glides. In order to account for this gap, Rochoń (2000) posits constraints which prohibit their occurrence. The constraints are presented in 24.

24. An additional onset constraint in Polish (Rochoń 2000: 125)

(24.a) NASAL + NASAL: A sequence of two nasals in the onset is prohibited.
(24.b) LIQUID + LIQUID: A sequence of two liquids in the onset is prohibited.
(24.c) GLIDE + GLIDE: A sequence of two glides in the onset is prohibited.

The constraints in (24.a), (24.b) and (24.c) are highly ranked. This means that when sonorant clusters occur intervocalically, 24 ensure that they are heterosyllabified. Such a set of constraints has particular consequences for phonological theory. Namely, it encourages views on a relatively simple, well-formed and unmarked structure of Polish phonotactics. This remark holds not only for sonorant clusters but also for strings of obstruents.

A number of hierarchies presented in 19 would evaluate obstruent + obstruent sequences as sonority-violating, offering evidence in favour a marked character of Polish phonotactics. However, as is argued in Rubach and Booij (1990a, b), the syllabification of medial obstruent clusters is arbitrary, as no sonority differential is required between plosives, affricates and fricatives. This remark is particularly important given that Polish features numerous obstruent-only clusters. Table 2.5 presents a quantitative overview of CC classes collected by Dobrogowska (1992). Initial obstruent + obstruent clusters are the most common in text corpora, and constitute 49% of all CC clusters in popular science texts, and 45% of all CC clusters in artistic prose.

Table 2.5 Initial CC clusters in scientific and artistic prose

Scientific text	Artistic prose
Voiceless obstruent + voiceless obstruent 8,543 (41.5%)	Voiceless obstruent + voiceless obstruent 6,820 (36.1%)
Voiceless obstruent + liquid 4,844 (23.5%)	Voiceless obstruent + liquid 4,128 (21.9%)
Voiced obstruent + voiced obstruent 1,519 (7.4%)	Voiced obstruent + voiced obstruent 1,578 (8.4%)
Voiced obstruent + liquid 4,699 (22.8%)	Voiced obstruent + liquid 4,976 (26.4%)
Liquid + voiceless obstruent 8 (0.04%)	Liquid + voiceless obstruent 7 (0.04%)
Liquid + voiced obstruent 22 (0.1%)	Liquid + voiced obstruent 12 (0.06%)
Liquid + liquid 966 (4.7%)	Liquid + liquid 1,353 (7.2%)

Adapted from Dobrogowska (1992: 69)

Adjacent obstruents are also common in longer sequences. A corpus study of Śledziński (2010) demonstrated that the most frequent initial CCC clusters have the following structure: fricative + plosive + liquid, fricative + plosive + glide, fricative + affricate + fricative and fricative + fricative + glide as in /fpr fpw stf zvj/. By the same token, the structure of the most frequent four-member clusters is represented by two fricatives followed by a plosive and a liquid, as in /vzgl/ (Śledziński 2010: 76f.).

Apart from the controversies involved in the treatment of obstruent clusters, one could justly reflect upon the ordering of sonorants in Polish. This issues is addressed in Szpyra-Kozłowska (1998), who investigates surface syllabification of CC and CCC intervocalic clusters.

> "(…) it appears that a distinction should be made between obstruent + glide and obstruent + liquid clusters on the one hand, and obstruent plus nasal clusters on the other hand. In the former case 36.3% of open syllable divisions can be observed, while in the latter only 15%. This makes obstruent + approximant clusters the optimal onsets in Polish, which is understandable in view of the fact that such sequences represent a sharp rise in sonority and are therefore universally favoured as syllable onsets." (Szpyra-Kozłowska 1998: 71)

Based on these observations, a more refined version of the sonorous end of the hierarchy is proposed.

25. Sonority distinctions between glides and liquids in Polish (Szpyra-Kozłowska 1998: 71)

    j > r > w > l

This ordering is consistent with the sonority scales in (19.b) through (19.k), which assume that glides are more sonorous than liquids, and liquids are more sonorous than nasals. This observation has not been explored in the phonological literature on Polish. I am not aware of any contribution which in the past two decades have investigated the validity of 25. This proposal requires empirical testing, which would be particularly important for the purpose of this book. Given the goal of identifying properties or principles which underlie the structure of Polish consonant clusters, the following questions arise: Is there a feature-based motivation for this ordering? Or do these sonority distinctions hold for a specific language domain, like the lexicon, perception or production? These ideas will re-emerge in Chaps. 3 and 6, where feature weight and ensuing rankings of preferences are discussed.

At this point, without considering the distinctions between /j r w l/, let me illustrate how various sonority hierarchies classify Polish clusters. Sections 2.4.1.2 and 2.4.1.3 present an analysis of initial and final phonotactics in terms of the SSG, where scales differing in the degree of detail are used.

2.4.1.2 The SSG Analysis of Initial Phonotactics

In Polish, word edge clusters cannot be equated with permissible syllable onsets and codas (Rubach and Booij 1990a; Szpyra-Kozłowska 2000). However, the sonority principle has also been applied to word-based phonotactics in Rubach (1996) and Steriade (1999). Therefore, I take the liberty to evaluate word edge clusters according to the three sonority scales, which have been used in the study on Polish so far, and which are given in 20 and 21.

On the assumption that fricatives, affricates and plosives are ordered freely in Polish, the scale in 20 predicts that a majority of clusters should follow the SSG, including some remarkable CCC and CCCC initials. A handful of examples is provided below.

(c) /bʒd/ in *brzdąc* 'tot'
(d) /kʃʧ/ in *Krzczonów* [village name]
(e) /ʑʥb/ in *źdźbeł* 'grass stalk' (gen pl)
(f) /gʒbj/ in *grzbiet* 'spine'
(g) /tkfj/ in *tkwiący* 'to be stuck' (ger)

According to the 6-point and 7-point scales in 21, clusters given above are classified as marked. Sequences composed of three obstruents are bound to violate hierarchies sensitive to obstruent classes. To compare how the selection of a scale influences the classification of clusters into SSG-obeying and SSG-violating, let me analyse a rich list of word-initial and word-final CCs, CCCs, and CCCCs, which were compiled for the purpose of this book. To avoid bias resulting from morphological complexity, the analysis focuses on unmotivated clusters, i.e. 336 initials and 131 finals listed in Tables 1.14 and 1.18, respectively.

Table 2.6 presents the analysis for word-initial clusters. The following groups were identified: SSG-obeying clusters exhibit a rise from the left-most consonant towards a vowel, SSG-violating clusters display the reverse pattern, and plateau clusters involve segments from the same class. It must be noted that the interpretation of well-formedness, and the resulting classification of clusters into well-formed, ill-formed and plateaus differs from one scale to another.

The 5-point scale in 20 (Rubach and Booij 1990a, b) posits that all combinations of plosives, fricatives and affricates are well-formed. Since the sonority differential is not required within the class of obstruents, sequences such as /ps sp tʃ ʃt fɕʨ/ are all

Table 2.6 Markedness-based classification of word-initial phonotactic clusters (N = 336) by three sonority scales

SSG profile	A: 5-point scale		B: 6-point scale		C: 7-point scale	
	No	%	No	%	No	%
Obeying CC	177	92	117	61	122	63
Violating CC	14	7	39	20	44	23
Plateau CC	2	1	37	19	27	14
Obeying CCC	96	75	44	34	41	32
Violating CCC	32	25	84	66	87	68
Obeying CCCC	13	87	5	33	5	33
Violating CCCC	2	13	10	67	10	67
Total obeying	286	85	168	50	168	50
Total violating	48	14	136	40	141	42
Total plateau	2	1	32	10	27	8

A = Rubach and Booij (1990a, b), B = Foley (1972), C = Goldsmith (1990)

considered to be SSG-obeying. Therefore, the term *plateau* is used only with reference to sonorants sharing the manner of articulation, namely nasal + nasal /mn mɲ/.

In the 6-point and 7-point scales by Foley (1972) and Goldsmith (1990), clusters with identical manner features are classified as plateaus, namely plosive + plosive /db kp kt/, affricate + affricate /ʤʤ ʧʨ ʧʧ/, fricative + fricative /ɕf vz sx/ and nasal + nasal. Additionally, adjacent affricates and plosives form plateau CCs (e.g. /gʥ kʦ ʨp ʧk/) in the 6-point scale. In this count, CC plateaus in combination with sonorants are classified as sonority-obeying (e.g. fricative + fricative + glide in /ʃfj/) or violating (e.g. nasal + plosive + plosive in /mpt ŋkt/).

For all the size groups, I provide the number of types ('No') and percentages ('%') calculated for all clusters in each size group, namely 193 CCs, 128 CCCs and 15 CCCCs. Additionally, the bottom rows summarize the results for the total of 336 initial clusters. Note the assignment of the scales: A = 20, B = (21.a), C = (21.b). The classification of initial clusters in terms of the three scales is found in Appendix A.

As expected, the more detailed hierarchies yield a more marked output. B and C classify only 50% of all phonotactic clusters as sonority-obeying. To the contrary, the 5-point scale classifies 85% of all clusters as sonority-obeying. The same tendency can be observed across the size groups. According to the general scale in A, well-formed clusters prevail among CCs, CCCs and CCCCs. For B and C, the propensity of a marked cluster increases with an increase in size. That is, more than 60% of CC types follow the SSG, and nearly 70% of CCC(C) types do not follow the principle.

The observation that a general hierarchy yields a less marked output in terms of sonority than a more detailed one is also supported statistically. I performed a Pearson's chi-squared test for scales A, B, C, where I crossed (a) the total number of obeying and violating clusters (the latter including plateaus[1]) and (b) obeying and violating clusters for the CC and CCC groups separately. The results are highly significant ($p < 0.00001$). To conclude, the selection of a sonority scale largely influences the division of initial clusters, and is key for the classification of Polish clusters in terms of well-formedness.

2.4.1.3 The SSG Analysis of Final Phonotactics

An analogous analysis was conducted for word-final clusters. According to the SSG-obeying, clusters should display a sharp fall in sonority from a vowel towards the last consonant in a sequence (i.e. C2 in CC or C3 in CCC) as in /wk rs jnt/. SSG-violating clusters should show a sonority rise, e.g. /kl lɕɲ xtr/. Again, for the 5-point scale in A, obstruent clusters are well-formed. In the remaining scales, the

[1]SSG-violating and plateau clusters are merged into a single category for two reasons. Firstly, plateaus are generally considered ill-formed. Secondly, performing a χ^2 analysis is not possible on numbers lower than 5.

Table 2.7 Markedness-based classification of word-final phonotactic clusters (N = 131) by three sonority scales

SSG profile	A: 5-point scale		B: 6-point scale		C: 7-point scale	
	No	%	No	%	No	%
Obeying CC	83	82	73	72	74	73
Violating CC	17	17	22	22	22	22
Plateau CC	1	1	6	6	5	5
Obeying CCC	17	57	16	53	16	53
Violating CCC	13	43	14	47	14	47
Total obeying	100	76	89	68	90	69
Total violating	30	23	36	27	36	27
Total plateau	1	1	6	5	5	4

A = Rubach and Booij (1990a, b), B = Foley (1972), C = Goldsmith (1990)

specific ordering of plosives, affricates and fricatives holds according to 21. The treatment of plateau clusters corresponds with the description in Sect. 2.4.1.2.

Table 2.7 presents the summary of the results for final phonotactic CCs and CCCs. Each cell lists the number of cluster types (‘No’) along with the percentages (‘%’) calculated for each size group, namely 101 CCs and 30 CCCs. The bottom-most rows summarize the results obtained for the total of 131 final clusters. Scales A, B and C correspond with 20, (21.a), and (21.b), respectively. The distribution of final clusters in the group of SSG-obeying, SSG-violating and plateau sequences in terms of each scale is included in Appendix B.

The most general scale in A yields the most sonority-satisfying output. The 5-point scale classifies 76% of all clusters as well-formed. Also, SSG-obeying clusters prevail among two-member and three-member sequences. Although the more detailed scales pose more challenging criteria of phonotactic well-formedness, they unambiguously show that final clusters are sonority-obeying, disregarding their size. A Pearson’s chi-squared tests performed on the data did not yield significant results ($p > 0.05$), which suggests that the differences in the classification of clusters are at a negligible level. That is, the selection of a scale has a lesser impact on final phonotactics than on initial phonotactics. This observation lends support to the fact that constraints, and well-formedness conditions are positional.

It must be borne in mind that the data include sonorant-initial and sC(C) clusters. In particular /s/ + stop sequences pose challenges for general phonological theory. A large body of research has been devoted to the atypical behaviour of /s/-initial clusters such as /sp str skfj/ in *spać* ‘to sleep’, *strach* ‘fear’ and *skwierczeć* ‘to crackle’. The complexity of such sequences has been attributed to the extrasyllabic status of the fricative in non-linear approaches to the syllable (Goad 2011, 2012; Kaye 1992; Kaye et al. 1990; Vaux and Wolfe 2009), and in language acquisition (Cardoso 2008; Yavaş 2006, 2013; Yavaş et al. 2008). Treating /s/ as a disjunct element external to the syllable is a solution proposed to account for /s/ + stop clusters in English, but leaves other Polish sC clusters unexplained, e.g. phonotactic /sf, ss, sts, sx/ in *sfera* ‘sphere’, *ssać* ‘to suck’, *scena* ‘scene’ and *schody* ‘stairs’.

Additionally, clusters such as /st sp/ occur in numerous common words (e.g. *spać* 'to sleep', *stać* 'to stand') and have high text and usage frequencies. What is more, in Polish the pre-initial /s/ signals the presence of a morphological boundary (see Chap. 1, Sect. 1.6.2.3). Morphologically-complex and sC clusters require special treatment in sonority-based approaches. In turn, word-based models have an easier task of incorporating such sequences into the analysis.

2.4.2 Net Auditory Distance

Polish phonotactics has been studied from the perspective of other approaches based on well-formedness conditions. *Net Auditory Distance* (henceforth NAD, Dziubalska-Kołaczyk 2009, 2014, in press) is an extension of *Beats-and-Binding Phonology* by Dziubalska-Kołaczyk (2002), a syllable-less model of phonology (Dziubalska-Kołaczyk 1995, 1996). The principle is a measure of auditory distances between pairs of segments in consonant clusters (consonants and neighbouring vowels). NAD formulates well-formedness conditions for preferred clusters. Such a priori statements are derived from the cross-linguistic preference for the canonical CV structure, and the prosodic principle of perceptual contrast (Donegan and Stampe 2009). According to both approaches, sequences of consonants are disfavoured (or marked). First, clusters are generally avoided in the languages of the world. Second, since fortitions enhance clarity, larger phonetic distances are expected to facilitate perception, and result in a preferred combination of segments. Therefore, NAD proposes well-formedness conditions which meet this requirement for two-member and three-member sequences.

NAD is an example of a principle which uses a wider array of criteria in cluster classification than the manner of articulation. A complex interplay of manner, place and laryngeal features results in a different classification of clusters compared to the SSG. That is, NAD shows that clusters with a widely acknowledged marked character do not necessarily have to be doomed to dispreferability. The principle allocates clusters to the most and least preferred groups, along with intervening preferability categories mediating between the two options. Note that NAD operates only on CCs and CCCs. It is unclear how distances should be arranged in longer sequences (e.g. sequences of four or five consonants).

NAD operates on word-level phonotactics, and thus incorporates sC(C) clusters into the analysis. Although the principle is more restrictive than sonority, it classifies sC clusters as dispreferred, while sCC as preferred. This difference results from systematically incorporating three properties into a calculation matrix, namely the manner of articulation (MOA), place of articulation (POA) and laryngeal features expressed by the sonorant / obstruent distinction (S/O). NAD predicts that a degree of (dis)preferability is a sum of transitions (or distances) between segments, and that larger distances are perceptually favoured. The size of a transition is computed along the scales given in 26. The distance of one holds between each consecutive manner category on the horizontal axis,[2] and place category on the vertical axis. The two dimensions are presented in (26.a) and (26.b), respectively. The original table which includes specific segments is given in (26.c).

26. Auditory distances for Polish consonants

(26.a) MOA distances

<table>
<tr><td>0</td><td>1</td><td colspan="2">2</td><td>3</td><td colspan="2">4</td><td>5</td></tr>
<tr><td>V</td><td>glide</td><td colspan="2">liquid</td><td>nasal</td><td colspan="2">fricative</td><td>plosive</td></tr>
<tr><td></td><td></td><td>rhotic
= 2</td><td>lateral
= 2.5</td><td></td><td></td><td>affricate
= 4.5</td><td></td></tr>
</table>

(26.b) POA distances

<table>
<tr><td>0</td><td colspan="2">1</td><td colspan="3">2</td><td colspan="2">3</td></tr>
<tr><td>V</td><td colspan="2">labial</td><td colspan="3">coronal</td><td colspan="2">dorsal</td></tr>
<tr><td></td><td>bilabial
= 1</td><td>labio-dental
= 1.5</td><td>dental
= 2</td><td>alveolar
= 2.3</td><td>alveolo-
palatal = 2.6</td><td>palatal
= 3</td><td>velar
= 3.5</td></tr>
</table>

(26.c) MOA, POA distances (Dziubalska-Kołaczyk 2014: 10)

<table>
<tr><td colspan="3">OBSTRUENT</td><td colspan="5">SONORANT</td><td colspan="3" rowspan="3">V</td></tr>
<tr><td colspan="2">STOP</td><td>FRIC</td><td>NAS</td><td colspan="2">LIQ</td><td colspan="2">GLIDE</td></tr>
<tr><td colspan="3">AFFRICATE</td><td></td><td>lat</td><td>rhot</td><td colspan="2"></td></tr>
<tr><td>5.0</td><td>4.5</td><td>4.0</td><td>3.0</td><td>2.5</td><td>2.0</td><td>1.5</td><td>1.0</td><td colspan="3"></td></tr>
<tr><td colspan="2">p b</td><td></td><td>m</td><td colspan="2"></td><td>w</td><td>w̃</td><td>1.0</td><td>bilabial</td><td rowspan="2">LAB</td></tr>
<tr><td colspan="2"></td><td>f v</td><td></td><td colspan="2"></td><td colspan="2"></td><td>1.5</td><td>labio-
dental</td></tr>
<tr><td>t d</td><td>ʦ ʣ</td><td>s z</td><td>n</td><td>l</td><td></td><td colspan="2"></td><td>2.0</td><td>(post-)
dental</td><td rowspan="3">COR</td></tr>
<tr><td></td><td>tʂ dʐ</td><td>ʂ ʐ</td><td></td><td></td><td>r</td><td colspan="2"></td><td>2.3</td><td>alveolar</td></tr>
<tr><td></td><td>ʨ ʥ</td><td>ɕ ʑ</td><td>ɲ</td><td colspan="2"></td><td colspan="2"></td><td>2.6</td><td>alveolo-
palatal</td></tr>
<tr><td colspan="2"></td><td></td><td></td><td colspan="2"></td><td>j</td><td>j̃</td><td>3.0</td><td>palatal</td><td rowspan="2">DOR</td></tr>
<tr><td colspan="2">k g</td><td>x</td><td>ŋ</td><td colspan="2"></td><td>w</td><td>w̃</td><td>3.5</td><td>velar</td></tr>
<tr><td colspan="2"></td><td></td><td></td><td colspan="2"></td><td colspan="2"></td><td>4.0</td><td></td><td>RAD</td></tr>
<tr><td colspan="2"></td><td></td><td></td><td colspan="2"></td><td colspan="2"></td><td>5.0</td><td></td><td>GLOT</td></tr>
</table>

[2]Note that affricates are treated as a class intervening between plosives and fricatives, which results in the MOA distance of 0.5 for all affricate-plosive and affricate-fricative sequences such as /ʣb/ in *dzban* 'jug' or /ʣv/ in *dzwon* 'bell'.

The MOA categories correspond with the sonority hierarchies in 21. POA categories are taken from Ladefoged (2006). A distance equal to one holds between broad place categories: labial – coronal – dorsal – radical – glottal. Additionally, the S/O distinction is expressed by 0 or 1 depending on whether neighbouring segments are both sonorants or obstruents (= 0), or whether they belong to different classes (= 1). The computation of distances follows a formula for a preferred sequence: NAD = |MOA| + |POA| + |S/O|. Note that NAD posits separate conditions for clusters of different length (CC, CCC) as well as for clusters in different word positions (initial, medial, final). An exhaustive description of all the hypotheses is out of the scope of this chapter. Therefore, I illustrate the working of NAD on the example of initial two-member clusters.

The preferred arrangement of distances in an initial CC is the following:

$$\begin{aligned}&\mathrm{NAD(C1,C2)} \geq \mathrm{NAD(C2,V)},\ \text{where :}\\&\mathrm{NAD\,C1C2} = |(\mathrm{MOA1}-\mathrm{MOA2})| + |(\mathrm{POA1}-\mathrm{POA2})| + |\mathrm{S/O}|,\ \text{and}\\&\mathrm{NAD\,C2V} = |(\mathrm{MOA2}-\mathrm{MOAV})| + |\mathrm{S/O}|.\end{aligned}$$

For initial /tl/ cluster, the following distances are calculated:

$$\begin{aligned}&\mathrm{NAD(t,l)} \geq \mathrm{NAD\ (l,V)},\ \text{where :}\\&\mathrm{NAD/tl/} = |5-2.5| + |2.0-2.0| + |1| = 3.5,\ \text{and}\\&\mathrm{NAD/lV/} = |2.5-0| + |0| = 2.5.\end{aligned}$$

For the /t/ to /l/ transition, MOA distance equals 2.5 (= 5.0 − 2.5), while POA distance equals 0 (= 2.0 − 2.0). What is more, a distance-contribution of 1 is assigned to the S/O distinction. For the /l/ to /V/ transition, a distance of 2.5 is assigned for the MOA dimension, and a distance of 0 for the S/O distinction. The sum of C1C2 distances (= 3.5) is compared with the sum of C2V distances (= 2.5), Overall, /tl/ meets the well-formedness condition for initial CC in that 3.5 $\geq$ 2.0 (for a detailed discussion on hypotheses and calculations see Dziubalska-Kołaczyk (in press).

Apart from a binary division into preferred and dispreferred sequences, NAD makes it possible to rank clusters based on the so-called *NAD product,* which is a preferability index denoting a degree to which a given well-formedness condition is observed. Clusters which display a similar O + S structure can be further subcategorized depending on finer degrees of preferability. For instance, obstruent + glide clusters such as /pw vj ʧw/, and obstruent + liquid clusters such as /kr fl ɕr/ can be ordered with respect to each other. The ranking /pw/ > /vj/ > /kr/ > /ʧw/ > /ɕr/ > /fl/reflects a decrease in the NAD product; hence, an increase in dispreferability (for related measures of sonority distances see Clements 1990; Harris 1983; Parker 2012a; Selkirk 1984; Steriade 1982).

Similarly to the SSG, /sp/ and /sk/ are dispreferred by NAD. This classification is attributed to the fact that for a cluster to be perceived, the distance between C1C2 (/s/ – /t/, /s/ – /p/) should be greater or equal than the distance between C2V (/t/

– V, /p/ – V). MOA distances for both /sp/ and /sk/ equal |4 − 5| = 1, while POA distances amount to |2 − 1| = 1 for /sp/and |2 − 3.5| = 1.5 for /sk/. In CCC, the medial consonant pair is required to have the largest perceptual distance. Therefore, in Polish, all sCC clusters are preferred, following the well-formedness condition for three-member clusters: NAD(C1,C2) < NAD(C2,V) $\geq$ NAD(C3,V).

In the sections to follow, I demonstrate how the principle groups initial and final Polish clusters into preferred and dispreferred on the basis the well-formedness conditions presented above. The goal of the analysis is to compare the classification of clusters in terms of NAD and the SSG. This task is particularly important given that the two approaches differ substantially in they way they formulate well-formedness conditions.

2.4.2.1 The NAD Analysis of Initial (Mor)Phonotactics

The analysis is based on cluster inventories presented in Tables 1.14 and 1.15. Since NAD operates within the domain of a word, it offers a possibility of evaluating morphonotactic clusters. Note that only CCs and CCCs are taken into account. Calculations were performed with help of the *NAD Phonotactic Calculator* (Dziubalska-Kołaczyk et al. 2014), an online tool which automatically computes distances between pairs of segments, determines preferability and the NAD product. NAD is embedded in the framework of Natural Phonology, which emphases the importance of gradient output. Therefore, Table 2.8 juxtaposes the classification of word-initial clusters into preferred and dispreferred, rather than well-formed and ill-formed. Percentages are calculated for each size group as well as for the total of 321 phonotactic and 172 morphonotactic clusters. The classification of clusters in terms of NAD product is given in Appendices C and D.

Compared with the SSG, NAD proposes more demanding well-formedness criteria. As a result, the principle classifies the majority of clusters as dispreferred. This tendency is observed in all the subdivisions of the data, with the exception of

Table 2.8 Markedness-based classification of word-initial phonotactic (N = 321) and morphonotactic (N = 172) clusters by NAD

NAD	Phonotactic		Morphonotactic	
	No	%	No	%
Preferred CC	81	42	12	19
Dispreferred CC	112	58	50	81
Preferred CCC	57	45	68	62
Dispreferred CCC	71	55	42	38
Total preferred	138	43	80	47
Total dispreferred	183	57	92	53

morphonotactic CCCs, where preferred clusters prevail. The results of 2 × 2 Pearson's Chi-square tests confirm the results at the $p < 0.1$ level for the differences between CCs versus CCCs, and phonotactic versus morphonotactic clusters. That is, size and morphological composition have an impact on the classification of clusters in terms of NAD. No significant results were obtained for the total number of observations ($p > 0.5$).

2.4.2.2 The NAD Analysis of Final (Mor)Phonotactics

The same analysis was conducted for word-final clusters. The results are summarized in Table 2.9. NAD product values obtained for phonotactic and morphonotactic clusters are given in Appendices E and F, respectively.

The classification of final phonotactic clusters is comparable for CCs and CCCs. The proportion of preferred and dispreferred clusters equals 1:1 within each size group, and for all final phonotactic clusters. Differences can be observed in the group of morphologically-motivated clusters, where dispreferred clusters prevail. In general, morphonotactic CCs largely violate the proposed well-formedness conditions. The differences are statistically significant at $p < 0.1$ level, which suggests that the interaction between size and preferability is related to the morphological complexity of clusters. What is more, when compared to the SSG, more clusters are classified as marked when the NAD principle is applied. This observation suggests that NAD poses demanding preferability conditions for clusters, which are more difficult to meet.

That NAD is a more restrictive and challenging principle than sonority was also observed in Zydorowicz and Orzechowska (2016). The authors analysed, inter alia, 145 word-initial types (106 phonotactic, 21 morphonotactic, 18 mixed) in Polish in terms of the SSG and NAD, and showed that more clusters were classified as dispreferred when evaluated by NAD. The present analysis summarised in Tables 2.8 and 2.9 carried out for twice as large a dataset as in Zydorowicz and Orzechowska (2016) lends support to the original findings.

Table 2.9 Markedness-based classification of word-final phonotactic (N = 131) and morphonotactic (N = 97) clusters by NAD

NAD	Phonotactic		Morphonotactic	
	No	%	No	%
Preferred CC	51	50	31	39
Dispreferred CC	50	50	48	61
Preferred CCC	16	53	10	56
Dispreferred CCC	14	47	8	44
Total preferred	67	51	41	42
Total dispreferred	64	49	56	58

In general, the presentation of the approaches based on well-formedness conditions leads to two observations. First, the classification of clusters can vary depending on the degree of detail employed in the analysis. Well-formedness conditions, which rely on more criteria and complex relations between them tend to classify at least a half or a majority of clusters as ill-formed or dispreferred. Second, this being said, the question is why such sequences are permitted in the language at all? If ill-formed clusters exist, and are tolerated by Polish speakers, one can expect that there exists a force which counteracts their elimination from the lexicon. What properties or principles motivate cluster structure then? This issue is addressed by approaches which are not based on well-formedness conditions. Section 2.5 focuses on the description of the theory of Government Phonology, as one of the major representatives of this type of phonotactic modelling.

2.5 Approaches *Not* Based on Well-Formedness Conditions

2.5.1 *Government Phonology*

Government Phonology (henceforth GP, Charette 1990; Harris 1990, 1994; Kaye 1989, 1990, 1995; Kaye et al. 1985, 1990; Lowenstamm 1996; Scheer 2004, 2012) is a CV theory of phonology, which stems from the generative tradition (see Chomsky and Lasnik 1993). GP does not rely on previously derived statements on well-formedness but looks for their sources in subsegmental properties. Since the syllable and syllabification are central to the theory, GP accounts for the underlying structure of sequences of consonants.

In order to explain the complexity of different syllable types, Kaye and Lowenstamm (1981) propose to distinguish between three types of linguistic systems. The first type of languages (I) permits only the canonical CV structure. The second type of languages (II) permits branching onsets, next to the canonical syllable, i.e. CV and CCV. The third type of languages (III) additionally allows for branching rhymes, i.e. CV, CCV, and CVC. Kaye and Lowenstamm (1981)

Table 2.10 Indexed markedness scale for different syllable types

Onset	Rime	Markedness
C	V	0
Ø	Ø	1
CC	VC	2
CCC	VCC	3
$C_1 \ldots C_n$	$VC_1 \ldots C_{n-1}$	n

Kaye and Lowenstamm (1981: 292)

calculate markedness indices for onsets and rhymes separately, and allocate the total markedness index to a syllable type. Table 2.10 presents an overview of such possible syllables spanned on a scale where markedness increases from 0 to n. The least marked onset and rhyme are placed at the top of the illustration. '∅' refers to V syllables, which are considered to be slightly more marked than CV.

In GP, the scale can be represented in terms of two types of complexity: substantive and formal. The first one refers to the infra-segmental properties of vowels and consonants, while the latter is expressed by dependency relations between segments.

Substantive (subsegmental) complexity is one of primary organizing properties of phonological representation in a language, which in GP is captured by Element Theory (henceforth ET, Harris 1994; Harris and Lindsey 1995). ET defines segments in terms of subsegmental primes, or the so-called *elements*, which are the smallest units of phonological representation. Primes express melodic complexity of segments, and have a phonetic interpretability: they serve as targets for the speaker, and as perceptual reference points for the listener. Harris and Lindsey (1995: 50) define them as "(…) cognitive objects which perform the grammatical function of coding lexical contrasts". The acoustic dimension is held the most adequate for the interpretation of primes as it represents a communicative experience between the speaker and the listener. An overview of the phonetic correlates of some basic primes is provided by Harris (1996) (Table 2.11).

In the description of vocalic systems, the place primes (A), (I), (U) correspond to "low", "coronal / palatal", "round", and are phonetically interpreted as /a/, /i/, /u/, respectively. These primes are also used to code place contrasts in consonants. Additionally, consonants are defined in terms of five manner primes, out of which only two are truly consonantal (ʔ) and (h). (ʔ) is best achieved by a complete glottal closure in the oral tract, while (h) is produced with a placeless / glottal fricative noise. Other consonant-describing primes involve nasality (N), and phonation types (H) and (L). A summary of consonantal primes is given in 27.

Table 2.11 The acoustic and articulatory interpretations of primes in Element Theory

	Acoustic pattern	Articulatory pattern
[A]	Mass: central spectral energy mass (convergence of F1 and F2)	Maximal expansion of oral tube; maximal constriction of pharyngeal tube
[I]	Dip: low F1 coupled with high spectral peak (convergence of F2 and F3)	Maximal constriction of oral tube; maximal expansion of pharyngeal tube
[U]	Rump: low spectral peak (convergence of F1 and F2)	Trade-off between expansion of oral and pharyngeal tubes
[ʔ]	Edge: abrupt and sustained drop in overall amplitude	Occlusion in oral cavity
[h]	Noise: aperiodic energy	Narrowed stricture producing turbulent airflow

Harris (1996: 314)

27. Primes in Element Theory (Cyran 2003b: 23ff.)

(27.a) place:

(I) = palatal, e.g. [j, ç, ʃ]
palatalized, e.g. [p', k']
(U) = labial, e.g. [p, b, v, f, w]
labialized, e.g. [k^w, g^w]
(A) = coronal, e.g. [r, t, s]
retracted (uvular, pharyngeal), e.g. [R, q, G, ʕ]
(_) = velar, e.g. [k, g, x]
velarization, e.g. dark [ɫ] in English

(27.b) manner:

(ʔ) = occluded, e.g. [p, t, k]
(h) = 'noisy', e.g. [s, ʃ, x]
(N) = nasal, e.g. [m, n, ŋ]
(H) = voiceless aspirated [p^h, t^h]
(L) = fully voiced [b, d, g]

The primes can describe simple representations or combine in more complex ones. For instance, vowel /a/ is represented by means of element (A), while /e/ is represented by (A, I). Among consonants, Polish /r/ is represented by (A), while /b/ by (U, h, ʔ, L) (Cyran 2003b: 32).

Under this view, complexity is associated with the number of elements contained in a segment, among which vowels and plosives form extremes. The *Complexity Condition* (Harris 1994, 1996; Harris and Lindsey 1995) states that vowels are simple and contain fewer elements (i.e. only (A), (I), (U) and their combinations), while plosives contain the greatest number of elements.[3] The relative sonority of segments is established on the basis of the number of constituent primes in that it is inversely proportional to subsegmental complexity. For instance, in the original account by Harris (1994, 1996), and Harris and Lindsey (1995), fricatives are composed of fewer primes than released stops, and liquids are composed of fewer primes than nasals, which suggest the following complexity, or sonority-based relations: released stops > fricatives, and nasals > liquids (where '>' means 'more complex than' or 'less sonorous than'). Generally, the ordering of segments in terms of their complexity corresponds with the sonority hierarchies presented in 19 but differs from 19 in that it is inferred from the intrinsic representational complexity of segments.

[3]Over the years, the theory has been in the state of constant flux resulting in different interpretations of complexity. For instance, Scheer (2004) demonstrates that sonorants involve greater complexity than initially suggested, and Cyran (2003b) proposes to determine complexity on the basis of place elements.

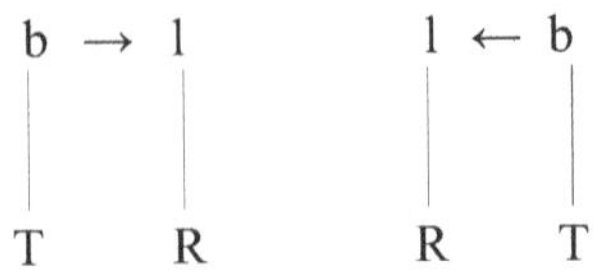

Fig. 2.1 Direction of government in GP (T = governor, R = governee)

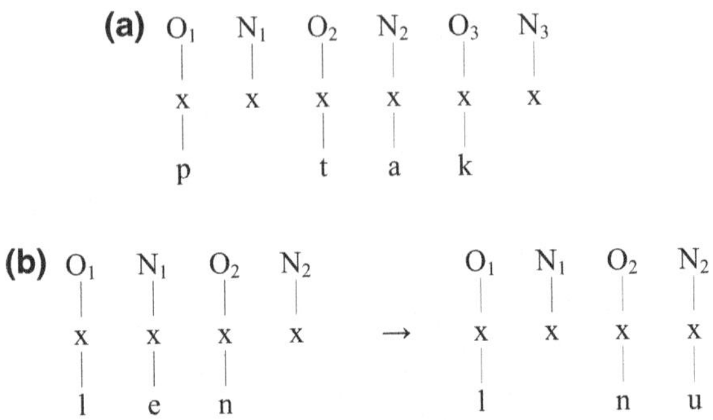

Fig. 2.2 Representation of empty nuclei in /pt/ and /ln/ (Cyran and Gussmann 1999: 220f.)

The way in which substantive complexity is incorporated into the structure of higher prosodic units, such as the syllable, is expressed in terms of *formal* complexity. This type of complexity refers to the interaction between the number of subsegmental primes, and governing (or dependency) relations between neighbouring segments. The sonority scale in GP is the basis for determining the governing relations between adjacent segmental slots. Such positions are asymmetrical with respect to each other: they act either as *governors* (T) or as *governees* (R). Both differ in their governing potential in that a governee is simpler (or less sonorous) than its governor in terms of the number of composite primes. In other words, GP predicts that a less sonorous segment always governs, or controls, a more sonorous one, disregarding their linear arrangement. This relation is captured in Fig. 2.1.

The directionality of government between plosives and liquids results in onsets such as /bl tl kr/ in *blok* 'block', *tlen* 'oxygen', *krok* 'step'. No such relation can be established for /pt ln/in *ptak* 'bird' and *lnu* 'flax' (gen sg), due to an insufficient sonority differential. As a result, clusters composed of segments with the same intrinsic complexity are viewed as singleton onsets separated by a nucleus which is empty, i.e. not realized phonetically. A representation of empty positions is provided in Fig. 2.2.

In *ptak,* initial obstruents /p/ and /t/ are split by a licensed empty nucleus (N_1). Additionally, there is a phonetically unrealized vowel word-finally (N_2). The presence of such empty slots is motivated historically. Complex clusters in Polish have arisen from the disappearance of *yers* (for descriptive and theoretical accounts see Bethin 2006; Osiewicz 2010; Rochoń 2000; Rubach 1984; Szpyra 1992a). The phenomenon of *yers* in Modern Polish is manifested in vowel—zero alternations, as in *len* (nom sg) → *lnu* (gen sg). What is more, empty nuclei are also found in sequences composed of three and four consonants. For instance, /tkn/ in *tknąć* 'to touch' (perf) consists of a simple onset /t/ separated by an empty nucleus from a licensed branching onset /kn/, while /drgn/ in *drgnąć* 'to vibrate' (perf) is a maximally branching sequence of two onsets.

A wide range of long consonant clusters in Polish offers an excellent study material for GP. This point is raised in Kijak (2008), who states that influential contributions on the topic have mainly dealt with long and sonority-violating sequences such as /tkn fstr drgn/. These clusters provide a testing ground for phonological theories (Bethin 1992; Cyran 2003a, b, 2006; Cyran and Gussmann 1999; Gussmann 1991, 1997, 2007; Gussmann and Cyran 1998; Gussmann and Kaye 1993; Lowenstamm 1996, 1999; Scheer 2004, 2012). Government Phonology has demonstrates that several principles which license empty nuclei can account for such unusual strings of consonants. These principles involve Proper Government (henceforth PG), Magic Licensing (henceforth 'magic') and Interonset Government (henceforth IO).

First, empty slots are licensed through *Proper Government* from a neighbouring nucleus which is phonetically realized. PG also accounts for alternations such as *len* 'flax' (nom sg) versus *lnu* 'flax' (gen sg), *lew* 'lion' (nom sg) versus *lwi* 'lion' (adj). The second type of licensing is referred to as *Magic Licensing*. The terms was introduced by Kaye (1992) to refer to the heterosyllabic status of sC clusters. Kaye (1992) argues that /s/ + stop represents a structure composed of a rhymal complement and an onset, rather than a branching onset. It is unclear why some languages permit sC initial clusters (e.g. Italian), while other languages require a prothetic vowel before the sequence (e.g. Spanish). Thus, the term "magical" indicates that the licensing mechanism of coda /s/ is unknown. Polish provides substantial evidence in favour of magically-licensed empty nuclei as the rhymal complement can be occupied not only by /s/ but also by voiced, palatal, and palatalised fricatives. It must be noted that the two licensing mechanisms allow for the emergence of sequences such as /pp nm jC/, which are attested neither in Polish nor generally in the languages of the world. Therefore, another licensing mechanism is required.

The *Interonset Government* (IO), originally proposed by Gussmann and Kaye (1993), has the capacity to account for sequences composed of consonants which cannot contract a governing relation, and which are ill-formed. Following Cyran and Gussmann (1999), I present examples of such clusters in 28.

28. Sequences containing two empty nuclei (after Cyran and Gussmann 1999: 228)

(28.a) /mkn/ in *mknąć* 'to speed'
(28.b) /pxw/ in *pchła* 'flea'
(28.c) /ʑʥbw/ in *źdźbło* 'grass stalk'

The authors suggest that the last two consonants contract an IO governing relation which licenses the intervening empty slot. That is, the vowel following a cluster has two functions. First, it makes the IO possible. Second, it properly governs the first empty slot. A vexing questions is which licensing mechanism

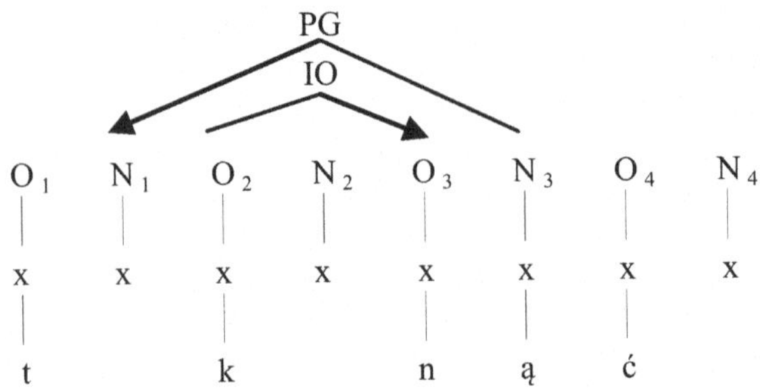

Fig. 2.3 Simultaneous licensing of IO and PG in /tkn/ (Cyran and Gussmann 1999: 229)

Table 2.12 A summary of cluster types and licensing mechanisms motivating them in Polish (Cyran and Gussmann 1999: 243), where O?=?onset, R?=?rhyme

	PG	IO	PG, IO	'magic'
CC	k Ø t o ?ł Ø b a	k Ø r a m Ø l e k o		R O Ø s t ó ł
CCC	O g r Ø g y k a		t Ø k Ø n ą ć	R O Ø s t r o n a
CCCC			O d r Ø g Ø n ą ć R O Ø ź dź Ø b Ø w o	O R O f Ø s t r ę t

should be selected. The problem can be illustrated on the example of /tkn/ in *tknąć* 'to touch' (perf) in Fig. 2.3.

As can be observed, N_2 is licensed by IO. However, it could be licensed only by Proper Government as the final full vowel could serve as a governor. Therefore, it is suggested that the Interonset Government should be applied whenever possible (i.e. prior to PG). This ranking reflects the importance of the licensing mechanisms, and the degree to which they are responsible for the emergence of consonant clusters. For expository reasons, Table 2.12 summarizes the relevant licensing mechanisms along with examples of clusters.

The proposed licensing mechanisms account for a wide range of sonority violating CCs, CCCs and CCCCs in Polish. Cyran and Gussmann (1999) claim to have *demystified* the complexity of Polish clusters, and showed that their apparently irregular and unusual character can be subsumed under several general principles. However, some reservations have been raised with regard to sonority-violating clusters composed of sonorants and obstruents.

Onsets starting with sonorants (conventionally referred to as #RT in GP), and codas ending with sonorants (TR#) have been studied extensively by Cyran (2006), Cyran and Gussmann (1999) and Scheer (2007, 2008). Their complexity cannot be fully captured by means of licensing. Polish features numerous sonorant-initial sequences, which are listed in Tables 1.14, 1.15 and 1.16. Recall some examples.

29. Sonorant-initial clusters in Polish

(29.a) /lʒ/ in *lżej* 'light' (compar)
(29.b) /mʃ/ in *msza* 'mass'
(29.c) /mʒ/ in *mrzonka* 'pipe dream'
(29.d) /wb/ in *łby* '(animal) head' (gen pl)

Scheer (2007) makes a point that the sequences form a natural class neither in Polish, nor in any Slavonic language. Disregarding which distinctive features or phonological criteria are selected for positing a natural class (e.g. nasality, coronality, sonority), the #RT sequences consequently resists their exhaustive assignment, and in such a way escape a formal description.

The views implemented in GP go in line with early remarks of Kuryłowicz (1952), who treats longer SSG-violating onsets in Polish as sequences of well-formed onsets. The only difference between Kuryłowicz's (1952) original proposal and GP is that the latter requires that onsets be separated by an empty nucleus. From this viewpoint, Polish follows the SSG at the level of sub-constituents.

A full exposition of further details of the theory and licensing mechanisms is not central to the present discussion. Generally, what we have seen is that GP employs a type of well-formedness principles, which are a manifestation of the intrinsic complexity of segments forming clusters. That is, government as well as the asymmetrical relation between a governor and a governee arise from segments' sonority, which, in turn, arises from the density of primes in a phonological expression. By providing an in-depth analysis of the infrasegmental properties of vowels and consonants, and the itersegmental relations between these properties, GP reveals the phonological structure of possible onset types. The observed effect of hundreds of long and sonority-violating clusters in Polish discussed in Chap. 1 is attributed to the underlying manipulation of such adjacent onsets. The capacity of Polish to host numerous empty nuclei is held responsible for consonant clusters in the language.

Let me remark that a number of similarities can be found between the theory and the method proposed in Chap. 3. GP employs a mechanism of headedness to represent the asymmetrical relation between composite primes in a phonological expression. The mechanism yields different segments depending on whether a prime occupies a head position (_) or an operator position, which is a formal way of capturing the fact that one prime dominates another. For instance, the combination of (A) and (I) elements can correspond either to /e/, when (I) is a head (A-I̲) or to /æ/ , when the reverse is true (A̲-I). This aspect of GP is related to the proposal of *weight of phonological features* put forward in this book. What makes the feature-based approach different from GP is that weight is expressed in graded terms, rather than a binary distinction between head versus non-head.

Apart from the asymmetrical relation between primes, GP also accounts for the asymmetrical relations between word and prosodic positions. For instance, Ségéral and Scheer (2001, 2005) present an analysis of weakening and strengthening, and emphasize the positional load of consonants. A strong position is word-initial and after a heterosyllabic segment (i.e. {#,C}__). Weak positions are word-final and before a heterosyllabic segment (i.e. __{#,C}) as well as intervocalic V__V. While the strong position favours fortition, the weak positions favour lenition. The positional load is incorporated into the proposal in Chap. 3. The asymmetrical relation between word positions is expressed in terms of *positional weight of features.*

2.5.2 *Examples of Other Approaches*

Apart from Element Theory, there are other methods of phonotactic modelling, which are not based on well-formedness conditions, and which rely on phonetic measurements. Two acoustic factors have been considered relevant in determining preferred and dispreferred strings of consonants (Ohala 1980; Kawasaki 1982, 1986): the magnitude of acoustic modulation and the degree of differences in modulations between adjacent segments. Ohala and Kawasaki-Fukumori (1997) propose an alternative to sonority and derive segmental sequential constraints from the modulations of amplitude, periodicity, spectral shape and F0. The authors demonstrate that preferred sequences display sufficient differences in the modulations of the acoustic parameters, which results in an increased trajectory that a sequence occupies in the acoustic space. In other words, preferred sequences have high magnitude of modulations, which makes them perceptually more salient. Additionally, preferred sequences are sufficiently different from each other, which makes them less confusable and counteracts their merger.

Another phonetically-based approach which accounts for static distribution patterns is the Onset Prominence framework proposed by Schwartz (2013, 2015, 2016). Segments and syllables emerge from a hierarchical tree structure, which encodes acoustic events associated with a C-V transition (i.e. stop-vowel). These events encompass closure, noise, the onset of a vowel and the vocalic target, all of which can be read off a waveform. The manner of articulation is represented in terms of nodes in a tree, while place and laryngeal specifications attach to the tree as active nodes. Although the SSG has no formal status in Onset Prominence, the approach successfully captures some generalizations related to sonority, for instance, sonority reversals, dispreference of /tl/ onsets and trapped sonorants in Polish.

These approaches share some similarities with the method proposed in the chapters to follow. In Ohala and Kawasaki-Fukumori (1997), sonority can be reconstructed from the size of modulations of acoustic parameters. In the Onset Prominence approach, sonority is derived from the acoustically-motivated manner-based specification. Similarly, in the present work, sonority is an epiphenomenon. Well-formedness conditions are inferred from feature-based patterns prevailing in the lexicon (Chap. 3), from minimum cognitive effort (Chap. 4) and from modifications of clusters in spontaneous speech (Chap. 5).

2.6 Conclusions

In this chapter, I have presented two major directions in the study of phonotactics, namely approaches which are based on well-formedness conditions, and approaches which are not based on well-formedness conditions. The bifurcation reflects the nature of phonotactic modelling. Consonant clusters can be analysed either from the perspective of previously derived principles, or in terms of subsegmental properties which can lead to the formulation of such new principles. The two traditions aim at answering different questions. Approaches based on well-formedness conditions offer a classification of clusters into those which obey or disobey the proposed set of markedness criteria. Approaches which do not employ statements on well-formedness aim at discovering the underlying motivation for the phonological structure of clusters, without positing requirements on what the structure should be like. The Sonority Sequencing Generalization and the Net Auditory Distance principle represent the first type of approaches, while Government Phonology is an example of the latter type.

As I have attempted to demonstrate, the models refer to different aspects of phonotactics (for analyses which bridge the gap between the formal and natural framework see Balas 2009; Haładewicz-Grzelak 2008; Michalski 2009). Disregarding the adopted approach, the analyses of the Polish data trigger the following questions:

(1) How would the classification of consonant clusters change if positional weight of features was employed in well-formedness conditions?
(2) Are there underlying language-specific or cross-linguistic properties, which can successfully account for core clusters and 'magical' clusters?
(3) Can phonotactic well-formedness in Polish be posited only for cluster sub-constrituents?

The focus of the analyses in the following chapters of the book is to explore the relevance of phonological features pertaining to the place, manner and voice dimension in constructing consonant clusters. If we had more insights into the role that subsegmental properties play in static distribution patterns in a phonotactically elaborate language such as Polish, maybe new constraints or preferences could be identified. With these views in mind, in Chap. 3. I propose to infer generalizations from the data at hand by providing an in-depth analysis of phonological features of consonants forming clusters.

References

Andersen, H. 2001. Markedness and the theory of linguistic change. In *Actualization: Linguistic change in progress*, ed. H. Andersen, 21–57. Amsterdam: John Benjamins.

Andersen, H. 2008. Naturalness and markedness. In *Naturalness and iconicity in language* [Iconicity in language and literature 7], eds. K. Willems, and L. De Cuypere, 101–119. Amsterdam, Philadelphia: John Benjamins.

Balas, A. 2009. Natural Phonology as a functional theory. *Poznań Studies in Contemporary Linguistics* 45 (1): 43–54.

Battistella, E.L. 1990. *Markedness: The evaluative superstructure of language*. Albany: SUNY Press.

Battistella, E.L. 1996. *The logic of markedness*. Oxford: Oxford University Press.

Bertinetto, P.M., Scheuer, S., Dziubalska-Kołaczyk, K., and M. Agonigi. 2007. Intersegmental cohension and syllable division in Polish. In *Proceedings of the 16th international congress of phonetic sciences, Saarbrücken,* 6–10 August 2007, eds. J. Trouvain, and W.J. Barry, 1953–1956. Saarbruecken: University of Saarbruecken.

Bethin, C.Y. 1992. *Polish syllables: The role of prosody in phonology and morphology*. Colombus, OH: Slavica Publishers.

Bethin, C.Y. 2006. *Slavic prosody: Language change and phonological theory* [Cambridge studies in linguistic, vol. 86]. Cambridge: Cambridge University Press.

Basbøl, H. 2005. *The phonology of Danish*. Oxford: Oxford University Press.

Bigi, B., and K. Klessa. 2015. Automatic syllabification of Polish. In 7th language and technology conference: Human language technologies as a challenge for computer science and linguistics. Poznań, Poland, eds. J. Mariani, and Z. Vetulani, 262–266. Poznań: Fundacja Uniwersytetu im. Adama Mickiewicza.

Calabrese, A. 1995. A constraint-based theory of phonological markedness and simplification procedures. *Linguistic Inquiry* 26 (3): 373–463.

Calabrese, A. 2005. *Markedness and economy in a derivational model of phonology* [Studies in generative grammar 80]. Berlin: Mouton de Gruyter.

Cardoso, W. 2008. The development of sC onset clusters in interlanguage: Markedness versus frequency effects. In *Proceedings of the 9th generative approaches to second language acquisition conference, Iowa, 18–20 May 2007*, eds. R. Slabakova, J. Rothman, P. Kempchinsky, and E. Gavrusev, 15–29. Somerville, MA: Cascadilla Proceedings Project.

Cetnarowska, B., and M. Żygis. 2004. Syllabification across a prefix-stem boundary in Polish: The role of semantic compositionality. *Zeitschrift für Slawistik* 49: 42–60.

Cetnarowska, B., and M. Żygis. 2007. Phonetic syllabification and morphological parsability: The case of prefixed words in Polish. In *Challenging tasks for psycholinguistics in the new century*, ed. J. Arabski, 149–163. Katowice: Uniwersytet Śląski.

Charette, M. 1990. Licence to govern. *Phonology* 7: 233–253.

Chomsky, N. 1986. *Knowledge of language: Its nature, origin and use*. New York: Praeger.

Chomsky, N., and M. Halle. 1968. *The Sound Pattern of English*. New York: Harper and Row.

Chomsky, N., and H. Lasnik. 1993. Principles and parameters theory. In *Syntax: An international handbook of contemporary research*, eds. J. Jacobs, A. von Stechow, W. Sternefeld, and T. Vennemann. Berlin: Walter de Gruyter.

Clements, G.N. 1990. The role of the sonority cycle in core syllabification. In *Papers in laboratory phonology 1: Between the grammar and physics of speech*, eds. J. Kingston, and M.E. Beckman, 283–333. Cambridge: Cambridge University Press.

Cser, 2000. Phonological models of sonority. *The Even Yearbook* 4: 1–18.

Cyran, E. 2003a. Licensing strength and syllable structure in Government Phonology. *Poznań Studies in Contemporary Linguistics* 38: 41–73.

Cyran, E. 2003b. *Complexity scales and licensing strength in phonology*. Lublin: Wydawnictwo Katolickiego Uniwersytetu Lubelskiego.

Cyran, E. 2006. Polish and English syllable structures. How different are they? *Zeszyty Wszechnicy Świętokrzyskiej Filologia Angielska* 1 (23): 151–160.

Cyran, E., and E. Gussmann. 1999. Consonantal clusters and governing relations: Polish initial consonant sequences. In *The syllable: Views and facts*, ed. H. van der Hulst and A.N. Ritter, 219–249. Berlin: Mouton de Gruyter.

De Lacy, P. 2002. *The formal expression of markedness*. PhD diss., Amherst: University of Massachusetts.

De Lacy, P. 2006. *Markedness: Reduction and preservation in phonology* [Cambridge studies in linguistics 112]. Cambridge: Cambridge University Press.

Dell, F., and M. Elmedlaoui. 1985. Syllabic consonants and syllabification in Imdlawn Tashlhiyt Berber. *Journal of African Languages and Linguistics* 7: 105–130.

Dobrogowska, K. 1992. Word initial and word final consonant clusters in Polish popular science texts and in artistic prose. *Studia Phonetica Posnaniensia* 3: 47–121.

Donegan, P.J. 1985. *On the Natural Phonology of vowels*. New York: Garland Publishing.

Donegan, P.J. 2002. Phonological processes and phonetic rules. In *Future challenges for natural linguistics*, ed. K. Dziubalska-Kołaczyk and J. Weckwerth, 57–82. Muenchen: Lincom Europa.

Donegan, P.J., and D. Stampe. 1979. The study of Natural Phonology. In *Current approaches to phonological theory*, ed. D.A. Dinnsen, 126–173. Bloomington, London: Indiana University Press.

Donegan, P.J., and D. Stampe. 2009. Hypotheses of Natural Phonology. *Poznań Studies in Contemporary Linguistics* 45 (1): 1–31.

Dressler, W.U. 1985. *Morphonology: The dynamics of derivation*. Ann Arbor: Karoma Publishers.

Dressler, W.U., W. Mayerthaler, O. Panagl, and W.U. Wurzel. 1987. *Leitmotifs in Natural Morphology*. Amsterdam: John Benjamins.

Dziubalska-Kołaczyk, K. 1995. *Phonology without the syllable: A study in the natural framework*. Poznań: Motivex.

Dziubalska-Kołaczyk, K. 1996. Natural Phonology without the syllable. In *Natural Phonology: The state of the art*, eds. B. Hurch, and R.A. Rhodes, 53–72. Berlin: Mouton de Gruyter.

Dziubalska-Kołaczyk, K. 2002. *Beats-and-Binding Phonology*. Frankfurt am Main: Peter Lang.

Dziubalska-Kołaczyk, K. 2009. NP extensions: B&B phonotactics. *Poznań Studies in Contemporary Linguistics* 45 (1): 55–71.

Dziubalska-Kołaczyk, K. 2014. Explaining phonotactics using NAD. *Language Sciences* 46 (A): 6–17.

Dziubalska-Kołaczyk, K., D. Pietrala, and G. Aperliński. 2014. The NAD phonotactic calculator—An online tool to calculate cluster preference in English, Polish and other languages. Online access: http://wa.amu.edu.pl/wa/files/The_NAD_Phonotactic_Calculator.pdf .

Eckman, F.R., E.A. Moravcsik, and J. Wirth (eds.). 1986. *Markedness*. New York: Plenum Press.

Foley, J. 1972. Rule precursors and phonological change by meta-rule. In *Linguistic change and generative theory*, eds. R. Stockwell, and R. Macauley, 96–100. Bloomington: Indiana University Press.

Fudge, E.C. 1969. Syllables. *Journal of Linguistics* 5: 253–287.

Goad, H. 2011. The representation of sC clusters. In *The Blackwell companion to phonology*, eds. M. van Oostendorp, C.J. Ewen, E. Hume, and K. Rice, 898–923. Malden, MA, Oxford: Wiley Blackwell.

Goad, H. 2012. sC Clusters are (almost always) coda-initial. *The Linguistic Review* 29 (3): 335–373.

Goldsmith, J.A. 1990. *Autosegmental and metrical phonology*. Oxford: Blackwell.
Greenberg, J.H. 1978. Some generalizations concerning initial and final consonant clusters. In *Universals of human language*, eds. J.H. Greenberg, C.A. Ferguson, and E.A. Moravcsik, 243–279. Stanford. CA: Stanford University Press.
Guitart, J.M. 1976. *Markedness and a cuban dialect of Spanish*. Washington, DC: Georgetown University Press.
Gurevich, N. 2001. A critique of markedness-based theories in phonology. *Studies in the Linguistic Sciences* 31 (2): 89–114.
Gussmann, E. 1991. Polish syllable structure: A hypothesis and its problems. In *Words are physicians for an ailing mind*, eds. M. Grochowski, and D. Weiss, 207–213. München: Sagner.
Gussmann, E. 1992. Resyllabification and delinking: The case of Polish voicing. *Linguistic Inquiry* 23 (1): 29–56.
Gussmann, E. 1997. Govern or perish. In *Language history and language modelling. Festschrift for Jacek Fisiak on his 60th birthday*, eds. S. Puppel, and R. Hickey, 1291–1300. Berlin, New York: Mouton de Gruyter.
Gussmann, E. 2007. *The phonology of Polish*. Oxford: Oxford University Press.
Gussmann, E., and E. Cyran. 1998. Polish consonantal sequences: A phonological testing ground. In *Structure and interpretation: Studies in phonology*, ed. E. Cyran, 127–138. Lublin: Folium.
Gussmann, E., and J. Kaye. 1993. Polish notes from a Dubrovnik Café I: The Yers. *SOAS Working Papers in Linguistics and Phonetics* 3: 427–462.
Hall, T.A. 1992. *Syllable structure and syllable-related processes in German*. Tübingen: Max Niemeyer Verlag.
Halle, M., and J.-R. Vergnaud. 1980. Three-dimensional phonology. *Journal of Linguistic Research* 1: 83–105.
Haładewicz-Grzelak, M. 2008. Direct effect in Beats-and-Binding Phonology. *Poznań Studies in Contemporary Linguistics* 44 (4): 503–544.
Harris, J.W. 1983. *Syllable structure and stress in Spanish: A nonlinear analysis*. Cambridge, MA: The MIT Press.
Harris, J. 1990. Phonological government. *Phonology* 7 (2): 255–300.
Harris, J. 1994. *English sound structure*. London: Blackwell Publishing.
Harris, J. 1996. Phonological output is redundancy-free and fully interpretable. In *Current trends in phonology: Models and methods*, eds. J. Durand, and B. Laks, 305–332. Salford, Manchester: European Studies Research Institute, University of Salford.
Harris, J., and G. Lindsey. 1995. The elements of phonological representation. In *Frontiers of phonology: Atoms, structures, derivations*, eds. J. Durand, and F. Katamba, 34–79. London, New York: Longman.
Haspelmath, M. 2006. Against markedness (and what to replace it with). *Journal of Linguistics* 42 (1): 25–70.
Hayes, B., and D. Steriade. 2004. Introduction: The phonetic bases of phonological markedness. In *Phonetically-based phonology*, eds. B. Hayes, R. Kirchner, and D. Steriade, 1–33. Cambridge: Cambridge University Press.
Herbert, R.K. 1986. *Language universals, markedness theory, and natural phonetic processes* [Trends in linguistics, studies and monographs 25]. Berlin, Boston: Mouton de Gruyter.
Hogg, R.M., and C.B. McCully. 1987. *Metrical phonology: A coursebook*. Cambridge, New York, Oakleigh: Cambridge University Press.
Hooper, J. 1976. *An introduction to natural generative phonology*. New York: Academic Press.
Hume, E. 2004. Deconstructing markedness: A predictability-based approach. In *Proceedings of the Berkeley Linguistics Society*, eds. M. Ettlinger, N. Fleisher, and M. Park-Doob, 182–198. Berkeley Linguistics Society: University of California.
Jakobson, R. 1941. *Kindersprache, aphasie, und allgemeine lautgesetze*. Uppsala: Almqvist och Wiksel.
Jany, C., M. Gordon, C.M. Nash, and N. Takara. 2007. How universal is the sonority hierarchy? A cross-linguistic acoustic study. In *Proceedings of the 16th international congress of phonetic*

sciences, Saarbrucken, 6–10 August 2007, eds. J. Trouvain, and W. J. Barry, 1401–1404. Saarbruecken: University of Saarbruecken.
Jespersen, O. 1904. *Lehrbuch der phonetik*, 2nd ed. Leipzig, Berlin: Teubner.
Kager, R. 1999. *Optimality Theory*. Cambridge: Cambridge University Press.
Katamba, F. 2009. How hierarchical and universal is consonant strength? *Theoretical Linguistics* 6 (1–3): 23–40.
Kawasaki, H. 1982. *An acoustical basis for universal constraints on sound sequences*. PhD diss., Berkeley: University of California.
Kawasaki, H. 1986. Phonetic explanations for phonological universals: The case of distinctive vowel nasalization. In *Experimental phonology*, eds. J.J. Ohala, and J.J. Jaeger, 81–103. Orlando, FL: Academic Press.
Kaye, J. 1979. On the alleged correlation of markedness and rule Function. In *Current approaches to phonological theory*, ed. D.A. Dinnsen, 272–280. Bloomington, London: Indiana University Press.
Kaye, J. 1989. *Phonology: A cognitive view*. Hillside, NJ: Lawrence Erlbaum Associates.
Kaye, J. 1990. Coda licensing. *Phonology* 7: 301–330.
Kaye, J. 1992. Do you believe in magic? The story of s+C sequences. *SOAS Working Papers in Linguistics and Phonetics* 2: 293–313.
Kaye, J. 1995. Derivations and interfaces. In *Frontiers of phonology: Atoms, structures, derivations*, eds. J. Durand, and F. Katamba, 289–332. London, New York: Longman.
Kaye, J., and J. Lowenstamm. 1981. Syllable structure and markedness theory. In *Theory of markedness in generative grammar. Proceedings of the 1979 GLOW conference*, eds. A. Belletti, and L. Rizzi, 287–315. Pisa: Scuola Normale Superiore di Pisa.
Kaye, J., J. Lowenstamm, and J.-R. Vergnaud. 1985. The internal structure of phonological elements: A theory of charm and government. *Phonology Yearbook* 2: 305–328.
Kaye, J., J. Lowenstamm, and J.-R. Vergnaud. 1990. Constituent structure and government in phonology. *Phonology* 7 (2): 193–231.
Kean, M.L. 1975. *The theory of markedness in generative grammar*. Ph.D diss., Massachusetts Institute of Technology.
Kenstowicz, M. 1994. *Phonology in generative grammar*. Cambridge, MA, Oxford: Blackwell Publishing.
Kijak, A. 2008. *Polish and English consonantal clusters: A contrastive analysis within the strict CV framework*. Katowice: Wydawnictwo Uniwersytetu Śląskiego.
Kilani-Schoch, M. 1988. Discontinuity or continuity of the morphological basis in Classical Arabic and in Tunisian Arabic? *Zeitschrift für Arabische Linguistik* 19: 81–92.
Klessa, K., and D. Śledziński. 2006. A study of chosen temporal relations within syllable structure in Polish. *Speech and Language Technology* 9 (10): 87–92.
Kuryłowicz, J. 1952. Uwagi o polskich grupach spółgłoskowych. *Biuletyn Polskiego Towarzystwa Językoznawczego* 11: 54–69.
Ladefoged, P. 2006. *A course in phonetics*. Boston: Heinle & Heinle.
Lombardi, L. 2002. *Markedness and the typology of epenthetic vowels*. College Park: University of Maryland.
Lowenstamm, J. 1996. CV as the only syllable type. In *Current trends in phonology: Models and methods*, eds. J. Durand, and B. Laks, 419–442. Salford: European Studies Research Institute, University of Salford Publications.
Lowenstamm, J. 1999. The beginning of the word. In *Phonologica 1996: Syllables!?*, eds. J. Rennison, and K. Kühnhammer, 153–166. The Hague: Thesus.
Ludwig, R. 2001. Markiertheit. In *Language typology and language universals: An international handbook* [Handbdcher zur Sprach—und Kommunikationswissenschaft 1], eds. M. Haspelmath, E. König, W. Oesterreicher, and W. Raible, 400–419. Berlin: Mouton de Gruyter.
Malisz, Z., and P. Wagner. 2012. Acoustic-phonetic realisation of Polish syllable prominence: A corpus study of spontaneous speech. In *Speech and language technology, Vol. 14/15. Rhythm,*

melody and harmony in speech. Studies in honour of Wiktor Jassem, eds. D. Gibbon, D. Hirst, and N. Campbell, 105–114. Poznań: Polish Phonetic Association.

Michalski, G. 2009. *Phonology with interfaces. The morphophonology and postlexical phonology of English and Polish*. PhD diss., Poznań: Adam Mickiewicz University.

Moravcsik, E.A., and J. Wirth. 1986. Markedness—An overview. In *Markedness*, eds. F.R. Eckman, E.A. Moravcsik, and J. Wirth, 1–12. New York: Plenum Press.

Murray, R.W., and T. Vennemann. 1983. Sound change and syllable structure in Germanic phonology. *Language* 59 (3): 514–528.

Ohala, J.J. 1980. The application of phonological universals in speech pathology. In *Speech and language: Advance in basic research and practice*, vol. 3, ed. N. Lass, 75–97. New York: Academic Press.

Ohala, J.J., and H. Kawasaki-Fukumori. 1997. Alternatives to the sonority hierarchy for explaining segmental sequential constraints. In *Language and its ecology: Essays in memory of Einar Haugen* [Trends in linguistics. Studies and monographs 100], eds. S. Eliasson, and E.H. Jahr, 343–365. Berlin: Mouton de Gruyter.

Orzechowska, P., and R. Wiese. 2015. Preferences and variation in word-initial phonotactics: a multi-dimensional evaluation of German and Polish. *Folia Linguistica* 49: 439–486.

Orzechowska, P., and P. Zydorowicz. 2019. Frequency effects and markedness in phonotactics. *Poznań Studies in Contemporary Linguistics* 55(1): 157–179.

Osiewicz, M. 2010. Kierunki przemian polszczyzny w zakresie fonetyki (propozycja rozdziału podręcznika do nauczania treści historycznojęzykowych na studiach I stopnia). *Kwartalnik Językoznawczy* 2010 (2): 58–86.

Parker, S. 2002. *Quantifying the sonority hierarchy*. PhD diss., Amherst: University of Massachusetts.

Parker, S. 2008. Sound level protrusions as physical correlates of sonority. *Journal of Phonetics* 36: 55–90.

Parker, S. 2012a. Sonority distance versus sonority dispersion—A typological survey. In *The sonority controversy*, ed. S. Parker, 101–166. Berlin: Walter de Gruyter.

Parker, S. (ed.). 2012b. *The sonority controversy*. Berlin: Walter de Gruyter.

Pawelec, P. 2012. The Sonority Sequencing Generalization and the structure of consonant clusters with trapped sonorants in Polish. *Anglica Wratislaviensia*. 50: 183–195.

Prince, A., and P. Smolensky. 1993. *Optimality Theory: Constraint interaction in generative grammar*. Cambridge, MA: The MIT Press.

Rice, K. 2007. Markedness in phonology. In *The Cambrdige handbook of phonology*, ed. P. de Lacy, 89–97. Cambridge: Cambridge University Press.

Rochoń, M. 2000. *Optimality in complexity: The case of polish consonant clusters* [Studia grammatica 48]. Berlin: Akademie Verlag.

Roussou, A. 2017. Markedness, naturalness and complexity. In *The Cambridge handbook of historical syntax* [Cambridge handbooks in language and linguistics], eds. A. Ledgeway, and I. Roberts, 360–380. Cambridge: Cambridge University Press.

Rubach, J. 1984. *Cyclic and lexical phonology*. Dordrecht: Foris Publications.

Rubach, J. 1996. Nonsyllabic analysis of voice assimilation in Polish. *Linguistic Inquiry* 27 (1): 69–110.

Rubach, J., and G. Booij. 1990a. Syllable structure assignment in Polish. *Phonology* 7: 121–158.

Rubach, J., and G. Booij. 1990b. Edge of constituent effects in Polish. *Natural Language and Linguistic Theory* 8 (3): 427–463.

Scheer, T. 2004. *A lateral theory of phonology 1: What is CVCV, and why should it be?* Berlin: Mouton de Gruyter.

Scheer, T. 2007. On the status of word-initial clusters in Slavic (and elsewhere). In *Annual workshop on formal approaches to Slavic linguistics: The Toronto Meeting 2006*, eds. R. Compton, M. Goledzinowska, and U. Savchenko, 346–364. Ann Arbor: Michigan Slavic Publications.

Scheer, T. 2008. Syllabic and trapped consonants in (Western) Slavic: Different but still the same. In *Formal description of Slavic languages*, eds. G. Zybatow, L. Szucsich, U. Junghanns, and R. Meyer, 149–167. Frankfurt am Main: Peter Lang.

Scheer, T. 2012. *Direct interface and one-channel translation. A non-diacritic theory of the morphosyntax-phonology interface. Vol. 2 of A Lateral Theory of Phonology*. Berlin: Mouton de Gruyter.

Schwartz, G. 2013. A representational parameter for onsetless syllables. *Journal of Linguistics* 49 (3): 613–646.

Schwartz, G. 2015. Who needs a nucleus? Tashlhiyt Berber syllabification in the onset prominence representational environment. *Poznań Studies in Contemporary Linguistics* 51 (2): 247–290.

Schwartz, G. 2016. On the evolution of prosodic boundaries—parameter settings for Polish and English. *Lingua* 171: 37–73.

Ségéral, P., and T. Scheer. 2001. La coda-miroir. *Bulletin de la Société de Linguistique de Paris* 96: 107–152.

Ségéral, P., and T. Scheer. 2005. What lenition and fortition tells us about Gallo-Romance *Muta cum Liquida*. In *Romance languages and linguistic theory* [Current issues in linguistic theory 270], eds. T. Geerts, I. van Ginneken, and H. Jacobs, 235–267. Amsterdam: John Benjamins.

Selkirk, E.O. 1984. On the major class features and syllable theory. In *Language sound structure*, eds. M. Aronoff, and R.T. Oehrle, 107–136. Cambridge, MA: The MIT Press.

Sievers, E. 1881. *Grundzüge der Phonetik*. Leipzig: Breitkopf und Hartel.

Stampe, D. 1979. *A dissertation on Natural Phonology*. Bloomington: IULC.

Steriade, D. 1982. *Greek prosodies and the nature of syllabification*. PhD diss., Cambridge, MA: The MIT Press.

Steriade, D. 1995. Underspecification and markedness. In *The handbook of phonological theory*, eds. J.A. Goldsmith, J. Riggle, and A.C.L. Yu, 114–174. Oxford, Cambridge: Blackwell.

Steriade, D. 1999. Alternatives to the syllabic interpretation of consonantal phonotactics. In *Item order in language and speech*, ed. O. Fujimura, B.D. Joseph, and B. Palek, 205–242. Columbus: The Karolinum Press.

Szpyra, J. 1992. Ghost segments in nonlinear phonology: Polish yers. *Language* 68 (2): 277–312.

Szpyra, J. 1995. *Three tiers in Polish and English phonology*. Lublin: Wydawnictwo Uniwersytetu Marii Curie-Skłodowskiej.

Szpyra-Kozłowska, J. 1998. The sonority scale and phonetic syllabification in Polish. *Biuletyn Polskiego Towarzystwa Językoznawczego* 54: 63–82.

Szpyra-Kozłowska, J. 2000. On some misconceptions concerning phonetic syllabifications in Polish. *Folia Linguistica Anglica* 2: 159–173.

Śledziński, D. 2010. Analiza struktury grup spółgłoskowych w nagłosie oraz w wygłosie wyrazów w języku polskim. *Kwartalnik Językoznawczy* 3–4: 61–84.

Śledziński, D. 2013. Podział korpusu tekstów na sylaby—analiza polskich grup spółgłoskowych. *Kwartalnik Językoznawczy* 3 (15): 48–100.

Śledziński, D. 2016. Tworzenie reguł dla programu dzielącego tekst w języku polskim na sylaby. *Biuletyn Polskiego Towarzystwa Językoznawczego* 72: 151–161.

Śledziński, D. 2017. Badanie odczucia subiektywnego związanego z dzieleniem na sylaby wyrazów języka polskiego—podział grup złożonych ze spółgłosek sonornych. *Acta Universitatis Lodziensis. Folia Linguistica* 51 (1): 109–127.

Śledziński, D., M. Szczerbiński, and J. Piotrowska. 2013. Przygotowanie i podział na sylaby korpusu tekstów dla dzieci. In *Scripta manent â res novae*, eds. S. Puppel and T. Tomaszkiewicz, 439–450. Poznań: Wydawnictwo Naukowe UAM.

Tomić, O.M. (ed.). 1989. *Markedness in synchrony and diachrony*. Berlin: Mouton de Gruyter.

Trask, R.L. 1996. *Dictionary of phonetic and phonology*. London, New York: Routledge.

Trubetzkoy, N.S. 1969. *Principles of phonology*. Berkeley: University of California Press. [Reprint of: *Grundzüge der Phonologie*, 1939. Travaux du Cercle Linguistique de Prague 7].

Vaux, B., and A. Wolfe. 2009. The appendix. In *Contemporary views on architecture and representations in phonology* [Current studies in linguistics], eds. E. Raimy, and C.E. Cairns, 101–143. Cambridge, MA: The MIT Press.

Vennemann, T. 1988. *Preference laws for syllable structure and the explanation of sound change*. Berlin, New York, Amsterdam: Mouton de Gruyter.

Whitney, W.D. 1865. On the relation of vowels and consonants. *Journal of the American Oriental Society* 8: 357–373. [Reprinted in Whitney, W.D. 1874. *Oriental and linguistic studies*. New York: Charles Scribner's Sons, 198–214.].

Wiese, R. 1988. *Silbische und lexikalische Phonologie. Studien zum Chinesischen und Deutschen*. Tubingen: Max Niemeyer Verlag.

Wurzel, W.U. 1984. *Flexionsmorphologie und natürlichkeit*. Berlin: Akademie Verlag.

Wurzel, W.U. 1998. On markedness. *Theoretical Linguistics* 24 (1): 53–71.

Yavaş, M. 2006. Sonority and the acquisition of #sC clusters. *Journal of Multilingual Communication Disorders* 4 (3): 159–168.

Yavaş, M. 2013. What explains the reductions in /s/-clusters: Sonority or [continuant]? *Clinical Linguistics and Phonetics* 27: 394–403.

Yavaş, M., A. Ben-David, E. Gerrits, K.E. Kristoffersen, and H.G. Simonsen. 2008. Sonority and cross-linguistic acquisition of initial s-clusters. *Clinical Linguistics and Phonetics* 22 (6): 421–441.

Zec, D. 1995. Sonority constraints on syllable structure. *Phonology* 12: 85–129.

Zydorowicz, P., and P. Orzechowska. 2016. The study of Polish phonotactics: Measures of phonotactic preferability. *Studies in Polish Linguistics* 11 (3): 97–136.

Chapter 3
Statistical Modelling of Phonotactic Constraints and Preferences

The important thing in science is not so much to obtain new facts as to discover new ways of thinking about them.
(Sir William Henry Bragg Nobel Prize in Physics, 1915)

3.1 Introduction

This chapter presents an analysis of Polish initial and final (mor)phonotactics in terms of an approach which is *not based on well-formedness conditions*. The proposed method consists in a meticulous analysis of subsegmental properties of consonants forming clusters, and leads to the formulation of heretofore unidentified constraints and preferences. The exploratory method advocated in this chapter is rooted in a feature-based description of large sets of clusters, in which markedness conditions are extrapolated from the intrinsic properties of adjacent consonants. Out of 26 properties related to the place of articulation, manner of articulation, voicing and structural complexity, statistical methods makes it possible to infer the relative importance of features in the construction of cluster inventories in different word positions. The analysis demonstrates that Polish phonotactics is a well-motivated phenomenon. Phonotactic generalizations that define the phonological structure of the lexicon are encoded in *positional weight of phonological features*. Overall, preferred initial and final clusters rely on featural specification pertaining to stridency, voicing and coronality. Additionally, lack of dorsals is preferred word-finally.

3.2 Theoretical Tenets of the Model

The analysis proposed in this chapter offers an alternative to the phonotactic models presented in Chap. 2. This approach is not based on well-formedness conditions. It focuses on a rigorous study of consonant clusters in terms of subsegmental

P. Orzechowska, *Complexity in Polish Phonotactics*, Prosody, Phonology and Phonetics, https://doi.org/10.1007/978-981-13-7299-5_3

characteristics. An unexpected corollary of the analysis is that heretofore unidentified phonotactic constraints and preferences emerge. Such generalizations are expressed in terms of phonological features which are ordered with respect to each other depending on their positional importance. The theoretical underpinnings of the method are presented below. First, I discuss the nature of phonotactic constraints and preferences which are employed in the model, and the unit they are refer to. Next, I argue how they can be extrapolated from the study of phonological features.

3.2.1 *Word as a Domain of Phonotactic Generalizations*

The selection of a domain for the study of phonotactics has several consequences for phonological theory. First, a syllable-based approach assumes the extrasyllabic status of initial and final consonants in sonority-violating clusters. For instance, fricatives in fricative + obstruent, sonorants in sonorant + obstruent clusters or glides in glide-final clusters are not adjoined to the syllable nodes but to higher prosodic units such as the phonological word (PW). Therefore, /sp lɕɲ sw/ in *spać* 'to sleep', *lśnić* 'to shine' and *niósł* 'to carry' (3rd sg past masc) are represented in the following way: *spać* → PW = s, σ = patɕ; *lśnić* → PW = l, σ = ɕɲitɕ; *niósł* → σ = ɲjus, PW = w. Second, clusters generated by morphological operations, e.g. /sp fkl vzbr/ in *s + padać* 'to decline', *w + kleić* 'to stick into', *wz + bronić* 'to prohibit' are not a part of the syllable. As a consequence, the inventory of all clusters which can be analysed in terms of the SSG is reduced to a sequence of an obstruent followed by a sonorant in onsets, or the reverse pattern in codas. However, as discussed in Chap. 1 in Sect. 1.4.5, there is a body of research (cf. Rubach 1996; Steriade 1999) which considers the domain of a word to be equally informative in the study of phonotactics in terms of the SSG (for other word-based approaches see Aronoff 1976; Halle 1973).

Recognizing that a word is a legitimate unit for formulating phonotactic generalizations provides an alternative to the view rooted in contemporary syllable-based phonological theory. In the analysis proposed in this chapter, phonotactic constraints and preferences emerge from prevalent feature-based patterns which hold in sequences of consonants found word-initially and word-finally. Thus, the analysis makes room for including larger cluster sets, which encompass sequences containing extra-syllabic consonants. What is more, word-based phonotactics clears the way for embracing morphologically-motivated clusters, which are found in abundance in Polish. The possibility of looking into such sequences is particularly important in Polish, whose morphologically-motivated clusters display varying degrees of markedness. Apart from clusters containing easily decomposable morphemes (i.e. overt affixes), a large variety of strings of consonants is generated by non-concatenative morphology. Given these facts, a model operating on the unit of a word has the capacity to generalize on hundreds of clusters varying in length and displaying unusual phonological characteristics, some of which are due to morphology.

3.2.2 *Discovering Constraints and Preferences*

In every-day usage, *constraint* and *preference* can be co-referential. In some phonological contributions, the terms have been used interchangeably (for an overview see Ritt 2001), although they have been primarily associated with Optimality Theory and Natural Phonology. Ritt (2001: 308) provides a comprehensive exposition of OT constraints and NP preferences, showing that the relationship between them is "anything but straightforward and that they certainly do not simply translate into each other".

A discussion on constraints and preferences in linguistic theories is offered in Dziubalska-Kołaczyk (2001b). The argument adduced in favour of preferences is that they imply the human agent, whose behaviour reflects the preferred linguistic options. Implicit in preferences is the notion of gradience. Structures can be described or evaluated on a scale from the least to the most preferred. The differences between constraints and preferences based on their ontology are delineated in the following way:

> - *an absolute constraint*: a non-violable, universal principle, e.g. "mechanical" constraint in Maddieson's (1999) terminology; defines the borders of the possible; ontologically *a law*, OR
>
> - *a violable constraint*: a violable, universal tendency, whose applicability is influenced by "ecological" factors (cf. Maddieson 1999) – leading to type-specific and system-specific differences; defines direction of selection from the possible; ontologically *a preference.* (Dziubalska-Kołaczyk 2001a: 75)

In the present model, I will show that both terms are relevant for the discussion of phonological patterns, as constraints and preferences emerge at the empirical level from a particular infrasegmental and intersegmental organizations of features. On the one hand, NP preferences are the most adequate measure of strategies that are cognitively favoured by speakers. Ritt (2001: 307) refers to this idea by emphasizing that "[t]he way from external constraints to language internal design leads right through the realm of human minds, which are under the influence of allegedly autonomous, free-willed human selves" . On the other hand, in OT specific phonological patterns emerge when conflicting constraints are optimally satisfied in a language. OT assumes a finite number of universally-ranked constraints, whose language-specific re-ordering results in a given linguistic structure. Also, ranked preferences and absolute constraints open up a path to discovering *elementary particles,* which define the backbone structure of phonotactics in Polish and other languages.

Recall the restrictions on the possible onset and coda clusters in Polish given in Chap. 1 in Sect. 1.4.

30. A summary of phonotactic constraints on Polish syllables

(30.a) onsets: adjacent stops must be heterorganic; /m l/ must be followed only by a sonorant; sC clusters must be preceded only by /m l/

(30.b) codas: adjacent obstruents must agree in voicing; sonorant-only geminates; voiceless and non-palatalized consonants finally.

Constraints in 30 account for the structure of a subset of clusters attested in Polish. If what is known about phonotactic restrictions in Polish can be recapitulated in 30, additional insights could possibly account for preferred patterns. Let me illustrate the claim with an example.

The total of word-initial phonotactic CCs collected for the purpose of the study equals 193 (see Chap. 1, Sect. 1.7.1). When we adopt a rather rigorous interpretation of the constraints in 30, and eliminate all sonorant + sonorant, sonorant + obstruent and obstruent + obstruent clusters, we are still left with as many as 89 obstruent + sonorant sequences. That is, the structure of more than a half of the inventory of initial CC sequences (which the constraints in 30 do not apply to) is not restricted in any way. The constraint allows for sequences such as /ʃj pm/, which are not attested in Polish. In fact, little is known about phonotactic preferences which underlie the phonological structure of these clusters. What is a preferred sequence or an optimal sequence of consonants? Which properties constitute the tiniest composite parts of clusters? And which properties determine the degrees of preferability in Polish phonotactics?

With 458 initial and 170 final clusters being subject to the analysis, identifying a force which motivates their structure requires exploratory methodology. A necessary turning point in the search of the synchronic mechanisms underlying the phonological structure of clusters lies the decomposition of segments into smaller constituents, on whose basis new principles of phonotactic organization can be formulated. The analysis eventually leads to three types of generalizations. *Minimal requirements* (or inviolable constraints) underlie the structure of all clusters, and reveal core phonological properties of the phonotactic grammar of a language. *Strong* and *weak preferences* apply to the (vast) majority of clusters, and specify structure types which are favoured in a language to varying degrees. This classification is based on the importance of phonological features, which I capture by the concept of *feature weight*.

3.2.3 Feature Weight and Featuretactics

The proposal of *feature weight* put forward in this volume originally emerged from the results of the study by Orzechowska and Wiese (2015). The authors compared Polish and German word-initial clusters in terms of 16 phonetic and phonological properties (the so-called *parameters*) pertaining to structural complexity, place of articulation, manner of articulation and voicing. The goal of the paper was to propose rankings of consonant clusters and discuss the structure of optimal initials in the two languages. The authors observed that fundamental differences between

Polish and German phonotactics and different rankings of consonant clusters are attributed to several preferences:

> (...) there are three preferences which hold particularly for Polish: the presence of one or more coronals, the cluster-final position of coronals and voicing agreement. For German, three other preferences play a more significant role, namely size, increase in opening and voicing in C1. These preferences combine to achieve sonority-based clustering in German, while in Polish, the preferences conspire to form clusters which have at least one or two coronals, and which are voiced throughout. (Orzechowska and Wiese 2015: 480)

The statement has inspired research on the relative importance of phonological features in phonotactics in different phonological systems and in different prosodic positions. The nature of this type of an analysis was captured by the term *featuretactics* (Orzechowska 2016) to refer to the infrasegmental organization of consonants forming clusters. Featuretactics is based on the premise that phonotactic constraints and preferences are encoded in *weighted phonological features* specified within a segments and across segments. Emphasis is placed on the distribution and co-occurrence of features in cluster constituents, and the role (expressed by weights and rankings) that they play in the formation of cluster inventories. The preliminary definition of the term emphasizes the potential of accounting for cross-linguistic phonotactic variability:

> The focal point of the reasoning adopted here is that a specific feature setting expressed by a set of preferences is responsible for the structure of consonant clusters in a given language and word position. The same set of phonological features (complexity, place, manner, voice) is universally available to all languages; however, each language selects a feature or a subset of features in the construction of clusters, which decide on the idiosyncratic character of [its] clusters. (Orzechowska 2016: 170)

Weight is a measure of importance of one feature relative to another, which is expressed in terms of rankings. In the original proposal of Orzechowska (2016), weights are allocated to features by means of statistical methods. In other words, weight expresses the degree to which a feature explains the variability of the data and discriminates between clusters. Features with higher weights have a greater share in creating phonotactic inventories in a language, i.e. they underly the structure of a majority of consonant clusters. As I will show in the following chapters of this book, lexical statistics is only one way of inferring the relative importance of features. The data presented in Chaps. 4 and 5 reveal that feature weight also holds in language as it happens, i.e. in processing and in production.

This type of phonotactic modelling gets support from theoretical and empirical analyses. Theoretical contributions have stressed the relevance of subsegmental properties in phonology and their asymmetrical relations (e.g. Hall 2001, 2007; Halle et al. 2000). For instance, non-linear phonology uses feature geometry (e.g. Clements 1985; Clements and Hume 1995; Halle 1995; Padgett 1995; Rice 1992; Rubach 2007; Sagey 1982) to express intrinsic complexity of segments, and dependency relations to represent major classes of segments (e.g. Anderson and Durand 1986; Ewen 1995, 1996). As a result, featural markedness has been proposed to account for the asymmetries of features within a class of segments. A comprehensive summary of views on the topic is presented in Rice (2003, 2007), and is listed in Table 3.1.

As can be observed, features can be ordered with respect to each other in terms of the marked versus unmarked options. The ordering is relative, i.e. [coronal] is universally unmarked compared to other place features, or voiceless obstruents are universally unmarked compared to voiced obstruents. A more detailed account of markedness specifications for consonants is provided in Singh (1976) (Table 3.2).

Phonological features have also been used to account for static distribution patterns. For instance, Hirst's (1980) *Single Segment Hypothesis* states that syllable constituents are underlyingly represented by a single segment. Segments are defined in terms of phonological features such as high, labial, coronal, nasal, continuant, sonorant, strident and voice. Also, in the *Phonotactic Learner* of Hayes and Wilson (2008), constraints are constructed on the basis of natural classes determined by phonological features such as [anterior], [back], [consonantal], [continuant], [labial], [lateral], [nasal], [sonorant], [strident], [voice]. Such a feature-based system has the capacity to learn phonotactic phenomena of natural languages. An implementation of the model in a later study of Hayes (2011) shows that even a modest feature system represented by [sonorant], [approximant] and [consonantal] can successfully acquire grammar of constraint-based languages.

Table 3.1 Markedness relations between phonological features

Unmarked	Marked
Coronal	Other places of articulation
Nasal	Other sonorants
Voiceless obstruents	Voiced obstruents
High tone	Low tone
High and low vowels	Mid vowels

Rice (2007: 81f.)

Table 3.2 Description of feature specifications in terms of markedness

Consonant	Voicing	Nasality	Place
p	U	U	U
b	M	U	U
t	U	U	U
d	M	U	U
k	U	U	M
g	M	U	M
m	M	M	U
n	M	M	U
ŋ	M	M	M

Singh (1976: 27)
where *M* marked, *U* unmarked

It is necessary to emphasize that the understanding of *feature weight* is not related to the meaning of the concept traditionally applied in phonology. For example, weight has been used to account for phenomena such as syllable structure and syllable constraints, stress assignment, allomorphy and reduplication or even the ordering of constituents in sentences (for overviews see Gordon 2002, 2006, 2016; Hyman 1985; Ryan 2011, 2016). Another implementation of weights, which is more closely related to the present understanding of the term, concerns phonotactic constraints. The *Maximum Entropy Model* and *Phonotactic Learner* of Hayes and Wilson (2008) constructs constraints on sequences of natural classes, and scales their importance in terms of numerical weights. Such weights indicate the probability of forms which can follow or violate natural constraints.

Further support in favour of the feature-based modelling of phonotactics is found in the realm of phonological typology. Viewed from a cross-linguistic perspective, Slavic and Germanic languages are phonotactically complex (Maddieson 2013), allowing for C(C)(C)VC(C)(C)(C) sequences. The classification, however, does not account for large disproportions found in the phonotactic inventories of the languages in terms of clusters' length and their phonological structure. To compare, English and German permit 50–60 initial clusters, while Polish and Russian nearly ten times as many (for a systematic comparison see Orzechowska 2018). What is more, similar disproportions are found in different prosodic positions (onsets vs. codas), word positions (word-initial vs. word-final clusters) and within a language. These observations suggests that cluster structure arises from language-specific properties at the subsegmental level. In other words, differences in the positional weight of phonological features are responsible for the emergence of clusters of different length and phonological make-up across word or prosodic positions, languages and language families. This claim gets further support from universal feature hierarchies.

Clements' (2001, 2009) work provides ample evidence in favour of the universal relevance of selected phonological features. For instance, the principle of *Marked Feature Avoidance* (Clements 2009) states that some values are omitted cross-linguistically. Based on the analysis of the UPSID database containing 451 languages, the author observes that nasal vowels, fricatives and sonorants are marked with respect to their unmarked equivalents: oral vowels, stops and obstruents. A similar idea is captured in the *Accessibility Hierarchy* (Clements 2001), and its refined version embraced in the *Robustness Scale* (Clements 2009), which show that some phonological features are favoured cross-linguistically in the formation of phonemic systems, while others are disfavoured.

Robustness scale proposes a universal hierarchy of phonological features from which languages draw when constructing their phonemic inventories. The highest ranks in the scale represent the most favoured contrast, which is present in the majority of the world's languages, and which reflects constraints on production and perception for all normal speakers. Robustness captures phonological contrast. Robust features maximize salience and involve low articulatory cost. Since they serve to distinguish between segments even in rapid speech or in noisy conditions, they tend to be mastered and produced relatively early in language acquisition. The most robust contrasts include: sonorant versus obstruent, labial versus coronal, coronal versus dorsal, nasal versus oral, stop versus continuant and voiced versus voiceless.

31. Robustness scale for consonant features (Clements 2009: 46f.)

[±sonorant]
[labial]
[coronal]
[dorsal]
[±continuant]
[±posterior]
[±voiced]
[±nasal]
[glottal]
others

From 31 it emerges that the distinction between a sonorant and an obstruent is universally more accessible than feature [glottal]. That is, all languages rely on the O/S contrast as it surfaces in early L1 acquisition and in basic phonological patterns. Features found at the bottom of the hierarchy are exploited in fewer languages, and only when higher-ranking contrasts are present.

Crucial for the present model is the relative importance of features. While Clements (2001, 2009) demonstrates that some features are preferred over other features in the construction of segment inventories, the method of phonotactic modelling discussed in this chapter infers such preferred features for different word positions in a language. Clements (2001, 2009) accounts for such a possibility by asserting that universally-given feature rankings can be overridden by language-particular hierarchies, although the universal ranking is expected to be largely respected across phonological systems.

3.3 The Phonotactic Model

3.3.1 Selection of Parameters

Methodology adopted in this study was first introduced in Orzechowska and Wiese (2015), and further developed in Orzechowska (2016, submitted a, b). Four *dimensions* are used in the description of consonant clusters: complexity, place of articulation (POA), manner of articulation (MOA) and voice (VOI).[1] Each dimension is represented by a set of *parameters* (P) and their *patterns* (also referred to as *values*). The general outline of the model is given in Fig. 3.1.

[1]The term *dimension* is used to refer to the general structure of the model. The term *feature* relates to the specifications of the place, manner and voice dimensions.

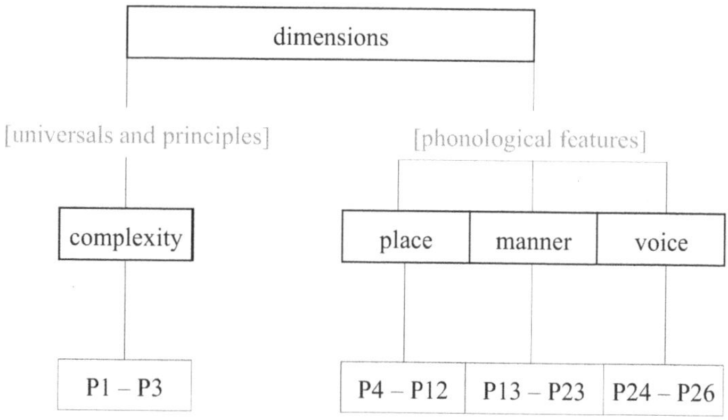

Fig. 3.1 An outline of the model

The analysis is based on 26 parameters. Three parameters represent the complexity dimension and the voice dimension. The place of articulation is represented by nine parameters, and the manner of articulation encompasses 11 parameters. (P4–P26) are feature-based and refer to place, manner and voice characteristics of clusters. (P1–P3) are motivated by cluster characteristics which go beyond phonological features, namely cluster size, decomposition of clusters into smaller constituents and their repeatability in strings.

This type of phonotactic modelling represents approaches which are not based on well-formedness conditions (Chap. 2). The goal of the analysis is to answer the following questions: What properties or principles motivate the phonological make-up of clusters, disregarding whether they are well-formed or ill-formed? The analysis consists in a rigorous analysis of large sets of initial and final clusters with a view to determining positional weight of phonological features. The corollary of the analysis is the identification of heretofore undiscovered constraints and preferences. This approach is open. It has the capacity to incorporate a large (virtually unlimited) set of defining parameters. The first attempt at providing a similar featural analysis of phonotactics was pursued in Orzechowska and Wiese (2015). The authors proposed 15 parameters based on [labial], [coronal], [dorsal], [±sonorant] and their specific realizations, e.g. bilabial, dental, velar, plosive, fricative, glide. A refinement of the method proposed in Orzechowska (2016) employed 19 parameters. In the analysis presented below, I propose to extend the number of variables to 26 parameters by including [±anterior], [±consonantal], [±continuant], and [±strident].

A complete list of 26 parameters employed in this study is given in Table 3.3. Naturally, one could argue for the inclusion of other consonant-related features into the analysis. For instance, phonological theory employs [±delayed release] to differentiate between plosives, in which an articulatory closure is released abruptly ([−del rel]) and affricates, in which a slow release of the obstruction results in friction noise ([+del rel]). Instead, the distinction between the obstruents is captured

Table 3.3 Parameters of cluster description

Dimensions	Parameters
Complexity	(P1) Size
	(P2) Compositionality
	(P3) Identity avoidance
Place of articulation (POA)	(P4) Place of articulation distance
	(P5) Directionality
	(P6) Labial C
	(P7) Coronal C
	(P8) Dorsal C
	(P9) Anterior—initial C
	(P10) Anterior—final C
	(P11) Initial C
	(P12) Final C
Manner of articulation (MOA)	(P13) Manner of articulation distance
	(P14) Articulatory opening
	(P15) Obstruent C
	(P16) Consonantal—initial C
	(P17) Consonantal—final C
	(P18) Continuant—initial C
	(P19) Continuant—final C
	(P20) Strident—initial C
	(P21) Strident—final C
	(P22) Initial C
	(P23) Final C
Voicing (VOI)	(P24) Initial C
	(P25) Final C
	(P26) Voice agreement

by continuancy (P18, P19) whereby plosives are marked for [−continuant] and affricates for [±continuant] feature. Similarly, a distinction between acute versus grave, compact versus diffuse is not included as the features correspond with [coronal] and [±anterior], which are here captured by (P7, P9, P10). The consonant inventory of Polish has also been defined in terms of features such as [±distributed], [±round], [±high], [±back] (Bethin 1992; Rochoń 2000) and [±spread glottis] (Schwartz and Arndt 2018). The list of nine features incorporated in the present analysis is based on approaches to phonotactics by Hirst (1980), and Hayes and Wilson (2008), and is at this stage considered to be sufficient for the description of Polish clusters.

Table 3.4 provides the definitions of the features used in this analysis. Each feature is binary and can be realized either with a plus '+' mark or a minus '−' mark. Such an interpretation diverges from the representation of features in feature geometry (among others, Clements 1985; Clements and Hume 1995; Lass 1976;

Table 3.4 Articulatory correlates of phonological features

Features	Articulatory correlates
Anterior versus posterior [±ant]	Anterior sounds are produced with a primary constriction at or in front of the alveolar ridge, while posterior sounds are produced with a primary constriction behind the alveolar ridge
Consonantal versus non-consonantal [±cons]	Consonantal sounds are produced with a sustained vocal tract constriction at least equal to that required in the production of fricatives; nonconsonantal sounds are produced without such a constriction
Continuant versus stop [±cont]	Continuants are formed with a vocal tract configuration allowing the airstream to flow through the midsagittal region of the oral tract; stops are produced with a sustained occlusion in this region
Coronal versus non-coronal [±cor]	Coronal sounds are produced by raising the tongue blade toward the teeth or the hard palate; noncoronal sounds are produced without such a gesture
labial versus non-labial [±lab]	Labial sounds are formed with a constriction at the lips, while nonlabial sounds are formed without such a constriction
Sonorant versus obstruent [±son]	Sonorant sounds are produced with a vocal tract configuration sufficiently open that the air pressure inside and outside the mouth is approximately equal. Obstruent sounds are produced with a vocal tract constriction sufficient to increase the air pressure inside the mouth significantly over that of the ambient air
Strident versus non-strident [±strid]	Strident sounds are produced with a complex constriction forcing the airstream to strike two surfaces, producing high-intensity fricative noise; nonstrident sounds are produced without such a constriction
Voiced versus voiceless [±voice]	Voiced sounds are produced with a laryngeal configuration permitting periodic vibration of the vocal cords; voiceless sounds lack such periodic vibration

Adapted from Halle and Clements (1994: 6–8)

McCarthy 1988; Sagey 1982), where (in)dependency relations in tree diagrams vary across the proposed models (for overviews see Halle et al. 2000; Dresher 2015, 2016; Rubach 2007). For instance, labiality is a privative feature in Clements and Hume (1995), but is expressed in terms of [±round] in Sagey (1982) and Halle (1995). The same holds true for coronality and dorsality, which are generally considered to be privative (e.g. Clements and Hume 1995; McCarthy 1988; Sagey 1982). Such an interpretation has consequences for the representation of all consonants in a language. For instance, when coronality is a privative feature, it does not apply to non-coronal segments (i.e. they are unmarked in terms of coronality). To the contrary, a binary division into [±coronal] entails the allocation of [−coronal] to labials and dorsals (e.g. Giegerich 1995). The validity of the latter proposal is refuted by Hall (1997), who argues that [−coronal] cannot exist as a feature.

Similar representational inconsistencies are related to stridency and anteriorness (cf. Halle et al. 2000). Feature [±strident] has been located either as a daughter of a root node or as a daughter of a coronal node. In the first case, the feature is used to specify all consonants and separate [+strident] high-noise fricatives and affricates from all other sounds. In the second case, it is contrastive only for coronal fricatives and affricates, and is therefore non-applicable to plosives and sonorants. As regards anteriorness, the specification [±anterior] has been used to specify either all consonants or coronals only.

The laryngeal properties of segments also pose challenges for a feature-based analysis. For example, in Polish there is no agreement on which laryngeal features should be used. A simplified version of feature geometry proposed by Bethin (1992) involves [+voice] versus [−voice] contrast, rather than spread glottis, which is considered to be non-contrastive in Polish. When viewed from the perspective of *Laryngeal Realism* (e.g. Beckman et al. 2013; Honeybone 2005), such a representation might be too simplistic. Cyran (2011) demonstrates that Polish represents two voicing systems which reflect the dialectal voicing properties. While Cracow-Poznan Polish involves sandhi voicing (e.g. *brat Adama* /brad adama/ 'Adam's brother'), Warsaw Polish does not (i.e. /brat adama/). On these grounds, Cyran (2011) posits the presence of both features in Polish, where [±voice] is indicated by full voicing, and [±spread glottis] is motivated by aspiration. Under the third, more radical view, Schwartz and Arndt (2018) propose to dispense with the [±voice] feature altogether. In their perception study, the authors investigate contrast between word-initial consonants /b d g/ and /p t k/, and conclude that Polish operates on a single feature of spread glottis which denotes voicelessness. Given the inconsistencies involved in the allocation of phonological features to consonants and different motivations, I follow the specification of Polish consonants provided by Bethin (1992), and Rochoń (2000).

Based on Table 3.5, I propose a set of parameters for the description of Polish phonotactics. Empty slots in the table indicate that a feature is non-applicable (NA) to a consonant. For instance, labiality is a privative feature that specifies six consonants /p b f v m w/ as [labial]. The remaining consonants are labelled **NA labial* to indicate that they are marked by other features such as coronality or dorsality. Similarly, anteriorness can have a binary realization [+anterior] and [−anterior] for coronal consonants, while labials and dorsals are labelled **NA anterior*. Positing the *NA* category is imperative in order to tease apart consonants with a minus value for a feature from consonants to which a feature does not apply. What is more, a marking for each consonant is necessary when performing a statistical analysis.

By now, the inquisitive reader should have noticed that the features discussed above are both phonetic and phonological. For example, parameters (P4) and (P5) make use of specific place features such bilabial and labio-dental which are phonetic subtypes of a broad phonological class of sounds produced with the lips. The same holds true for parameters (P13) and (P14) based on specific manners of articulation such as plosives, fricatives and affricates. While such fine-grained categories have been traditionally associated with the phonetic level (as captured by the IPA classification of consonants), phonologically they have been subsumed under features of labiality and sonorance.

Table 3.5 Polish consonant features

	p	b	f	v	m	w	t	d	tɕ	dʑ	s	z	ɕ	ʑ	ts	dz	n	ɲ	l	r	j	ʃ	ʒ	tʃ	dʒ	k	g	x
[cons]	+	+	+	+	+	−	+	+	+	+	+	+	+	+	+	+	+	+	+	+	−	+	+	+	+	+	+	+
[son]	−	−	−	−	+	+	−	−	−	−	−	−	−	−	−	−	+	+	+	+	+	−	−	−	−	−	−	−
[cont]	−	−	+	+	−	+	−	−	−/+	−/+	+	+	+	+	−/+	−/+	−	−	−	+	+	+	+	−/+	−/+	−	−	+
[voice]	−	+	−	+	+	+	−	+	−	+	−	+	−	+	−	+	+	+	+	+	+	−	+	−	+	−	+	−
[nasal]	−	−	−	−	+	−	−	−	−	−	−	−	−	−	−	−	+	+	−	−	−	−	−	−	−	−	−	−
[labial]	+	+	+	+	+	+																						
[coronal]							+	+	+	+	+	+	+	+	+	+	+	+	+	+	+	+	+	+	+			
[anter]						−	+	+	−	−	+	+	−	+	+	+	+	−	+	+	−	−	−	−	−			
[distr]							−	−	+	+	−	−	+	+	−	−	−	+	−	−	+	−	−	−	−			
[lateral]																			+									
[dorsal]																										+	+	+
[high]	−	−	−	−	−	+	−	−	+	+	−	−	−	−	−	−	−	−	−	−	+	+	+	+	+	+	+	+
[back]	+	+	+	+	+	+	+	+	−	−	+	+	+	+	+	+	+	+	+	+	−	+	+	+	+	+	+	+

Based on Bethin (1992: 19) and Rochoń (2000: 278)

An analysis involving both phonetic and phonological features is considered more insightful. Let me illustrate the role of a phonetic and phonological description on the example of (P4) ands (P13). The parameters measure the distances between adjacent consonants in terms of places and manners of articulation. A distance of one holds between consecutive articulatory types on the following place scale: bilabial – labio-dental – dental – alveolar – palato-alveolar – palatal – velar, and the manner scale: plosives – affricates – fricatives – nasals – liquids – glides. The smallest distances (equal to zero) involve the same articulatory types such as velar + velar or plosive + plosive. The largest distances hold between extreme types of articulation, e.g. bilabial – velar or glide – plosive. Determining distances between neighbouring segments is less insightful when based on three place features and two manner features. Examples in 32 juxtapose all the phonetic realizations [(32.a), (32.b)] of two broad phonological patterns, namely [coronal] + [coronal] in (32.c) and [−sonorant] + [−sonorant] in (32.d). The phonetic articulations representing the overarching feature [coronal] involve: dental, alveolar, alveolo-palatal and palatal, while [−sonorant] is an umbrella term for fricatives, affricates and plosives. The resulting distance count is more accurate for the phonetic categories.

32. Accuracy of distance measures

(32.a) phonetic place distances:

= 0 (dental + dental, alveolar + alveolar, alveolo-palatal + alveolo-palatal)
/st/ *staw* ‘pond’
/ʃʧ/ *deszcz* ‘rain’
/ɕɲ/ *śnieg* ‘snow’
= 1 (dental + alveolar, alveolar + alveolo-palatal, palatal + alveolo-palatal)
/tr/ *trawa* ‘grass’
/rʨ/ *śmierć* ‘death’
/jɕ/ *czyjś* ‘somebody’s’
= 2 (alveolo-palatal + dental, palatal + alveolar)
/ɕl/ *ślub* ‘wedding’
/jʧ/ *pejcz* ‘riding crop’

(32.b) phonetic manner distances:

= 0 (fricative + fricative, affricate + affricate, plosive + plosive)
/sf/ *sfera* ‘sphere’
/ʤʤ/ *dżdżownica* ‘earthworm’
/kt/ *nikt* ‘nobody’
= 1 (fricative + affricate, affricate + plosive, plosive + affricate)
/ʃʧ/ *szczotka* ‘brush’
/ʦk/ *Płock* [place name]
= 2 (fricative + plosive)

/sk/ *wosk* 'wax'
/dʒ/ *drzwi* 'door'

(32.c) phonological place distances:

= 0 [coronal] + [coronal]
/st ʃʧ ɕɲ tr rtɕ jɕ ɕl jʧ/

(32.d) phonological manner distances:

= 0 [−sonorant] + [−sonorant]
/sf ʤʤ kt ʃʧ ʦk sk dʒ/

As can be observed, the broad categories based on phonological features do not distinguish between specific phonetic types, and result in a more general description. Naturally, the model could dispense with one type of features. However, in order to provide a more complete description of phonotactics, reference is made to both phonetic and phonological categories. Phonetic features are here employed in computing parameters which require a fine-grained classification of consonants. Phonological features, in turn, are used to determine feature weight.

3.3.2 *Interpretation of Parameters*

The parameters proposed in the model are qualitative and quantitative. They specify the first cluster segment (initial, C1) and the last cluster segment (final, C-fin) or characteristics which define the whole cluster (i.e. the number of labials, coronals, dorsals, distance, directionality). Parameter patterns represent possible realizations of a parameter. Some patterns are binary. For instance, a cluster-initial consonant can be characterized either as [+continuant] or as [−continuant]. Other patterns are n-ary and express an overall presence of a feature. For example, the number of labials, coronals or dorsals in a cluster can range from zero to three. Finally, patterns can have a descriptive character (e.g. directionality of articulation: forward, backward, level).

The number of clusters representing a particular parameter pattern is expressed in percentages calculated for the total number of observations in a given cluster group (e.g. initial phonotactic clusters, N = 336). The percentages are further transformed into percentage scores assigned to all sequences representing a particular pattern. That is, if the proportion of [+voice] to [−voice] C cluster-initially is 151 to 185, clusters starting with a voiced C score 0.45 (45% = 151 out of 336), while clusters starting with a voiceless C are assigned a score equal to 0.55 (55% = 185 out of 336) for the voicing in C1 parameter (P24). If all clusters with no exception display one pattern, each cluster receives a score of 1 (= 100%).

Individual scores and their sum ($\sum$) are used to formulate generalizations on the phonological structure of the left and right word edge. Since scores are calculated for a large inventory of clusters for two word positions (initial and final) and morphological contexts (phonotactic and morphonotactic), they reveal areas of feature (co-)occurrence and distribution for four data sets. The interpretation of the scores is the following:

(1) individual scores show prevalent patterns for parameters (P1–P26)
(2) a sum of scores ($\sum_{P1-P26}$) for a cluster expresses whether, and to what degree, the cluster follows the set of prevalent patterns
(3) a sum of scores ($\sum_{P1-P26}$) for the whole inventory expresses the overall degree to which all clusters follow prevalent patterns.

To provide insights into why specific restrictions hold in a language, I derive a set of parameters which motivate the structure of the (vast) majority of clusters. Depending on their weight, parameter patterns function either as obligatory components or graded preferences in a phonotactic grammar. A preference is viewed in quantitative terms as a parameter pattern which is followed by at least 60% ($\geq$ 60%) of clusters. This threshold has no empirical basis but offers a convenient and tentative split of parameter patterns into those which define a larger and smaller majority of clusters. Note that the verification of the actual weight of features and preferences is possible with the help of statistical modelling performed at a later stage of the analysis.

The strength of a preference increases from 60 to 99%. Patterns which define all clusters with no exception (i.e. 100%) are viewed as phonotactic prerequisites. The percentage-based ranges are informative only when the data under scrutiny is sufficiently large, or preferably complete. That is, a large list of clusters ensures that inferred generalizations are not based on a random selection of clusters. The classification of patterns into prerequisites and preferences follows from the interpretation of scores presented in Sects. 3.3.3.1 through 3.3.3.4. I propose the following hierarchy of phonotactic preferability.

33. Scale of phonotactic preferability

(33.a) prerequisites: parameter patterns that are absolute and apply by default to *all* cluster types within a given inventory (100% of clusters)
(33.b) strong preferences: parameter patterns that apply as strong default and are found in the vast majority of cluster types within a given inventory (towards 99%)
(33.c) weak preferences: parameter patterns that apply as weak default and are found in more than 60% of types within a given inventory (starting at 60%).

Phonotactic prerequisites are non-contrastive and function as mandatory components of a phonological grammar. Prerequisites are included into the preferability scale in (33.a), although they do not have the status of preferences per se: rather, they should be viewed as obligatory, inviolable building blocks of phonotactics, which guarantee that a cluster survives in a language. The obligatoriness of a parameter decreases from (33.a) to (33.c). Parameters subsumed under (33.b) and (33.c) are contrastive and apply to a larger and smaller majority of clusters within a particular cluster set. Such prerequisites and preferences contrast clusters in different word positions (initial vs. final), clusters with different morphological composition (phonotactic vs. morphonotactic) and clusters belonging to different systems. It must be stressed that although defaults and preferences tend to be defined as *typical* and *favoured* constraints, respectively, they are not fixed values. Gibbon (2001: 143) makes a crucial point: "[a] preference may not be favoured under all conditions, and a default may be overridden by other considerations in specific situations". Therefore, the scale of preferability in 33 constitutes the first attempt at a ranking of phonotactic generalizations. A detailed exposition of constraints and graded preferences is pursued in the following sections of the chapter.

3.3.3 Analysis

The data used in this study is based on the inventories of word-initial and final clusters. I used 336 initial phonotactic and 189 morphonotactic clusters listed in Chap. 1 in Tables 1.14 and 1.15, and 131 final phonotactic and 103 morphonotactic clusters given in Tables 1.18 and 1.19. Separate analyses are carried out for each cluster set.

3.3.3.1 Complexity Dimension

The dimension of *complexity* is represented by three parameters. Cluster *size* (P1) is motivated by the CV universal (Donohue et al. 2013; Greenberg 1978; Maddieson 2013). The parameter specifies the number of consonants in a cluster, where 2 corresponds with CC, 3 with CCC, and 4 CCCC.

The second parameters, referred to as *compositionality* (P2), is based on Greenberg's (1978) principle of 'resolvability' (cf. Harley's (2006) *substrating rule*). The principle states that longer clusters are decomposable into shorter constituents. Greenberg (1978) discusses this property on the example of a four-member cluster /fstr/.

> [T]he property of resolvability (…) was first suggested by Hjelmslev. A sequence is here said to be completely resolvable if every continuous subsequence also occurs. (…) For example, if in a language initial fstr occurs then if fs, st, tr, fst and str all occur, it is completely resolvable. If some of these occur but not otherwise, it is partially resolvable, and if non occurs, it is non resolvable. Every initial and final sequence of length m contains at least one continuous subsequence of length m-1. (Greenberg 1978: 250)

The statement suggests that three-member clusters C1C2C3 are completely resolvable into existing C1C2 and C2C3. For the purpose of this study, the principle is extended to account for clusters of length two to five, where the following is assumed:

(1) all clusters are fully decomposable into single consonants found in a language-specific inventory, C1C2 are thus composed of two existing singletons, namely C1 and C2
(2) C1C2C3 are fully compositional if formed of two attested doubles with independent existence (i.e. C1C2 and C2C3) and singletons
(3) C1C2C3C4 are fully compositional if formed of two attested triples (i.e. C1C2C3, C2C3C4), three doubles (i.e. C1C2, C2C3, C3C4) with independent existence and singletons
(4) C1C2C3C4C5 are fully compositional if formed of two attested four-member clusters, three triples, four doubles and attested singletons
(5) a cluster is partially compositional if at least one of the constituent clusters fails to occur in the phonotactic inventory in a given word position.

Note that the parameter partially corresponds with an early analysis of Polish phonotactics by Kuryłowicz (1952), who posits a bipartite structure of clusters longer than CC. For instance, initial /vzdr/ is fully compositional as it contains existing two-member clusters /vz zd dr/ and three-member clusters /vzd zdr/ word initially, e.g. *wzór* 'pattern', *zdobić* 'to decorate', *drewno* 'wood', *wzdychać* 'to sigh' and *zdrowie* 'health'. Conversely, final /lɕɲ/ is partially compositional as it contains one non-existent initial sequences /lɕ/, apart from a sequence /ɕɲ/ found in *śnieżka* 'snowball'.

Finally, *identity avoidance* (P3) investigates the occurrence of identical segments within a cluster. The parameter is a modification of the strict version of the *Obligatory Contour Principle* (henceforth OCP, Leben 1973; McCarthy 1986), which prohibits like segments in phonological units, and its extension Place-OCP, which refers to non-adjacent homorganic (but not totally identical) consonants (McCarthy 1988; Mester 1986; Yip 1988). In the present analysis, identity refers to the same place, manner and voice specification of at least two (non-)adjacent segments. With this interpretation, patterns labelled *total*, *partial* and *none* describe clusters such as /drvj/, /sks/ and /vv/, respectively.

A synopsis of the results for initial and final cluster types is given in Tables 3.6 and 3.7, respectively. In these and the following tables, I present the number of

Table 3.6 Complexity parameters: initial clusters

P	Parameters	Patterns	Phon		Morph	
			no	%	no	%
1.	Size	CC	193	57	62	33
		CCC	128	38	110	58
		CCCC	15	5	17	9
2.	Compositionality	full	299	89	180	95
		partial	37	11	9	5
3.	Identity avoidance	total	332	99	182	96
		none	4	1	3	2
		partial	-	-	4	2

Table 3.7 Complexity parameters: final clusters

P	Parameters	Patterns	Phon		Morph	
			no	%	no	%
1.	Size	CC	101	77	79	77
		CCC	30	23	18	17
		CCCC	-	-	5	5
		CCCCC	-	-	1	1
2.	Compositionality	full	129	98	99	96
		partial	2	2	4	4
3.	Identity avoidance	total	131	100	102	99
		none	-	-	1	1

clusters adhering to a particular pattern ('No'), and their percentage share ('%') calculated for the total number of clusters in a particular dataset, i.e. phonotactic ('Phon') and morphonotactic ('Morph'). For clarity of presentation, shaded cells mark the patterns which define more than 60% of cluster types, and which are at this point tentatively referred to as preferences.

The results show that initial and final clusters differ primarily in terms of cluster size. There is a preference for shorter clusters to occur finally: 77% of word-final clusters are composed of two consonants. No such preference can be inferred from the word-initial data: 43% of clusters are represented by CCCs and CCCCs. As far as parameters (P2) and (P3) are concerned, both word edges exhibit strong preferences for full compositionality and avoidance of identical segments. As regards phonotactic and morphonotactic clusters, both groups follow the same patterns for each parameter.

3.3.3.2 Place of Articulation Dimension

The place dimension is represented by nine parameters. The classification of places of articulation into broad articulatory types is based on Bethin (1992) and Rochoń (2000), and is summarized in Table 3.8.

Specific place features are employed in four parameters (P4, P5, P9, P10). Parameter (P4) measures the place of articulation *distances* (see

Table 3.8 Classification of places of articulation

Labial		Coronal				Dorsal
Bilabial	Labio-dental	Dental	Alveolar	Alveolo-palatal	Palatal	Velar
1	2	3	4	5	6	7
p b m (w)	f v	t d s z ʦ ʣ n l	ʃ ʒ ʧ ʤ r	ɕ ʑ ʨ ʥ ɲ	c ɟ j	k g ŋ x (w)

Dziubalska-Kołaczyk 2009, 2014, in press). A distance of one holds between all adjoining articulations: bilabial – labio-dental – dental – alveolar – alveolo-palatal – palatal – velar. The smallest distance of zero is found in clusters sharing the place feature (e.g. /dn st ɕtɕ/). The largest distance of six is exemplified by the most peripheral articulations involving the combination of a bilabial gesture and a velar gesture (e.g. /mk gb kp/). For clusters containing /w/ (/kw gw/), a mean distance is computed for the labial and dorsal gesture separately, i.e. (velar /g/-velar /w/) + (velar /g/-bilabial /w/) = (0 + 6) /2 = 3. An averaging procedure is also applied to calculate distances for C1C2C3(C4). For example, /skr/ has two transitions: dental + velar and velar + alveolar = (4 + 3) /2 = 3.5. Decimal numbers are rounded to the closest whole number, resulting in a distance equal to four for /skr/.

Specific places of articulation are also used to calculate the *directionality* (P5) of articulatory movement from the first (C1) to the final (C-fin) consonant in a cluster. The parameter investigates whether the tongue slides towards the front or rear part of the mouth cavity, or whether articulation is made towards or outwards from the lips. A *forward* gesture proceeds towards a fronted region (e.g. velar → alveolar/dental/ bilabial in /kʃ kt km/), while a *backward* gesture proceeds towards a retracted region (e.g. dental → alveolar / palatal/velar in /lʒ tj sx/). I also posit the third articulatory type, referred to as *level*, which embraces homorganic clusters in which constituent consonant share the same POA (e.g. /sl rʒ ʃʧ/). A *mixed* pattern is found in clusters with combined directionality (e.g. forward + backward /spj ʃtr kfj/) and containing / w/. In the latter case, articulation proceeds simultaneously in two opposite directions: towards the lips and the soft palate (e.g. dental + bilabial and dental + velar in /dw tw sw/). The only exception to this pattern is the group of sequences such as /pw bw mw/, which are subsumed under the backward gesture due to the simultaneity of the level (bilabial + bilabial) and backward (bilabial + velar) gestures.

As regards the general place categories, *labial*, *coronal* and *dorsal* are expressed by two sets of parameters. (P6–P8) capture an overall presence of a particular articulatory type in a cluster (e.g. 1 coronal + 1 dorsal in /sk tj gr/), while (P11, P12) specify cluster onset (C1) and offset (e.g. C2 in C1C2, C3 in C1C2C3, C4 in C1C2C3C4). Although phonetically /w/ has dual articulation, at the phonological level the consonant is classified as [labial], in line with Table 3.5.

Moreover, in order to distinguish between subtypes of coronals, I propose two parameters referring to the presence of an *anterior* consonant (P9, P10). A division into anterior and posterior consonants is made depending on whether they are produced in the front or rear part of the mouth cavity, respectively. Definitions of the feature vary across frameworks. For instance, in Cairns (1988) and Chomsky and Halle (1968), [+anterior] specifies not only coronals but also labials (i.e. articulations starting with bilabial to alveolar), while [−anterior] includes dorsals (i.e. from alveolo-palatal to velar articulation). In contrast, Fant (1969) and Sagey (1982) argued that the feature can apply only to coronals. Following the classification in Table 3.5, in Polish [+anterior] is allocated to dentals and alveolars, and [−anterior] is allocated to alveolo-palatals and palatals. The feature is non-applicable to labials and dorsals, which is expressed in an additional pattern labelled as **NA*.

Table 3.9 Place parameters: initial clusters

P	Parameters	Patterns	Phon		Morph	
			no	%	no	%
4.	Distance	0	24	7	13	7
		1	57	17	41	22
		2	79	23	44	23
		3	87	26	48	25
		4	60	18	34	18
		5	20	6	8	4
		6	9	3	1	1
5.	Directionality	forward	95	28	17	9
		backward	106	32	62	33
		level	24	7	13	7
		mixed	111	33	97	51
6.	Number of labial C	0	143	43	54	29
		1	178	53	99	52
		2	15	4	35	18
		3	-	-	1	1
7.	Number of coronal C	0	20	6	14	7
		1	151	45	69	37
		2	143	42	93	49
		3	22	7	13	7
8.	Number of dorsal C	0	217	65	133	70
		1	119	35	56	30
9.	Anterior initial C	[+anterior]	160	47	96	51
		[-anterior]	29	9	5	3
		*NA	147	44	88	46
10.	Anterior final C	[+anterior]	150	45	86	46
		[-anterior]	119	35	65	34
		*NA	67	20	38	20
11.	Initial C	[labial]	92	27	87	46
		[coronal]	184	55	99	52
		[dorsal]	60	18	3	2
12.	Final C	[labial]	74	22	45	24
		[coronal]	247	74	133	70
		[dorsal]	15	4	11	6

The results of the analyses of initial and final clusters are presented in Tables 3.9 and 3.10, respectively.

3.3.3.3 Manner of Articulation Dimension

The MOA dimension is represented by 11 parameters. They largely correspond with the place of articulation dimension, and account for specific and broad features. The classification of consonants based on Table 3.5 is summarised in Table 3.11.

Table 3.10 Place parameters: final clusters

P	Parameters	Patterns	Phon		Morph	
			no	%	no	%
4.	Distance	0	18	14	15	15
		1	38	29	38	36
		2	26	20	17	17
		3	36	27	21	20
		4	11	8	8	8
		5	2	2	2	2
		6	-	-	2	2
5.	Directionality	forward	44	33	47	46
		backward	51	39	29	28
		level	18	14	15	14
		mixed	18	14	12	12
6.	Number of labial C	0	73	56	51	49
		1	50	38	47	46
		2	8	6	4	4
		3	-	-	1	1
7.	Number of coronal C	0	11	8	7	7
		1	60	46	42	41
		2	47	36	42	41
		3	13	10	12	11
8.	Number of dorsal C	0	100	76	87	84
		1	24	18	15	15
		2	6	5	1	1
		3	1	1	-	-
9.	Anterior initial C	[+anterior]	56	43	54	53
		[-anterior]	40	30	24	23
		*NA	35	27	25	24
10.	Anterior final C	[+anterior]	80	61	48	47
		[-anterior]	14	11	14	15
		*NA	37	28	39	38
11.	Initial C	[labial]	41	31	25	24
		[coronal]	76	58	70	68
		[dorsal]	14	11	8	8
12.	Final C	[labial]	21	16	32	31
		[coronal]	92	70	62	60
		[dorsal]	18	14	9	9

Table 3.11 Classification of manners of articulation

Obstruents			Sonorants		
Plosives	Affricates	Fricatives	Nasals	Liquids	Glides
1	2	3	4	5	6
p b t d c ɟ k g	ʦ ʣ ʧ ʤ ʨ ʥ	f v s z ʃ ʒ ɕ ʑ x	m n ŋ ɲ	l r	w j

Broad and specific manner categories are employed in different parameters. The overarching division into obstruents and sonorants is used in (P15, P22, P23). The *number of obstruents* (P15) states the proportion of sonorants to obstruents (S/O) in a cluster. Percentages are calculated separately for two-, three-, four-, and five-member clusters in (15a, 15b, 15c, 15d), respectively. This division ensures that the S/O proportion in a sequence is captured adequately. Parameters (P22, P23) specify the presence of a sonorant or an obstruent in cluster initial and final position. It must be noted that (P15, P22, P23) provide partially overlapping information. If a two-member cluster contains only one obstruent, which is expressed in (15a), and this obstruent is found in C1 (P22), then the C2 slot must obviously contain a sonorant: a distribution pattern repeated in (P23). Nevertheless, to make the manner parameters comparable to the place dimension, where segments at cluster edges are considered, (P15, P22, P23) are included in the analysis.

The distinction into specific manners of articulation is used in the description of the remaining parameters. Parameter (P14), related to sonority distances (for similar proposals see Clements 1990; Dziubalska-Kołaczyk 2002; Harris 1983; Selkirk 1984; Steriade 1982), calculates manner *distances* between consecutive segments on the sonority scale given in Table 3.11. A distance of one holds between plosives − affricates − fricatives − nasals − liquids − glides. Distances for three-member and four-member clusters are obtained by averaging over distances for the consecutive pairs. For instance, in a four-member cluster /bʒmj/, the distances C1C2 + C2C3 + C3C4 entail the following computation: (plosive + fricative) + (fricative + nasal) + (nasal + glide) = $(2 + 1 + 2) / 3 = 1.67 \approx 2$.

Specific places are also used in determining the *articulatory opening* (P14), which describes the constriction of the vocal tract from C1 towards a vowel. In other words, (P14) reflects the degree to which clusters follow the SSG, according to the sonority scale in Table 3.11. Four patterns are distinguished. In word-initial position, an *increase* in opening defines core clusters (Clements 1990) (e.g. /tw smr dʒvj/), a *decrease* corresponds to reversals (Clements 1990) (e.g. /sp lɲ mʃʧ/), and *plateau* articulation involves an identical degree of stricture across cluster members (e.g. /db ʤʤ fsʃ/). Word-finally, the reverse ordering is assumed, where an increase defines sonority-violating clusters such as /ks tm rw/ and a decrease encompasses sonority-obeying clusters such as /mp ŋk j̃ɕtɕ/. Additionally, *mixed* clusters which involve two or three transitions belonging to different classes are kept distinct. Such clusters are exemplified by decrease + increase in /wbj lɕɲ/ and plateau + decrease + increase in /fstʃ/.

Phonological theory subdivides sonorants and obstruents by means of features such as *consonantal*, *continuant* and *strident*, which are incorporated into the present model in parameters (P16–P19, P20, P21), Depending on the degree of stricture in the vocal tract, [+consonantal] obstruent, nasal and liquid consonants are distinguished from [−consonantal] glides /w j/.

Continuancy can be viewed in articulatory terms (Chomsky and Halle 1968; Halle and Clements 1994) where [+continuant] specifies segments articulated with no occlusion in the mid-sagittal region (i.e. glides, rhotics, fricatives). On the other hand, the feature can be defined in terms of the sonority hierarchy as it separates continuant nasal and fricative consonants from non-continuant affricates and plosives. The ambivalence of the feature is discussed in Mielke (2004, 2005), who shows that lateral and nasal consonants can be [+continuant] in some languages, but [−continuant] in others. In this analysis, I follow the featural specification in Table 3.5 where nasal consonants are defined as [−continuant, +consonantal] (the same interpretation is found in Carr 1993; Halle and Clements 1994; Hayes 2009; Kenstowicz 1994), similarly to laterals. The feature is also used to distinguish between obstruents: the two-way specification in affricates (i.e. [−/+ continuant]) reflects their complex structure.

The last parameter used in the description of the manner dimension is stridency. The articulatory and acoustic description of the feature, and the allocation [+strident] and [−strident] to consonants is ambiguous. The definition of the feature adopted in the present analysis comes from the SPE:

> Strident sounds are marked acoustically by greater noisiness than their non-strident counterparts. When the air stream passes over a surface, a certain amount of turbulence will be generated depending upon the nature of the surface, the rate of flow and the angle of incidence. A rougher surface, a faster rate of flow an angle of incidence close to ninety degrees will all contribute to greater stridency. Stridency of a feature is restricted to obstruent continuants and affricates. Plosives and sonorants are non-strident. (Chomsky and Halle 1968: 329)

Generally, stridency characterizes a subclass of fricatives and affricates. [+strident] specifies high-intensity fricative coronal sibilants /s z ʃ ʒ ɕ ʑ ʦ ʣ ʧ ʤ ʨ ʥ/, and [−strident] specifies /f v x/. The feature is non-applicable to plosives and sonorants, which are subsumed under a category labelled as **NA strident*. This additional pattern should not be mistaken with typical [−strident] consonants such as /f v x/. Although the feature is not included in Bethin (1992) and Rochoń (2000), it is particularly important for the specification of morphonotactic initials, many of which start with [+strident] prefixes /s z/.

The synopsis for the manner-defining parameters in initial and final (mor) phonotactics is given in Tables 3.12 and 3.13, respectively.

3.3.3.4 Voice Dimension

The last three parameters capture the laryngeal properties of cluster members. *Initial C* (P24) and *final C* (P25) provide the [±voice] specification at cluster edges. Again, C1 corresponds to the first consonant in a cluster, while C-fin refers to the last consonant. Parameter referred to as *voice agreement* (P26) characterizes the voicing profile across cluster segments, for which three patterns can be distinguished. Disregarding their length, initial clusters with *total* agreement are uniformly voiced (e.g. /gl vzn ʑʥbw/) or voiceless (e.g. /kt xʃʧ pʃt/), while a group labelled *none* contains segments which disagree in voicing (i.e. /fr ʨm xj/). Most sequences longer than CC display a pattern of *partial* agreement since they contain sequences which both agree and disagree in voicing (e.g. /stl/, /st/ = total, /tl/ = none).

Table 3.12 Manner parameters: initial clusters

P	Parameters	Patterns	Phon		Morph	
			no	%	no	%
13.	Distance	0	27	8	22	12
		1	66	20	47	25
		2	113	34	61	32
		3	78	23	35	18
		4	38	11	21	11
		5	14	4	3	2
14.	Articulatory opening	increase	171	51	50	26
		decrease	52	15	33	18
		plateau	27	8	22	12
		mixed	86	26	84	44
15.	Number of obstruents	a) CC: 2/2	87	45	40	65
		1/2	98	51	20	32
		0/2	8	4	2	3
		b) CCC: 3/3	28	22	32	29
		2/3	70	55	71	65
		1/3	30	23	7	6
		c) CCCC: 4/4	-	-	2	12
		3/4	10	67	10	59
		1/2	5	33	5	29
16.	Consonantal initial C	[+consonantal]	331	99	187	99
		[-consonantal]	5	1	2	1
17.	Consonantal final C	[+consonantal]	259	77	147	78
		[-consonantal]	77	23	42	22
18.	Continuant initial C	[+continuant]	156	46	167	88
		[-continuant]	151	45	19	10
		-/+	29	9	3	2
19.	Continuant final C	[+continuant]	175	52	115	61
		[-continuant]	131	39	64	34
		-/+	30	9	10	5
20.	Strident initial C	[+strident]	126	38	92	49
		[-strident]	45	13	76	40
		*NA	164	49	21	11
21.	Strident final C	[+strident]	66	20	40	21
		[-strident]	30	9	20	11
		*NA	240	71	129	68
22.	Initial C	obstruent	297	88	182	96
		sonorant	39	12	7	4
23.	Final C	obstruent	143	43	81	43
		sonorant	193	57	108	57

The results of the analysis are juxtaposed in Tables 3.14 and 3.15. The voice characteristics of initial and final clusters are unsurprising. For instance, the prevalence of voiceless segments in absolute word-final position (P25) reflects the rule of the obstruent-final devoicing. Also, the preference for voice agreement word-initially is unsurprising. Obstruent-only phonotactic clusters must agree in voicing, and prefixes in morphonotactic clusters must display voice agreement with stem-initial segments.

Table 3.13 Manner parameters: final clusters

P	Parameters	Patterns	Phon		Morph	
			no	%	no	%
13.	Distance	0	5	4	5	5
		1	21	16	19	18
		2	46	35	40	39
		3	32	24	21	20
		4	21	16	13	13
		5	6	5	5	5
14.	Articulatory opening	increase	24	18	23	22
		decrease	90	69	62	60
		plateau	3	2	3	3
		mixed	14	11	15	15
15.	Number of obstruents	a) CC: 2/2	20	20	23	29
		1/2	68	67	47	60
		0/2	13	13	9	11
		b) CCC: 3/3	3	10	3	17
		2/3	19	63	13	72
		1/3	8	27	2	11
		c) CCCC: 4/4	-	-	2	40
		3/4	-	-	3	60
		d) CCCCC:4/5	-	-	1	100
16.	Consonantal initial C	[+consonantal]	96	73	85	83
		[-consonantal]	35	27	18	17
17.	Consonantal final C	[+consonantal]	129	98	99	96
		[-consonantal]	35	2	4	4
18.	Continuant initial C	[+continuant]	76	58	60	58
		[-continuant]	54	41	40	39
		-/+	1	1	4	3
19.	Continuant final C	[+continuant]	51	39	38	37
		[-continuant]	62	47	46	45
		-/+	18	14	19	18
20.	Strident initial C	[+strident]	15	11	20	19
		[-strident]	9	7	8	8
		*NA	107	82	75	73
21.	Strident final C	[+strident]	41	31	30	29
		[-strident]	14	11	16	16
		*NA	76	58	57	55
22.	Initial C	obstruent	42	32	45	44
		sonorant	89	68	58	56
23.	Final C	obstruent	93	71	76	74
		sonorant	38	29	27	26

3.3.4 *Deriving Preferability Scales*

On the basis of the analysis, preliminary percentage-based rankings of parameters can be established for word-initial and word-final phonotactic and morphonotactic clusters. It must be noted that the rankings constitute the first attempt at proposing a preferability ranking, along the scale in 33.

Table 3.14 Voice parameters: initial clusters

P	Parameters	Patterns	Phon		Morph	
			no	%	no	%
24.	Initial C	[+voice]	151	45	99	52
		[-voice]	185	55	90	48
25.	Final C	[+voice]	253	75	139	74
		[-voice]	83	25	50	26
26.	Voice agreement	total	214	64	143	76
		partial	64	19	39	20
		none	58	17	7	4

Table 3.15 Voice parameters: final clusters

P	Parameters	Patterns	Phon		Morph	
			no	%	no	%
24.	Initial C	[+voice]	89	68	58	56
		[-voice]	42	32	45	44
25.	Final C	[+voice]	13	10	9	9
		[-voice]	118	90	94	91
26.	Voice agreement	total	55	42	54	52
		partial	24	18	17	17
		none	52	40	32	31

3.3.4.1 Preferability Scales in Initial Phonotactics

Tables 3.16 and 3.17 present the rankings of parameters for initial phonotactic and morphonotactic clusters, respectively. The ranks (labelled 'R') decrease from 1 to 9 and 1 to 11, reflecting the decreasing degree of parameter obligatoriness. In other words, the higher the position of a parameter in the ranking, the more preferred its status. I report only on the parameters which define more than 60% of clusters.

Each ranking is subdivided into three parts. Absolute parameters underlie the structure of all clusters (100%; percentage score = 1) in a given inventory, and are viewed as structural prerequisites. Parameters considered to be preferences apply as strong and weak default, i.e. they determine the structure of a larger (towards 99%) and smaller (starting at 60%) majority of clusters, respectively. Note that the percentage ranges are not based on any principled premises but they reflect a relative strength of a preference.

Tables 3.16 and 3.17 distinguish 9 and 11 ranks of preferability, respectively. Parameter patterns with the same percentages are subsumed under the same rank. For instance, 14 preferences identified for morphonotactic initials are grouped into 11 ranks. As can be observed, in both sets preferences representing the manner of articulation prevail. Out of ten parameters identified in the phonotactic group, four represent the manner of articulation features. In the morphonotactic group, there are eight manner-defining parameters. What is more, MOA parameters, along with complexity, are classified as strong default. That is, (consonantal) obstruents (P16, P22) which display full compositionality (P2) and total avoidance of identical

Table 3.16 Percentage ranking of parameters: initial phonotactic clusters

	R	Dimension	Parameter pattern	Parameter
absolute				
		---	---	---
strong default	1	complexity	total identity avoidance	P3
		manner	consonantal C cluster-initially	P16
	2	complexity	full compositionality	P2
	3	manner	obstruent C cluster-initially	P22
	4	manner	consonantal C cluster-finally	P17
	5	voice	voiced C cluster-finally	P25
	6	place	coronal C cluster-finally	P12
	7	manner	3 obstruents in CCCC	P15c
weak default	8	place	no dorsals	P8
	9	voice	total voice agreement	P26

Table 3.17 Percentage ranking of parameters: initial morphonotactic clusters

	R	Dimension	Parameter pattern	Parameter
absolute				
		---	---	---
strong default	1	manner	consonantal C cluster-initially	P16
	2	complexity	total identity avoidance	P3
		manner	obstruent C cluster-initially	P22
	3	complexity	full compositionality	P2
	4	manner	continuant C cluster-initially	P18
	5	manner	consonantal C cluster-finally	P17
	6	voice	total voice agreement	P26
	7	voice	voiced C cluster-finally	P25
	8	place	coronal C cluster-finally	P12
		place	no dorsal C	P8
	9	manner	*NA strident cluster-finally	P21
	10	manner	2 obstruents in CC	P15a
weak default		manner	2 obstruents in CCC	P15b
	11	manner	continuant C cluster-finally	P19

segments (P3) define more than 80% of all initial clusters. Note that the strongest parameters determine the structure of the first consonant in a cluster (word-initial C in initials; post-vocalic C in finals).

Phonotactic and morphonotactic clusters also share parameter patterns subsumed under the weak-default extremes of the ranking. Weak preferences define the right-most edge of clusters (prevocalic C and word-final C). That is, there is a preference for voiced, coronal, consonantal segments (P12, P17, P25) before a vowel. This specification is indirectly supported by (P8), which captures a preference for a lack of dorsals in a cluster. Apart from the voicing specification for the cluster-final slot, voice agreement (P26) is another defining property of phonotactic and morphonotactic clusters. Additionally, both groups exhibit preferences regarding the number of obstruents which are expressed by the group of parameters numbered (15). Overall, if n stands for a number of consonants in a cluster, a favoured pattern is to have $n - 1$ obstruents in clusters longer than CC. In turn, full obstruency is preferred in two-member sequences (i.e. obstruent + obstruent).

The status of the preferences (P16, P17) requires a clarification. Given the characteristics of the consonant inventory of Polish, a logical conclusion could be drawn that a strong preference for consonantal segments is a reflection of a systemic dispreference for non-consonantal segments. That is, since only two glides represent this class of consonants in Polish (2 out of 31 C = 6%), the propensity of their emergence in a cluster is expected to be low. In word-initial phonotactics, this line of reasoning is supported by parameter (P16), which shows that 99% of clusters start with a [+consonantal] C. However, note that the prevocalic position is less commonly occupied by a consonantal C (73%). Thus, theoretically, the potential of filling the prevocalic slot with /j/ and /w/ could be exploited to a larger extent. Such a tendency was observed in English. In an analogous feature-based study of word-initial clusters, Orzechowska (submitted b) notes that although /j/ and /w/ constitute only 8% of the English consonant inventory (2 out of 25 C), 45% (25 out of 58) of consonant clusters contain a glide before a vowel. This observation supports the argument that the parameters listed in Tables 3.16 and 3.17 reflecta preferred type of clusters that the system produces.

As regards the place of articulation, out of nine place parameters available in the analysis, only (P8) and (P12) show to contribute to cluster structure. These parameters suggest that preferred clusters should be composed of non-dorsal segments, especially a coronal cluster-finally.

Tables 3.16 and 3.17 show that phonotactic clusters share parameter patterns with morphonotactic clusters, with the exception of continuancy and stridency. Feature [±continuant] leads to a preference only in the morphonotactic group. That is, morphologically-motivated clusters tend to start and end with a continuant consonant (P18, P19). The preference for [+continuant] cluster-initially follows from the phonetic realization of the prefixes, i.e. /f v s z/. A continuant consonant in prevocalic position ensures a gradual transition towards a continuant vowel. Finally, the group of morphonotactic clusters displays a weak preference to end with a *NA strident segment (P21), i.e. with plosives or sonorants (to which the feature does not apply). This preference, in combination with (P19), indicates that initial morphonotactic clusters tend to end with a glide or a rhotic (/r j w/ are [+continuant] and *NA strident). Such a specification suggests that a consonant released into a vowel should preferably display vocalic properties to ensure a smooth transition from the left cluster edge towards a peak.

At this point, a preferred profile can be posited for initial clusters. The first group of preferences subsumed under (34.a) is shared by all initials. Preferences identified exclusively for phonotactic and morphonotactic clusters are given in (34.b) and (34. c), respectively.

34. Summary of favoured parameter patterns in initial clusters

(34.a) shared:
voice agreement, full compositionality, avoidance of identical segments, lack of [dorsal], start with: [+consonantal] / [−sonorant], end with: [+voice] / [coronal] / [+consonantal]

(34.b) only phonotactic clusters:
maximization of obstruents but not full obstruency in CCCC

(34.c) only morphonotactic clusters:
maximization of obstruents but not full obstruency in CCC, full obstruency in CC, start with: [+continuant], end with: [+continuant] / *NA strident.

The preferences in (34.a) shared by phonologically- and morphologically-motivated clusters refer to a preferred or expected feature setting for initial clusters disregarding whether they are phonotactic or morphonotactic. Table 3.18 summarizes the distribution of features of the most preferred word-initial clusters. The top-down ordering of features reflects the strength of a preference based on the percentage rankings.

To sum up, there is a preference for Polish initial clusters to start with an obstruent and end with a voiced consonantal coronal. What is more, there is no parameter pattern which would define all clusters with no exception. The top-most category, which corresponds with absolute constraints, is empty in both rankings in Table 3.16 and 3.17. Thus, initial position seems to be open to clusters of any phonological characteristics, and operates on several preferences. Let me now proceed to the analysis of parameters defining right-edge phonotactics.

3.3.4.2 Preferability Scales in Final Phonotactics

A summary of the results for word-final phonotactic and morphonotactic clusters is given in Tables 3.19 and 3.20, respectively. The lists of preferences embrace only parameter patterns which are found in at least 60% of clusters in each inventory. Compared to word-initial position, final phonotactics is motivated by more preferences and absolute constraints. 16 preferability parameters were identified for each cluster set and subsumed under 13 ranks in the phonotactic group, and 11 ranks in the morphonotactic group.

Table 3.18 Preferred cluster structure for initial phonotactics: 1st attempt

C-initial	C-final
[+cons]	[+cons]
[−son]	[+voice]
	[coronal]

In general, final phonotactics is structured on the basis of the manner features. Eight manner-defining preferences were identified in the phonotactic set and in the morphonotactic one. The remaining dimensions are represented by one to three parameters. As regards phonotactic prerequisites, one absolute pattern requires that phonotactic clusters avoid the repetition of an identical segment. The second pattern given in Table 3.20 is not considered to be an obligatory constraint as it refers to a single cluster type /mpstf/.

A general picture that emerges from the rankings is that the majority of preferred parameters, and all parameters shared by the two groups specify the cluster-final consonant, i.e. the absolute word-final position. This absolute final position tends to be filled with a voiceless consonantal obstruent with a coronal place of articulation (P12, P17, P23, P25). This structure is also supported by (P8) which specifies an overarching preference for a lack of dorsal consonants in a cluster. Also, word-final phonotactics largely follows the SSG by displaying a decrease in articulatory opening from a vowel rightward (P14). This preference is partially reflected in (P15), which specifies the number of obstruents in a cluster. A preferred pattern which holds for clusters of all sizes is $n - 1$. That is, CCs, CCCs and CCCCs tend to contain one, two and three obstruents, respectively. Finally, both groups of clusters display a preference to start with a *NA strident segment (P20), i.e. with a plosive or sonorant. The remaining parameters are group-specific, and are summarized in 35.

Table 3.19 Percentage ranking of parameters: final phonotactic clusters

	R	dimension	parameter pattern	parameter
absolute				
		complexity	total identity avoidance	P3
strong	1	complexity	full compositionality	P2
default		manner	consonantal C cluster-finally	P17
↑	2	voice	voiceless C cluster finally	P25
	3	manner	*NA strident cluster-initially	P20
	4	complexity	CC size	P1
	5	place	no dorsals	P8
	6	manner	consonantal C cluster-initially	P16
	7	manner	obstruent C cluster-finally	P23
	8	place	coronal C cluster-finally	P12
	9	manner	decrease in articulatory opening	P14
	10	voice	voiced C cluster-initially	P24
		manner	sonorant C cluster-initially	P22
	11	manner	1 obstruent in CC	P15a
weak	12	manner	2 obstruents in CCC	P15b
default	13	place	anterior C cluster finally	P10

Table 3.20 Percentage ranking of parameters: final morphonotactic clusters

	R	dimension	parameter pattern	parameter
absolute				
		manner	4 obstruents in CCCCC	P15d
strong	1	complexity	total identity avoidance	P3
default	2	complexity	full compositionality	P2
		manner	consonantal C cluster-finally	P17
↑	3	voice	voiceless C cluster finally	P25
	4	place	no dorsals	P8
	5	manner	consonantal C cluster-initially	P16
	6	complexity	CC size	P1
	7	manner	obstruent C cluster-finally	P23
	8	manner	*NA strident cluster-initially	P20
	9	manner	2 obstruents in CCC	P15b
	10	place	coronal C cluster-initially	P11
	11	place	coronal C cluster-finally	P12
		manner	1 obstruent in CC	P15a
weak		manner	3 obstruents in CCCC	P15c
default		manner	decrease in articulatory opening	P14

35. Summary of favoured parameter patterns in final clusters

(35.a) shared:
CC size, full compositionality, avoidance of identical segments, maximization of the number of obstruents but not full obstruency, SSG-obeying, lack of [dorsal], start with: [+consonantal] / *NA strident, end with: [−voice] / [coronal] / [+consonantal] / [−sonorant]

(35.b) only phonotactic clusters:
start with: [+voice] / [+sonorant]
end with: [+anterior]

(35.c) only morphonotactic clusters:
start with: [coronal]

An illustration of a preferred feature specification for word-final phonotactics is given in Table 3.21. The table accounts for the parameters in (35.a), which are shared by both phonotactic and morphonotactic clusters. Since a preference for two-member sequences was identified in parameter (P1), the grid is most likely to apply to CCs.

When this specification is compared with the grid for initial clusters in Table 3.18, three major areas of differences can be observed. First, word-initial and word-final clusters end with [+voice] and [−voice] consonants, respectively. That is, voiced segments are preferred before a vowel, and voiceless segments are preferred in the absolute word-final position in a word. Second, while there is a strong preference for [+consonantal] feature in C2 in both word positions, word-finally the specification excludes [±strident] consonants. Finally, a general distribution of

Table 3.21 Preferred cluster structure for final phonotactics: 1st attempt

C-initial	C-final (C2)
[+cons]	[+cons]
*NA strident	[-voice]
	[−son]
	[coronal]

features in Tables 3.18 and 3.21 suggests that the majority of two-member clusters have an obstruent + obstruent structure word-initially and a sonorant + obstruent structure word-finally. The percentage-based analysis provide preliminary insights into the backbone structure of Polish phonotactics. In order to establish the ultimate set of parameters which play a role in static distributional patterns, a statistical analysis is required.

In Sect. 3.3.5 I propose a method of deriving the strength of parameters (P1–P26). The results for initial and final phonotactics are presented in Sects. 3.3.5.1 and 3.3.5.2, respectively. For each word position, phonotactic and morphonotactic clusters are analysed separately.

3.3.5 *Statistical Weight of Parameters*

In order to establish a ranking of statistically-relevant parameters in clustering, the *Principal Component Analysis* (henceforth PCA) was performed. The method allows to analyse the structure of the data by converting a large number of variables (N = 26 parameters) into linearly uncorrelated principal components (N = 26 components), among which only several have the greatest explanatory power. The principle behind the method is that variables with very small variances are negligible, i.e. they do not contribute to the classification of the input data. Each component (Comp) explains some portion of the observations (i.e. consonant clusters). Since PCA maximizes the variance of the first component, Comp1 explains the largest portion of the data, while each successive component accounts for the data which is not explained by the preceding component(s). That is, Comp2 explains some portion of the data not explained by Comp1, Comp3 explains some data variability which was explained neither by Comp1 nor by Comp2. Detailed PCA calculations for initial and final clusters are provided in Appendix I.

3.3.5.1 PCA Loadings in Initial Phonotactics

In PCA, a scree plot is used to visually assess which components explain the variability in the data. The plot in Fig. 3.2 displays the eigenvalues associated with Comp1–10 in decreasing order. Since the first three components show to have the greatest explanatory power in phonotactic clusters, only they will enter further computation (variances for the fourth and following components drop below 8%). Comp1 explains 20% (cumulative proportion = 0.2000984) of the variability in the data, Comp2 and Comp3 explain 14% (cumulative proportion = 0.1329446) and

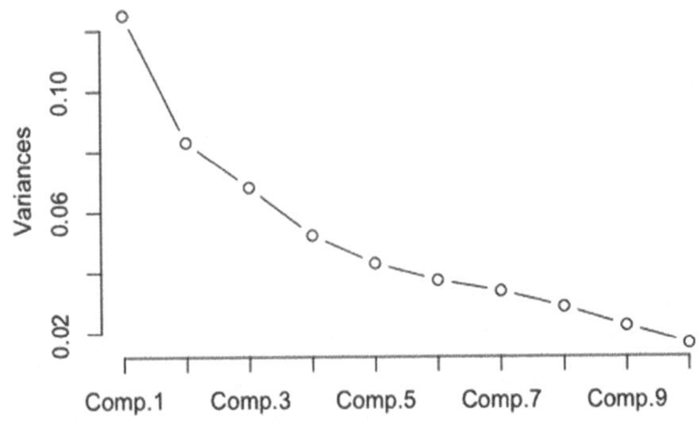

Fig. 3.2 Variances of principal components: initial phonotactic clusters

11% (cumulative proportion = 0.1089918) of the variability that is not covered by the previous components. In total, Comp1–3 generalize on of 44% (cumulative proportion = 0.4420348) of phonologically-motivated clusters under scrutiny.

Comp1–3 are used to weight 26 parameters with the help of PCA loadings. The loading values range from 0 to 1 or −1, and reflect a degree to which a variable discriminates the input observations. Thus, weight points to these parameters which best capture the variability of the data. The higher the value of a loading, the greater the weight of a parameter. In this chapter, statistical weight is interpreted as the strength of a phonotactic preference, i.e. its active role in constructing the cluster inventories, and in introducing phonological contrast. It must be noted that although finding the strongest predictors of cluster structure is our ultimate goal, statistically speaking no loading value is expected to approximate 1 or −1. Such a result would suggest that a single variable explains the structure of all clusters. Since the loading values are relatively low in Comp1 (the highest = 0.564 for P21), I follow Orzechowska (2016), and set the threshold of > 0.4 for data interpretation. The same procedure was adopted in all the datasets. Table 3.22 shows that the following parameters have the greatest weight: (P21, P25) in Comp1, (P22, P2) in Comp2, (P12) in Comp3. Loading values ('Load') turned into percentages ('%'), and rounded to the nearest whole number, indicate a degree to which a particular parameter explains data variability. A rank of a parameter for each component is indicated by 'R'.

Table 3.22 Statical rankings of parameters: initial phonotactic clusters

R	Dimension	Preference	Load	%
Comp1				
1	Manner	P21: *NA strident C cluster-finally	0.564	32
2	Voice	P25: voiced C in cluster-finally	0.449	20
Comp2				
1	Manner	P22: obstruent C in C1	0.688	47
2	Complexity	P2: full compositionality	0.554	31
Comp3				
1	Place	P12: coronal in cluster-finally	−0.818	67

The ranking of parameters encompasses parameters representing all the dimensions. The ordering (P21) > (P25), followed by (P22) > (P2), and finally (P12) makes it possible to establish the hierarchy of dimensions that the parameters represent. Comp1 reveals the parameters which are the most important for statistical discrimination, followed by Comp2 and Comp3. This ordering reads: the manner of articulation discriminates between clusters better than voice (MOA > VOI). Comp2 provides supporting parameters serving discrimination, where the manner of articulation and complexity are found. Since MOA has already been allocated to the top the hierarchy, the complexity dimension is added, resulting in: MOA > VOI > COMPLEX. Finally, the place feature expressed by (P12) in Comp3 makes it possible to extend the hierarchy to MOA > VOI > COMPLEX > POA. The hierarchy reflects the role that the dimensions play in cluster discrimination at the statistical level.

This ordering corroborates the relevance of the manner and complexity parameters in the percentage-based ranking in Table 3.16. What is more, the results suggest that the specification of the prevocalic segment in terms of *NA stridency (P21), voicing (P25) and coronality (P12) is key for cluster discrimination. Finally, discrimination is facilitated by the sonorant / obstruent distinction in C1. Based on Table 3.22, I propose a formula which summarizes a preferred featural specification which facilitates discrimination. The left-to-right ordering of features in brackets is based on their decreasing weight. Note that the formula specifies only the first and last consonant in a cluster.

36. Preferred feature specification in initial phonotactics

$$\mathbf{C1([-son]) + C{-}fin({*}NA\ strid\ [+voice][cor]) + V}$$

Let me now proceed to the presentation of the results for morphologically-motivated clusters. Figure 3.3 plots the variances for the first ten components, among which components 1, 2 and 3 account for 18, 14 and 10% of data variability (cumulative proportions = 0.1781405, 0.1417285 and 0.1035948), respectively. As can be seen in Fig. 3.3, there is a relatively steep drop between Comp1–2 and Comp2–3, and a mild difference in variance between Comp3 and Comp4. However, to make the analysis directly comparable to the group of phonotactic clusters, the first three components are selected for the interpretation of the results.

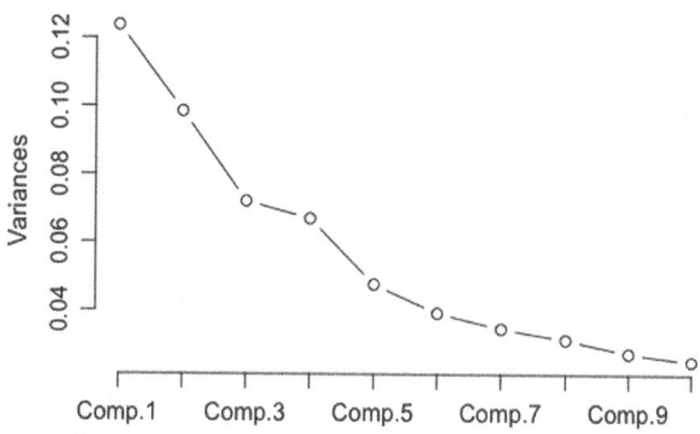

Fig. 3.3 Variances of principal components: initial morphonotactic clusters

PCA loadings for Comp1–3 explain 42% of the data pool (cumulative proportion = 0.4234638). The parameters which discriminate between morphonotactic clusters partially overlap with the parameters which were identified in initial phonotactics in Table 3.22. Both statistical rankings of weighted parameters point to the same hierarchy of dimensions: MOA > VOI > COMPLEX > POA. This ordering supports the tentative percentage-based ranking in Table 3.16.

Parameters (P17, P18, P26) are specific for morphonotactic clusters. The weight of (P26) is attributed to the presence of prefixes assimilating in voice to stem-initial consonants. Table 3.23 shows the preferred structure of morphonotactic clusters is also determined by continuancy cluster-initially and a consonantal character of the prevocalic segment. On this basis, I propose the following statistically-based featural organization of preferred morphonotactic clusters. Since the parameters do not specify cluster length, the equation represents edges in clusters of varying length, where C-fin can refer to C2, C3, and C4 in CC, CCC and CCCC, respectively. Again, the *NA strident specification characterizes plosives and sonorants.

37. Preferred feature specification in initial morphonotactics

$$\mathbf{C1}([+\mathbf{cont}]) + \mathbf{C{-}fin}(*\mathbf{NA\ strid}\ [+\mathbf{voice}][+\mathbf{cons}][\mathbf{cor}]) + \mathbf{V}$$

Generally, the statistically-based analysis validates the percentage-based rankings. Parameters with the greatest weight defined for phonotactic and morphonotactic groups apply by stronger and weaker default (see Tables 3.16 and 3.17). It must be noted that the percentages corresponding with PCA loadings elucidate possible preferences but are not ultimate. Parameters classified as weak default show to have greater statistical weight than parameters classified located at the top of the percentage-based ranking.

3.3.5.2 PCA Loadings in Final Phonotactics

An analogous analysis was performed for word-final clusters. Let me start with the presentation of the results for phonotactic clusters. As is shown in Fig. 3.4, the explanatory power of the first components is comparable to word-initial position. Components 1, 2, 3 and 4 account for 21, 14, 12 and 11% of data variability (cumulative proportions = 0.2122251, 0.1436195, 1204227, 0.1082245), respectively.

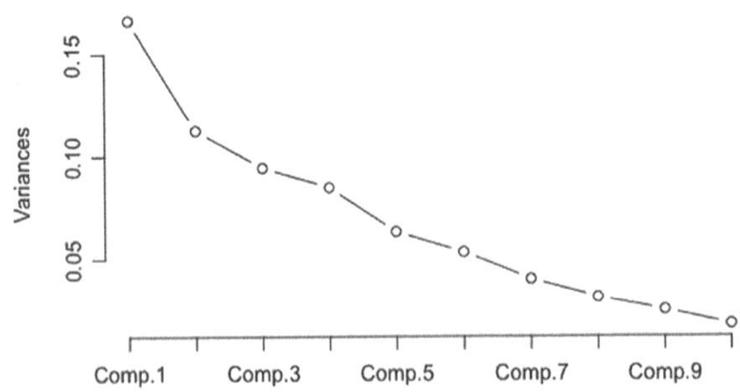

Fig. 3.4 Variances of principal components: final phonotactic clusters

Since the variance of Comp5 drops to 8%, the interpretation of the results is based on the first four components (the analysis of initial clusters also disregarded components with variances lower than 10). The parameters with the greatest statistical weight are listed in Table 3.24. They explain 58% of the data.

Similarly to word-initial position, the PCA loading values are relatively low. The cut-off point equal to >0.4 makes it possible to identify parameters which have the greatest discriminatory power. The manner features in Comp1 have the highest PCA loading, and are the strongest predictors of cluster structure, followed by the place features prevailing in Comp2–4. To recapitulate, final phonotactic clusters are structured along the following hierarchy of dimensions: MOA > POA > VOI > COMPLEX. This ordering largely corresponds with the preliminary percentage-based ranking in Table 3.19.

The results suggest that the primarily criterion which serves cluster discrimination is (P20). The post-vocalic segments are favourably represented by plosives and sonorants. The SSG profile is equally informative: a decrease in articulatory opening in (P14) suggests a falling sonority slope. The remaining parameters define the right-most consonant in a cluster. A voiceless coronal is preferred at the very end of a word. Since [dorsal] is a privative feature and cannot be expressed in binary terms, there is no formal way in which a lack of dorsal segments could be indicated. For this reason, this property is marked with an asterisk (*). On the basis of PCA loading values, I propose a formula which captures a featural specification which best discriminates between final phonotactic clusters.

38. Preferred feature specification in final phonotactics

$$\mathbf{V + C1(*NA\ strid,\ *dors) + C2(*dors\ [-voice][cor])}$$

It must be emphasized that the ranking of parameters accounts for length: (P2) surfaces as a predictor of cluster structure in Comp4. Therefore, 38 holds primarily for CCs.

As regards morphonotactic clusters, the first four components are selected for the interpretation of the results. Comp1–4 explain 54% of the data. The explanatory force of the first components is comparable to the phonotactic group. Comp1, 2, 3 and 4 explain 18, 13, 12 and 10% of the input data (cumulative proportions equal 0.1817760, 0.1338155, 0.1185892 and 0.1022289, respectively). The variances are presented in a scree plot in Fig. 3.5.

On the basis of Comp1–4, Table 3.25 lists the variables which discriminate between clusters. Parameters with PCA loading values larger than 0.4 are selected for each component.

The ranking suggests the following hierarchy of dimensions: COMPLEX > POA > MOA > VOI. This ordering differs substantially from the previous rankings in that cluster size in (P1) comes to the forefront as a discriminatory criterion. (P8) specifies the overall absence of dorsals in a cluster, while (P20) and (P16) refer to the presence of plosives and sonorant (or consonantal segments) in post-vocalic

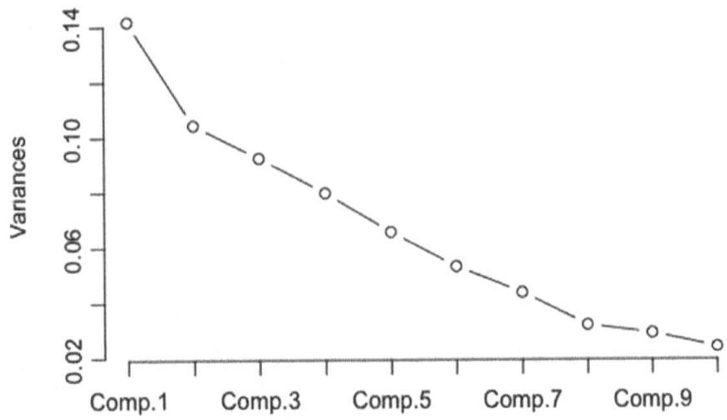

Fig. 3.5 Variances of principal components: final morphonotactic clusters

position. Finally, there are (weak) preferences for the right-most consonant to be occupied by a voiceless obstruent (P25, P23).

Based on the ranking in Table 3.25 it is possible to propose a formula which captures preferred features serving the discrimination of final morphonotactic clusters. Again, 39 is most likely to refer to two-member clusters.

39. Preferred feature specification in final morphonotactics

$$\mathbf{V + C1(*dors\ *NA\ strid\ [+cons]) + C2(*dors\ [-voice][-son])}$$

To sum up, the rankings in Tables 3.22 and 3.23 describe 40–44% of the initial data, and Tables 3.24 and 3.25 generalize on 54–58% of the final data. The rankings offer new insights into the structure of Polish (mor)phonotactics, which are summarized in several points.

(a) Parameters (P1–P26), and features they represent, are exploited in phonotactics to different degrees.
(b) Phonological features differ in statistical weight depending on word position. For instance, in initial phonotactics, parameters defining the prevocalic (or

Table 3.23 Statical rankings of parameters: initial morphonotactic clusters

R	Dimension	Preference	Load	%
Comp1				
1	Manner	P21: *NA strident C cluster-finally	−0.516	27
2	Voice	P26: total voice agreement	0.436	19
3	Voice	P25: voiced C cluster-finally	−0.423	18
4	Manner	P17: consonantal C cluster-finally	0.414	17
Comp2				
1	Complexity	P2: full compositionality	0.402	16
2	Manner	P18: continuant C cluster-initially	0.740	55
Comp3				
1	Place	P12: coronal C cluster-finally	−0.759	58

Table 3.24 Statical rankings of parameters: final phonotactic clusters

R	Dimension	Preference	Load	%
Comp1				
1	Manner	P20: *NA strident C cluster-initially	0.509	26
2	Manner	P14: decrease in articulatory opening	0.472	22
Comp2				
1	Place	P8: no dorsal C	−0.487	24
2	Voice	P25: voiceless C cluster-finally	0.483	23
3	Place	P12: coronal C cluster-finally	−0.452	20
Comp3				
1	Place	P12: coronal C cluster-finally	−0.557	31
2	Voice	P25: voiceless C cluster-finally	−0.495	25
Comp4				
1	Place	P8: no dorsal C	−0.538	29
2	Complexity	P1: CC size	−0.454	21

Table 3.25 Statical rankings of parameters: final morphonotactic clusters

R	Dimension	Preference	Load	%
Comp1				
1	Complexity	P1: CC size	−0.471	22
Comp2				
1	Place	P8: no dorsal C	−0.498	25
Comp3				
1	Manner	P20: *NA strident cluster-initially	0.470	22
2	Place	P8: no dorsal C	−0.464	22
3	Manner	P16: consonantal C cluster-initially	−0.407	17
Comp4				
1	Complexity	P1: CC size	−0.480	23
2	Voice	P25: voiceless C cluster-finally	−0.470	22
3	Manner	P23: obstruent C cluster-finally	−0.418	17

C-fin) consonant are key for cluster structure: they reveal the importance of the transition from the prevocalic position towards a vowel. In final phonotactics, (P2) referring to size is the most relevant defining property of cluster structure.

(c) Phonological features differ in statistical weight depending on morphological complexity. In initial and final phonotactics, only morphologically-motivated clusters contain a [+consonantal] segment in the immediate proximity to the vowel (i.e. C-fin in initials and C1 in finals).

These observations have some consequences for phonological theory, and for markedness principles. They pave the way for possible extensions of well-formedness conditions discussed in Chap. 2. At least one cannot discredit the proposal that criteria implemented in phonotactic principles can contribute to cluster structure to various degrees. The following section discusses the role of the rankings and statistical weight in relation to phonological theory.

3.3.6 *Inducing Feature Weight*

In this section, I explore the underlying structure of consonant clusters. The analysis offers new insights into the Polish feature system and its role in phonotactics. Two directions in the study of phonotactics involving approaches which are *based on well-formedness conditions*, and approaches *not based on well-formedness conditions* (Chap. 2, Sects. 2.4 and 2.5) provide a factual, conceptual and methodological frame for the model. The analysis shows that some parameters are mandatory for the existence of clusters, while other parameters have the status of graded preferences. Given that combinations of consonants are universally marked, obviously there must exist a force which motivates their preservation at least at the lexical level discussed in this chapter. The method proposed afore serves to discover such force. The synopsis of the results presented in Sects. 3.3.6.1 and 3.3.6.2 accounts for the relevance of phonological features.

3.3.6.1 Feature Weight in Initial Phonotactics

Statistically active features in Polish phonotactics are derived from the rankings in Tables 3.22, 3.23, 3.24 and 3.25. Separate specifications capture the phonological properties that characterize initials and finals. As before, slots C1 and C-fin denote the first (absolute word initial) and the last (prevocalic) segment in a sequence. Therefore, 'x' refers to C2 in a three-member cluster or C2C3 in a four-member cluster. The ordering of features in a specification reflects their PCA loading values, i.e. the top-most features have the greatest weight as their explanatory potential is the greatest.

The specification in 40 is based on features shared by initial phonotactic and morphonotactic clusters revealing the very basic structure of preferred types occurring at the left word edge. As can be seen, *NA strident voicing and coronality have the greatest discriminatory power, and are therefore assigned the greatest weight word-initially.

40. Feature weight specification for initial phonotactics

C1	x	C-final
		*NA strident
		[+voice]
		[coronal]

This specification goes in line with Clements' (2001, 2009) universal *Accessibility Hierarchy* (see 31), which lists features used cross-linguistically in the formation of consonant systems. The top of the hierarchy is occupied by coronality, followed by [consonant], [sonorant], and further by [labial] > [dorsal] > [strident] > [nasal] > [posterior] > [lateral]. Voicing is found at the very bottom of the hierarchy, suggesting that the laryngeal features are exploited the least in the languages of the world in the construction of phoneme inventories. That is, they are the least favoured features serving contrast.

It must be emphasized that 40 diverges from Clements' work in that the specification does not generalize from universal consonant inventories, but it defines preferred consonant combinations for one word position in a language. However, a common point of reference can be found. Similarly to Clements, 40 embraces a ranking of feature preferability, or degrees of preferability. This default phonological make-up of Polish clusters points to the exploitation of a limited number of features in phonotactics.

The importance of selected features has been generally agreed upon among phonologists. The markedness relations in Tables 3.1 and 3.2 are not easily violated across the languages of the world. This point is raised by Lombardi (2001) who observes that the place constraints are universal, i.e. fixed in the Universal Grammar, and proposes a ranking of place constraints. The idea that the coronal place of articulation is unmarked cross-linguistically is uncontroversial, and goes back to Hall (1997) and Paradis and Prunet (1991). Also de Lacy (2002) demonstrates that place features are always neutralized to coronal or glottal. Compare the major place hierarchies in 41.

41. Constraints on place of articulation

(41.a) dorsal > labial > coronal > glottal (de Lacy 2002: 173)
(41.b) dorsal, labial > coronal > glottal (Lombardi 2001: 29)

The rankings point to the relevance of coronal articulation. With the rankings proposed in this chapter, it is possible to specify a favoured position for coronal consonants in cluster. The overall picture that emerges from Tables 3.22 and 3.23 is that pre-vocalic (left edge) position shows to be crucial in Polish word-initial clusters. The C-fin slot constitutes the transition from the left-most segment towards a vowel. The position is favourably occupied by all *NA strident (i.e. plosives and sonorants), voiced and coronal segments. In line with the sonority scales which distinguish between less sonorous voiceless consonants and more sonorous voiced ones, the preferences for [+voice] prevocalically points to a smooth release of a voiced consonant into a voiced vowel. Additionally, coronal segments are unmarked in relation to other places of articulation. Although no shared preferences were identified for C1, in the statistical rankings [+consonantal] was a defining property in phonotactic clusters, and [+continuant] in morphonotactic clusters.

The question that arises at this point is how the weight specification is related to cluster well-formedness. The statistical rankings demonstrate that Polish phonotactics is governed mainly by manner features, among which *NA strident,

Table 3.26 Initial phonotactic CCs which adhere to Table 3.22, where C1 = [−sonorant], C2 = [+voice], [coronal] plosive / sonorant

All possible	Model-generated	Attested
29 × 29 = 841	21 × 6 = 126	/dɲ, pɲ, sn, vd, vj, vl, vn, vɲ, vr, zd, zj, zl, zn, zɲ, zr/ = 15

[−sonorant], [+consonantal], [+continuant] play the greatest role. The profile of clusters does not unambiguously point to the rising sonority slope. These observations shed light on the phonotactic inventory of Polish, which can be viewed as a well-motivated phenomenon following a set of new preferences.

The features in the specification are rather general. However, when combined, they severely delimit the full phonotactic potential of Polish. For instance, *NA strident in combination with [+voice] specify 14 out of 29 cluster-forming consonants in Polish (cf. Jassem 2003).[2] The preference for [+coronal] reduces this set to six segments preferred in prevocalic position only, i.e. /j n ɲ l r d/.

How does this observation relate to the cluster inventory? If we set the goal of compiling a list of preferred two-member clusters of the preferred structure *NA strident plus [+voice] plus [coronal], this model generates 174 legitimate CCs (= 29 C cluster-initially × 6 C preferred cluster-finally) out of the total of 841 (29 C × 29 C) logically possible CCs. Interestingly, 168 phonotactic CC and 90 morphonotactic CC combinations respecting this structure are attested word-initially.

This set of clusters can be further narrowed down by applying the parameters found in the PCA-driven rankings. That is, the prevocalic consonant is preferably represented by either of six consonants /j n ɲ l r d/. What is more, (P22) ensures the presence of an obstruent in C1, i.e. either of 21 consonants /f v s z ʃ ʒ ɕ ʑ x p b t d k g ʦ ʣ ʧ ʤ ʨ ʥ/. Overall, the number of preferred two-member sequences is narrowed down to 126 (= 21 C preferred in C1 × 6 C preferred in C-fin). In the dataset, only 17 CC clusters with this structure are attested. That is, the full potential of constructing optimal clusters is exploited successfully (17 attested CCs vs. 126 possible CCs). As can be observed in Table 3.26, the method provides tools which extract preferred combinations of segments from a large set.

The analysis does not reveal any absolute parameters. Initial phonotactics features no obligatory requirements which would define all clusters with no exception. This observation is particularly striking given that some parameters used in the model are very general, such as the classification into broad place and manner features. The number and character of parameters can be further explored. Therefore, at present, I refrain from making any generalizations on the most elementary structure of clusters and keep the conclusions simple: voice and coronality have the greatest weight in initial phonotactics, and contribute substantially to cluster structure.

[2]Jassem's (2003) phonemic inventory contains 31 consonants. However, palatal plosives /c ɟ/ are excluded from the list of segments forming clusters, as they are represented by a plosive + glide sequence /kj gj/.

3.3.6.2 Feature Weight in Final Phonotactics

Let me now proceed to the presentation of the feature weight specification for right edge phonotactics. 42 is based on the features shared by final phonotactic and morphonotactic clusters. The core structure of final preferred clusters relies on size, voice cluster-finally, presence of plosives and sonorants (*NA strident) in post-vocalic position, and a lack of dorsals (*dorsal). Note that the (*) refers to segments to which features [±strident] and [dorsal] cannot be allocated. In general, [−voice] has the greatest weight in final phonotactics. The presence of a voiceless segment in word-absolute position is attributed to the phonological rule of obstruent devoicing.

42. Feature weight specification for final phonotactics

C1	x	C2
*NA strident		[−voice]
*dorsal		*dorsal

What is more, the specification is most likely to hold for two-member clusters. Parameter (P2) expresses a preference for two adjacent consonants, and shows to be a statistically relevant measure in clusters discrimination. The preference for shorter clusters word-finally can be explained in prosodic and morphological terms. First, word-final position is the least salient and is therefore more susceptible to change such as alternation, assimilation and reduction. Second, final morphonotactic clusters are more marked with respect to initial congeners as the first involve covert morphological markers (e.g. truncation). Sense 3 of Haspelmath's (2006) classification refers specifically to this type of markedness, whereby covert morphological expressions are more marked. Therefore, it is argued that the degree of complexity in final morphonotactic clusters must be neutralized . A possible way to minimize complexity is to ensure that a cluster does not violate universals and universal principles. CCs offend the sonority-obeying CV structure only minimally.

3.3.7 *Parameters as Exponents of Sonority*

In the previous sections, emphasis was placed on the features which are relevant for the statistical modelling of Polish phonotactics. The proposed preferences provide a more detailed picture of cluster structure than generalizing principles discussed in Chap. 2. It is suggested that phonotactic markedness does not need to relate only to well-formedness conditions such as sonority but stem from a set of criteria which might be associated with the principle. This point was made in earlier contributions by Orzechowska and Wiese (2011, 2015) and Orzechowska (2016, 2018), who suggest that the SSG profile does not suffice in accounting for the structure of clusters in phonotactically elaborate systems. For example, Orzechowska and Wiese (2011) reconstructed the sonority hierarchy into nine constituent scales and provided a more insightful analysis of German phonotactics than a manner-based SSG analysis. The inventory of German word-initial clusters was shown to be structured on the basis of several preferences, the strongest of which require: two-member sequences, a coronal C in cluster onset, absence of stop + stop sequences, rising sonority, and a voiceless and voiced segments in cluster onset and offset, respectively. The results of this study were confirmed in a comparative study by Orzechowska and Wiese (2015), who demonstrated that German initial clusters favour parameters that conspire to create a sonority-obeying profile. In contrast, Polish has been suggested to rely on place and voice parameters such as the presence of one or more coronals, the presence of a coronal segment cluster-finally and voicing agreement. In other words, Polish favours clusters that have at least one or two dental, alveolar, alveolo-palatal or palatal consonants, and which are voiced throughout.

That sonority in its generalized form is not necessarily the most adequate principle to account for phonotactic patterns was also demonstrated in English. For instance, in his study on the acquisition of initial sC clusters, Yavaş (2013) notes that reduction is not related to sonority as such, but to continuancy. In particular, in two-member clusters children maintain C2 in /s/ + [−continuant] targets, and retain C1 in /s/ + [+continuant] targets. The role of sonority was also investigated in neurolinguistic experiments involving electroencephalography by means of which electrophysiological responses (event-related potentials, ERPs) were recorded. In two parallel experiments on Polish (Wiese et al. 2017) and German (Ulbrich et al. 2016), speakers were tested on the learnability of nonce words containing SSG-obeying and SSG-violating final CCs (for a detailed description see Chap. 4). Final existent clusters were present in both languages (e.g. well-formed /sp/ vs. ill-formed /ps/), while non-existent clusters were potential but attested neither in Polish nor in German (e.g. well-formed /ʧk/ vs. ill-formed /kʧ/). The results obtained from the ERP signal demonstrated the main effect for sonority only in German participants, and lowered sensitivity to sonority violations in Polish participants. That is, the learning process at the neural-physiological level is strongly affected by sonority only in a phonotactically simpler language.

Although the percentage-based and PCA-based rankings are only lists of preferences having their source in lexical statistics, they demonstrate the elementary structure of the lexicon. High ranked preferences do not unambiguously point to a sonority-based profile of clusters. Approaches which are based on well-formedness conditions propose generalizing statements which overshadow the role of specific features in phonotactics. As it turns out, weighted feature specifications are more detailed: they reveal properties (or substructure) of sonority, which play a role in static distribution patterns in a language. That is, parameters can conspire to form a sonority-based profile in terms of, for instance, voicing or obstruency. The question is: Which parameters describe sonority most adequately in Polish, and how do they contribute to cluster markedness? Parameter (P14) is associated with the SSG as it describes the articulatory opening from the word-edge segment towards a vowel.

For instance, in initial phonotactic clusters, an *increase* in aperture holds for 50% of clusters (see Table 2.6). If a half of initial clusters disobey the principle by displaying a fall in sonority (i.e. *decrease*), no difference in sonority (i.e. *plateau*), or a combination of gestures (i.e. *mixed*), how relevant are other parameters which contribute strictly to (P14)?

The aforementioned observations go in line with the proposal that sonority per se does not provide the most accurate account of cluster patterning. The preferred parameters identified for initial and final clusters (i.e. stridency, voice) are not in conflict with the SSG but are more detailed than the requirement of the SSG. The established preferences for a voiced consonant adjacent to a vowel can be directly derived from the SSG. Also, the specification {*NA strident, voiced} prevocalically can be characteristic of consonantal sonorants, as predicted by the SSG. However, preferences related to the place of articulation (i.e. coronality, dorsality) provide new insights into the structure of clusters, which sonority requirements neither assume nor predict.

What is more, another difference between the SSG and the proposed approach is that the SSG offers conditional statements on what is permitted. For example, the sonority principle makes the following prediction on initial clusters: if C2 is filled by a glide, C1 can be filled by a nasal as in /mj/ in *miód* ‘honey’. The reverse ordering of segments is rejected by the principle. The analysis proposed in this chapter does not relate C1 to C2 or vice versa. Rather, it shows the features which can occupy specific positions in cluster types that Polish phonotactics can produce.

The question whether sonority-based analyses would benefit more from decomposing the sonority hierarchy into constituent criteria was tentatively tested from a cross-linguistic perspective in Orzechowska (2018). The author analysed initial clusters in Slavic and Germanic languages in terms of eight parameters: (P1) cluster length, (P2) the number of obstruents, (P3, P4) the S/O distinction cluster-initially and cluster-finally, (P5) manner of articulation distances, (P6, P7) voicing at cluster edges and (P8) voice agreement. The criteria are treated as exponents of sonority as they refer to general distinctions between the manner of articulation classes and voicing captured by various sonority hierarchies. Orzechowska (2018) shows that sonority is manifested by different criteria in different languages. Sonority in English is based on the number of obstruents, where obstruent maximization (but not full obstruency) is favoured. Sonority in German is best expressed in terms of cluster size (i.e. CCs). In Slavic languages, sonority is best manifested by means of the voicing profile.

The preferences identified in the previous section get further support from statistical and computational models. Below, I provide a brief overview of other statistical methods which show that Polish phonotactics is well-structured. The classification of clusters along the proposed set of parameters can be illustrated with the help of heatmaps and random forests.

3.4 Statistical Methods of Representing Phonotactics

3.4.1 Heatmaps

Complex heatmaps and dendrograms constitutes another statistical approach to illustrating the inherent structure of consonant clusters. They provide graphical representations of associations between the variables, and have the potential of revealing the structure of the data, which otherwise would be too cumbersome to present in the form of a regular graph. Colours in heatmaps communicate the relationship between individual data points. The darker the colour, the stronger the interaction of the parameter patterns.

Consonant clusters, together with percentage scores for parameters (P1–P26), were entered into the *R* software (R Development Core Team 2018, version 1.1.456) as variables. I used the *gplots* package (Warnes et al. 2016, version 3.0.1). The heatmap.2 function offers a number of extensions to the standard R heatmap, such as the inclusion of dendrograms. The colour histogram reflects the values in the matrix, and how they correspond to the colours in the heatmap. Here, values range from −1 (the red range) to 1 (the violet range). The dendrograms are generated by means of the Cluster Analysis, and illustrate the internal structure of consonant clusters. In the description below, two types of clusters are distinguished. To avoid confusion, the term "statistical cluster" is used to describe groups of clusters generated by the heatmap, while "consonant clusters" refer to target word-initial and word-final clusters in the datasets.

Figure 3.6 shows the intrinsic organization of initial clusters. Generally, as it turns out there is a lot of structure in the data. The vertical and horizontal axes represent the same data points, resulting in the highest correlation (equal to 1.0) for the same parameters (violet points in the line that slants from the bottom left corner towards the top right corner). Each colour section (square or rectangle) communicates a data subset characterized by a specific feature or a set of features. The structure of the phonotactic and morphonotactic cluster sets is comparable. Yet, some differences are noticeable, for instance, in the left bottom-most squares which contain more feature-based subclasses in the phonotactic group compared to the morphonotactic group.

Figure 3.7 presents the analysis of clusters in word-final position. As can be observed, phonotactic and morphonotactic clusters have a similar structure. The colouring in the panels in Fig. 3.7 is brighter than in initial clusters, which suggests that final clusters are defined by parameters with lower values, and display fewer highly correlated parameters. Generally, the visualizations lend support to the observation that Polish phonotactics, disregarding word position and morphological composition, is well-motivated. Note that coloured subsections are not scattered randomly in the panels but form a structure. Also, dendrograms presented at the top and left side of each heatmap show the internal organization of phonotactics. Each cluster set is categorized into several broad classes determined by sets of parameters.

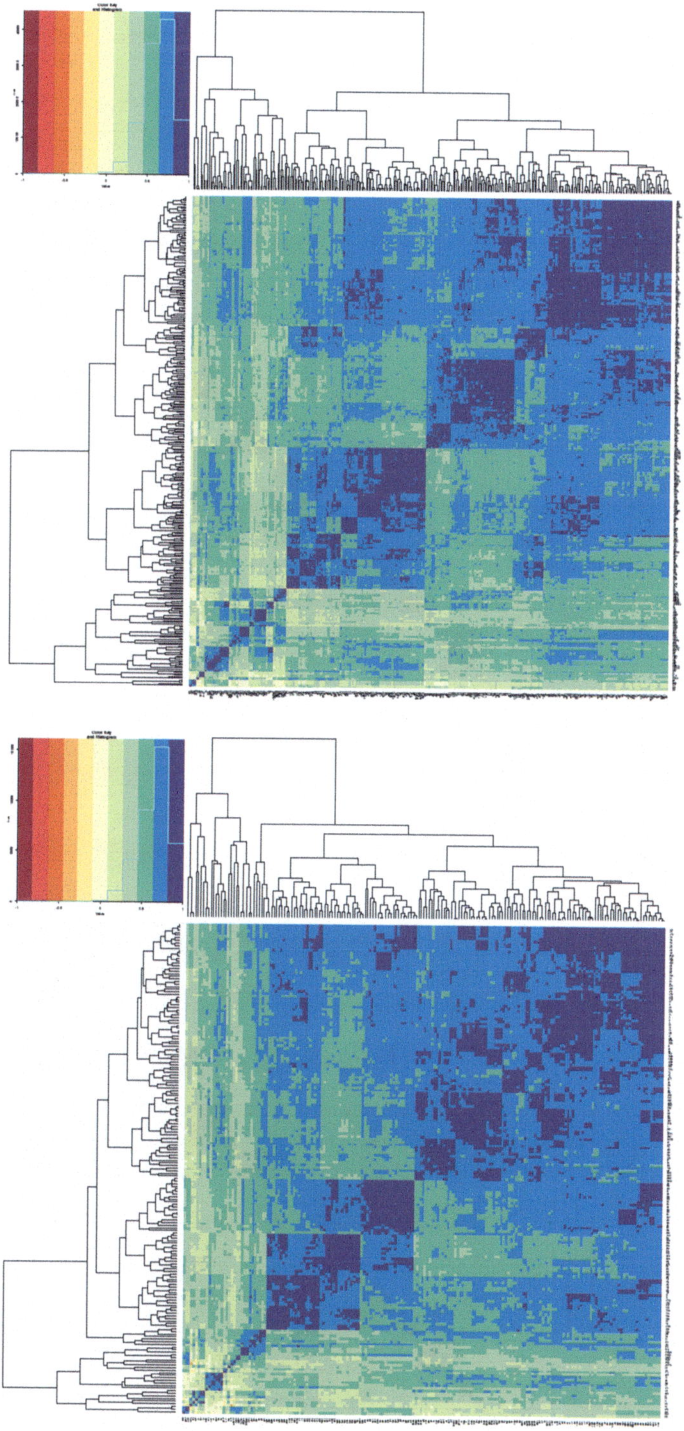

Fig. 3.6 Heatmaps for Polish initial clusters. The top panel shows phonologically-motivated clusters, while the top panel shows morphologically-motivated clusters. Darker shades (violet) indicate higher values

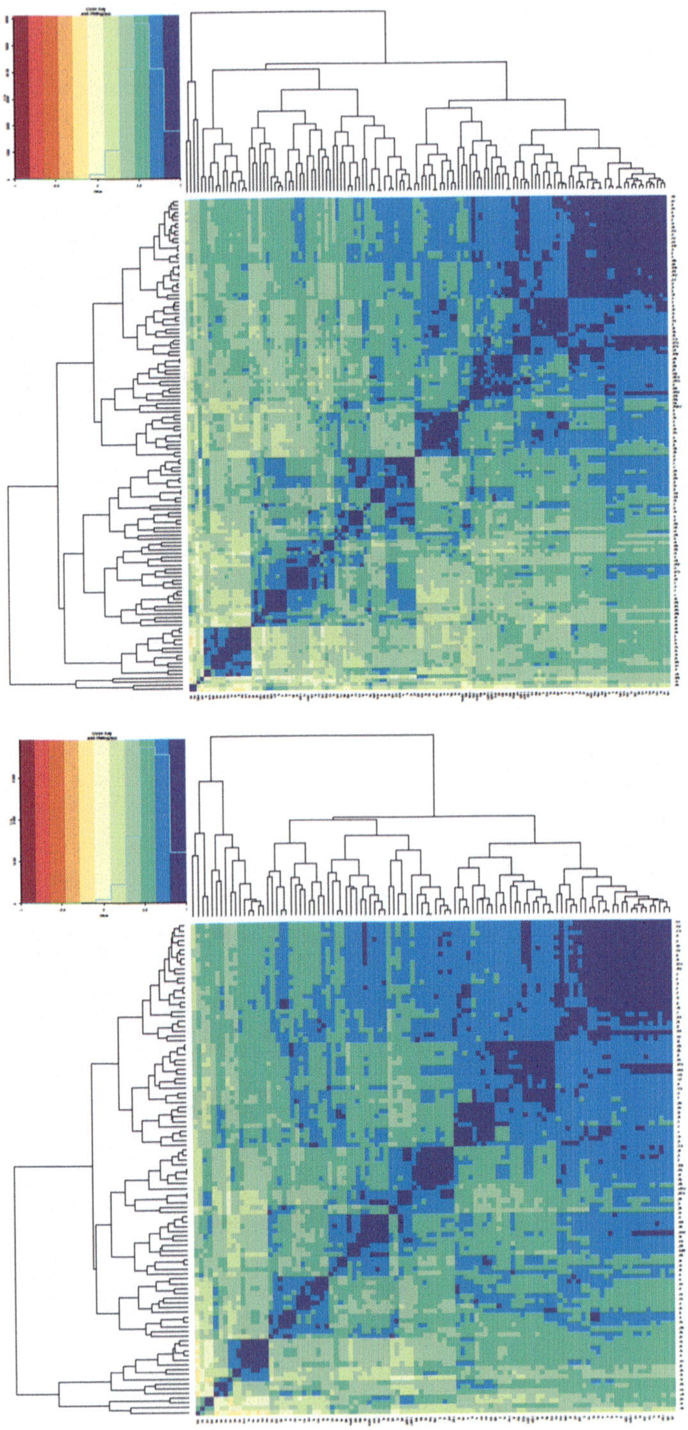

Fig. 3.7 Heatmaps for Polish final clusters. The top panel shows phonologically-motivated clusters, while the top panel shows morphologically-motivated clusters. Darker shades (violet) indicate higher values

3.4.2 Random Forests

Another statistical method used for data classification constitute random forests, which implement forests of conditional inference trees. This tree-based classification consists in the recursive partitioning of the data by means of performing a binary split on the dependent variable. The structure of a tree starts with a root node, branches, and ends in terminal nodes. The procedure of recursive partitioning involved in building a tree is the following. Given a dataset with an x number of variables, the variable which best splits the data (x′) is selected. This variable forms a root node of the tree and divides the data into two branches. The procedure is recursively repeated on the subsets of the data at each node until all the observations have been classified. Note that at each node, a single variable is selected. Such a tree specifies the output variables which achieve the best split (for a detailed description see Hothorn et al. 2006, 2018; Sardá-Espinosa et al. 2017; Strobl et al. 2007, 2008). That is, with each sub-tree created, the pool of variables is narrowed down until a single prediction on the structure of the dataset can be done. The variables found at the very top of the tree lead to the best split.

Random forests are considered to be an appropriate method for dealing with the present data for several reasons. The method runs efficiently on large number of observations (i.e. cluster types) and input variables (i.e. 26 parameters). What is more, random forests provide estimates of the variables which are key for the classification, and the relation between such variables. In the present case, random forests lead to the unsupervised clustering of consonant clusters and the identification of parameters which are of prime importance in distinguishing between the input cluster inventories (initial vs. final, phonotactic vs. morphonotactic). Below, two types of random forests are presented.

Several random forest analyses were performed. I used the R *party* package (Hothorn et al. 2018; version 1.3-1) which serves recursive partitioning of the data. The results of the analysis are presented in Figs. 3.8 and 3.9.

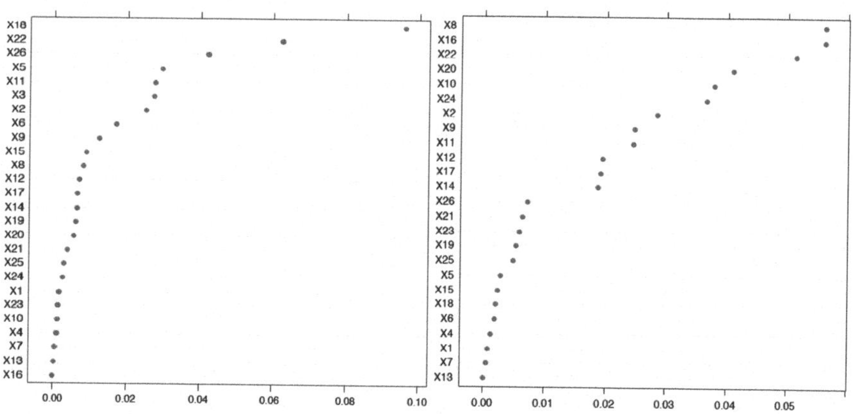

Fig. 3.8 Variable importance in initial and final clusters depending on the morphological structure. The left panel shows the classification for initial phonotactic versus initial morphonotactic clusters in terms of 26 parameters. The right panel shows the classification for final phonotactic versus final morphonotactic clusters

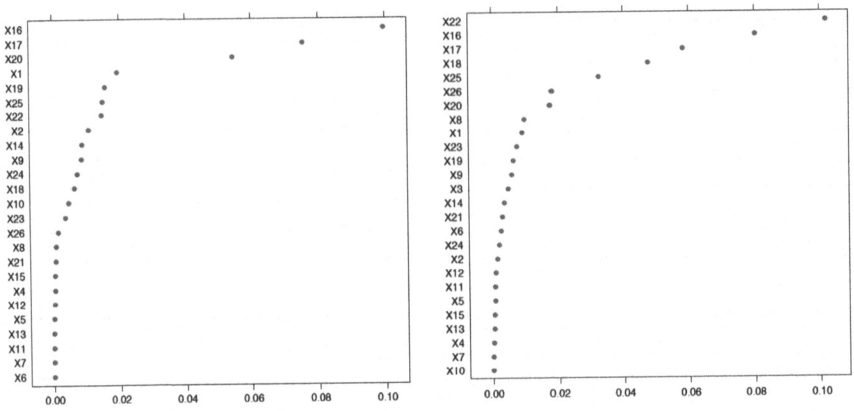

Fig. 3.9 Variable importance in phonotactic and morphonotactic clusters depending on the word position. The left panel shows the classification for initial phonotactic versus final phonotactic clusters. The right panel shows the classification for initial morphonotactic versus final morphonotactic clusters

In Fig. 3.8, the left panel presents the classification of initial phonotactic and morphonotactic clusters. The vertical axis lists parameters (P1–P26). As can be observed, the best split is achieved by (P18), which refers to continuance. The presence of a continuant C cluster-initially (P18) provides the best split of the data, and is a strong indicator of the presence of a morphological boundary. Continuance provides the most important classification benchmark for more than 95% of clusters. The remaining parameters are weaker predictors of cluster motivation. For instance, the presence of an obstruent in C1 (P22) and voicing agreement (P26) discriminate between the datasets in 60 and 40%, respectively. The preferences for [−sonorant] in C1 and total voice agreement define the majority of both cluster groups.

The results for word-final clusters are presented in the right panel in Fig. 3.8. The computation was performed on 25 parameters. (P3) was excluded from the set of variables. Total identity avoidance characterizes all final phonologically-motivated sequences, and therefore it provides the best split of the data. Among the remaining 25 parameters, the major split is obtained at a lower level than in initial clusters (50%). The distinction between phonotactic and morphonotactic clusters word-finally can be made on the basis of parameters (P8) and (P16), which correspond to the absence of dorsal segments in a cluster, and the presence of consonantal segments in C1.

Random forests are also generated to distinguish between word positions. Figure 3.9 presents the importance of variables for the discrimination of phonotactic initial versus phonotactic final clusters (left panel), and morphonotactic initial versus morphonotactic final clusters (right panel). Again, for reasons mentioned above, the first analysis was run on 25 variables. (P3) was excluded as it distinguishes final phonologically-motivated clusters from the remaining groups.

Table 3.27 Importance of parameters in the discrimination of cluster inventories

Input inventory →	Discriminatory parameter →	Inventory 2
Initial phonotactic	[+continuant] in C1	Initial morphonotactic
	Total identity avoidance	Final phonotactic
Final morphonotactic	Total identity avoidance	Final phonotactic
	[−sonorant] in C1	Initial morphonotactic
Final phonotactic	[+consonantal] in C1	Initial phonotactic

Based on Fig. 3.9, two observations can be made. Parameter (P16) provides the best split among phonotactic clusters. The presence of a consonantal C cluster-initially makes it possible to distinguish between word-initial and word-final sequences. Second, (P22), which corresponds to the presence of an obstruent cluster-initially, is the most important variable distinguishing between initial and final clusters in the morphonotactic group. Both random forests achieve splits at a high level.

The results of the analyses have the predictive power. Parameters which lead to the first binary split indicate the assignment to a group. This means that the presence of a specific parameter pattern decides on the classification of a cluster. The summary of the results is presented in Table 3.27.

The arrow indicates the direction of the classification if a discriminatory parameter pattern is identified in a cluster. For instance, word-initial sequences in which the first segment in a continuant are most likely to be morphologically-motivated, while morphonotactic sequences which start with an obstruent are most likely to be word-initial. The importance of features [±continuant], [±sonorant] and [±consonantal] in the classification of clusters is corroborated in feature-based rankings of cluster types.

3.5 Cluster Rankings

On the basis of the scores obtained for parameters (P1–P26), it is possible to rank consonant clusters. A rank is established by averaging over all percentage scores. Note that all parameters contribute to cluster structure to the same degree. The lowest contribution is expressed by values close to 0, while the greatest contribution approximates 1. For each cluster, individual percentage points express the degree to which a particular parameter is followed, while the sum of scores ($\sum_{\mathrm{P1-P26}}$) expresses the degree to which a full set of preferences is followed.

Tables below present the highest-scoring and lowest-scoring clusters, which should be viewed the most preferred ten (here referred to as best) and the least preferred ten (worst) clusters in terms of 26 parameters. Each table lists percentage scores obtained for each parameter, and the sum ($\sum$). Parameter patterns marked in bold type are shared by 10 best and 10 worst clusters. Tables 3.28 and 3.29 present the best initial phonotactic and morphonotactic sequences, respectively. The highest scoring clusters share a number of parameter patterns, in contrast to the lowest-scoring clusters.

Table 3.28 Highest-scoring and lowest-scoring initial phonotactic clusters

Best		1	2	3	4	5	6	7	8	9	10	11	12	13
1	zr	0.57	**0.89**	**0.99**	0.17	0.32	0.43	0.42	**0.65**	0.47	0.45	0.55	**0.74**	0.34
2	ʒl	0.57	**0.89**	**0.99**	0.17	0.28	0.43	0.42	**0.65**	0.47	0.45	0.55	**0.74**	0.34
3	dr	0.57	**0.89**	**0.99**	0.17	0.32	0.43	0.42	**0.65**	0.47	0.45	0.55	**0.74**	0.11
4	br	0.57	**0.89**	**0.99**	0.26	0.32	0.53	0.45	**0.65**	0.44	0.45	0.27	**0.74**	0.11
5	bl	0.57	**0.89**	**0.99**	0.23	0.32	0.53	0.45	**0.65**	0.44	0.45	0.27	**0.74**	0.11
6	dɲ	0.57	**0.89**	**0.99**	0.23	0.32	0.43	0.42	**0.65**	0.47	0.35	0.55	**0.74**	0.23
7	zbr	0.38	**0.89**	**0.99**	0.26	0.33	0.53	0.42	**0.65**	0.47	0.45	0.55	**0.74**	0.23
8	ʒr	0.57	**0.89**	**0.99**	0.07	0.07	0.43	0.42	**0.65**	0.47	0.45	0.55	**0.74**	0.34
9	ʑl	0.57	**0.89**	**0.99**	0.23	0.28	0.43	0.42	**0.65**	0.09	0.45	0.55	**0.74**	0.34
10	sr	0.57	**0.89**	**0.99**	0.17	0.32	0.43	0.42	**0.65**	0.47	0.45	0.55	**0.74**	0.34
Worst		1	2	3	4	5	6	7	8	9	10	11	12	13
1	mkɲ	0.38	0.11	0.99	0.18	0.33	0.53	0.45	0.35	0.44	0.35	0.27	0.74	0.23
2	mkn	0.38	0.11	0.99	0.06	0.33	0.53	0.45	0.35	0.44	0.45	0.27	0.74	0.23
3	xʃtɕ	0.38	0.11	0.99	0.23	0.33	0.43	0.42	0.35	0.44	0.35	0.18	0.74	0.2
4	ʧʧ	0.57	0.89	0.01	0.07	0.07	0.43	0.42	0.65	0.47	0.45	0.55	0.74	0.08
5	skrf	0.05	0.11	0.99	0.26	0.33	0.53	0.42	0.35	0.47	0.2	0.55	0.22	0.23
6	xf	0.57	0.89	0.99	0.06	0.28	0.53	0.06	0.35	0.44	0.2	0.18	0.22	0.08
7	mdw	0.38	0.11	0.99	0.26	0.33	0.04	0.45	0.65	0.44	0.35	0.27	0.22	0.11
8	wg	0.57	0.89	0.99	0.26	0.32	0.53	0.06	0.35	0.09	0.2	0.27	0.04	0.04
9	mgw	0.38	0.11	0.99	0.06	0.33	0.04	0.06	0.35	0.44	0.35	0.27	0.22	0.11
10	wk	0.57	0.89	0.99	0.26	0.32	0.53	0.06	0.35	0.09	0.2	0.27	0.04	0.04

(continued)

Table 3.28 (continued)

14	15	16	17	18	19	20	21	22	23	24	25	26	∑
0.51	0.51	**0.99**	**0.77**	0.46	0.6	0.38	**0.71**	**0.88**	**0.57**	0.45	**0.75**	0.64	**15.21**
0.51	0.51	**0.99**	**0.77**	0.46	0.6	0.38	**0.71**	**0.88**	**0.57**	0.45	**0.75**	0.64	**15.17**
0.51	0.51	**0.99**	**0.77**	0.45	0.6	0.49	**0.71**	**0.88**	**0.57**	0.45	**0.75**	0.64	**15.08**
0.51	0.51	**0.99**	**0.77**	0.45	0.6	0.49	**0.71**	**0.88**	**0.57**	0.45	**0.75**	0.64	**14.99**
0.51	0.51	**0.99**	**0.77**	0.45	0.6	0.49	**0.71**	**0.88**	**0.57**	0.45	**0.75**	0.64	**14.96**
0.51	0.51	**0.99**	**0.77**	0.45	0.4	0.49	**0.71**	**0.88**	**0.57**	0.45	**0.75**	0.64	**14.96**
0.26	0.55	**0.99**	**0.77**	0.46	0.6	0.38	**0.71**	**0.88**	**0.57**	0.45	**0.75**	0.64	**14.9**
0.51	0.51	**0.99**	**0.77**	0.46	0.6	0.38	**0.71**	**0.88**	**0.57**	0.45	**0.75**	0.64	**14.86**
0.51	0.51	**0.99**	**0.77**	0.46	0.6	0.38	**0.71**	**0.88**	**0.57**	0.45	**0.75**	0.64	**14.85**
0.51	0.51	**0.99**	**0.77**	0.46	0.6	0.38	**0.71**	**0.88**	**0.57**	0.55	**0.75**	0.17	**14.84**
14	15	16	17	18	19	20	21	22	23	24	25	26	∑
0.26	0.23	0.99	0.77	0.45	0.4	0.49	0.71	0.12	0.57	0.45	0.75	0.17	**11.71**
0.26	0.23	0.99	0.77	0.45	0.4	0.49	0.71	0.12	0.57	0.45	0.75	0.17	**11.69**
0.51	0.22	0.99	0.77	0.46	0.4	0.13	0.2	0.88	0.43	0.55	0.25	0.64	**11.58**
0.08	0.45	0.99	0.77	0.09	0.4	0.38	0.2	0.88	0.43	0.55	0.25	0.64	**11.51**
0.26	0.67	0.99	0.77	0.46	0.6	0.38	0.09	0.88	0.43	0.55	0.25	0.19	**11.23**
0.08	0.45	0.99	0.77	0.46	0.6	0.13	0.09	0.88	0.43	0.55	0.25	0.64	**11.17**
0.26	0.23	0.99	0.23	0.45	0.6	0.49	0.71	0.12	0.57	0.45	0.75	0.64	**11.09**
0.15	0.51	0.01	0.77	0.46	0.4	0.49	0.71	0.12	0.43	0.45	0.75	0.64	**10.5**
0.26	0.23	0.99	0.23	0.45	0.6	0.49	0.71	0.12	0.57	0.45	0.75	0.64	**10.2**
0.15	0.51	0.01	0.77	0.46	0.4	0.49	0.71	0.12	0.43	0.45	0.25	0.17	**9.53**

Table 3.29 Highest-scoring and lowest-scoring initial morphonotactic clusters

Best		1	2	3	4	5	6	7	8	9	10	11	12	13
1	zbr	**0.58**	**0.95**	**0.96**	0.25	0.51	0.52	**0.49**	0.7	0.51	0.46	0.52	**0.7**	0.18
2	zvr	**0.58**	**0.95**	**0.96**	0.23	0.51	0.52	**0.49**	0.7	0.51	0.46	0.52	**0.7**	0.25
3	zbl	**0.58**	**0.95**	**0.96**	0.23	0.51	0.52	**0.49**	0.7	0.51	0.46	0.52	**0.7**	0.18
4	vdr	**0.58**	**0.95**	**0.96**	0.22	0.33	0.52	**0.49**	0.7	0.46	0.46	0.46	**0.7**	0.18
5	zvl	**0.58**	**0.95**	**0.96**	0.22	0.51	0.52	**0.49**	0.7	0.51	0.46	0.52	**0.7**	0.25
6	vzr	**0.58**	**0.95**	**0.96**	0.22	0.33	0.52	**0.49**	0.7	0.46	0.46	0.46	**0.7**	0.25
7	spr	**0.58**	**0.95**	**0.96**	0.25	0.51	0.52	**0.49**	0.7	0.51	0.46	0.52	**0.7**	0.18
8	zgr	**0.58**	**0.95**	**0.96**	0.18	0.51	0.29	**0.49**	0.3	0.51	0.46	0.52	**0.7**	0.18
9	zmr	**0.58**	**0.95**	**0.96**	0.25	0.51	0.52	**0.49**	0.7	0.51	0.46	0.52	**0.7**	0.25
10	zvj	**0.58**	**0.95**	**0.96**	0.25	0.51	0.52	**0.49**	0.7	0.51	0.34	0.52	**0.7**	0.32
Worst		1	2	3	4	5	6	7	8	9	10	11	12	13
1	skrf	0.09	0.05	0.96	0.25	0.51	0.52	0.49	0.3	0.51	0.2	0.52	0.24	0.18
2	drgɲ	0.09	0.05	0.96	0.23	0.51	0.29	0.07	0.3	0.51	0.34	0.52	0.7	0.11
3	vv	0.33	0.95	0.02	0.07	0.07	0.18	0.07	0.7	0.46	0.2	0.46	0.24	0.12
4	lv	0.33	0.95	0.96	0.22	0.09	0.52	0.37	0.7	0.51	0.2	0.52	0.24	0.32
5	wbj	0.58	0.95	0.96	0.18	0.51	0.18	0.37	0.7	0.03	0.34	0.46	0.7	0.02
6	krfj	0.09	0.05	0.96	0.25	0.51	0.52	0.49	0.3	0.46	0.34	0.02	0.7	0.18
7	pwtɕ	0.58	0.05	0.96	0.25	0.51	0.18	0.37	0.7	0.46	0.34	0.46	0.7	0.02
8	wb	0.33	0.95	0.96	0.25	0.09	0.18	0.07	0.7	0.03	0.2	0.46	0.24	0.02
9	krf	0.58	0.05	0.96	0.25	0.09	0.52	0.37	0.3	0.46	0.2	0.02	0.24	0.18
10	mx	0.33	0.95	0.96	0.01	0.33	0.52	0.07	0.3	0.46	0.2	0.46	0.06	0.25

(continued)

Table 3.29 (continued)

14	15	16	17	18	19	20	21	22	23	24	25	26	∑
0.44	0.65	**0.99**	0.78	**0.88**	0.61	0.49	**0.68**	**0.96**	**0.57**	0.52	**0.74**	0.76	**16.4**
0.26	0.65	**0.99**	0.78	**0.88**	0.61	0.49	**0.68**	**0.96**	**0.57**	0.52	**0.74**	0.76	**16.27**
0.44	0.65	**0.99**	0.78	**0.88**	0.34	0.49	**0.68**	**0.96**	**0.57**	0.52	**0.74**	0.76	**16.11**
0.44	0.65	**0.99**	0.78	**0.88**	0.61	0.4	**0.68**	**0.96**	**0.57**	0.52	**0.74**	0.76	**15.99**
0.26	0.65	**0.99**	0.78	**0.88**	0.34	0.49	**0.68**	**0.96**	**0.57**	0.52	**0.74**	0.76	**15.99**
0.26	0.65	**0.99**	0.78	**0.88**	0.61	0.4	**0.68**	**0.96**	**0.57**	0.52	**0.74**	0.76	**15.88**
0.44	0.65	**0.99**	0.78	**0.88**	0.61	0.49	**0.68**	**0.96**	**0.57**	0.48	**0.74**	0.2	**15.8**
0.44	0.65	**0.99**	0.78	**0.88**	0.61	0.49	**0.68**	**0.96**	**0.57**	0.52	**0.74**	0.76	**15.7**
0.26	0.06	**0.99**	0.78	**0.88**	0.61	0.49	**0.68**	**0.96**	**0.57**	0.52	**0.74**	0.76	**15.7**
0.26	0.65	**0.99**	0.22	**0.88**	0.61	0.49	**0.68**	**0.96**	**0.57**	0.52	**0.74**	0.76	**15.68**
14	15	16	17	18	19	20	21	22	23	24	25	26	∑
0.44	0.59	0.99	0.78	0.88	0.61	0.49	0.11	0.96	0.43	0.48	0.26	0.2	**12.04**
0.44	0.29	0.99	0.78	0.1	0.34	0.11	0.68	0.96	0.57	0.52	0.74	0.76	**11.96**
0.12	0.65	0.99	0.78	0.88	0.61	0.4	0.11	0.96	0.43	0.52	0.74	0.76	**11.82**
0.18	0.32	0.99	0.78	0.1	0.61	0.11	0.11	0.04	0.43	0.52	0.74	0.76	**11.62**
0.44	0.06	0.01	0.22	0.88	0.61	0.11	0.68	0.04	0.57	0.52	0.74	0.76	**11.62**
0.44	0.29	0.99	0.22	0.1	0.61	0.11	0.68	0.96	0.57	0.48	0.74	0.04	**11.1**
0.44	0.65	0.99	0.78	0.1	0.05	0.11	0.21	0.96	0.43	0.48	0.26	0.04	**11.08**
0.18	0.32	0.01	0.78	0.88	0.34	0.11	0.68	0.04	0.43	0.52	0.74	0.76	**10.27**
0.44	0.65	0.99	0.78	0.1	0.61	0.11	0.11	0.96	0.43	0.48	0.26	0.04	**10.18**
0.18	0.32	0.99	0.78	0.1	0.61	0.11	0.11	0.04	0.43	0.52	0.26	0.04	**9.39**

As regards the phonologically-motivated group, the best sequence is represented by /zr/. The cluster scores 15.21 percentage points out of 26, i.e. it meets the established set of preferences in 58%. The highest-scoring clusters are mainly two-member obstruent + sonorant sequences, represented by fricative + liquid, plosive + liquid, plosive + nasal. The lowest-scoring cluster /wk/, with a score of 9.53 points, follows the preferred parameter patterns in 37%. Similarly to /wk/, other clusters found at the bottom-most end of the ranking either have an S + O structure or are composed of three or four consonants. As for the SSG, the least preferred clusters are represented by plateaus, or clusters which display a falling or mixed sonority profile.

The group of morphonotactic clusters meets a larger set of preferred parameter patterns than the phonotactic group. All top-ranked clusters score higher than the best phonotactic sequence /zr/, in spite of the fact that they are all CCCs. The best cluster in Table 3.29, /zbr/, scores 16.4 points, which corresponds to 63% of the total score for (P1–P26). Preferred clusters are due to prefixation, and are mainly composed of /z/ followed by /br bl dr zr/: doubles, which have been identified among the best clusters in Table 3.28. The least preferred extreme of this ranking is occupied by clusters which are due to non-concatenative morphological operations, and which for this reason exhibit rather varied phonological composition. The least preferred cluster /mx/ follows the preferred patterns in 36%. There is no pattern shared by the worst clusters in either dataset. As can be observed, the best phonotactic clusters and the best morphonotactic clusters are characterized by the same set of parameters, namely (P12, P16, P21, P22, P23, P25). These parameters surface in the statistical analyses as critical conditions for preferred initial phonotactics in Polish.

The inventories of final phonotactic and morphonotactic clusters are presented in Tables 3.30 and 3.31, respectively. Clusters occupy preferability ranges between 56 and 37% for the phonologically-motivated context, and between 54 and 29% for the morphologically-motivated context. The top-scoring extremes are represented by the same clusters in both datasets, namely /lt nt rt rs rʃ rʦ/. It must be noted that the remaining preferred clusters are also CCs, with the exception of /rst/ in Table 3.31. On this dimension, initial and final clusters differ from each other substantially. As was demonstrated in Table 3.29, initial morphonotactic clusters are composed of three consonants suggesting that the intervention of morphology contributes to quantitative complexity of phonotactics. This observations does not hold word-finally. Among morphonotactic clusters, the least preferred group contains CCCs and CCCCs, next to five two-member clusters. What is more, the comparison of the highest-scoring and lowest-scoring clusters in Table 3.31 reveals the morphological properties of clusters. The first set is due to non-concatenative morphological operations such as genitive plural or imperative singular formation. The latter set involves non-concatenative morphology as well as contexts for clear morphological parsing. /w/-final clusters arise in the 3rd person singular past (masc) formation as in *niós+ł* 'to carry' (3rd sg past masc).

As far as sonority is concerned, the best final clusters are SSG-obeying, and represented by combinations such as liquid + plosive, liquid + fricative,

Table 3.30 Highest-scoring and lowest-scoring final phonotactic clusters

Best		1	2	3	4	5	6	7	8	9	10	11	12	13
1	rt	**0.77**	**0.98**	**1**	0.29	0.33	**0.56**	**0.36**	**0.76**	**0.43**	0.61	**0.58**	**0.7**	0.16
2	rs	**0.77**	**0.98**	**1**	0.29	0.33	**0.56**	**0.36**	**0.76**	**0.43**	0.61	**0.58**	**0.7**	0.35
3	lʃ	**0.77**	**0.98**	**1**	0.29	0.39	**0.56**	**0.36**	**0.76**	**0.43**	0.61	**0.58**	**0.7**	0.35
4	nt	**0.77**	**0.98**	**1**	0.14	0.14	**0.56**	**0.36**	**0.76**	**0.43**	0.61	**0.58**	**0.7**	0.24
5	nʃ	**0.77**	**0.98**	**1**	0.29	0.39	**0.56**	**0.36**	**0.76**	**0.43**	0.61	**0.58**	**0.7**	0.16
6	rʃ	**0.77**	**0.98**	**1**	0.14	0.14	**0.56**	**0.36**	**0.76**	**0.43**	0.61	**0.58**	**0.7**	0.35
7	lt	**0.77**	**0.98**	**1**	0.14	0.14	**0.56**	**0.36**	**0.76**	**0.43**	0.61	**0.58**	**0.7**	0.16
8	nʧ	**0.77**	**0.98**	**1**	0.29	0.39	**0.56**	**0.36**	**0.76**	**0.43**	0.61	**0.58**	**0.7**	0.35
9	rts	**0.77**	**0.98**	**1**	0.29	0.33	**0.56**	**0.36**	**0.76**	**0.43**	0.61	**0.58**	**0.7**	0.24
10	rɕ	**0.77**	**0.98**	**1**	0.29	0.39	**0.56**	**0.36**	**0.76**	**0.43**	0.11	**0.58**	**0.7**	0.35
Worst		1	2	3	4	5	6	7	8	9	10	11	12	13
1	xʃ	0.77	0.98	**1**	0.27	0.33	0.56	0.46	0.18	0.27	0.61	0.11	0.7	0.04
2	ĵsk	0.23	0.02	**1**	0.08	0.14	0.56	0.36	0.18	0.3	0.28	0.58	0.14	0.24
3	tw	0.77	0.98	**1**	0.27	0.14	0.38	0.46	0.76	0.43	0.11	0.58	0.16	0.05
4	fk	0.77	0.98	**1**	0.02	0.39	0.38	0.08	0.18	0.27	0.28	0.31	0.14	0.35
5	psk	0.23	0.98	**1**	0.27	0.39	0.38	0.46	0.18	0.27	0.28	0.31	0.14	0.3 5
6	tsk	0.77	0.98	**1**	0.08	0.14	0.56	0.1	0.05	0.27	0.61	0.11	0.7	0.16
7	xtr	0.23	0.98	**1**	0.27	0.14	0.56	0.36	0.18	0.27	0.61	0.11	0.7	0.24
8	ʃx	0.77	0.98	**1**	0.27	0.39	0.56	0.46	0.18	0.43	0.28	0.58	0.14	0.04
9	sw	0.77	0.98	**1**	0.27	0.14	0.38	0.46	0.76	0.43	0.11	0.58	0.16	0.24
10	kx	0.77	0.98	**1**	0.14	0.14	0.56	0.08	0.05	0.27	0.28	0.11	0.14	0.35

(continued)

Table 3.30 (continued)

14	15	16	17	18	19	20	21	22	23	24	25	26	∑
0.69	**0.67**	**0.73**	**0.98**	0.58	0.47	**0.82**	0.58	**0.68**	**0.71**	**0.68**	**0.9**	**0.4**	**14.44**
0.69	**0.67**	**0.73**	**0.98**	0.58	0.39	**0.82**	0.31	**0.68**	**0.71**	**0.68**	**0.9**	**0.4**	**14.28**
0.69	**0.67**	**0.73**	**0.98**	0.41	0.39	**0.82**	0.31	**0.68**	**0.71**	**0.68**	**0.9**	**0.4**	**14.17**
0.69	**0.67**	**0.73**	**0.98**	0.41	0.47	**0.82**	0.58	**0.68**	**0.71**	**0.68**	**0.9**	**0.4**	**14.01**
0.69	**0.67**	**0.73**	**0.98**	0.41	0.39	**0.82**	0.31	**0.68**	**0.71**	**0.68**	**0.9**	**0.4**	**13.98**
0.69	**0.67**	**0.73**	**0.98**	0.58	0.39	**0.82**	0.31	**0.68**	**0.71**	**0.68**	**0.9**	**0.4**	**13.94**
0.69	**0.67**	**0.73**	**0.98**	0.41	0.47	**0.82**	0.58	**0.68**	**0.71**	**0.68**	**0.9**	**0.4**	**13.93**
0.69	**0.67**	**0.73**	**0.98**	0.41	0.14	**0.82**	0.31	**0.68**	**0.71**	**0.68**	**0.9**	**0.4**	**13.92**
0.69	**0.67**	**0.73**	**0.98**	0.58	0.14	**0.82**	0.31	**0.68**	**0.71**	**0.68**	**0.9**	**0.4**	**13.92**
0.69	**0.67**	**0.73**	**0.98**	0.58	0.39	**0.82**	0.31	**0.68**	**0.71**	**0.68**	**0.9**	**0.4**	**13.84**
14	15	16	17	18	19	20	21	22	23	24	25	26	∑
0.02	0.2	0.73	0.98	0.58	0.39	0.07	0.31	0.32	0.71	0.32	**0.9**	0.42	**10.59**
0.69	0.63	0.27	0.98	0.58	0.47	0.82	0.58	0.68	0.71	0.68	**0.9**	0.18	**10.52**
0.18	0.67	0.73	0.02	0.41	0.39	0.82	0.58	0.32	0.29	0.32	**0.9**	0.42	**10.5**
0.69	0.2	0.73	0.98	0.58	0.47	0.07	0.58	0.32	0.71	0.32	**0.9**	0.42	**10.48**
0.11	0.1	0.73	0.98	0.41	0.47	0.82	0.58	0.32	0.71	0.32	**0.9**	0.42	**10.47**
0.69	0.2	0.73	0.98	0.1	0.47	0.11	0.58	0.32	0.71	0.32	**0.9**	0.42	**10.42**
0.11	0.63	0.73	0.98	0.58	0.39	0.07	0.58	0.32	0.29	0.32	**0.9**	0.42	**10.33**
0.02	0.2	0.73	0.98	0.58	0.39	0.11	0.11	0.32	0.71	0.32	**0.9**	0.42	**10.23**
0.18	0.67	0.73	0.02	0.58	0.39	0.11	0.58	0.32	0.29	0.32	**0.9**	0.42	**10.15**
0.18	0.2	0.73	0.98	0.41	0.39	0.82	0.11	0.32	0.71	0.32	**0.9**	0.42	**9.72**

Table 3.31 Highest-scoring and lowest-scoring final morphonotactic clusters

Best		1	2	3	4	5	6	7	8	9	10	11	12	13
1	rt	0.77	**0.96**	**0.99**	0.36	0.46	0.49	0.41	**0.84**	**0.53**	0.47	**0.68**	0.6	0.13
2	rs	0.77	**0.96**	**0.99**	0.36	0.46	0.49	0.41	**0.84**	**0.53**	0.47	**0.68**	0.6	0.39
3	rʃ	0.77	**0.96**	**0.99**	0.15	0.14	0.49	0.41	**0.84**	**0.53**	0.47	**0.68**	0.6	0.39
4	rp	0.77	**0.96**	**0.99**	0.2	0.46	0.46	0.41	**0.84**	**0.53**	0.38	**0.68**	0.31	0.13
5	nt	0.77	**0.96**	**0.99**	0.15	0.14	0.49	0.41	**0.84**	**0.53**	0.47	**0.68**	0.6	0.2
6	rts	0.77	**0.96**	**0.99**	0.36	0.46	0.49	0.41	**0.84**	**0.53**	0.47	**0.68**	0.6	0.2
7	lt	0.77	**0.96**	**0.99**	0.15	0.14	0.49	0.41	**0.84**	**0.53**	0.47	**0.68**	0.6	0.13
8	rst	0.17	**0.96**	**0.99**	0.36	0.46	0.49	0.12	**0.84**	**0.53**	0.47	**0.68**	0.6	0.39
9	ls	0.77	**0.96**	**0.99**	0.15	0.14	0.49	0.41	**0.84**	**0.53**	0.47	**0.68**	0.6	0.39
10	lp	0.77	**0.96**	**0.99**	0.17	0.46	0.46	0.41	**0.84**	**0.53**	0.38	**0.68**	0.31	0.13
Worst		1	2	3	4	5	6	7	8	9	10	11	12	13
1	kf	0.77	0.96	0.99	0.02	0.46	0.46	0.07	0.15	0.24	0.38	0.08	0.31	0.39
2	sw	0.77	0.96	0.99	0.2	0.12	0.46	0.41	0.84	0.53	0.15	0.24	0.6	0.2
3	psk	0.17	0.96	0.99	0.2	0.28	0.46	0.41	0.15	0.24	0.38	0.24	0.09	0.39
4	pstf	0.05	0.96	0.99	0.36	0.12	0.04	0.41	0.84	0.24	0.38	0.24	0.31	0.39
5	xm	0.77	0.96	0.99	0.02	0.46	0.46	0.07	0.1S	0.24	0.38	0.08	0.31	0.18
6	ĵstf	0.05	0.04	0.99	0.17	0.46	0.46	0.12	0.84	0.23	0.38	0.68	0.31	0.39
7	xɕ	0.77	0.96	0.99	0.17	0.46	0.49	0.41	0.15	0.24	0.15	0.08	0.6	0.05
8	ʦtf	0.17	0.04	0.99	0.36	0.46	0.46	0.41	0.84	0.53	0.38	0.68	0.31	0.39
9	kw	0.77	0.96	0.99	0.2	0.12	0.46	0.07	0.15	0.24	0.15	0.24	0.09	0.05
10	fstf	0.05	0.04	0.01	0.36	0.12	0.04	0.41	0.84	0.24	0.38	0.24	0.31	0.18

(continued)

Table 3.31 (continued)

14	15	16	17	18	19	20	21	22	23	24	25	26	∑
0.6	0.6	**0.83**	**0.96**	0.58	0.45	**0.73**	0.55	**0.56**	**0.74**	**0.56**	**0.91**	0.31	**13.93**
0.6	0.6	**0.83**	**0.96**	0.58	0.37	**0.73**	0.29	**0.56**	**0.74**	**0.56**	**0.91**	0.31	**13.85**
0.6	0.6	**0.83**	**0.96**	0.58	0.37	**0.73**	0.29	**0.56**	**0.74**	**0.56**	**0.91**	0.31	**13.53**
0.6	0.6	**0.83**	**0.96**	0.58	0.45	**0.73**	0.55	**0.56**	**0.74**	**0.56**	**0.91**	0.31	**13.52**
0.6	0.6	**0.83**	**0.96**	0.39	0.45	**0.73**	0.55	**0.56**	**0.74**	**0.56**	**0.91**	0.31	**13.49**
0.6	0.6	**0.83**	**0.96**	0.58	0.18	**0.73**	0.29	**0.56**	**0.74**	**0.56**	**0.91**	0.31	**13.47**
0.6	0.6	**0.83**	**0.96**	0.39	0.45	**0.73**	0.55	**0.56**	**0.74**	**0.56**	**0.91**	0.31	**13.42**
0.6	0.72	**0.83**	**0.96**	0.58	0.45	**0.73**	0.55	**0.56**	**0.74**	**0.56**	**0.91**	0.17	**13.42**
0.6	0.6	**0.83**	**0.96**	0.39	0.37	**0.73**	0.29	**0.56**	**0.74**	**0.56**	**0.91**	0.31	**13.34**
0.6	0.6	**0.83**	**0.96**	0.39	0.45	**0.73**	0.55	**0.56**	**0.74**	**0.56**	**0.91**	0.31	**13.33**
14	15	16	17	18	19	20	21	22	23	24	25	26	∑
0.22	0.29	0.83	0.96	0.39	0.37	0.73	0.16	0.44	0.74	0.44	**0.91**	0.52	**10.39**
0.22	0.6	0.83	0.04	0.58	0.37	0.19	0.55	0.44	0.26	0.44	**0.91**	0.52	**10.35**
0.15	0.17	0.83	0.96	0.39	0.45	0.73	0.55	0.44	0.74	0.44	**0.91**	0.52	**10.17**
0.15	0.4	0.83	0.96	0.39	0.37	0.73	0.16	0.44	0.74	0.44	**0.91**	0.52	**10.14**
0.22	0.6	0.83	0.96	0.58	0.45	0.08	0.55	0.44	0.26	0.44	**0.91**	0.52	**10.02**
0.15	0.6	0.17	0.96	0.58	0.37	0.73	0.16	0.56	0.74	0.56	**0.91**	0.17	**9.97**
0.03	0.29	0.83	0.96	0.58	0.37	0.08	0.29	0.44	0.74	0.44	**0.91**	0.52	**9.96**
0.15	0.17	0.83	0.96	0.03	0.37	0.19	0.16	0.44	0.74	0.44	**0.91**	0.52	**9.7**
0.22	0.6	0.83	0.04	0.39	0.37	0.73	0.55	0.44	0.26	0.44	**0.91**	0.52	**8.72**
0.15	0.4	0.83	0.96	0.58	0.37	0.08	0.16	0.44	0.74	0.44	**0.91**	0.52	**7.57**

nasal + plosive, nasal + fricative, and liquid + affricate. The lowest-scoring clusters differ in term of length and phonological make-up. As for the SSG, the least preferred clusters are represented by plateaus, or clusters which display a falling or mixed sonority profile.

Since the data presented above embrace only a limited set of clusters, let me present exhaustive rankings of clusters for both word positions. A full exposition of phonotactic and morphonotactic clusters is presented in Tables 3.32, 3.33, 3.34 and 3.35. The rankings show that the majority of cluster types accumulate in the mid ranges of preferability. The most preferred and the least preferred extremes of the rankings are represented by several clusters. This means that there are a lot of types which are moderately preferred but few types which either maximally or minimally follow the established set of preferences. As can be observed, word-initial position features more top-ranked clusters (ranks 1–4) compared to word-final position.

Table 3.32 Ranking of initial phonotactic clusters (N = 336)

Rank	Cluster
1	zr
2	ʒl, dr, br, bl, dɲ
3	zbr, ʒr, ʑl, sr, vr, ʃl, ʑr, vl, ʒɲ, dl, tr
4	dn, pr, zvj, dvj, dʒ, pl, tɲ, spr, ʃpr, tkl, zn, pn, bʒ, sl, ʃr, ɕl, bz, fr, ʃn, gr, dj, vzr, smr, vn, vɲ
5	zgl, zgr, ɕr, fl, ʒd, dm, gl, pɲ, tl, zdr, tkn, bʑ, tkɲ, gn, sxl, ʒm, tn, sfj, tʃn, vzn, tfj, gɲ, zm, pxl, zmj, dmj, brd, tʃ, sj, zw, ʒw
6	sn, ʃkr, pʃ, bʒd, zd, kr, bj, dw, ps, skl, skr, ʃkl, vj, bzd, vd, kl, ʃt, ʃtr, ʦl, ʦn, str, gʒ, xr, kn, pɕ, ʃm
7	gz, ʦfj, xl, kɲ, sm, skn, ʒb, tʧ, vbr, gʑ, mr, ts, zb, ml, ɕfj, dv, sw, ʃw, drj, drʒ, ʥvj, tj, vzdr, gvd, gvj, zgj, spj, ʃpj, pj, tw, pt, st, pʃt, ʧm, pstr, ɕɲ, fj, gʒm, gj, grd, ʦm, zdj
8	fkr, spʃ, ft, prj, bʒm, zvw, db, ptɕ, rd, ʧkɲ, kʃ, txn, zgʒ, lʒ, txɲ, fkl, gd, gʥ, ʧt, vʒd, ks, bʑʥ, ʃp, ɕm, kɕ, trj, ʨfj, tkfj, vʒ, drv, sp, drvj, ʃtfj, tf, kfj, skj, ʃkj, lj
9	vz, ɕmj, vʣ, vʑ, rj, brn, kpj, vʥ, skfj, ʥb, ʒg, sxn, ʦw, ʧw, dʒv, mʒ, stj, sxɲ, kj, rvj, brɲ, rʒn, kln, zg, klɲ, ʨm, ɕpj, ʥv, rʣ, rʒ, rʒɲ, pʃʧ, kʃt, kʦ, skʃ, xfj, mj, krj, xj
10	kt, ktɕ, xt, gm, ʒv, mn, sʦ, ʃʧ, ʦf, fʃ, kmj, fst, fʧ, zv, ɕp, ʃkw, ʨmj, fɕ, ʑʥ, gw, stʃ, ʃk, ʦkl, mɲ, ʥv, fʃʧ, bw, tx
11	ʧf, fɕtɕ, sk, rv, ʦkɲ, xmj, brʥ, krt, dʒvj, ʧtɕ, vw, fkʃ, km, tʃmj, ʃf, tʃpj, kʃʧ, sʦj, sf, rt, gv, gʒmj, mdl, tk
12	ʑʥbl, gʒbj, ɕtɕ, kw, xʃ, bʒmj, pw, ʨf, psk, ʨp, tkf, zz, krn, ʃʧf, xʦ, ʧk, xʃʧ, xw, ʃkf, xtɕ, ʥg, klv, drg
13	xm, lgn, mʃ, ɕf, plv, lgɲ, gb, mʦ, mgl, kf, mgɲ, px, tʃtɕ, sx
14	pxw, ss, ʑʥb, skf, wz, wʒ, ʧx, ʑʥbw, mʃʧ, mw, lɕɲ, wʑ, kp, ʤʤ, fsp, mɕtɕ
15	trf, mst, mgj, mkɲ, mkn, xʃtɕ
16	ʧʧ
17	skrf, xf, mdw
18	wg
19	mgw
20	wk

Table 3.33 Ranking of initial morphonotactic clusters (N = 189)

Rank	Cluster
1	zbr, zvr
2	zbl, vdr, zvl
3	vzr, spr
4	zgr, zmr, zvj, sfr, vgr, vzl, vzn, zbj, zbʒ, zdr, spl, vzɲ, fɕr
5	zbʑ, zgn, ʒgn, vzbr, ftr, sfl, zgɲ, zr, zmɲ, vr, fɕl, vgɲ
6	vgl, zdw, vzdr, fpr, vzgl, skr, vd, ʃfj, spʃ, vzd, zgj, zmj, fkr, vbj, sxr, vl, spj, zdm
7	str, spɕ, vgj, vn, zɲ, zgʒ, fpl, skl, skn, vɲ, zdj, fskr, vgʒ, zd, vzbj, zvw, vdm, zbw, sxl, zʒ, zdʒ
8	zl, vʒ, vz, vzm, zʑ, zgw, zn, stw, ft, fstr, zj, fst, sxj, vmj
9	skj, stl, fpj, vj, zw, fpʃ, skʃ, vvj, zb, ʥgn, zdv, sʧ, fʧ, vzdw, stfj, st, zʥ, vzmj, sʃ, fspj, vʥ, zmw
10	ʥgɲ, zm, spw, fsʃ, fʃ, fs, ftʃ, ʧkn, sɕ, vzb, sxw, fɕ, zgv, skw, fsw, ftw, bz
11	fʃʧ, sn, sxʃ, sp, stf, zv, vgw, fʦ, fskʃ, zg, stʃ, dɲ, fʨ
12	vzg, vw, fsp, fstʃ, vb, fpw, sʦ, sks, ps
13	zz, zʥv, vg, vm, skf, ʃf, brvj, sf, brv, pɕ, stx, sk, fxw, fkw
14	fsk, lvj, sxf, fp
15	ss, pɲ, ɕʨ, fk, sst, sx, fsx, pxɲ
16	vzv, pxn, xʃt, lɲ
17	fx, ln, drgn
18	skrf, drgɲ
19	vv, lv, wbj
20	krfj, pwʨ
21	wb
22	krf
23	mx

Let me now focus on the top-ranked clusters. A striking observation is that in all the datasets, the prevocalic and postvocalic position is occupied by the same classes of consonants. Nasals and liquids seem to constitute the most natural transition between cluster margins and a vowel. That is, in initial clusters /r l m n ŋ/ are best released into a vowel. These consonants are also favoured in postvocalic position word-finally. Glides, in turn, neighbour on vowels mainly in the group of the least preferred clusters. This result could be attributed to the artefact of the selected parameters. However, it must be noted that glides, in contrast to other sonorants, are classified as [−consonantal]. This property of clusters is captured by (P17) in initials and (P16) in finals. Thus, it is possible that Polish phonotactics strives at an optimal distribution of manner distances between vowels and consonants. A slope from an obstruent towards a vowel is more steady and gradual when nasals and liquids intervene. To the contrary, the sonority rise from cluster margins is more sharp when /j/ and /w/ are found in prevocalic or postvocalic position. These observations partially support some measures of distance.

Table 3.34 Ranking of final phonotactic clusters (N = 131)

Rank	Clusters
1	rt
2	rs, lʃ
3	nt, nʃ, rʃ, lt, nʧ, rʦ
4	rɕ, rʃt, ls, jt
5	ɲʦ, ns, rʧ, js, nʦ, lft, rn, rʨ, rp, mʃ, lʦ
6	ms, w̃s, w̃ʃ, jʦ, lp, wt, jʧ
7	mpt, rk, ʃt, j̃ɕ, jn, rf, rɲ, ws, wʃ, jst, lf, tr, wʧ, ɲʨ, jl
8	rʃʧ, nr, nf, rɕʨ, lk, rx, st, jnt, ntʃ, tl, wst, w̃ʃt, ft, ŋkt, wn, rm, pl, jk, pr, ɕl, lx, lsk, rsk,
9	wl, pʃ, lm, pt, wnt, wr, ps, jf, wʨ, fl, ʃp, j̃ɕʨ
10	jx, ltr, ntr, tm, mn, fr, ʃʧ, fn, mp, pɲ, w̃ʃʧ, jm
11	fʦ, wp, kr, xt, mf, kl, tf, str, wk, sk
12	mpl, ŋks, ŋk, kt, ɕɲ, ks, sm, mpr, ɕʨ, stʃ
13	wf, w̃x, wx, wm, kst
14	ŋkr, lɕɲ, stm
15	xʃ
16	j̃sk, tw, fk, psk, ʦk, xtr
17	ʃx, sw
18	kx

Table 3.35 Ranking of final morphonotactic clusters (N = 103)

Rank	Clusters
1	rt
2	rs
3	rʃ, rp, nt, rʦ, lt, rst
4	ls, lp, rf, nʧ, ʃt, ɲʧ, rʧ, nʦ
5	lf, lʧ, rn, rʨ, st, jt
6	sp, ʃp, tʃ
7	rm, mst, rʃʧ, ɲʨ, rɲ, ɕp, tr, rk, ʧt, jʦ, tl, tm, lm, jɕ, ɕl
8	lɲ, tf, lk, mɕ, rtf, ft, ʃʧ, sn, jʨ
9	wt, ntʃ, lsk, w̃s, w̃ʃ, sm, ʧp, ntf, pt, ps, rstf, jm
10	sk, ɕm, pr, jɕʨ, j̃ɕʨ, mp
11	ɕʨ, fr, xt, pʧ, wn, fʦ, sf, str
12	wp, kt, ʃtr, mn, ntr, stf, wnt, fʨ, jx, kr
13	jsʦ, jsk, jstf, ŋk, mpstf
14	tw, rw, km, kf, sw
15	psk, pstf, xm
16	j̃stf, xɕ
17	ʦtf
18	kw
19	fstf

Table 3.36 Rankings of sonority distances in demisyllables

Rank	Combination
1	Obstruent + liquid + vowel
2	Obstruent + glide + vowel
2	Obstruent + nasal + vowel
3	Nasal + glide + vowel
3	Nasal + liquid + vowel
4	Liquid + glide + vowel

Based on Clements (1990: 304ff.)

Clements' (1990) *Sonority Dispersion Principle* asserts that an optimal structure of CCV and VCC should exhibit a sharp rise in sonority from the left-most consonant towards a vowel, and a minimum fall in sonority from a vowel rightwards. Clements (1990) calculates distances between pairs of segments in a demisyllable, based on the following sonority scale: vowels (V) > glides (G) > liquids (L) > nasals (N) > obstruents (O). The principle makes it possible to determine degrees of cluster naturalness in terms of a ranking. A combination of segments C1 − C2 − V with a steady and gradual rise in sonority is universally most preferred. Consonant combinations ranked 1 should be dispersed along the whole sonority scale, ensuring a maximum distance between C1 and a vowel. This is true for OLV clusters, which display a large distance between obstruents and vowels, and where liquids exhibit a 2-step distance towards the neighbouring segments. A less natural combination (rank 2) is exemplified by OGV clusters, since the intermediate distances between C1–C2 and C2−V are unsymmetrical. LGV represents the least natural cluster type as it involves a steady but small (only 1 distance) rise in sonority. The summary of the ranking is presented in Table 3.36, where (1) and (4) stand for the least and the most complex combinations, respectively.

The group of highest-scoring initial clusters, where obstruent + liquid sequences prevail, largely supports the hypothesis of Clements (1990). Similarly, the most preferred word-final clusters feature a liquid in post-vocalic position and an obstruent in absolute word-final position. The structure of the C − V transition is the same as for the V − C transition, suggesting that preferred clusters exhibit a gradual increase in sonority from cluster margins towards a vowel.

3.6 Conclusions

The goal of this chapter was to present a feature-based analysis of Polish initial and final (mor)phonotactics leading to the formulation of new constraints and preferences for phonologically- and morphologically-motivated clusters. Preferences provide insights into subsegmental properties which motivate the phonotactic grammar of a language notorious for complex clusters by revealing the positional weight of phonological features. I have shown that the dimensions of complexity, place of articulation, manner of articulation and voice contribute to cluster structure to varying degrees. Only a subset of features, their well-defined distribution and co-occurrence have the capacity to account for the phonological make-up of Polish consonant clusters. Overall, word-initial clusters favour [+voice] and [coronal] segments in prevocalic position, while word-final clusters exhibit a preference for a [−voice] consonant in cluster-final position. What is more, there is a preference for avoiding dorsals word-finally. Also, consonants to which the feature of stridency cannot be allocated (i.e. plosives and sonorants) are favoured in both word positions. I conjure that the apparent markedness of consonant clusters can be easily decomplexified when they are studied at their prime level, i.e. in terms of phonological features. Such intrinsic properties are expected to account for cross-linguistic phonotactic variation. The idea of positional weight of phonological features opens an area for large-scale typological studies where tiny subsegmental properties define groups of systems.

There still is a major lacuna in the statistically-based generalizations. The methods employed in the analysis have revealed the underlying structure of cluster types attested in Polish. The themes which still remain unexplored are related to how the feature-based specifications proposed in the chapter contribute to theoretical phonology, and to what extent they are reflected in various types of external evidence. In order to test whether the established set of preferences for an optimal cluster holds in processing and production, the chapters to follow provide feature-based analyses of clusters using psycholinguistic and casual speech data. Are native speakers of Polish fine-attuned to the same set of parameters at the cognitive level? Which preferences have the greatest weight in motor control, and facilitate articulation? Or, possibly, is there a tiny subsegmental property of clusters which underlies phonotactics in the psychological domain? The questions related to processing are addressed in Chap. 4, where I examine the psychological reality of sonority and place of articulation distances.

References

Anderson, J.M., and J. Durand. 1986. Dependency phonology. In *Dependency and non-linear phonology*, ed. J. Durand, 1–54. London: Croom Helm.

Aronoff, M. 1976. *Word formation in generative grammar* [Linguistic inquiry monograph 1]. Cambridge, MA: The MIT Press.

Beckman, J., M. Essen, and C. Ringen. 2013. Empirical evidence for laryngeal features: Aspirating vs. true-voice languages. *Journal of Linguistics* 49 (2): 259–284.

Bethin, C.Y. 1992. *Polish syllables: The role of prosody in phonology and morphology.* Colombus, OH: Slavica Publishers.

Cairns, C.E. 1988. Phonotactics, markedness and lexical representation. *Phonology* 5 (2): 209–236.

Carr, P. 1993. *Phonology.* London: Macmillan.

Chomsky, N., and M. Halle. 1968. *The Sound Pattern of English.* New York: Harper and Row.

Clements, G.N. 1985. The geometry of phonological features. *Phonology Yearbook* 2: 225–252.

Clements, G.N. 1990. The role of the sonority cycle in core syllabification. In *Papers in laboratory phonology. 1: Between the grammar and physics of speech*, eds. J. Kingston, and M.E. Beckman, 288–333. Cambridge: Cambridge University Press.

Clements, G.N. 2001. Representational economy in constraint-based phonology. In *Distinctive feature theory*, ed. T.A. Hall, 71–146. Berlin: Mouton de Gruyter.

Clements, G.N. 2009. The role of features in phonological inventories. In *Contemporary views on architecture and representations in phonological theory*, eds. E. Raimy, and C. Cairns, 19–68. Cambridge, MA: The MIT Press.

Clements, G.N., and E.V. Hume. 1995. The internal organization of speech sounds. In *The handbook of phonological theory*, eds. J.A. Goldsmith, J. Riggle, and A.C.L. Yu, 245–306. Oxford, MA: Blackwell.

Cyran, E. 2011. Laryngeal realism and laryngeal relativism: Two voicing systems in Polish? *Studies in Polish Linguistics* 6 (1): 45–80.

De Lacy, P. 2002. *The formal expression of markedness*. Ph.D. diss., Amherst: University of Massachusetts.

Donohue, M., R. Hetherington, J. McElvenny, and V. Dawson. 2013. *World phonotactics database*. Department of Linguistics, The Australian National University. Online access: http://phonotactics.anu.edu.au. Accessed on 20 Nov 2017.

Dresher, B.E. 2015. The motivation for contrastive feature hierarchies in phonology. *Linguistic Variation* 15 (1): 1–40.

Dresher, B.E. 2016. Contrast in phonology 1867–1967: History and development. *Annual Review of Linguistics* 2: 53–73.

Dziubalska-Kołaczyk, K. 2001a. Phonotactic constraints are preferences. In *Constraints and preferences*, ed. K. Dziubalska-Kołaczyk, 69–100. Berlin: Mouton de Gruyter.

Dziubalska-Kołaczyk, K. (ed.). 2001b. *Constraints and preferences* [Trends in linguistics. Studies and monographs 134]. Berlin, New York: Mouton de Gruyter.

Dziubalska-Kołaczyk, K. 2002. *Beats-and-binding Phonology*. Frankfurt am Main: Peter Lang.

Dziubalska-Kołaczyk, K. 2009. NP extensions: B&B phonotactics. *Poznań Studies in Contemporary Linguistics* 45 (1): 55–71.

Dziubalska-Kołaczyk, K. 2014. Explaining phonotactics using NAD. *Language Sciences* 46 (A): 6–17.

Dziubalska-Kołaczyk, K. (in press). On the structure, survival and change of consonant clusters.

Ewen, C.J. 1995. Dependency relations in phonology. In *The handbook of phonological theory*, ed. J.A. Goldsmith, 570–585. Oxford: Blackwell.

Ewen, C.J. 1996. Dependency phonology. In *The encyclopaedia of language and linguistics*, ed. R.E. Asher, 864–867. Amsterdam: Elsevier.

Fant, G. 1969. Distinctive features and phonetic dimensions. *Speech Transmission Laboratory: Quarterly Progress and Status Report* 2–3: 1–18.

Gibbon, D. 2001. Preferences as defaults in computational phonology. In *Constraints and preferences*, ed. K. Dziubalska-Kołaczyk, 143–199. Berlin: Mouton de Gruyter.

Giegerich, H.J. 1995. *English phonology: An introduction*. Cambridge: Cambridge University Press.

Gordon, M. 2002. Weight-by-position adjunction and syllable structure. *Lingua* 112: 901–931.

Gordon, M. 2006. *Syllable weight: Phonetics, phonology, typology*. New York, London: Routledge.

Gordon, M. 2016. *Phonological typology*. Oxford: Oxford University Press.

Greenberg, J.H. 1978. Some generalizations concerning initial and final consonant clusters. In *Universals of human language*, eds. J.H. Greenberg, C.A. Ferguson, and E.A. Moravcsik, 243–279. Stanford. CA: Stanford University Press.

Hall, T. A. 1997. *The phonology of coronals* [Current issues in linguistic theory 149]. Amsterdam: John Benjamins.

Hall, T.A. 2001. *Distinctive feature theory*. Berlin: Mouton de Gruyter.

Hall, T.A. 2007. Segmental features. In *The Cambridge handbook of phonology*, ed. P. de Lacy, 311–334. Cambridge: Cambridge University Press.

Halle, M. 1973. Prolegomena to a theory of word formation. *Linguistic Inquiry* 4 (1): 3–16.
Halle, M. 1995. Feature geometry and feature spreading. *Linguistic Inquiry* 26: 1–46.
Halle, M., and G.N. Clements. 1994. *Problem book in phonology. A workbook for introductory courses in linguistics and modern phonology,* 7th printing. Cambridge, MA: The MIT Press.
Halle, M., B. Vaux, and A. Wolfe. 2000. On feature spreading and the representation of place of articulation. *Linguistic Inquiry* 31 (3): 387–444.
Harley, H. 2006. *English words: A linguistic introduction*. Malden, Oxford, Carlton: Blackwell Publishing.
Harris, J.W. 1983. *Syllable structure and stress in Spanish: A nonlinear analysis*. Cambridge, MA: The MIT Press.
Haspelmath, M. 2006. Against markedness (and what to replace it with). *Journal of Linguistics* 42 (1): 25–70.
Hayes, B. 2009. *Introductory phonology*. Malden, MA: Wiley-Blackwell.
Hayes, B. 2011. Interpreting sonority-projection experiments: The role of phonotactic modeling. In *Proceedings of the 17th international congress of phonetic sciences, Hong Kong, 17–21 August 2011*, eds. W.S. Lee, and E. Zee, 835–838. Hong Kong: City University of Hong Kong.
Hayes, B., and C. Wilson. 2008. A maximum entropy model of phonotactics and phonotactic learning. *Linguistic Inquiry* 39 (3): 379–440.
Hirst, D. 1980. Linearisation and the single-segment hypothesis. In *Grammatical representation*, eds. J. Guéron, H.-G. Obenauer, and J.-Y. Pollock, 87–99. Dordrecht, Cinnaminson: Foris Publications.
Honeybone, P. 2005. Diachronic evidence in segmental phonology: The case of laryngeal specifications. In *The internal organization of phonological segments* [Studies in generative grammar 77], eds. M. van Oostendorp, and J. van de Weijer, 319–354. Berlin, New York: Mouton de Gruyter.
Hothorn, T., K. Hornik, and A. Zeileis. 2006. Unbiased recursive partitioning: A conditional inference framework. *Journal of Computational and Graphical Statistics* 15 (3): 651–674.
Hothorn, T., K. Hornik, C. Strobl, and A. Zeileis. 2018. *Package 'party'. A laboratory for recursive partytioning. R package version 1.3-1.* Online access: https://cran.r-project.org/web/packages/party/vignettes/party.pdf.
Hyman, L. 1985. *A theory of phonological weight*. Dordrecht: Foris Publications.
Jassem, W. 2003. Polish. *Journal of the International Phonetic Association: Illustrations of the IPA* 33 (1): 103–107.
Kenstowicz, M. 1994. *Phonology in generative grammar*. Cambridge, MA, Oxford: Blackwell Publishing.
Kuryłowicz, J. 1952. Uwagi o polskich grupach spółgłoskowych. *Biuletyn Polskiego Towarzystwa Językoznawczego* 11: 54–69.
Lass, R. 1976. *English phonology and phonological theory: Synchronic and diachronic studies* [Cambridge studies in linguistics 17]. Cambridge: Cambridge University Press.
Leben, W. R. 1973. *Suprasegmental phonology*. Ph.D. diss., Cambridge, MA: The MIT Press.
Lombardi, L. 2001. Why place and voice are different: Constraint-specific alternations in Optimality Theory. In *Segmental phonology in Optimality Theory: Constraints and representations*, ed. L. Lombardi, 13–45. Cambridge: Cambridge University Press.
Maddieson, I. 1999. In search of universals. In *Proceedings of the 14th international congress of phonetic sciences, San Francisco, CA, 1–7 August 1999*, eds. J.J. Ohala, Y. Hasegawa, M. Ohala, D. Granville, and A.C. Bailey, 2521–2528. Berkeley: University of California.
Maddieson, I. 2013. Syllable structure. In *The World Atlas of Language Structures online*, eds. M. Dryer, and M. Haspelmath. Munich: Max Plank Digital Library. Online access: http://wals.info/. Accessed on 21 July 2017.
McCarthy, J.J. 1986. OCP effects: Gemination and antigemmination. *Linguistic Inquiry* 17: 207–263.
McCarthy, J.J. 1988. Feature geometry and dependency: A review. *Phonetica* 43: 84–108.
Mester, R. A. 1986. *Studies in tier structure*. Ph.D. diss., Amherst, MA: The MIT Press.

Mielke, J. 2004. *The emergence of distinctive features*. Ph.D. diss., Columbus: The Ohio State University.
Mielke, J. 2005. Ambivalence and ambiguity in laterals and nasals. *Phonology* 22: 169–203.
Orzechowska, P. 2016. In search of phonotactic preferences. *Yearbook of the Poznań Linguistic Meeting* 2: 167–193.
Orzechowska, P. 2018. Exponents of sonority in Slavic and Germanic languages. In *Proceedings of the 9th international conference on speech prosody, Poznań, 13–16 June 2018*, eds. K. Klessa, J. Bachan, A. Wagner, M. Karpiński, and D. Śledziński, 999–1003. Poznań: Adam Mickiewicz University.
Orzechowska, P. (submitted a). Complexity of initial clusters in Polish: An exploratory feature-based approach.
Orzechowska, P. (submitted b). Feature activity in English phonotactics.
Orzechowska, P., and R. Wiese. 2011. Reconstructing the sonority hierarchy. In *Proceedings of the 17th international congress of phonetic sciences, Hong Kong, 17–21 August 2011*, eds. W. S. Lee, and E. Zee, 1542–1545. Hong Kong: City University of Hong Kong.
Orzechowska, P., and R. Wiese. 2015. Preferences and variation in word-initial phonotactics: A multi-dimensional evaluation of German and Polish. *Folia Linguistica* 49: 439–486.
Padgett, J. 1995. Feature classes. In *University of Massachusetts occasional papers 18. Papers in Optimality Theory*, eds. J.N. Beckman, S. Urbanczyk, and L. Walsh, 385–420. Amherst: GLSA-Graduate Linguistic Student Association, University of Massachusetts.
Paradis, C., and J.-F. Prunet. 1991. *The special status of coronals: Internal and external evidence*. San Diego: Academic Press.
R Development Core Team. 2013. *R: A language and environment for statistical computing. R foundation for statistical computing*. Vienna, Austria. Online access: http://www.R-project.org/.
Rice, K. 1992. On deriving sonority: A structural account of sonority relationships. *Phonology* 9 (1): 61–99.
Rice, K. 2003. Featural markedness in phonology: Variation. In *The second glot international state-of-the-article book* [Studies in generative grammar 61], eds. L. Cheng, and R. Sybesma, 389–430. Berlin, Boston: Mouton de Gruyter.
Rice, K. 2007. Markedness in phonology. In *The Cambridge handbook of phonology*, ed. P. de Lacy, 89–97. Cambridge: Cambridge University Press.
Ritt, N. 2001. Are optimality theoretical "constraints" the same as natural linguistic "preferences"? In *Constraints and preferences* [Trends in linguistics. Studies and monographs 134], ed. K. Dziubalska-Kolaczyk, 291–310. Berlin, New York: Mouton de Gruyter.
Rochoń, M. 2000. *Optimality in complexity: The case of Polish consonant clusters* [Studia Grammatica 48]. Berlin: Akademie Verlag.
Rubach, J. 1996. Nonsyllabic analysis of voice assimilation in Polish. *Linguistic Inquiry* 27 (1): 69–110.
Rubach, J. 2007. Feature geometry from the perspective of Polish, Russian, and Ukrainian. *Linguistic Inquiry* 38: 85–138.
Ryan, K.M. 2011. Gradient syllable weight and weight universals in quantitative metrics. *Phonology* 28 (3): 413–454.
Ryan, K.M. 2016. Phonological weight. *Language and Linguistics Compass* 10: 720–733.
Sagey, E. 1982. *The representation of features and relations in non-linear phonology*. Ph.D. diss., Cambridge, MA: The MIT Press.
Sardá-Espinosa, A., S. Subbiah, and T. Bartz-Beielstein. 2017. Conditional inference trees for knowledge extraction from motor health condition data. *Engineering Applications of Artificial Intelligence* 62: 26–37.
Schwartz, G., and D. Arndt. 2018. Laryngeal realism vs. modulation theory—Evidence from VOT discrimination in Polish. *Language Sciences* 69: 98–112.
Selkirk, E.O. 1984. On the major class features and syllable theory. In *Language sound structure*, eds. M. Aronoff, and R.T. Oehrle, 107–136. Cambridge, MA: The MIT Press.
Singh, S. 1976. *Distinctive features: Theory and validation*. Baltimore: University Park Press.

Steriade, D. 1982. *Greek prosodies and the nature of syllabification*. Ph.D. diss., Cambridge, MA: The MIT Press.

Steriade, D. 1999. Alternatives to the syllabic interpretation of consonantal phonotactics. In *Item order in language and speech*, eds. O. Fujimura, B.D. Joseph, and B. Palek, 205–242. Columbus: The Karolinum Press.

Strobl, C., A.-L. Boulesteix, A. Zeileis, and T. Hothorn. 2007. Bias in random forest variable importance measures: Illustrations, sources and a solution. *BMC Bioinformatics* 8 (1): 25–45.

Strobl, C., A.-L. Boulesteix, T. Kneib, T. Augustin, and A. Zeileis. 2008. Conditional variable importance for random forests. *BMC Bioinformatics* 9 (1): 307–317.

Ulbrich, C., P. Alday, J. Knaus, P. Orzechowska, and R. Wiese. 2016. The role of phonotactic principles in language processing. *Language, Cognition and Neuroscience* 31 (5): 662–682.

Warnes, G.R., B. Bolker, L. Bonebakker, R. Gentleman, W.H.A. Liaw, T. Lumley, and M. Schwartz. 2016. *Various R programming tools for plotting data. R package version 3.0.1. The comprehensive R archive network*. Online access: https://cran.r-project.org/web/packages/gplots.

Wiese, R., P. Orzechowska, P. Alday, and C. Ulbrich. 2017. Structural principles or frequency of use? An ERP experiment on the learnability of Polish consonant clusters. *Frontiers in Psychology—Auditory Cognitive Neuroscience* 7: 2005.

Yavaş, M. 2013. What explains the reductions in /s/-clusters: Sonority or [continuant]? *Clinical Linguistics and Phonetics* 27: 394–403.

Yip, M. 1988. The Obligatory Contour Principle and phonological rules: A loss of identity. *Linguistic Inquiry* 19 (1): 65–100.

Chapter 4
Sonority and Place Constraints in Phonotactics: Evidence from Reaction Time Experiments

There seems to be a paradox in Polish: speakers tolerate extraordinarily complex consonant clusters except when they do not.
(Christina Bethin 1992)

4.1 Introduction

This chapter discusses the role of phonological principles in online processing of CC phonotactics in Polish. Two reaction time experiments explore the psycholinguistic reality of three factors: (1) *existence*, (2) *well-formedness* and (3) *distance* in word-initial clusters (Experiment 1) and in word-final clusters (Experiment 2). Existence distinguishes between clusters which are part of the phonotactic inventory of Polish, and which are hypothetical. Well-formedness is associated with the sonority profile of CC clusters, which is either sonority-violating or sonority-obeying following the hierarchy: plosive – affricate – fricative – nasal – liquid – glide. The concept of distance is represented by the proximity of places of articulation on a scale bilabial – labio-dental – dental – alveolar – alveolo-palatal – palatal – velar. For each experiment, two types of data were collected: accuracy rates and response latencies. The studies offer new data for Polish phonotactics, from which the following conclusions are drawn. First, it is shown that sonority and existence affect only accuracy rates, and do not contribute to the processing of word-edge phonotactics. In turn, response latencies are facilitated by the place of articulation distances. Reaction times are the longest for medial distances, and the shortest for large distances. Processing of large contrast (e.g. bilabial – velar, bilabial – palatal, dental – velar) involves the least cognitive effort, and it lends support to the principle of the clarity of perception. The findings contribute to the ongoing discussion on sources of phonotactic knowledge, an underlying feature-based composition of clusters, and conflicting forces related to place and manner features in online processing and intuitive judgement.

P. Orzechowska, *Complexity in Polish Phonotactics*, Prosody, Phonology and Phonetics, https://doi.org/10.1007/978-981-13-7299-5_4

4.2 State of the Art

One of the primary strategies employed in the collection of linguistic data is to record intuitions of native speakers. Introspective data provide insights not only into the cognitive abilities of speakers, but also into the general mechanisms that underlie the grammatical knowledge in a linguistic population. With the advances in psycholinguist methodology, it has become possible to investigate linguistic judgments through experimentation.

Numerous tools have been developed to allow to research the dynamics of language processing. In the realm of phonology, on-line methodologies such as cross-modal priming, eye-tracking and neurophysiological techniques have been in demand as they allow to measure factors that are operative in the processing of language just at the moment it happens (for overviews see Kawahara 2016; Marinis 2003). Off-line techniques have also been used in the form of word-likeliness or naturalness judgements (e.g. Frisch et al. 2000). Phonotactics presents an excellent testing ground for deploying both types of strategies.

A large body of research has used non-existent words to study the psychological reality of phonological principles (for reviews and syntheses on artificial phonology and language learning, see Moreton and Pater 2012a, b; Myers and Padgett 2014). Linguists have explored the possibility of replicating existent combinations of sounds with hypothetical words, successfully demonstrating that whenever scalar ratings of linguistic forms are available native speakers provide gradient judgments on the acceptability of nonce words in their mother tongue. Such gradient responses are particularly powerful in the realm of phonotactics.

Let us illustrate a possible judgment scheme with a seminal example of Chomsky and Halle (1968). *Brick* /bɹɪk/ is an existent and sonority-obeying word in English. Its modification to *blick* /blɪk/ is unattested but still phonotactically legitimate as the syntagmatic relation between # – /b/, /b/ – /l/, /l/ – /ɪ/, /ɪ/ – /k/ and /k/ – # can be reconstructed from other existent words such as *bliss* and *lick*. However, *bnick* /bnɪk/ is both unattested and outlawed by phonotactic constrains. Intuitive judgements of native speakers of English reflect the hierarchy according to which *brick* is considered phonologically well-formed, *bnick* ill-formed, and *blick* —as a form mediating between the two extremes—possibly acceptable. Such a gradient classification is supported by experimental data on English onset clusters.

Pitt (1998) shows that perceptual illusions in the mother tongue are triggered by well-formedness and existence. American English speakers misperceive marked unattested obstruent + liquid + vowel sequences, such as /tlæ/, as their disyllabic counterparts, such as /tela/, while no such effects are observed for unmarked existent syllables. Moreton (2002) measures the perceptual biases against /dl/ and /bw/, both of which are unattested onsets in English. American English speakers showed a significant phonotactic bias only against the /dl/ cluster, suggesting that the sonority differential between adjacent consonants is recognized as a subtle cue of cluster goodness. That is, a smaller distance in /dl/ makes the cluster worse.

In another study on illicit phonotactics, Berent et al. (2007) investigate perceptual illusions of English speakers to universally preferred and dispreferred clusters. Similarly to Pitt (1998), the authors observe that sequences containing ill-formed non-existent onsets such as /lbɪf/ tend to be confused with their epenthetic equivalents and repaired to /ləbɪf/. Interestingly, the illusory schwa is less likely to be heard in nonce words containing onsets which are relatively preferred across languages (such as /bdɪf/), although obviously the speakers have been exposed to neither sequence in their mother tongue. The constraints tested in a functional Magnetic Resonance Imaging experiment corroborated the results. Berent et al. (2014) report that the hemodynamic response in the brain is modulated by phonological well-formedness in terms of sonority (i.e. large rise, small rise, plateau, and fall), reflecting the universal hierarchy of the syllable structure, namely blif > bnif > bdif > lbif. Dispreferred syllables are more difficult to identify, and lead to more errors.

As far as the psychological reality of the sonority principle is concerned, the SSG constitutes a benchmark for the classification of existent and non-existent forms in terms of well-formedness or markedness. For instance, Daland et al. (2011) show that English speakers provide judgements on sonority in non-existent items. That is word initial clusters with falling sonority tend to be evaluated as worse than clusters with no sonority differential (plateaus). The experimental data unarguably demonstrate the speakers' capacity to provide fine-grained judgement of varying linguistic forms. It was observed that speakers provide principled responses not only to existence, distinguishing between licit and illicit phonotactics, but also to items of different well-formedness conditions. Apart from existence and phonological structure, gradient phonotactic judgement has been also shown to be affected by frequency, or its interaction with other factors.

Classic contributions by Coleman (1996) and Coleman and Pierrehumbert (1997) demonstrate the relation between well-formedness and frequency. Frisch et al. (2000) show that nonce words in English are more likely to be judged as real words if they are shorter and composed of high-frequency subunits. A body of research also demonstrated that probabilistic phonotactics and neighbourhood density play a role in processing times and correctness rates. Vitevitch et al. (1999) report that nonce words with high probability segments and sequences of segments involve faster processing times than nonce words composed of (sequences of) segments with relatively low frequency in spoken words. The results are confirmed in Vitevitch and Luce (1999), who show that higher phonotactic probability facilitates the processing of spoken stimuli. In both studies, the positive effects of neighbourhood density are observed as well.

One interpretation of the extant processing data states that principles of phonological organization (such as sonority) constitute a deeply-rooted linguistic universal (see Berent et al. 2004). The misperception of errors in cross-linguistically dispreferred onset clusters in Pitt (1998), Moreton (2002) and Berent et al. (2007, 2014) can reflect the clusters' ill-formed status in the grammars of all speakers, disregarding their linguistic competence, experience or exposure. What is more, sonority is not the only principle investigated with respect to phonotactic markedness. Another principle of syntagmatic organization involves constraints on (non-)identical place of articulation (Leben 1973; McCarthy 1986, 1988; Mester 1986; Sommerstein 1974; Yip 1988). Although this topic has been explored particularly in relation to Arabic, who are fine-tuned to OCP-Place effects in the judgement of nonce words (e.g. Frisch and Zawaydeh 2001; Frisch et al. 2004), constraints on homorganic consonants have been identified in various typologically unrelated languages such as English, Javanese and Ngbaka (for an extended discussion see Frisch 2004).

With these views in mind, words of different phonological structure and (non-) existence are expected to be processed differently. The phonological structure embraces different features, based either on the manner or place of articulation or voicing. These themes of investigation have also beed pursued in Polish phonotactics in Wagner et al. (2012) and Wiese et al. (2017). In an ERP study on the perception of /pt/ by native English and Polish speakers, Wagner et al. (2012) show that the cluster found in onset position is correctly identified only by Polish speakers. That is, speakers distinguish between nonce words starting with /pt/ (which is attested in Polish in *ptak* 'bird') and the same sequence split by a vowel /pEt/ (as in *petycja* 'petition'). In English speakers, the absence of onset /pt/ results in the misperception of the cluster in spite of the existing contrast between /pt/ – /pEt/ word-finally in *trumped* and *trumpet* (sic!).[1] The results suggest that the exposure of phoneme sequences in a specific prosodic position is a prerequisite for accurate perception. This result is relevant for the present analysis which investigates positional constraints.

Another ERP study on Polish phonotactics is reported in Wiese et al. (2017). The experiment aimed at testing the learnability of final CC clusters in nonce monosyllables depending on two factors; existence of a cluster (CC attested in Polish vs. non-existent) and sonority (well-formed vs. ill-formed). The learnability paradigm involved recording electro-physiological and behavioural responses during two EEG sessions separated by the interval of 2–3 days, during which learning took place. The study demonstrates that sonority as a factor is not significant in early N400 time window (450–550 ms) but contributes to processing in the later component belonging to the P600 family (700–1050 ms). What is more, existence shows to be significant only in interactions. These findings suggests that sonority has a more a facilitative effect on perception than cluster existence. The lack of effect in the early time window is attributed to the fact that native speakers of Polish are generally exposed to long and sonority-violating clusters. Overall, well-formed clusters, disregarding whether they are existent or non-existent, are easier to learn.

Note that Wagner et al. (2012) and Wiese et al. (2017) discuss electro-physiological responses to the conditions under scrutiny. So far, no studies I am aware of have tested online processing of existence and sonority violations in

[1]sic! The words exemplifying the sequences, as quoted in the paper, are not combinations of /pt/ and /pVt/ but /mpt/ and /mpVt/.

Polish consonant clusters explicitly in terms of reaction times. Therefore, this chapter reports on two experiments, which investigate the psychological reality of three factors: existence, sonority and place of articulation distances. Given a wealth of research on the interaction between existence and sonority (see above), I propose to include a variable related to the place of articulation. The POA distance can be viewed as another aspect of well-formedness (like the OCP). What is more, it has never been studied with respect to the processing of phonotactics.

Experiment 1 (henceforth Exp 1) refers to word-initial phonotactics, while Experiment 2 (henceforth Exp 2) refers to word-final phonotactics. Given the complexity of Polish consonant clusters, the experiments are aimed at answering the following questions:

(1) Do existent phonotactic patterns generalize to novel words?
(2) Which phonological factors facilitate (and to what degree) the processing of clusters?
(3) Does the processing of nonce words reflect grammatical knowledge or can it be modelled by means of lexical analogy?

4.3 Hypotheses

Apart form the investigation of the role that sonority, place distance and existence play in online processing, there are larger issues at hand which the experiments have the potential to address, namely gradience, positionality of constraints and sources of phonotactic knowledge.

Previous accounts on the processing of phonotactics have demonstrated that speakers respond differently to phonotactic patterns which are exemplified in their mother tongue, in contrast to patterns which are non-existent. However, it has also been established that judgement can be gradient, depending on the degree of phonotactic violations resulting from a sonority distance (e.g. small vs. medium vs. large) as well as the severeness of the OCP violations (e.g. involving a complex interplay of relations between consonants sharing place vs. identical consonants, and immediately adjacent consonants or not). Exp 1 and Exp 2 have the power of providing insights into gradient responses in two ways. First, the structure of the stimuli enables a gradient evaluation of the distance condition. The POA distance encompasses seven levels (distances 0–6), which can be subsequently analysed on a scale, or in terms of broader categories of small, medium and large distances. Second, with respect to the statistical methods employed in the processing of the data (quantile regression), a fine-grained analysis of the predictors is possible by looking into consecutive deciles of the observed latencies. Traditional psycholinguistic methodology makes use of models which operate on averages, which results in losing insights into the importance of factors at early and late reaction times.

The second issue of interest constitutes the comparison between initial and final clusters. Exp 1 and Exp 2 are expected to provide systematic insights into positional constraints in Polish. Since phonotactic constraints are formulated separately for syllable onsets and codas, different factors are likely to affect word-initial and word-final clusters. It is possible that initial phonotactics is governed by a different set of restrictions than final phonotactics. Care was taken to construct two identical experiments for two word positions, and to supply two sets of comparable stimuli.

Finally, the experiments contribute to the debate on the sources of phonotactic knowledge. This topic has been debated in phonological theory, leading to two hypotheses. One interpretation of constraints is that they are stored in the mental lexicon. Viewed from this perspective, nonce words containing non-existent clusters in Polish are bound to have a significant impact on acceptability ratings and response latencies. When confronted with a consonant cluster not exemplified in Polish, speakers should immediately recognize its obsolete status and respond accordingly. This will entail differences in correctness rates and increased cognitive costs in non-existent clusters.

Another interpretation assumes that phonotactic constraints have their source not only in the lexicon but also in phonological principles such as sonority. If speakers consult only lexical statistics when making lexical judgement, sonority should be a strong predictor in final phonotactics, and a weaker predictor in initial phonotactics. As I noted in Chap. 1, Polish speakers have been life-long exposed to long and sonority-violating clusters, many of which are common and have high usage frequency. However, the sonority profile of clusters varies in word-initial and word-final position. This property of Polish phonotactics was discussed in Chap. 2, where clusters were evaluated in terms of three sonority scales (cf. Tables 2.6 and 2.7). The analysis based on more detailed sonority hierarchies (i.e. involving six or seven sound classes) revealed that the proportion of SSG-obeying and SSG-violating types word-initially is comparable (50% : 50%). Different results are obtained in word-final position, where SSG-violating types prevail (70%). If sonority shows to have no effect on response latencies, it will suggest that the principle does not motivate the phonological structure of the lexicon. In consequence, it cannot be extrapolated as a principle and generalized to nonce items tested in the experiments. Overall, if phonotactic constraints are the domain of the lexicon, sonority-violating clusters should affect neither judgement ratings nor cognitive effort required in their processing.

The design of Exp 1 and Exp 2 offers a comparison of phonotactics at two word edges. Hypotheses outlined in 43 refer to reaction times (latency responses, RT). In line with previous psycho- and neurolinguistic studies on Polish (e.g. Wagner et al. 2012; Wiese et al. 2017) and feature weight discussed in Chap. 3, the following hypotheses are put forward for reaction times.

43. Hypotheses for reaction times

    (43.a) Existent versus non-existent
    No differences in the processing of existent and non-existent clusters are expected.

(43.b) Well-formed versus ill-formed clusters
Weak differences are expected to be observed in the processing of well-formed and ill-formed clusters. The SSG is likely to affect RTs in interaction with other factors.
Word-final position is expected to be more sensitive to sonority violations. SSG-violating clusters are likely to be immediately rejected resulting in shorter reaction times.

(43.c) Distances 0–6
The principle which governs the clarity of perception is sufficient contrast. Clusters exemplifying larger place of articulation distances are expected to facilitate perception resulting in shorter reaction times.

The subject literature suggests that behavioural data (i.e. accuracy responses, ACC) tend to be less sensitive with respect to subtle linguistic properties. Therefore, I expect that the hypotheses for reaction times are likely to hold for accuracy rates but the effects can be weaker.

4.4 The Experiments

Two reaction time experiments were designed to test the processing of clusters in the word-initial (Exp 1) and word-final (Exp 2) context. Since response latencies tend to be affected also by non-experimental factors, care was taken to design two largely comparable experiments. Therefore, the structure of the stimuli is identical. To neutralize the semantic bias and frequency effects, both studies are based solely on nonce words. In order to minimize the influence of fatigue, distorted attention, sleepiness, and time of the day, the same group of subjects was requested to take part in both experimental session on the same day. The experiments were separated by a break, whose length depended on participants' preferences. Also, I used the same sensory modality by presenting auditory stimuli.

4.4.1 Subjects

Thirty-eight native speakers of Polish (33 women) volunteered to take part in each experiment. Subjects, aged between 20 and 26 (average age: 21), were registered undergraduate students at Adam Mickiewicz University in Poznań (AMU), who reported no visual or hearing impairments, and who were mainly right-handed (89%). The largest group of students (42%) came from Great Poland, the region where the experiment was conducted. All subjects were brought up as monolingual speakers of Polish. Subjects provided informed consent for their participation and were financially gratified for their contribution. It must be noted that all subjects were advanced speakers of English, and four subjects reported proficiency in

French and Spanish. Among other languages mastered at basic or intermediate level, subjects listed Russian, German, Icelandic, French, Italian, and Spanish. Since none of the languages is phonotactically more complex than Polish, proficiency in other languages was not a disqualifying criterion. Responses from all subjects were used in the statistical analysis.

The sessions took place in the *Language and Communication Laboratory* at the Faculty of English (AMU) which is a research facility suited to conduct controlled interdisciplinary experiments. Computer stations equipped with the *E-Prime* software (E-Prime 2.0 Psychology Software Tools, Inc., Pittsburgh, PA, USA, Schneider et al. 2012) allow to collect behavioural and latency responses from eight subjects simultaneously. For both sessions, three to eight students were tested at a time. Subjects were monitored from a control room separated from the test room by a glass window. Those tested in booths were monitored by ceiling-mounted video cameras. In such a way, subjects were attended to during a break between experimental blocks.

4.4.2 Material

Word-final stimuli were originally designed for the purpose of two learnability experiments aimed at comparing Polish and German speakers' responses in two ERP studies (cf. Ulbrich et al. 2016 for German; Wiese et al. 2017 for Polish). The EEG experiments involved a learning paradigm in which subjects were requested to learn new words as names of objects. The stimuli were nonce monosyllables containing final CC clusters, which were designed to test two factors: existence and well-formedness. The two-by-two comparison of the factors made it possible to test micro-voltage and behavioural responses to the following phonotactic conditions: existent × well-formed, existent × ill-formed, non-existent × well-formed and non-existent × ill-formed.

It must be noted that the original stimuli prepared for the purpose of the EPR studies accounted for the place of articulation distance. This criterion was used in Wiese et al. (2017) to select cluster types, and avoid the prevalence of clusters composed solely of coronal consonants, which are more common than labials and dorsals in both Polish and German (Jassem 2003; Kohler 1990). Due to the complexity of the experimental design, Ulbrich et al. (2016) and Wiese et al. (2017) report only on the role of existence and well-formedness in online processing, and do not discuss the influence of distance. Therefore, to complement the previous results, the present reaction time experiments include the place of articulation distance as a variable.

Since the goal of Ulbrich et al. (2016) and Wiese et al. (2017) was to provide a systematic cross-linguistic comparison between German and Polish, it was ensured that the critical stimuli match both phonological systems. Thus, clusters used as stimuli in Wiese et al. (2017) were composed only of segments found in both languages (see this chapter, Section "Experiment 2: Word-Final Stimuli"), which substantially limited the inventory of existent and non-existent clusters to be used in the ERP studies. In Sect. 4.4.2.1, I present the general outline of the conditions investigated in Exp 1 and Exp 2. A detailed description of critical clusters and stimuli constructed for word-initial and word-final position is presented in “Experiment 1: Word-Initial Stimuli” and “Experiment 2: Word-Final Stimuli”, respectively.

4.4.2.1 Conditions

In each experiment, stimuli were 252 nonce monosyllables which were carefully constructed according to three factors: *existence* × *sonority* × *place of articulation distance*.

Existence. The factor distinguishes between two conditions: clusters that are found at edges of real words (labelled existent, EX), and clusters that are not exemplified in Polish (non-existent, NEX). Existent clusters included rare and obsolete sequences such as initial /lɲ mx rt/, which occur only in one word *lniany* ‘linen’ (adj), *mchu* ‘moss’ (gen sg) and *rtęć* ‘mercury’. In order to explore the full phonotactic potential of Polish, morphonotactic clusters were included in the list. This procedure broadened the range of cluster types to be used in the experiments by 122 initials and 39 finals, which made it possible to compile a sufficient number of types matching all the criteria.

Sonority. This two-level factor determines the sonority profile of clusters. Two conditions specify CCs that follow the SSG by displaying a gradual sonority rise from cluster margins towards a vowel (well-formed, WF), and CCs that violate the principle by exhibiting a rising slope from the nucleus outward (ill-formed, IF). The hierarchy used in the classification of clusters is given in 44.

44. The sonority scale used in stimulus construction
    plosives < affricates < fricatives < nasals < liquids < glides < vowels

Six classes of consonants make it possible to capture subtle differences between obstruent-only clusters, where affricates mediate between plosives (e.g. /bʣ ʦp ʧt/) and fricatives (/ʨx ʑʥ ʥv/). It must be noted that plateau clusters composed of segments with an identical manner of articulation (e.g. /ss pk mn/) were regarded as ill-formed due to their insufficient sonority differential (Parker 2012). While sonority and existence are uncontroversial factors in psycholinguistic studies, little is known about the role of the place of articulation in Polish phonotactics. Therefore, Exp 1 and Exp 2 report on yet another phonological factor which can possibly affect reaction times, namely the POA distance.

Place of articulation distance. The concept of phonetic and phonological distance has been explored from various perspectives. Distance has served to account for dialectal change in sociolinguistics (Chambers and Trudgill 1998; Heeringa 2004) and to group languages depending on their featural, lexical or geographical differences (Gibbon 2014, 2016). In phonology, it has been used to measure the relationship between phonotactic complexity and stress placement (e.g. Orzechowska et al. 2018, 2019). Phonetically-determined distances have been used to account for perceptual confusion (Miller and Nicely 1955) and predict cross-linguistic phonotactic constraints (Kawasaki 1982; Ohala and Kawasaki-Fukumori 1997). The sonority principle has implemented phonetic distances to capture degrees of phonotactic preferability, e.g. the *Sonority Dispersion Principle* (Clements 1990), *Minimal Sonority Distance* (Selkirk 1984; Steriade 1982), *Minimum Sonority Difference* (Harris 1983) or *Sonority Differential* (Parker 2012). While these approaches focus on the manner of articulation, in the present experiments distances are calculated for the place of articulation. Place distances have been explored in Dziubalska-Kołaczyk (2014) on par with manner and voice distances. Place distances have also been indirectly addressed by the *Obligatory Contour Principle*, whose version prohibits consecutive homorganic segments from underlying representations (McCarthy 1988; Mester 1986; Yip 1988). Note that a more strict version of the hypothesis originally proposed by Leben (1973) and McCarthy (1986) bans adjacent segments with total identity (i.e. with a distance of zero in terms of place, manner and voice properties). It must be emphasized that this variable serves a double function in the Exp 1 and Exp 2. Apart from being a factor under investigation, place distances constitute a control criterion for a balanced set of critical clusters.

A random selection of clusters could be biased by segment frequency as well as segment commonness in clusters and in different word positions. As to the second point, Zydorowicz et al. (2016) investigated the positional occupancy of consonants in a cluster. On the basis of large lists of initial, medial and final clusters, the authors inspected the occurrence of consonants in different cluster positions, as illustrated in Table 4.1. For each word position, several consonantal slots are given (e.g. 1–4 word-initially, 1–5 word-finally). These slots correspond to the number of consecutive consonants. An asterisk marks the presence of a consonant in a given cluster slot. From Table 4.1 it emerges that while some segments show not to form clusters in a given word position (e.g. /j̃ w̃ ŋ/ initially, /ʤ ʣ ʥ ʒ/ finally), other segments (e.g. /f t/) emerge freely in almost all consonant slots across a word.

A related point is that evidence has been provided in favour of the unmarked status of coronals (Hall 1997; Paradis and Prunet 1991; Rice 2007), which constitute the largest group of segments in Polish (N = 18), next to labials (N = 5) and dorsals (N = 6) in the classification of Jassem (2003). This means that a random selection of clusters could possibly lead to stimuli composed primarily of adjacent, say, dentals and alveolars. Therefore, distances constitute a control criterion for including a whole range of place features and their combinations. Clusters used as stimuli are composed of consonants articulated in different areas of the mouth cavity, and involve different directionality of the articulatory movement (i.e. towards a front or back part of the mouth cavity, see 3.3.3.2). The calculation of distances is based on the scale presented in Chap. 3, which is repeated in 45.

Table 4.1 Positional order of consonants in Polish clusters

C	initial				medial						final				
	1	2	3	4	1	2	3	4	5	6	1	2	3	4	5
j		*	*	*	*	*	*	*	*	*	*				
p	*	*	*		*	*	*	*	*	*	*	*	*		
r	*	*	*	*	*	*	*	*	*		*	*	*		
s	*	*	*		*	*	*	*	*		*	*	*		
t	*	*	*		*	*	*	*	*		*	*	*	*	
k	*	*	*		*	*	*	*	*		*	*	*		
m	*	*	*		*	*	*	*			*	*	*		
ʃ	*	*	*	*	*	*	*	*	*		*	*	*		
n		*	*	*	*	*	*	*			*	*			
ɕ	*	*	*		*	*	*	*			*	*	*		
w	*	*	*	*	*	*	*	*	*		*	*	*		
w̃					*						*				
tɕ	*	*	*		*	*	*	*				*	*		
v	*	*	*		*	*	*	*	*		*				
ɲ		*	*	*	*	*	*	*	*		*	*			
z	*	*			*	*	*	*			*	*			
b	*	*	*		*	*	*	*			*	*			
ts	*	*			*	*	*	*			*	*	*		
l	*	*	*	*	*	*	*	*	*		*	*	*		
d	*	*	*		*	*	*	*			*	*			
f	*	*	*	*	*	*	*	*	*		*	*	*	*	*
g	*	*	*		*	*	*	*			*	*			
tʃ	*	*	*		*	*	*	*			*	*	*		
ʒ	*	*	*		*	*	*	*	*						
x	*	*	*		*	*	*	*			*	*			
dʑ	*	*	*		*	*	*	*			*				
dz	*	*			*	*	*								
ʑ	*	*	*		*	*	*				*				
ŋ					*	*					*				
j̃					*	*					*				
dʒ	*	*			*	*	*								

Adapted from Zydorowicz et al. (2016: 85f.)

Table 4.2 Conditions tested in experiment 1 and experiment 2

	Existent clusters (EX)	Non-existent clusters (NEX)
Well-formed clusters (WF)	Distances (0–6)	Distances (0–6)
Ill-formed clusters (IF)	Distances (0–6)	Distances (0–6)

45. Place distances used in stimulus construction

bilabial < labio-dental < dental < alveolar < alveolo-palatal < palatal < velar
1 2 3 4 5 6 7

The procedure of calculating POA distances was introduced in Chap. 3. The distance of one holds between successive classes of consonants on the scale. For instance, distances of one, two and three hold for clusters /vm/ (labio-dental + bilabial), /bz/ (bilabial + dental), and /js/ (palatal + dental), respectively. The smallest difference in distance equals zero for combinations of segments with the same place of articulation (e.g. bilabial + bilabial /mp/, alveolo-palatal + alveolo-palatal /ɕɲ/), while the largest distance of six is found between the most extreme articulations combining the bilabial and velar gestures (e.g. /px gm kp/).

It must be emphasized that it is rather dubious that place distances can be adequately expressed in terms of an arithmetic system as the one given in 45. The proximity of specific places of articulation depends on the geometry of the vocal tract. For instance, a distance of one holds between labial consonants such as bilabial + labio-dental as well as between labial and coronal articulations such as labio-dental + dental, although labial and coronal gestures differ with respect to active articulators. In spite of this fact, the distance measure is treated as an approximation. What is more, the interpretation of the results accounts for coarse categories of small, medium and large distances.

When preparing the stimuli, I firstly automatically generated a list of all potential two-member combinations based on the consonantal inventory of Polish (Jassem 2003), resulting in 841 (29 × 29) CC items. Nasalized glides were eliminated from the list as they constitute a phonetic realization of nasal vowels {ą, ę} followed by fricatives. All the cluster types were grouped based on their existence and sonority, i.e. WF-EX, WF-NEX, IF-EX, IF-NEX. Next, for each item the place of articulation distance was calculated. An overview of the conditions is given in Table 4.2.

The number of clusters used in Exp 1 was determined by the number of two-member sequences originally used in Exp 2.

4.4.2.2 Stimuli

Experiment 1: Word-Initial Stimuli

Having compiled a list of 42 real initial clusters, I was left with around 300 combinations from the automatically generated list of 841 items. From this list, I eliminated 458 existing sequences found word-initially in Polish (see Tables 1.14 and 1.15). Given such a variety of clusters, the construction of non-existent congeners adhering to the three criteria turned out to be a challenging task. Additionally, an attempt was made to maximize phonetic similarity between EX and NEX items by matching non-existent clusters with real ones according to the manners and places of articulation. This procedure largely limited the number of possible but unattested sequences. Whenever possible, non-existent equivalents of existent clusters were constructed by introducing a minimal change of one feature (in terms of the place of articulation, manner of articulation or voicing). However, in order to be able to compile a list of 21 items per each condition WF-EX, WF-NEX, IF-EX, IF-NEX, a compromise had to be made with respect to the voicing profile, illegal combinations and frequency.

Target clusters display a varying profile in terms of voicing. For instance, the list of initial clusters includes /bx gf kv xʒ/, although phonotactic constraints require voice agreement between adjacent obstruents. Other examples of illegal clusters involve combinations which violate the phonotactic constraints listed in Chap. 1 in Sect. 1.4.1, namely initial /bg pk jm ŋv/. Finally, the lists incorporate existent clusters which are found in obsolete and morphologically complex words (e.g. /ln lɲ mx/ in *lnu* 'flax' (gen sg), *lniany* 'linen', *mchu* 'moss' (gen sg)).

A complete list of initial clusters compiled for Exp 1 is presented in alphabetical order in Table 4.3. Note that the structure of the stimuli constitutes an improvement on the word-final cluster set (Section "Experiment 2: Word-Final Stimuli"), whose construction was guided by the need to enable a cross-linguistic comparison between Polish and German. This goal resulted in eliminating some consonants (e.g. syllabic nasals and liquids in German) from the list of possible stimuli. The critical clusters used in Exp 1 explore the full phonotactic potential of Polish by using 29 consonants as initial input.

All the initial CCs were embedded in three types of monosyllabic nonce words of the structure CCVC. In order to increase the number of stimuli to be used in the

Table 4.3 Experiment 1: word-initial CC clusters used in stimulus construction

	Existent clusters (EX)	Non-existent clusters (NEX)
Well-formed clusters (WF)	0: dl, tl, ɕɲ	0: dʥ, pm, ʦs
	1: ʥv, tr vm	1: ʥr, fm, nr
	2: bz, dɲ, pn	2: bʥ, ʥɲ, ʨx
	3: br, lj, ʃm	3: ʤm, kʧ, xʒ[a]
	4: bʑ, fj, kl	4: pʨ, ʦx, xn
	5: gv, kf, pj	5: gf, kv, vŋ
	6: gm, px, xm	6: bŋ, bx, pŋ
Ill-formed clusters (IF)	0: ɕʨ, ln, ʑʥ	1: mp, rʃ, xk
	1: lv, rt, ʧt	2: mf, rd, rʑ
	2: lɲ, pt, zʥ	3: mz, ʦp, ʦʨ
	3: fʨ, mʒ, ʃp	4: mʤ, nk, xʧ
	4: ɕp, sk, xt	5: ʥg, lk, nx
	5: fk, vg, xf	6: jm, ŋv, vx
	6: gb, kp, mx	7: bg, pk, xp

[a]/xʒ/ was mistakenly classified as well-formed at the stage of data construction. In the phonetic analysis of the stimuli and the statistical analysis of the results, the cluster was analysed together with ill-formed non-existent clusters, along with other plateau sequences

Table 4.4 Experiment 1: summary of conditions

Clusters	Distance	Suffixes	Existence	Sonority
3	0-6 7	/es/ vs /ot/ vs /um/ 3	EX vs NEX 2	WF vs IF 2
Σ = 21				
Σ = 63				
Σ = 126				
Σ = 252				

experiment, the VC suffix was represented by three different vowels and consonants. The vowels selected for the nuclear position involved a low-front /e/, low-back /o/ and high back /u/. In the Polish vowel space, only these vowels ensure maximum articulatory distance. Vowels /i/ and /ɨ/ had to be disregarded as potential nuclei due to their palatalizing effect on the preceding consonant. Also, it was ensured that the final consonant of a nonce word was represented by different manners of articulation and relatively neutral places of articulation such as a dental fricative /s/, a dental plosive /t/ and a bilabial nasal /m/. The combination of the vowels and the consonants led to three VC suffixes, namely /es/, /ot/ and /um/.

Each nonce word was composed of a critical CC cluster followed by the suffixes, e.g. /ɕɲes/, /ɕɲot/, /ɕɲum/ and /bges/, /bgot/, /bgum/. Two words had to be presented with a different vowel. /pjas/ was used to substitute for /pjes/, which is an existing word meaning 'dog' (*pies*), while /kfet/ was used to replace /kfot/, which is a genitive plural form of the noun *kwota* 'sum' (of money). All words used in the study are tabulated in Appendix G. All critical clusters differing in terms of the place of articulation distance (3 clusters × 7 distances = 21) were presented with two existence values (21 × 2 = 42), three suffixes (42 × 3 = 126) and two sonority types (126 × 2 = 252). The overview of the stimuli per condition is presented in Table 4.4.

The resulting lists of 252 nonce words was recorded by a trained phonetician coming from the Great Poland region. The recordings of the stimuli for Exp 1 took place in the *Center for Speech and Language Processing* at the Faculty of English (AMU) in a sound-proof cabin. The items were recorded directly onto a Mac computer using the *Amadeus* software (HairerSoft, Kenilworth, UK; version 2.1, 1523; Hairer 2009), and were digitized at 44.1 kHz with a 16-bit sampling depth (mono format). The words were spoken at a normal speech rate.

Psycholinguistic research shows that processing latencies differ for real and hypothetical words (e.g. Bentin et al. 1999; Domahs et al. 2009; Friederici 2002). Since the data contain some demanding non-existent clusters (e.g. /ŋv jm pŋ dʥ/), whose articulation could be exaggerated (e.g. unnaturally slow), the recordings were supervised by a linguistically-trained assistant, and further judged by two evaluators with respect to naturalness. In case of unclear, exaggerated or prolonged pronunciation, some items were re-recorded until judged authentic.

Experiment 2: Word-Final Stimuli

Word-final stimuli used in Exp 2 were originally compiled for the ERP study by Wiese et al. (2017). The selection of critical clusters was guided by the necessity to provide a cross-linguistic comparison between Polish and German. In order to account for the differences in the consonant and cluster inventories between the languages, some sequences were disregarded. Since in German sonorants can be syllabic word-finally, combinations such as /tn fr ml/ were eliminated from the set of possible stimuli. Also, final clusters emerging from the realization of {ą, ę} + fricative sequences in Polish (e.g. /j̃s w̃ʃ/) were disregarded (for a detailed exposition see Sect. 1.5.2). Since /w/ is absent in German and /j/ is a fricative (Wiese 1996), clusters which can arise in asynchronic articulation of the vowels were eliminated from the stimulus set.

From the list of all possible two-member sequences, first I extracted existent final clusters matching the four main conditions WF-EX, WF-NEX, IF-EX, IF-NEX. The maximum number of available CCs was 21, with the exception of the EX-IF group for which only 19 real items were found. Therefore, some existent clusters were used twice but in combination with different prefixes. Morphologically-motivated and low frequency clusters were used. For instance, /fn km kf nr/ are found in isolated words such as *hafn* 'hafnium' (a chemical element), *flegm* 'phlegm' (gen pl), *strzykw* 'sea cucumber' (gen pl), *henr* 'henry' (a unit of electrical inductance). Since Polish features no syllabic consonants, obstruent + sonorant sequences such as /fn kl pɲ/ are legitimate tautosyllabic clusters. Also, attention was paid to matching existent and non-existent clusters in terms of places and manners of articulation. Finally, an insufficient number of real clusters made it impossible to provide the same number of items for each place distance ranging from zero to six: a criterion which was satisfied in Exp 1.

A list of target final clusters (ordered alphabetically) used in the construction of the stimuli in Exp 2 is given in Table 4.5.

The clusters were embedded in monosyllabic nonce words of the CVCC structure. Each word was composed of a CV prefix followed by a critical cluster. Three different prefixes were used, namely /ge/, /fa/, and /no/. Care was taken to

Table 4.5 Experiment 2: word-final CC clusters used in stimulus construction

	Existent clusters (EX)	Non-existent clusters (NEX)
Well-formed clusters (WF)	0–1: ɕtɕ, ɲtɕ, ʃʧ, rs, ʃt, ʧt	0–1: ŋx, sʦ, xk, fp, sʧ, ʃʦ
	2–4: lm, sp, ftɕ, js, mʃ, rk, ʧp, ɕp, lk, mɕ, sk	2–4: fʧ, np, ŋʧ, rŋ, ʃk, ʧk, xʧ, lŋ, nk, nx, ŋʦ
	5–6: fk, jm, jp, mx	5–6: ŋf, mk, ŋp, xp
Ill-formed clusters (IF)	0–1: kx, fn, nr, tf, tr	0–1: sʃ, ʦf, ʦʃ, ʧs, ʧʦ
	2–4: ɕl, fr, mn, ps, pt, pʧ, ʃx, xʃ, kl, pɲ, ptɕ	2–4: fʃ, pʦ, ʃf, tp, ʧf, kʃ, kʧ, ʧx, tk, ʦx, tx
	5–6: kf (2x), km (2x), xm (2x)	5–6: fx, xf, kp, pk, px

employ vowels maximally dispersed in the vowel space, which ensures large contrast. As to the consonants, /g/, /f/ and /n/ represent different places of articulation (velar, labio-dental, dental) and manners of articulation (plosive, fricative, nasal), which guarantees sufficient variation. The prefixes were attached to the critical clusters resulting in three different words such as /gekʧ/, /fakʧ/, /nokʧ/ and /gejp/, /fajp/, /nojp/. Due to an insufficient number of clusters with a large POA distance in the EX-IF group, /km/ and /xm/ were repeated using different vowels. That is, apart from /gekm fakm nokm/ and /gexm faxm noxm/, additional three stimuli /gakm foxm nekm/ were introduced. Also, /kf/ was used twice with different CV prefixes, namely /gekf fakf nokf/ and /gakf fokf nekf/. A complete list of nonce words created for the purpose of Exp 2 is given in Appendix H.

252 stimuli were recorded by the same phonetician as in Exp 1. The recordings took place in the phonetic lab at the Institute of Germanic Linguistics (University of Marburg). Words were recorded directly onto a Mac computer using the *Amadeus Pro* software (Hairer 2009) set to a 16-bit mono channel, digitized with a sampling frequency of 44,100 Hz. Some clusters which were articulatorily challenging (e.g. /km ŋʧ ʧʦ/) were recorded in the presence of another phonetician who evaluated their naturalness.

4.4.3 Procedure

Exp 1 and Exp 2 were divided into 2 blocks, each containing a fixed set of 126 trials. Within each block, the trials were randomised in terms of item order presentation, and counterbalanced for response buttons. The randomization of the trial lists and handedness was coded in E-Prime, which resulted in 38 different experimental versions automatically generated for all subjects. Prior to the task proper, subjects were required to complete a training session in order to familiarize themselves with the experimental design. The training session consisted of ten trials constructed to match the investigated conditions. Instructions were given prior to the training and repeated on instruction slides before the trials were played. After the training, subjects had the possibility to ask questions, or continue with the experiment, if desired.

The task of participants in each trial was to judge whether the word they heard sounded as if it could exist in Polish by pressing a 'yes' or 'no' button. Correctness of responses was coded according to the *existence* condition. That is, stimuli containing existent clusters were classified as possible ('yes' = correct response), while trials with non-existent clusters were coded as those which could not exist in Polish ('no' = correct response). Responses were coded in <left Ctrl> and <right arrow> keyboard buttons. Subjects who were assigned even identification numbers were automatically provided with the version where correct and incorrect responses were coded in <arrow> and <Ctrl>, respectively. A reverse response button assignment was allocated to subjects coded with uneven numbers. A resting phase

Table 4.6 The structure of a single trial in experiment 1 and experiment 2

Stimulus presentation	Response	Transition between trials
→ Fixation star (800 ms) → Blank (500 ms) → Audio	→ Timeout (5,000 ms, including audio)	→ Logger and blank screen (2,000 ms)

following the first block made it possible for students to rest, and continue with the second block whenever ready.

During the experiment, subjects were comfortably seated in front of a 15-in. computer screen. The presentation of an audio stimulus was accompanied by an image of a loudspeaker, followed by a fixation star, and a blank screen, after which the next trial started. The response timeout set at stimulus onset was 5,000 ms. The time-line of a trial in both experiments is presented in Table 4.6.

Responses were collected from the stimulus onset. The transition between trails was separated by a 2,000 ms blank screen. Each experiment took approximately 20 min, including the training session and the break.

4.5 Results

4.5.1 Experiment 1: Word-Initial Clusters

The experiment investigated the role of existence, sonority and place of articulation distances in the processing of word-initial two-member clusters. In the sections to follow, I provide the results of the analyses for reaction times and correctness rates for Exp 1, preceded by a discussion on the selection of the statistical model.

4.5.1.1 Statistical Model Considerations

The psycholinguistic experimentation predominantly makes use of generalized linear mixed models (henceforth GLMMs) and generalized additive models (henceforth GAMs) in the study of the relationship between the response and the predictors. GLMMs include fixed effects as well as random effects. This usual linear relationship is in GAMs substituted by non-linear smooth functions fitted to capture non-linear data. GLMMs, in turn, impose certain requirements on the data, which cannot be always fulfilled. The complexity of psycholinguistic methodology and experimental design generate data that can become rather demanding to handle. One of the problems is a skewed distribution.

The data collected in Exp 1 was first tested in terms of its normality using the *R* language (R Development Core Team 2013, version 1.1.456, Vienna, AT). The pre-processing of the data entailed eliminating trials coded as training, rest phase,

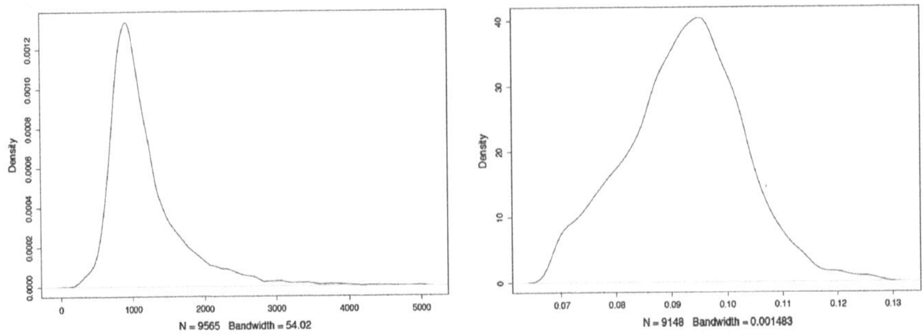

Fig. 4.1 Experiment 1: the distribution of RT responses. The left panel shows the right-skewed distribution of all the data (N = 9,565); the right panel shows the transformed distribution for the range 400–2,500 ms (N = 9,148), which approximates normality

and failure to react (the latter = 11 trials altogether). The distribution of the reaction time data (RT) is shown in Fig. 4.1. The density plot in the left panel shows that the symmetric Gaussian distribution does not hold as the distribution for all RT responses is right-skewed. The classic approach of dealing with skewness is to perform power transformations. The log transformation has been extensively used in psycholinguistic research to make the data fit more a Gaussian distribution (i.e. the familiar bell curve) and reduce variability (although see Feng et al. 2014). The range of the observed latencies varies from 97 to 4,998 ms, with a heavy tail starting at approximately 3,000 ms. The selection of the central fraction of the curve set at 400–2,500 ms leads to the loss of 417 observations. The normalized distribution using the Box-Cox transformation is given in the right panel.

As can be observed, the transformed reaction times approximate a normal distribution. Therefore, in order to find the model which would describe the structure of the data most adequately, several statistical analyses were performed. I run a generalized additive model using the *mgcv* package (Wood 2018). The package offers the scat family (or the so called scaled t-distribution) which successfully deals with outliers. Given that the data are heavy-tailed, I used a scat model which provides greater precision.

Based on the measurement of the goodness of fit REML and Akaike information criterion (AIC), the best formula was selected. Reaction times were entered as a dependent variable (with scaled t). *Existence* (existent vs. non-existent), *sonority* (well-formed vs. ill-formed) and their interaction were entered into the model as fixed factors. The GAM includes smooth terms for *POA distance* (0–6) and *audio* (i.e. the stimuli), the combination of *existence* and *subject* as well as the combination of *distance* and *subject*. Smooths involve those predictors for which no hypotheses can be put forward due to their unknown influence on RTs. The subject literature does not discuss the role of the place of articulation in online processing. Therefore, no predictions were made with respect to the role that POA distances play in response latencies. Similarly, it is unclear how RTs should be influenced by the combination of subjects and existence, as well as subjects and distance.

Table 4.7 Experiment 1: results of the generalized additive model fitted to the inverse-transformed RTs, where RT = (reaction time)$^{-0.343}$

Family: Scaled t (14.925,0.008)					
Link function: identity					
Formula:					
RT ~ Existence * Sonority + s(Distance, k = 3) + s(Audio, bs = "re") + s(Subject, Existence, bs = "re") + s(Subject, Distance, bs = "re")					
Parametric coefficients:					
	Estimate	Std. error	t-value	Pr (>|t|)	
Intercept	9.226e−02	1.094e−03	84.301	<2e−16	***
ExistenceEX	−3.609e−04	1.533e−03	−0.235	0.814	
SonorityWF	8.834e−05	3.922e−04	0.225	0.822	
ExistenceEX:SonorityWF	8.083e−04	5.546e−04	1.458	0.145	
–					
Signif. codes: 0 (***) 0.001 (**) 0.01 (*) 0.05 (.) 0.1 ( ) 1					
Approximate significance of smooth terms:					
	edf	Ref.df	F	*p*-value	
s(Distance)	1.882	1.922	5.310	0.0147	***
s(Audio)	151.795	247.000	1.685	<2e−16	***
s(Existence, Subject)	72.378	74.000	268.651	<2e−16	***
s(Distance, Subject)	22.184	37.000	138.095	2.69e−05	***
–					
Signif. codes: 0 (***) 0.001 (**) 0.01 (*) 0.05 (.) 0.1 ( ) 1					
R-sq.(adj) = 0.359; deviance explained = 35.3%					
fREML = 13910; scale est. = 1; n = 9148					

Interactions are marked in bold type

Nevertheless, the factors are expected to account for at least some variance in the data, and are therefore included into the model as smooths. The analysis was performed on 9,148 observations. Note that the difference in REML scores between different models tested did not exceed 8. The results are summarized in Table 4.7.

Let me first focus on the parametric part of the model summarized in the upper part of Table 4.7. The *p*-table lists regression coefficients, their standard error, t-statistic and corresponding *p*-values. The results show that no main effects are found. *Existence*, *sonority*, and their interaction do not contribute to the model. No t-value is larger than 2 and smaller than −2, which are borderline values used as indicators of statistical significance (Baayen et al. 2008). At the level of online processing, the results suggest that the sonority profile and existence of a cluster do not affect judgement. In other words, speakers are not sensitive to the distinction between words with real and hypothetical consonant sequences. Similarly, well-formed clusters do not facilitate processing, while ill-formed clusters do not hinder it: a result which would be expected in a sonority-governed language.

The lower part of Table 4.7 provides a list of smooth terms, marked with 's' on the predictor. The table includes effective degrees of freedom (edf), which largely correspond to the number of variables that enter the calculation of smooth terms. There are highly significant differences in response latencies for the relationship between *subjects*' reaction times and *existence,* and *subjects*' reaction times and *POA distance*. There is a substantial inter-speaker variation depending on items with existent and non-existent clusters, and items with clusters varying in the manipulation of the place features. Speakers react in a similar way to a similar set of audio stimuli. Some subjects immediately spot the difference between real and unattested clusters, and some are sensitive to the size of perceptual contrast. What is more, smooth terms involving *audio* and *POA distance* also show to contribute to the model. Response latencies are thus affected by audio stimuli and the size of perceptual contrast.

This results demonstrate that the place of articulation distance is a relevant principle in intuitive judgements. In fact, it is more relevant than well-formedess in terms of the SSG. The illustration of the smooth for *POA distance* is given in Fig. 4.2. The distribution suggests that medial distances are most costly for the processing. While clusters with distances 2–4 involve the longest reaction times (lower values on the *y* axis), a steady rise towards the POA distance of 6 points to the least cognitive cost, and ensuing shorter response latencies (higher values on the *y* axis).

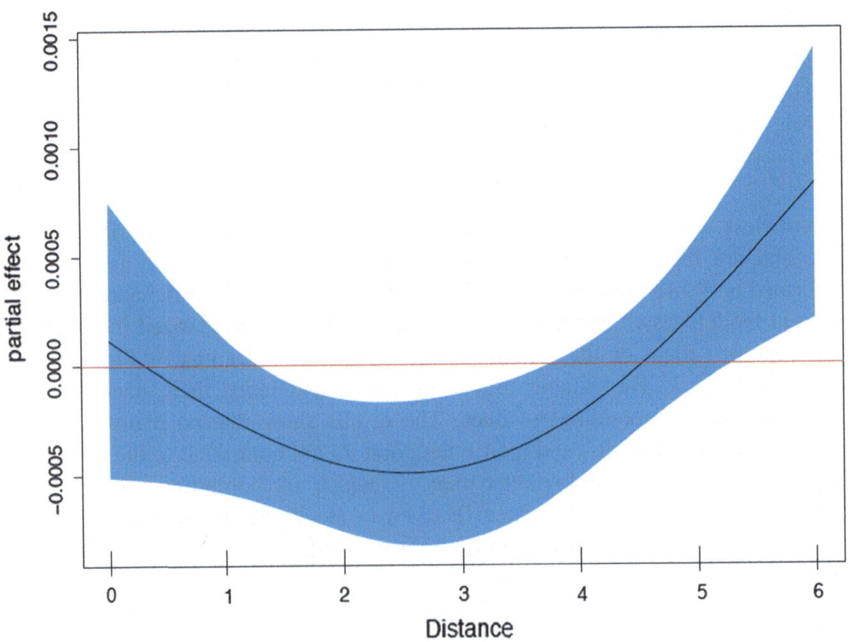

Fig. 4.2 Experiment 1: the partial effects of the POA distance smooth in a generalized additive model

Table 4.8 Major differences between linear and quantile regression

Linear regression	Quantile regression
Predicts the conditional mean	Predicts the conditional quantile and the median
Assumes a normal distribution	Is distribution-free
Conditional mean changes under transformation	Conditional quantiles are preserved under transformation
Is sensitive to outliers	Is less influenced by outliers

Based on Rodriguez and Yao (2017)

The GAM results show a general effect of the place of articulation on the processing of phonotactics. The question is how this and other factors influence perception in different windows of reaction times. The method that has been suggested to capture the influence of predictors in a fine-grained manner is quantile regression (Koenker and Bassett 1978, for introductions and overviews see Koenker 2010; Rodriguez and Yao 2017). The method has numerous advantages and in many ways surpasses the standard regression models. A summary of the most important differences between linear and quantile regression is given in Table 4.8.

One of the main advantages of the quantile regression is that it allows to detect a complex interplay between predictors for the quantiles of interest. The method has been suggested to be the most adequate one in the study of language and language processing in Baayen (to appear), who provides three arguments in favour of the modelling. Below, I summarize Baayen's arguments and make reference to the domain of reaction times.

(1) For every quantile, the effect sizes of predictors can vary. That is, the variables can take or lose effect as one moves from lower to higher quantiles. This information is lost when operating on the mean in GLMMs and GAMs. In terms of response latencies, different predictors can affect word recognition at different RTs (e.g. short, medial, long responses).
(2) If (1) is the case, the comparison of extreme quantiles of a response can be of particular relevance. The analysis of the lowest and highest quantiles can provide additional insights into the uneven predictive power of variables. Very early lexical access can be due to, for instance, sub-lexical cues rather than factors under scrutiny.
(3) The method is applicable to skewed data. Quantile GAMs are distribution agnostic, and therefore require no transformations to conform to a normal distribution.

In the present experiment, the use of quantile regression has two consequences. First, I can model the effects of the variables across all quantiles, and observe how the activation of the factors of existence, sonority and distance changes over time (e.g. from lower to higher quantiles). Secondly, I can detect a distinct set of predictors at each quantile level. For instance, given that the average duration of the stimuli in Exp 1 is 600 ms, a response at the 400–500 ms window can suggest a reaction just to the critical cluster, rather than the whole word. The analysis of the other quantile extreme, in turn, can expose factors which affect long response latencies involved in more carefully and consciously made decisions. A quantile-based analysis was argued for in Pham and Baayen's (2015) study on visual perception of Vietnamese compounds, and Baayen's (to appear) reanalysis of Ernestus and Cutler's (2015) auditory data on Dutch compounds.

4.5.1.2 Reaction Times

The analysis to follow employs a quantile GAM (with t-distribution) using the *qgam* package for R (Fasiolo et al. 2017). The package combines GAMs and quantile regression, and allows to run smooth additive quantile regression models. The model was based on the formula established in the GAM (see Table 4.7). It must be noted that quantiles constitute a convenient way of dividing the distribution into equal groups, all of which contain the same fraction of observations. *Quantile* (henceforth Q) is an umbrella term for different subdivisions of the data:

(1) deciles, i.e. the division into tenths (0.1–0.9)
(2) quantiles, i.e. the division into fifths (0.2, 0.4, 0.6, 0.8)
(3) quartiles, i.e. the division into quarters (0.25, 0.5, 0.75)
(4) percentile, i.e. the division into hundredths.

In order to provide the most detailed analysis, the response variables are analysed in terms of deciles. The data is thus divided into nine equal subsets (Q 0.1, 0.2, 0.3, …, 0.9).

I shall first focus on the description of the results obtained for intercept and fixed factors in Table 4.9. For each variable, the first column presents the estimated value, while the second column refers to the *p*-value. Each row corresponds to a quantile, i.e. the first 10, 20, 30, …, 90% of the duration of reaction times.

Table 4.9 Experiment 1: results of quantile regression for fixed factors and the intercept. The formula used: RT ~ Existence * Sonority + s(Distance, k = 3) + s(Audio, bs = "re") + s(Subject, Existence, bs = "re") + s(Subject, Distance, bs = "re")

Q	Intercept		Existence (EX)		Sonority (WF)		Existence * Sonority (EX, WF)	
0.1	0.0809	0	−3e−04	0.8237	0	0.9985	3e−04	0.6356
0.2	0.085	0	−7e−04	0.6611	1e−04	0.7698	6e−04	0.3422
0.3	0.0882	0	−7e−04	0.6752	−2e−04	0.6628	0.001	0.1139
0.4	0.0906	0	−7e−04	0.6432	−1e−04	0.8801	0.0012	0.053
0.5	0.0927	0	−6e−04	0.7106	2e−04	0.6681	0.001	0.0846
0.6	0.0947	0	−3e−04	0.8326	3e−04	0.5032	8e−04	0.1593
0.7	0.0968	0	−2e−04	0.8825	1e−04	0.7322	0.001	0.0786
0.8	0.0991	0	0	0.9992	1e−04	0.8482	9e−04	0.0981
0.9	0.102	0	4e−04	0.7789	2e−04	0.5689	5e−04	0.339

The results show that the predictors do not contribute to cluster processing (p-values > 0.05). A borderline case constitutes the interaction between existence and sonority with the p-value = 0.053 in the fourth quantile (0.4). Generally, however, the model does not reveal a linear relationship between existence, sonority and response latencies. As regards the intercept, it increases gradually from the lowest (0.1) to the highest (0.9) quantile. Significant p-values for each quantile suggest that the rise in the intercept constitutes the main factor which contributes to the increase in RTs.

Let me now proceed to the discussion on the smooth terms generated for the model. Figures 4.3, 4.4 and 4.5 show the impact of individual predictors on RTs. For each figure, nine panels correspond to nine quantiles. The left top-most panel generalizes on quantile 0.1 and the isolated panel in the fifth row generalizes on quantile 0.9. In brackets, degrees of freedom (df) are stated. The presentation of the results starts with *distance*, which is of great interest for the purpose of the present study. For reasons of space, further details of the analysis for each quantile are given in Appendix J.

The quantile analysis for *POA distance* yields statistically significant results for each quantile. It must be borne in mind that the input data was subject to the inverse transformation. As a result, the lowest quantile corresponds to the weakest RTs, which, in turn, are interpreted as the shortest reaction times. Therefore, the lower the values on the y axis, the more negative the effect of the variable on RTs, and the longer the reaction time.

Viewed from this perspective, the following observations can be made. First, there is a discrepancy in the processing of small, medium and large distances. The distribution of the data resembles the U-shaped curve, particularly in quantiles 0.5 and 0.7. As can be observed, distances 2–4 involve the longest reaction times depending on the quantile. The influence of these distances on RTs is negative, i.e. they lead to the lengthening in response latencies. Second, the distribution suggests that the largest distance equal to 6 involves the shortest reaction times. Weaker RTs can be also observed for distances 0 and 5, although the tendency is stronger in distance 6. It must be noted that the aforementioned observations do not hold for the most extreme quantiles (0.1 and 09), which are likely to be influenced by other non-linguistic factors.

Generally, the lower the quantile, the stronger the effect of distance on reaction times. This effect, however, varies depending on distance size. This observation can be explained in the following terms: the lower the quantile, the stronger the negative effect of distances 1, 2 and 3 on reaction times, and the stronger the positive effect of distances 5 and 6 on reaction times.

At this point, a clarification is required. The results for the place distances are here viewed in terms of a regular interval scale. However, it must be remembered that the interpretation of the scale is by no means straightforward. Distances 0–6 between consonants forming clusters are not directly comparable. That is, the distance of one between two regions such as bilabial and labio-dental in /fp/ cannot be treated as identical to the distance between velar and alveolo-palatal regions exemplified by /kɕ/. These discrepancies are attributed to the geometry of the mouth

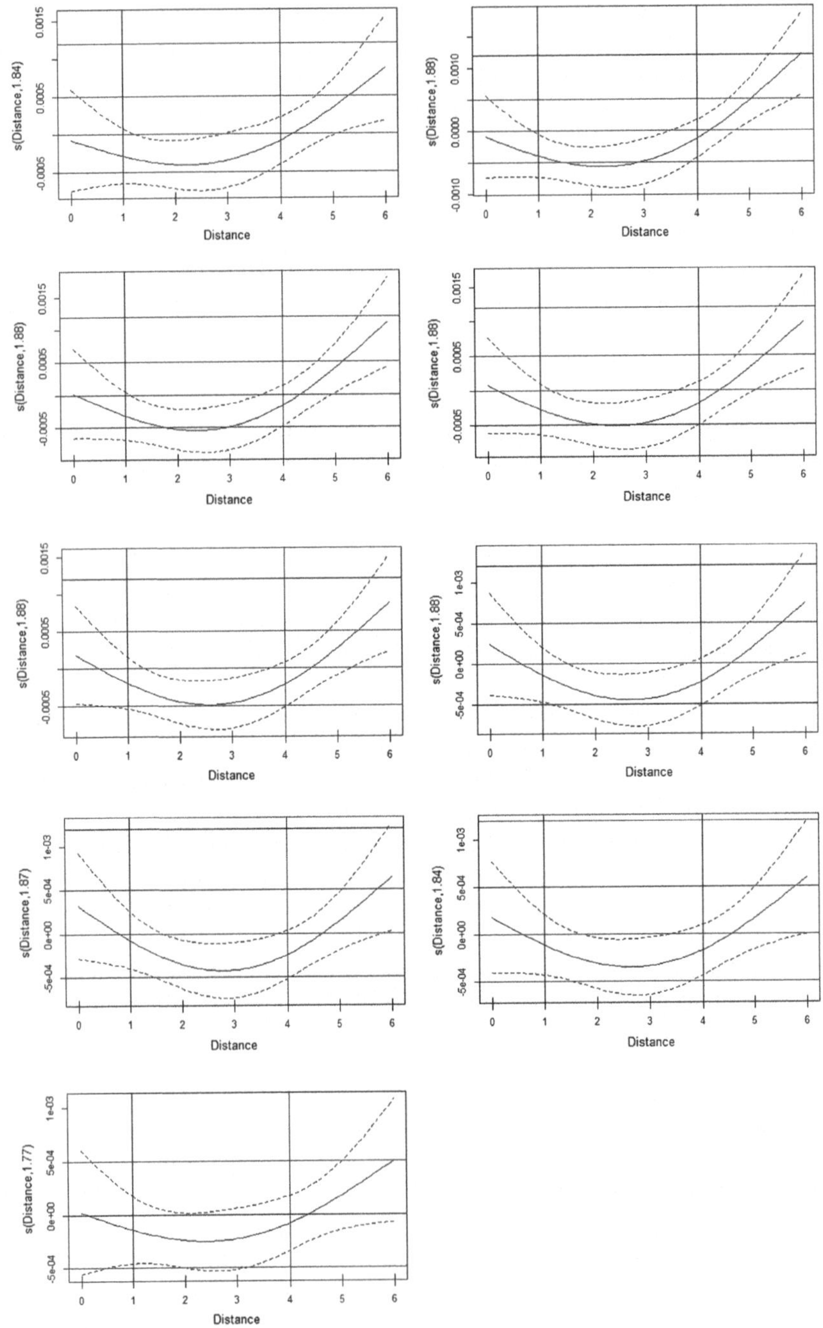

Fig. 4.3 Experiment 1: smooth terms for POA distances for quantiles 0.1–0.9

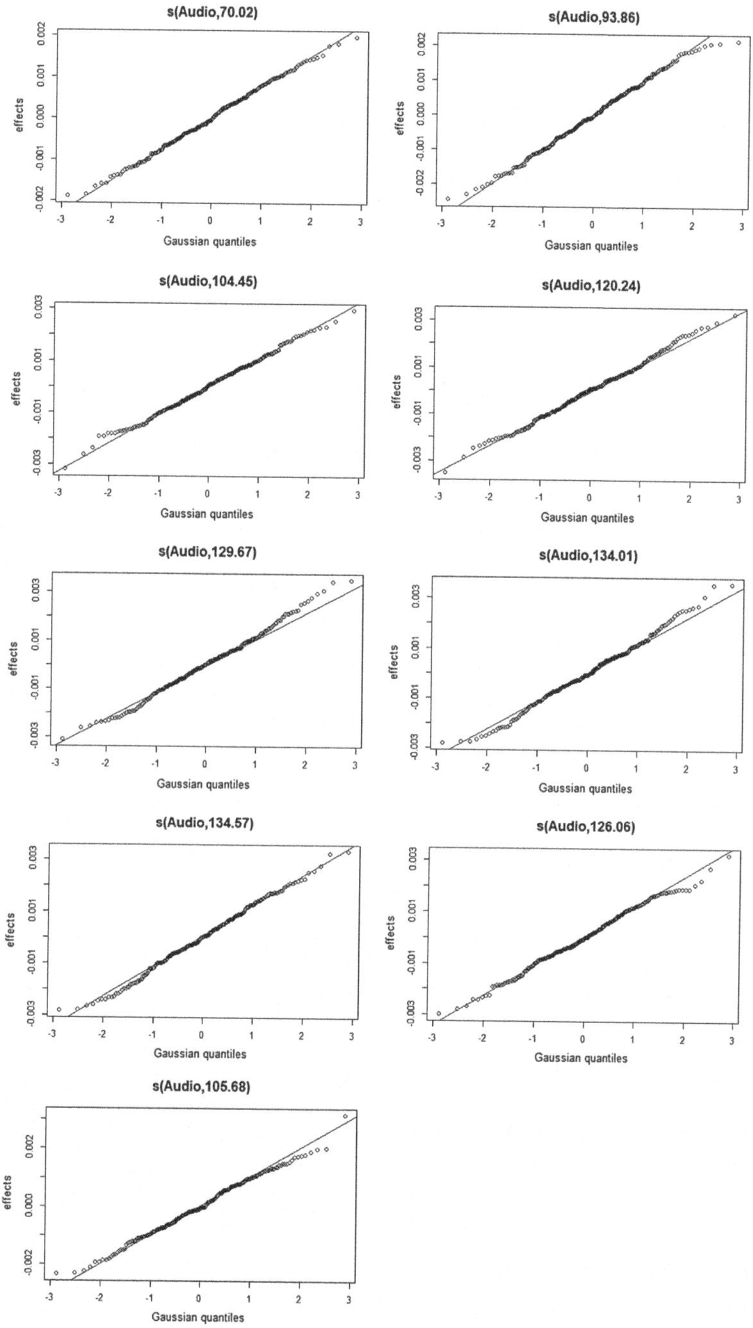

Fig. 4.4 Experiment 1: smooth terms for audio for quantiles 0.1–0.9

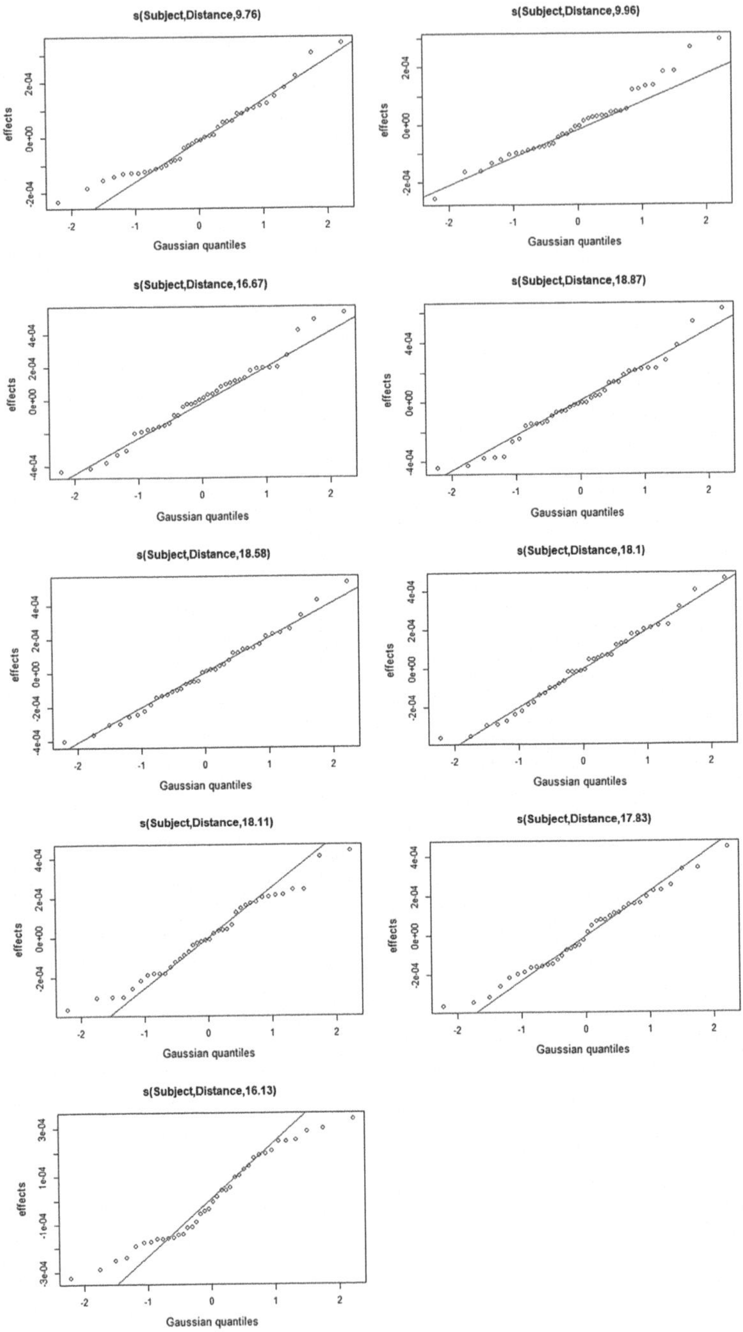

Fig. 4.5 Experiment 1: smooth terms for the combination of subject and distance for quantiles 0.1–0.9

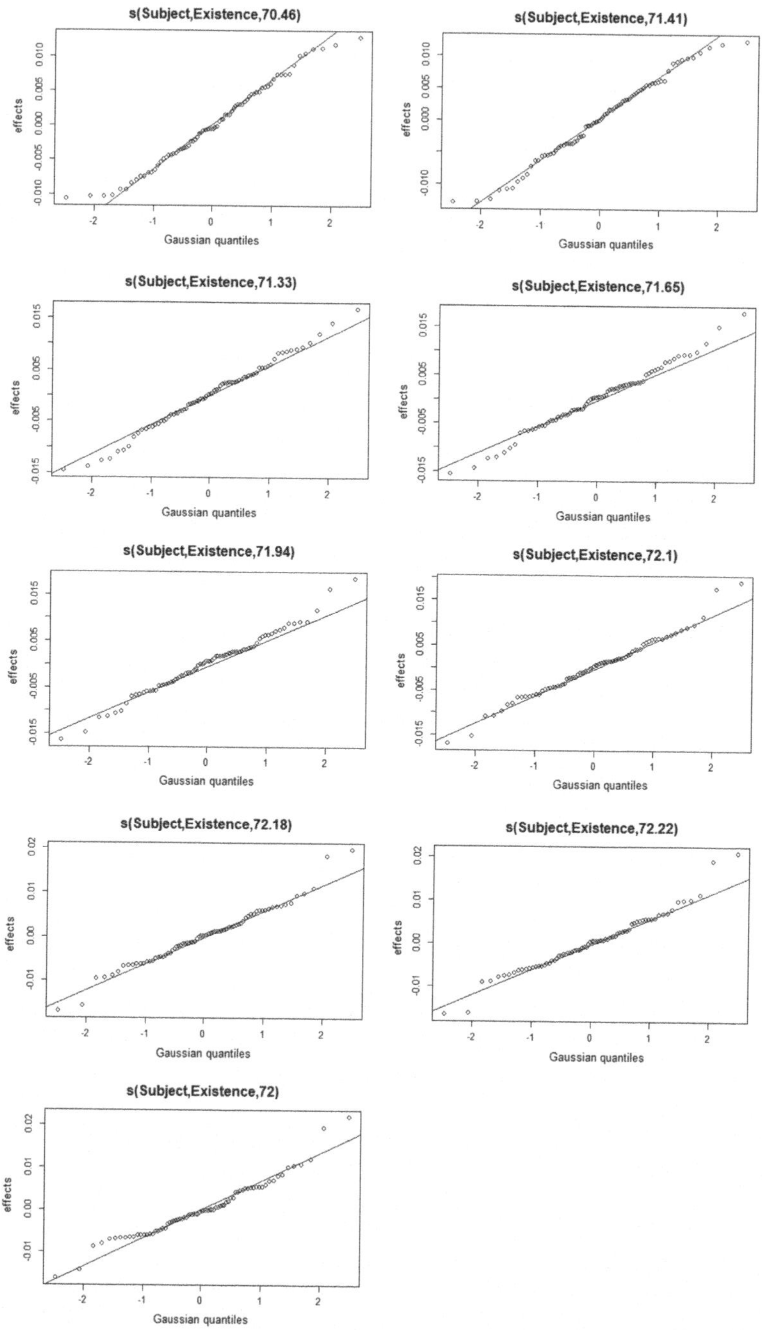

Fig. 4.6 Experiment 1: smooth terms for the combination of subject and existence for quantiles 0.1–0.9

cavity. I am aware of the fact that only a study involving specialist methodology, such as (electro)palatography, would be able to provide objectively valid insights into what is here discussed in terms of articulatory distances.

The proposed scale from zero (bilabial) to seven (velar) should not be viewed strictly in terms of a proper quantitative measure but as a reference point. The scale constitutes a conventional way of capturing the size of articulatory movement which is covered mainly by the tongue. That is, a large movement is involved in the gesture which proceeds from the back part of the mouth cavity (e.g. the velar region) towards the front part of the mouth cavity (e.g. the lips), or the reverse.

Overall, medial place distances are particularly costly for the processing of Polish initial phonotactics, while the largest distance involves the least cognitive effort. For lower quantiles, the effect is stronger, which points to fact that the reaction to the stimuli takes place relatively quickly. In phonological theory, perception is facilitated by maximum contrast. The principle of clarity of perception gets strong support in the study.

Another smooth was identified for *audio,* which has a statistically significant impact on RTs. The results are presented in Fig. 4.4. As can be seen, the data approach normal distribution as the distribution of samples is most dense in the medial RT range. Note that the extreme quantiles (Q 0.1, 0.2, 0.9) involve the range from 2 to −2. These quantiles are to a large extent affected by non-experimental factors, and play a lesser role in online processing.

Finally, the combination of subjects and distance as well as subject an existence contribute to reaction times, which is shown in Figs. 4.5 and 4.6, respectively. For some reaction times, subjects react to the place distances collectively, rather than individually. That is, the majority of subjects react in the same manner. Medial quantiles are the closes to normal distribution. As regards the combination of subjects and existence, there is a significant impact of the two factors on reaction times, which depends on the quantile. Figure 4.6 shows that the combination has the strongest effect for quantiles 0.3–0.6.

Let me now proceed to the discussion of accuracy rates. While reaction times provide insights into cognitive processing and the cognitive load that the conditions entail, correctness rates provide information on intuitive judgements. Section 4.5.1.3 presents the results obtained for the behavioural data and compares them to reaction times.

4.5.1.3 Accuracy Rates

Another set of data collected in Exp 1 involves correctness rates. The behavioural data represent subjects' decision on whether a word could possibly exist in Polish or not (by pressing a keyboard button). Accuracy was coded on the basis of clusters' existence. Namely, the correct answer for real CCs was existence (i.e. a word sounds like a possible a possible one in Polish), while the correct response for unattested CCs was non-existence (i.e. a word does not sound like a possible one in Polish). Subjects responded correctly to 63% of trials (i.e. 6,038 out of 9,565).

Table 4.10 Experiment 1: accuracy rates

	WF		IF		Total
	No	%	No	%	
EX	1,380	14	1,176	12	2,556
NEX	1,603	17	1,879	20	3,482
Total	2,983	31	3,055	32	6,038

Accuracy responses for existence and sonority are given in Table 4.10. Percentages of correct responses are calculated for the total of 9,569 observations.

Accuracy rates were analysed in a GAM with integrated smoothness estimation, using the *mgcv* package (Wood 2018). I employed the *bam*() function, which is a version of *gam*() for large datasets. The *logit* function transforms the probability value into a logarithm of the odds. Accuracy was entered into the model as a binomial variable with two levels: correct vs. incorrect. *Existence* (existent vs. non-existent) and *sonority* (well-formed vs. ill-formed) were entered as fixed factors, while *audio* as well as the combination of *subject* and *existence* were coded as smooth terms. The model was run on 9,565 observations. The differences between different GAM formulas yielded REML scores ranging from 2 to 700. Note that the formula selected for the statistical analysis based on the lowest AIC does not include the place of articulation distance. The overview of the results is given in Table 4.11.

A general picture that emerges from the statistical analysis is that *existence*, *sonority* and their interaction contribute substantially to the model, i.e. affect correctness rates. What is more, responses are influenced by *audio*. A significant result of the smooth for the combination of *subjects* and *existence* suggests that speakers reacted similarly to words containing existent and non-existent clusters. In order to investigate this relationship between sonority and existence in greater detail, Fig. 4.7 presents the distribution of correct and incorrect responses depending on the EX-NEX and WF-IF conditions.

The transformation into a logarithm of the odds (*logit* function) generates values higher than one and lower than zero. Values > 0 correspond to greater probability. On this basis, it can be stated that the difference between the ease with which EX and NEX items are classified correctly is greater for WF than for IF items. The distance on the y axis (*existence*) is smaller for sonority-violating clusters (approximately 1.15 for EX and 1.45 for NEX). In sonority-obeying clusters, the difference is larger (below zero for NEX and 0.75 for EX).

What is more, for the IF condition it is easier to correctly classify NEX items, while for the WF condition it is easier to respond correctly to EX items. In other words, when confronted with a word starting with a sonority-obeying cluster, subjects stand a greater chance of correctly identifying it as real. The fact that non-existent clusters are more difficult to recognize when they are well-formed suggests that sonority plays a crucial role in the decision making process.

Table 4.11 Experiment 1: results of the generalized additive model for accuracy

Family: binomial					
Link function: logit					
Formula:					
ACC ~ Existence * Sonority + s(Audio, bs = “re”) + s(Subject, Existence, bs = “re”)					
Parametric coefficients:					
	Estimate	Std. error	t value	Pr(>|t|)	
(Intercept)	−1.4176	0.2130	−6.655	2.84e−11	***
ExistenceEX	1.4524	0.3005	4.834	1.34e−06	***
SonorityWF	0.3012	0.1513	1.990	0.046555	*
ExistenceEX:SonorityWF	−0.7559	0.2112	−3.580	0.000344	***
–					
Signif. codes: 0 (***) 0.001 (**) 0.01 (*) 0.05 (.) 0.1 ( ) 1					
Approximate significance of smooth terms:					
	edf	Ref.df	F	p−value	
s(Audio)	191.4	248	1501	<2e−16	***
s(Existence, Subject)	71.0	74	1744	<2e−16	***
–					
Signif. codes: 0 (***) 0.001 (**) 0.01 (*) 0.05 (.) 0.1 ( ) 1					
R-sq.(adj) = 0.292; deviance explained = 26.4%					
fREML = 13871; scale est. = 1; n = 9565					

Interactions are marked in bold type

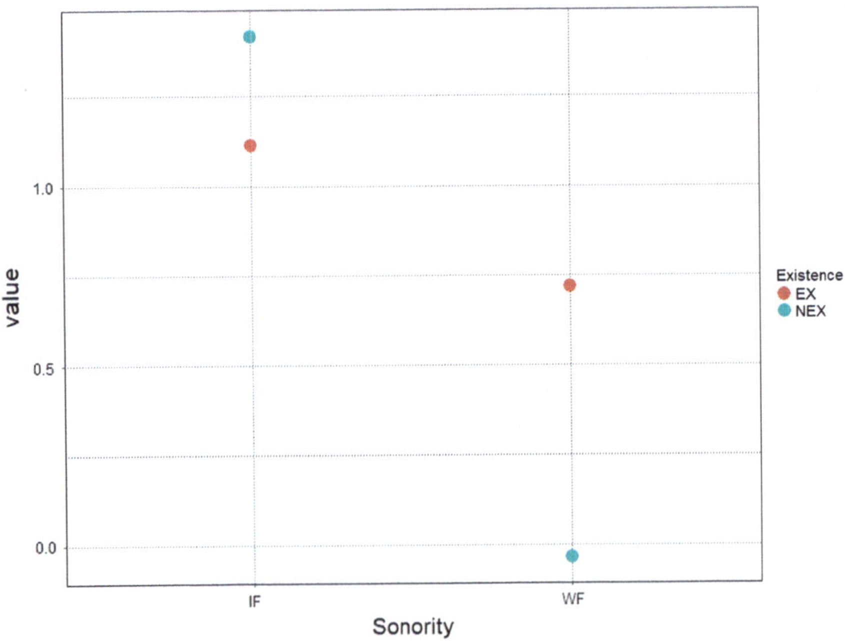

Fig. 4.7 Experiment 1: the influence of sonority and existence on accuracy

The results presented for word-initial position will now be contrasted with the results for word-final position. Sect. 4.5.2 discusses reaction times and accuracy rates for experiment 2.

4.5.2 *Experiment 2: Word-Final Clusters*

4.5.2.1 Reaction Times

The analysis of reaction times was conducted according to the procedure presented in Sect. 4.4. Latency responses collected in Exp 2 were first tested in terms of their normal distribution. The analysis was performed on the data from which trials coded as training items, rest phase and failure to react (the latter = 30 trials) were excluded. As is shown in the left panel of Fig. 4.8, subjects varied substantially in terms of reaction times: the shortest responses were provided at 1, 10 and 30 ms post-stimulus onset, while the longest responses reached 4,975 ms. Similarly to Exp 1, the data display skewness to the right, where a heavy tail starts at about 3,000 ms. The selection of the range between 400 and 2,500 ms leads to the loss of 720 observations. A normalized distribution using the Box-Cox transformation is illustrated in the right panel.

The transformed observations were analysed in terms of a GAM using the *mgcv* package for R (Wood 2018). Based on the measurement of the goodness of fit REML and AIC, the formula selected for Exp 1 showed to match the word-final data best. Reaction times were entered into the model as a dependent variable (with scaled t-distribution). *Existence* (existent vs. non-existent), *sonority* (well-formed vs. ill-formed) and the interaction between the two predictors served as fixed factors. Given the unknown influence of other predictors on reaction times, *POA distance* (0–6), *audio,* the combination of *existence* and *subject* as well as the combination of *distance* and *subject* were included as smooth terms. The analysis

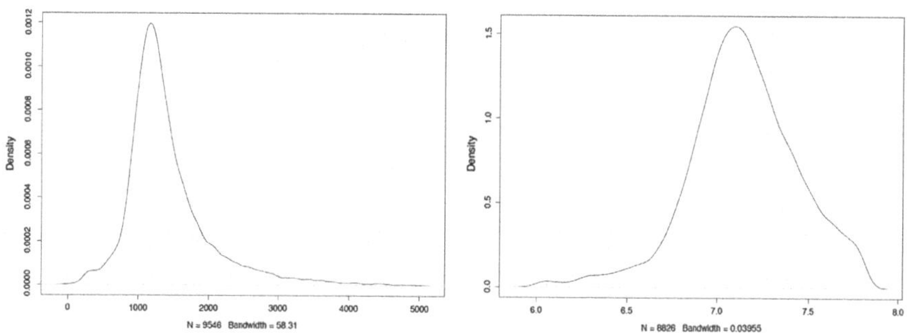

Fig. 4.8 Experiment 2: the distribution of RT responses. The left panel shows the right-skewed distribution of all the data (N = 9,546); the right panel shows the transformed distribution for the range 400–2,500 ms (N = 8,826), which approximates normality

Table 4.12 Experiment 2: Results of the generalized additive model fitted to the inverse-transformed RTs, where RT = $(\text{reaction time})^{-0.343}$

Family: scaled t (11.575,0.206)					
Link function: identity					
Formula:					
RT ~ Existence * Sonority + s(Distance, k = 3) + s(Audio, bs = "re") + s(Subject, Existence, bs = "re") + s(Subject, Distance, bs = "re")					
Parametric coefficients:					
	Estimate	Std. error	t-value	Pr(>|t|)	
(Intercept)	7.154674	0.034358	208.237	<2e−16	***
ExistenceEX	−0.027219	0.048423	−0.562	0.574	
SonorityWF	0.003307	0.011309	0.292	0.770	
ExistenceEX:SonorityWF	−0.25971	0.015977	−1.626	0.104	
–					
Signif. codes: 0 (***) 0.001 (**) 0.01 (*) 0.05 (.) 0.1 ( ) 1					
Approximate significance of smooth terms:					
	edf	Ref.df	F	*p*-value	
s(Distance)	1.823	1.878	8.975	0.00195	**
s(Audio)	158.879	247.000	1.988	<2e−16	***
s(Existence, Subject)	72.951	74.000	156.940	<2e−16	***
s(Distance, Subject)	11.254	37.000	34.261	0.07833	.
–					
Signif. codes: 0 (***) 0.001 (**) 0.01 (*) 0.05 (.) 0.1 ( ) 1					
R-sq.(adj) = 0.413; deviance explained = 37.9%					
fREML = 13562; scale est. = 1; n = 8826					

Interactions are marked in bold type

was performed on 9,148 observations. Note that the difference in REML score between different models tested did not exceed 6. The results are summarized in Table 4.12.

As far as the parametric part of the model is concerned, no main effects were found for *existence*, *sonority* and their interaction. That is, reaction times are neither facilitated by a well-formed sonority profile nor hindered by SSG violations. By the same token, the identification of an existent or non-existent cluster does not contribute to response latencies. These findings lead to the same conclusions as in Exp 1. Polish speakers' judgement is not affected by factors which have been demonstrated to play a crucial role in the processing of phonotactically simpler languages (such as Germanic). In turn, *POA distance* and *audio* contribute to the model significantly. This means that speakers are sensitive to the size of perceptual contrast and types of recorded stimuli. Also, a statistically significant result obtained for the combination of *subject* and *existence* suggests that speakers react in a similar way to existent and non-existent clusters.

In order to gain insights into the effects of the variables on specific reaction time windows, the word-final data was analized in terms of quantile regression. In parallel to Exp 1, the quantile GAM (with scaled t-distribution function) was run using the formula established for the GAM. The data range selected for the purpose of the *qgam* analysis (Fasiolo et al. 2017) was selected in such a way that the range is directly comparable to Exp 1. That is, the quantiles of reaction times are found in the range between 0.0081 and 0.964 of the input data, which corresponds to 310–2,870 ms.

Table 4.13 presents the results for intercept and fixed factors for *qgam*. For each decile of reaction times (Q 0.1–0.9), the estimated values and the *p*-values are given in the first column and the second column, respectively. The quantile regression results confirm that neither existence, sonority nor their interaction contribute to the processing of final phonotactics. The *p*-values are larger than 0.05 for each quantile, with one exception of quantile 0.9 for the interaction. That is, the interaction of existence and sonority plays a role in the latest reaction times: for an existent cluster, the influence of well-formedness is greater. However, this isolated result does not suffice in considering the interaction to be significant. Additionally, the intercept is statistically significant. On this basis, I conclude that the gradual rise in the intercept from the lowest to the highest quantile constitutes the main factor resulting in an increase in RTs.

So far, I have demonstrated that initial and final data lead to the same results in terms of the main factors. The question is how smooth terms contribute to the processing of final clusters. In Exp 1, the most important factor facilitating response latencies were small and large POA distances. The results for the final data are presented in Figs. 4.9, 4.10 and 4.11.

The description of the results starts with several observations regarding the smooth terms for *POA distances*. As is shown in Fig. 4.9, the extreme quantiles 0.1 and 0.9, which correspond to the first and the last decile of reaction times, are the least stable ones in terms of a confidence interval. This is a rather typical effect: the

Table 4.13 Experiment 2: results of quantile regression for fixed factors and the intercept. The formula used: RT ~ Existence * Sonority + s(Distance, k = 3) + s(Audio, bs = "re") + s(Subject, Existence, bs = "re") + s(Subject, Distance, bs = "re")

Q	Intercept		Existence (EX)		Sonority (WF)		Existence * Sonority (EX, WF)	
0.1	0.4686	0	4e−04	0.8954	−3e−04	0.7046	9e−04	0.3568
0.2	0.4751	0	9e−04	0.74	−7e−04	0.2676	0.0011	0.2121
0.3	0.4797	0	8e−04	0.7777	−7e−04	0.2639	0.0015	0.0992
0.4	0.4829	0	0.0011	0.6887	−3e−04	0.6559	0.0014	0.0965
0.5	0.4857	0	0.0015	0.572	0	0.9331	0.0012	0.1431
0.6	0.4883	0	0.0018	0.5051	0	0.9473	0.0013	0.1032
0.7	0.491	0	0.0018	0.5142	1e−04	0.8148	0.0015	0.0671
0.8	0.494	0	0.0018	0.5251	3e−04	0.6481	0.0016	0.0663
0.9	0.4981	0	0.0018	0.5375	3e−04	0.6782	0.0019	0.0347

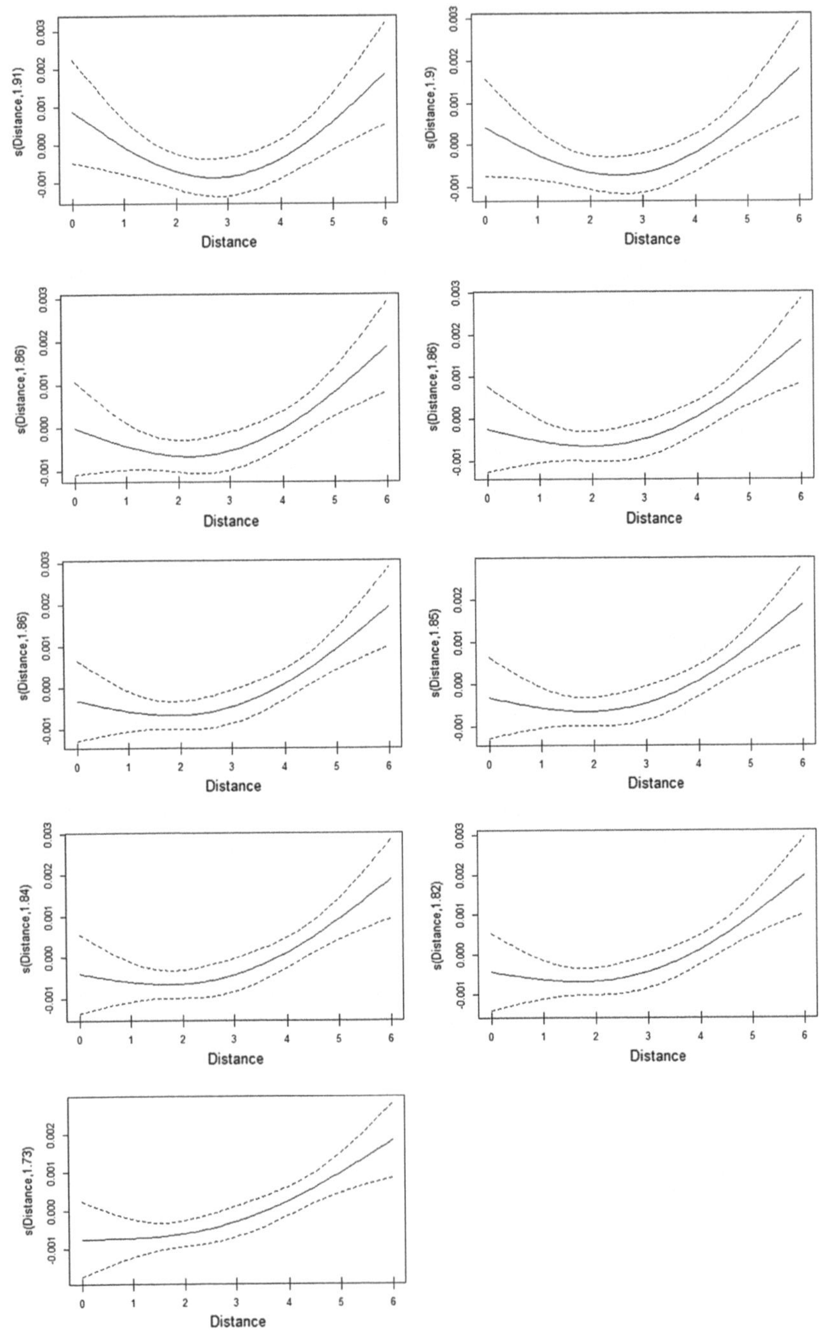

Fig. 4.9 Experiment 2: smooth terms for distance for quantiles 0.1–0.9

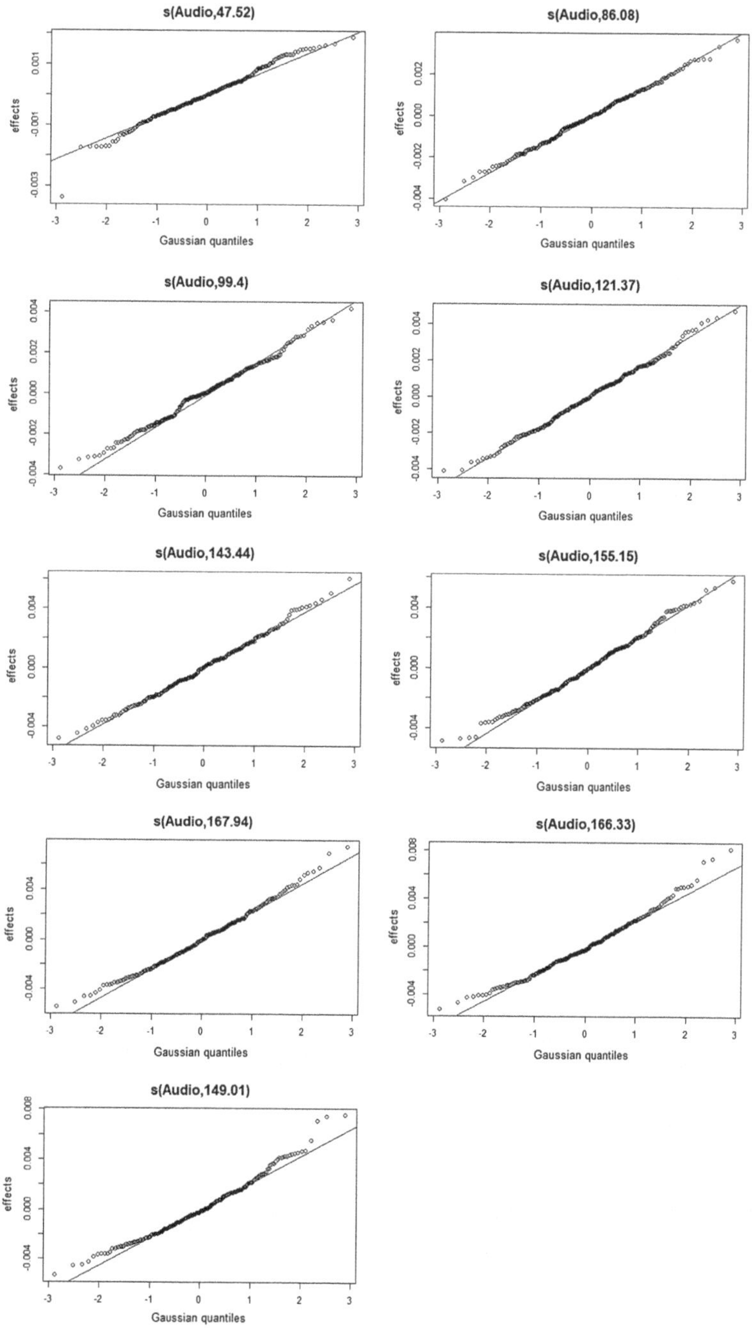

Fig. 4.10 Experiment 2: smooth terms for audio for quantiles 0.1–0.9

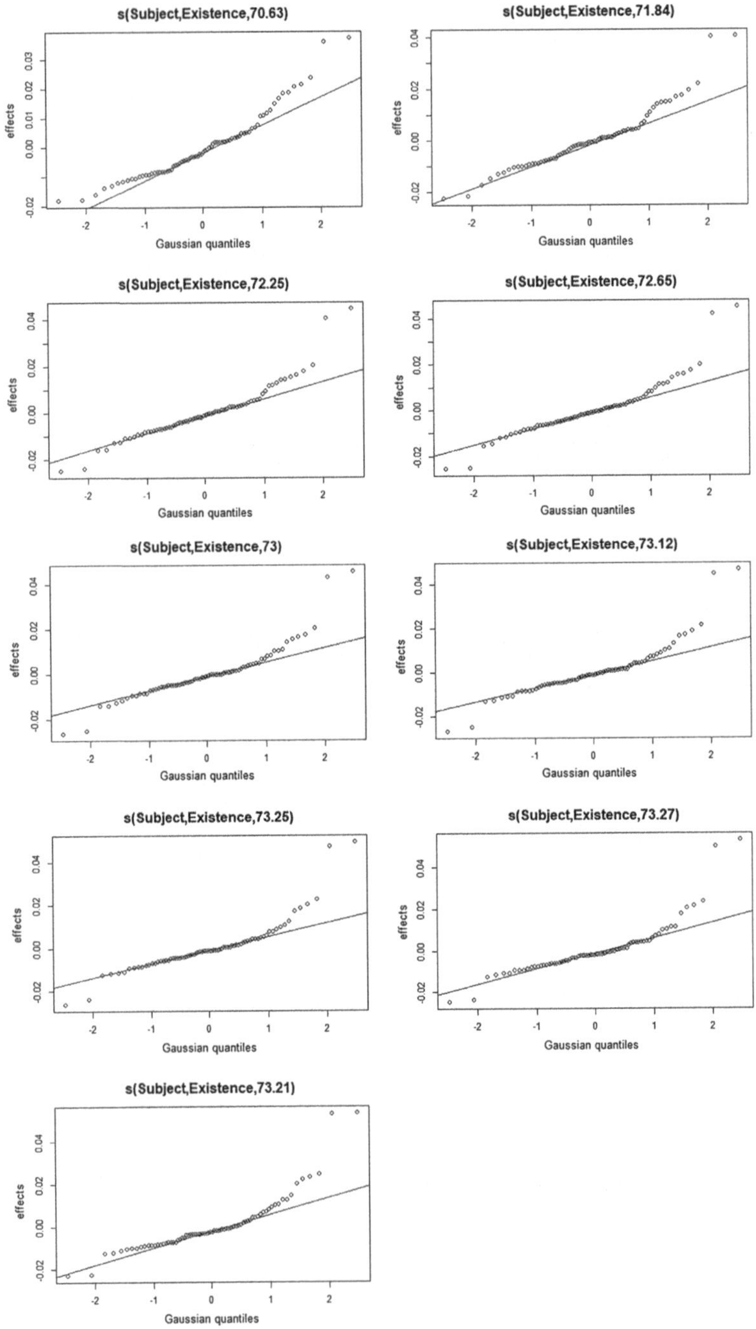

Fig. 4.11 Experiment 2: smooth terms for the combination of subject and existence for quantiles 0.1–0.9

extremes of the data tend to be anomalous, and frequently display the greatest standard deviation.

POA distances 2 and 3 always trigger an decrease in RT values, and henceforth contribute to longer reaction times. This effect is the strongest for quantiles 0.2 and 0.3, although it is also strong for quantile 0.4. The effect is weaker for higher quantiles, but it is still noticeable. POA distances equal to 1 and 4 also have a negative effect on reaction times. This effect is weaker than that observed for distances 2 and 3, however, the tendency occurs with high probability ($\sim$80–95%) in each quantile. The reverse pattern, resulting in an increase in RTs and the shortening of reaction times can be observed for clusters with distance 6. This result is statistically significant for each quantile with the exception of 0.9, where it appears with the probability of approximately 95%. What is more, the influence of distance 0 slightly diverges from 0 for some quantiles. From the statistical perspective, this result suggests that distance = 0 does not affect RTs, and that it can be considered to be referential.

Overall, the analysis lends support to the results in experiment 1. Latency responses are not affected by sonority and existence. In turn, online processing of word-initial phonotactics is facilitated by small and large distances. The same pattens holds word-finally, with the exception of place distance = 0, which is referential. In other words, large perceptual contrast entails the least cognitive effort.

As far as other smooth terms are concerned, statistically significant results are obtained for *audio,* and the combination of *subject* and *existence*. In both cases, the distribution of samples is the most dense in the medial RT range, i.e. medial quantiles are the most stable ones and approach normality. It can be concluded that medial reaction times show the greatest sensitivity to the audio stimuli. Also, for some reaction times, subjects react to cluster existence collectively, rather than individually. A detailed statistical account of the analysis for each quantile is given in Appendix K.

The second set of data collected in Exp 2 refers to accuracy rates. Psycholinguistic research has shown that processing and behavioural reposes provided by the same population in the same study can differ. Exp 1 showed that latency and behavioural responses are affected by different factors. In Sect. 4.5.2.2, I investigate the role of sonority, existence and POA distances in intuitive judgements of Polish speakers, and compare the findings with reaction times.

4.5.2.2 Accuracy Rates

Behavioural data collected in Exp 2 are related to correctness rates (for a detailed description see Sect. 4.5.1.3). A summary of the results is presented in Table 4.14. Subjects responded correctly to 60% of trials (i.e. 5,742 out of 9,546). Percentages of correct responses are calculated for the total of 9,546 observations.

In the statistical analysis of correctness rates, a generalized additive model with smooth functions was used. The analysis was performed with the help of the *mgcv* package for R (Wood 2018), see Sect. 4.5.1.3. The formula used in the analysis was

Table 4.14 Experiment 2: accuracy rates

	WF		IF		Total
	No	%	No	%	
EX	1234	13	831	9	2,065
NEX	1,750	18	1,927	20	3,677
Total	2,984	31	2,758	29	5,742

Table 4.15 Experiment 2: results of the generalized additive model for accuracy

Family: binomial					
Link function: logit					
Formula:					
ACC ~ Existence * Sonority + s(Audio, bs = "re") + s(Subject, Existence, bs = "re")					
Parametric coefficients:					
	Estimate	Std. error	t value	Pr(>|t|)	
(Intercept)	−2.0400	0. 0.2782	−7.331	2.28e−13	***
ExistenceEX	3.0488	0.3907	7.802	6.08e−15	***
SonorityWF	0.5007	0.1749	2.864	0.00419	**
ExistenceEX:SonorityWF	−1.5017	0.2439	−6.156	7.44e−10	***
–					
Signif. codes: 0 (***) 0.001 (**) 0.01 (*) 0.05 (.) 0.1 () 1					
Approximate significance of smooth terms:					
	edf	Ref.df	F	*p*-value	
s(Audio)	197.24	247	2180	<2e−16	***
s(Existence, Subject)	71.12	74	2097	<2e−16	***
–					
Signif. codes: 0 (***) 0.001 (**) 0.01 (*) 0.05 (.) 0.1 () 1					
R-sq.(adj) = 0.414; deviance explained = 37.4%					
fREML = 13265; scale est. = 1; n = 9546					

Interactions are marked in bold type

identical to that in Exp 1, as it showed to describe the word-final data most adequately. Accuracy was entered into the model as a binomial variable with two levels: correct vs. incorrect. *Existence* (existent vs. non-existent) and *sonority* (well-formed *vs*. ill-formed) were coded as fixed factors, while *audio* as well as the combination of *subject* and *existence* were coded as smooth terms. The model was run on 9,546 observations. The results are presented in Table 4.15.

Generally, the statistical analysis reveals that *existence, sonority* and their interaction contribute substantially to the model. Correctness rates are influenced by cluster status and its sonority profile. What is more, significant results were obtained for two smooth functions: *audio* as well as the combination of *subject* and *existence*. First, Polish speakers react to audio stimuli. Second, they react similarly to cluster (non-)existence. Figure 4.12 presents the results for correct and incorrect

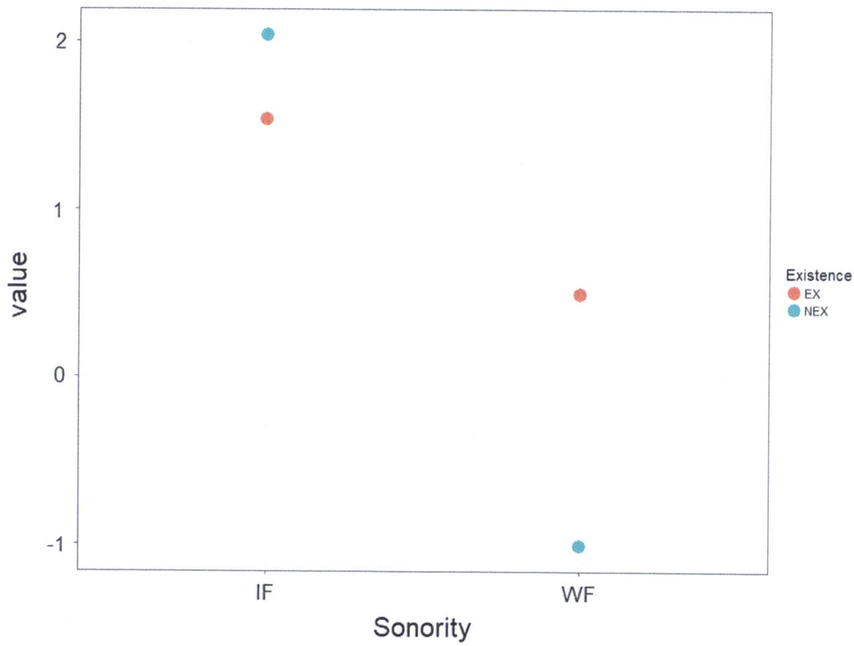

Fig. 4.12 Experiment 2: the influence of sonority and existence on accuracy

responses depending on two conditions: EX-NEX and WF-IF. Values > 0 indicate greater probability.

Generally, Fig. 4.12 confirms the tendencies which were observed in word-initial phonotactics. Namely, the difference with which items are correctly classified as EX and NEX is greater for the WF condition than for the IF one. What is more, in the group of ill-formed clusters, it is easier to correctly identify non-existent clusters (value larger than 2). In turn, in the group of well-formed clusters it is easier to correctly identify existent clusters. In other words, when confronted with a word ending with a sonority-obeying cluster, Polish speakers are more likely to correctly identify it as real. Given that non-existent clusters are more difficult to identify when they are well-formed suggests that sonority plays a crucial role in intuitive judgement. Note that there are larger differences in the intuitive evaluation of hypothetical clusters depending on whether they are well-formed or ill-formed. Sonority seems not to be such a relevant discriminatory criterion in existent clusters, and rightly so: Polish speakers are exposed to hundreds of sonority violating clusters on a regular basis.

Although Exp 1 and Exp 2 present identical results, they differ with respect to the probability values. In Exp 1, the probability for an IF cluster to be classified correctly is greater. The values are larger for non-existent clusters (a NEX increase from 1.5 in Exp 1 to 2 in Exp 2) and for existent clusters (an EX increase from 1.2 in Exp 1 to 1.5 in Exp 2). In turn, the probability of an incorrect response increases as well for WF NEX clusters to −1. The value drops for WF-EX clusters (from 0.7

in Exp 1 to 0.5 in Exp 2). In other words, in word-final position, the probability of correctly evaluating non-existent clusters (both WF and IF) increases, while the probability of correctly evaluating existent clusters (stronger for EX-IF, weaker for EX-WF) decreases, compared to word-initial phonotactics.

4.6 Discussion

4.6.1 Phonological Principles in Processing

The goal of the chapter was to provide insights into the psychological reality of existence, well-formedness and place of articulation distances in phonotactics. Existence distinguishes between clusters which are part of the phonotactic inventory of Polish and clusters which are hypothetical. Well-formedness is represented by the Sonority Sequencing Generalization (Selkirk 1984), which distinguishes between sonority-violating or sonority-obeying clusters following the scale of Goldsmith (1990). The concept of distance is here expressed by the place of articulation distances between sequences of consonants. Although the literature on the topic is vast, little is known about the processing of Polish phonotactics. What is more, this study provides new data, which go beyond the previous analyses: positional constraints in Polish phonotactics are investigated in terms of reaction times and in relation to the place of articulation distances.

Separate conclusions are formulated for latency and behavioural responses. Exp 1 and Exp 2 unambiguously demonstrate that POA distances are critical in the processing of word-initial and word-final CC clusters. Disregarding the prosodic position, medial distances entail the greatest articulatory effort. Clusters, in which adjacent consonants are separated by medial distances of 2, 3 and 4 intervening places of articulation (e.g. dental – alveolo-palatal, alveolar – bilabial) involve the longest reaction times. Large distances, in particular represented by the combination of extreme places such as bilabial + velar, involve the shortest reaction times. These findings offer support for the principle of the clarity of perception (Donegan and Stampe 2009). Just as minimum effort is relevant for the motor system, perception requires clear cut divisions of larger prosodic units. At the level of phonotactics, enhanced intersegmental differences, i.e. increased contrast, serves as a factor facilitating perceptibility. The principle can be illustrated on the example of a minimum syllable structure.

Maximum contrast is best represented by the CV structure, which is the basic syllable template (Gordon 2016; Greenberg 1978; Itô 1986). Across the language of the world, CV tends to be represented by a combination of an obstruent and a vowel. At the level of articulation, obstruents are produced with an occlusion in the vocal tract. Vowels involve no constriction, thanks to which the airflow in the vocal tract is not inhibited. Such contrast is articulatorily acute for a speaker as it involves an adjustment for different articulatory gestures. On the other hand, at the level of perception, contrast enhances the division of a prosodic unit into smaller constituents, and hence serves perception (Donegan and Stampe 2009). A native speaker of Polish finds it easier to recognize and access a phonological structure composed of distinct sounds, which is reflected in shorter reaction times and lesser cognitive effort. Similar observations were made in Flemming (2002, 2004), Łubowicz (2007, 2012, 2016), and Padgett (2001, 2003) who view contrast as a core organizing principle of a phonological grammar. The results of the present experiments lend support to the relevance of contrast in terms of the place of articulation.

Large articulatory place distances involve the following transitions in the vocal tract of a Polish speaker: bilabial + velar (distance = 6), bilabial + palatal, or labio-dental + velar (distance = 5). The repertoire of such transitions attested in Polish is limited. In Chap. 3, it was demonstrated that out of 458 cluster types, nine display distance = 6 and 20 distance = 5. Example of such clusters involve /km kp gb/ with distance = 6 and /fk gv mj jp/ with distance = 5. As regards word-final position, the cluster inventories in Tables 1.18, 1.19 and 1.20 contain two cluster types with distance = 6, namely /hm km/, and thee with distance = 5, namely /jm fk kf/. As regards perception, speakers immediately detect spectral differences between the compression force at the lips and further back in the mouth cavity in the velar region. For processing, this contrast is more important than contrast captured in terms of the manner features (although see approaches in which the manner of articulation constitutes the structural core in phonological units, e.g. Clements 1985; Schwartz 2013; Steriade 1993).

Given various interpretations of cognitive effort in psychological research (for an overview see Westbrook and Braver 2015), less effort is associated with activities which are less demanding, less difficult, requiring less attention. In the domain of phonology, the identification of large, or at least sufficient, differences between neighbouring segments contributes to more automatic decisions on the acceptability of a form. To the contrary, medial distances are the most costly in terms of processing. Clusters such as /br lj ʃp/ and /fj kl sk/ which represent place distances equal to 3 and 4 respectively, facilitate a contrary force, namely the ease of articulation. In other words, medial place distances involve shorter transitions that articulators (in particular the tongue) have to cover. Smaller articulatory gestures are certainly speaker-friendly, but hinder accurate perception of an item, which results in a longer decision-making process and in longer reaction times.

Another consideration is directionality. In Chap. 3, Sect. 3.3.3.2, the parameter of directionality was proposed to account for the articulatory movement from the first to the final consonant in a cluster. The parameter was used to specify whether the tongue slides towards the front or rear part of the mouth cavity, or whether articulation is made with the lips (i.e. bilabial), towards the labial place of articulation (e.g. from the back part of the mouth cavity towards the lips as in /sm kp/) or outward of the labial place of articulation (e.g. starting at the lips as in /mr pɕ/). I cannot rule out the possibility that the forward or backward movement of the tongue could have had some impact on the results. The same holds true for the transition between a consonant and a neighbouring vowel. Although the experiments aimed at investigating the distance between adjacent consonants, processing could have also been affected by the vowel qualities of the CV prefix and VC suffix. These aspects of processing require separate investigation.

Apart from the psychological reality of place distances, the experiments demonstrate the importance of other factors in behavioural data. Existence and sonority affect only accuracy rates and do not contribute to online processing of word-edge phonotactics. The results agree with a large body of theoretical and empirical evidence supporting the role of sonority in deep-level syllable structure (Cyran and Gussmann 1999; Gussmann 1991, 1992, 2007; Rubach and Booij 1990a, b), surface syllabification (Bertinetto et al. 2007; Cetnarowska and Żygis 2004, 2007; Szpyra 1995, Szpyra-Kozłowska 1998, 2000). The results partially support Wiese et al. (2017), who investigated online processing in terms of the electrophysiological responses of the nervous system. The ERP study showed that sonority is a main factor in the processing of final CC clusters in Polish (not only in behavioural responses). It must be borne in mind that the word-final stimuli used in Exp 2 are identical to Wiese et al. (2017). Therefore, comparable results would be expected for both studies. Let me now look closer into the areas which could have influenced the results.

The first issue to be considered in the analysis of electrophysiological responses are different time windows. Wiese et al. (2017) show that the SSG is the main factor only in the late time window (i.e. late positive component, P600). In the early time window (i.e. early negative component, N400), sonority is significant in the interaction with session (i.e. the first and the second EEG), which means that it facilitates learning over time. Exp 2 presented in this chapter and the ERP study differ in terms of the experimental design in that the first involves no learning paradigm. Therefore, the results are not directly comparable with Wiese et al. (2017).

What is more, the late positive component in EEG studies is associated with learning, memorization and recollection implicit in the experimental task. In the time window 700–1,050 ms, well-formedness shows to be a statistically significant factor in modulating phonotactic learning. Sonority facilitates online processing not only as a sole factor but also in interaction with session and existence. Again, this result cannot be directly compared to the present experiments, which rely on response latencies. These observations lead to two conclusions. First, the effects of the SSG on phonotactics are task-dependent and should be interpreted only in relation to a specific experimental setting. Second, sonority is not consulted in the evaluation of words but is required when learning new lexical items.

Another interpretation of the ERP results is related to the nature of the early negativity. In Wiese et al. (2017), the time window 450–550 ms is considered to reflect the processing of nonce words and pseudowords in opposition to existing words (Domahs et al. 2009). The fact that sonority does not surface as a predictor at an early stage of processing can be related to the presence of hypothetical words. That is, words with an obviously foreign status require consulting sonority. This interpretation suggests that when the decision is made on the acceptability of nonce words, sonority is not required. The SSG does not function as a sieve for rejecting a form or accepting it. This observation is supported by the historical development of complex clusters in Polish.

Phonotactic complexity in Polish emerged due to the deletion of *yers* (for references see Bethin 1992, 2006; Długosz-Kurczabowa and Dubisz 2006; Klemensiewicz et al. 1981; Rubach 2016; Szpyra 1992; Walczak 1999). The loss of yer resulted in the emergence of new syllable structures and changes in the phonemic inventory (Rochoń 2000). The increased phonotactic complexity was not compensated for by cluster simplification, which points to Polish speakers' acceptance of complex structures. On the other hand, sonority is a facilitative factor in learning-related tasks. There is a body of evidence offering support to the claim. Apart from the experimental learnability settings in Wiese et al. (2017), L1 constitutes a natural learning environment. Research on L1 shows that Polish children generally favour syllables which follow the SSG (Jarosz 2017; Jarosz and Rysling 2017; Łukaszewicz 2006, 2007, 2010).

4.6.2 Sources of Phonotactic Knowledge

Apart from the psychological reality of existence, sonority and POA distances, Exp 1 and Exp 2 offer some insights into the sources of phonotactic knowledge (Berent et al. 2004; Shademan 2006; Vitevitch and Luce 1999). As I discussed earlier, a possible interpretation of phonotactic constraints is that they are stored in the mental lexicon. The question is whether responses of speakers correspond with statistical proprieties of the lexicon. If phonotactic knowledge should be based exclusively on lexical statistics, then speakers should master language-specific phonotactic patterns and extrapolate lexical statistics as phonological generalizations. Viewed from this perspective, nonce words or words containing non-existent clusters should be immediately recognized as foreign as their phonotactic and statistical probability in a language is equal to zero. That is, real and hypothetical clusters should have a significant impact on acceptability ratings and response latencies. When confronted with a consonant cluster not exemplified in Polish (syntagmatically implausible or unattested), speakers should immediately recognize its obsolete status, and respond accordingly. This interpretation of the lexicon gets support from neighbourhood density (Vitevitch and Luce 1999), which confirms that phonotactic probabilities affect lexical judgement. Increased cognitive cost should be observed in the processing of non-existent clusters. The analysis of latency reposes in Exp 1 and Exp 2 shows the opposite: existence is statistically significant neither in initial nor in final word position. On this basis, I conjure that phonotactic constraints are not stored only in the mental lexicon in Polish speakers.

The second interpretation of phonotactic constraints attributes phonotactic judgement to a more complex interplay of lexical statistics and phonological principles. For instance, Hayes and White (2013) recorded native English speakers' judgements on lexical gaps representing phonologically natural and unnatural phonotactic constraints. The study showed that lexical statistics lead to phonological generalizations only when they are consistent with principles of phonological naturalness. That is, if speakers respond differently to lexical gaps of a varying phonological structure, most probably they consult a grammar, apart from the list of word forms stored in the lexicon. Principles of higher order thus seem to be operative in the processing non-existent items. The case of Polish demonstrates that phonotactic constraints are not only stored in the mental lexicon but are also the product of phonological principles. This claim is supported by two arguments.

First, the accuracy results related to sonority confirm that the SSG, as an over-arching principle of phonotactic preferability, is consulted in intuitive judgements. If native speakers of Polish access only lexical statistics when deciding on the status of a cluster, sonority would not surface as a predictor at all. Accuracy rates in both experiments show that sonority is operative. What is more, the predictive power of the SSG is related to a prosodic position. Let me recall the sonority-based classification of all available cluster types in Polish according to three sonority scales (see Chap. 2, Sects. 2.4.1.2 and 2.4.1.3). The analysis demonstrated that the proportion of well-formed clusters to ill-formed clusters (including plateaus) is 50–50% word-initially and 70–30% word-finally. In a similar vein, correctness ratings are higher in the word-final context. Sonority has a greater influence on accuracy rates in final clusters, compared to initial clusters: the results are statistically significant for both word positions, however, the p-value is lower for final phonotactics. This result supports *sonority projection*, which states that the effects observed in the grammar of a language are projected onto nonce items (Daland et al. 2011; Hayes 2011) and speakers' sensitivity to linguistic universals (Tamasi and Berent 2015).

Finally, when these remarks are placed against the results of reaction times, a clear picture emerges. Both the mental lexicon and phonological principles are operative in Polish phonotactics. Although judgement involves accessing lexical statistics, processing requires consulting some kind of organizational principles of higher order. Although sonority constitutes an obvious example of such a generalizing principle, the processing data suggests that Polish phonotactics is largely governed by subtle distinctions between consonants related to the place of articulation. These results provide new insights into perception, and pave the way for an area of phonological investigation focusing on factors other than sonority in perception and production.

4.6.3 Phonological Features in Processing

A type of investigation which accounts for a wide array of phonological features in the study of consonant clusters is strictly related to *featuretactics* introduced in Chap. 3. Let me recall that the analysis of Polish word-initial and word-final clusters in terms of lexical statistics demonstrated that different manner of articulation features (i.e. [sonorant], [strident], [continuant]) contribute most to cluster structure by discriminating between hundreds of existent CCs, CCCs and CCCCs. The results of Exp 1 and Exp 2 provide further empirical evidence in favour of the relative *weight of phonological features*. The importance of POA distances in processing confirms the assertion I made earlier, namely that sonority (in its present form) cannot be the ultimate mechanism underlying phonological structure. Whether the method proposed in Chap. 3 is insightful enough requires further investigation. However, unarguably it demonstrates that all languages cannot be measured in terms of the same principle which imposes the same requirements on all languages, and—what is more—on different prosodic positions (see Chap. 6). In languages, whose phonotactics poses challenges to phonological theory, one should make an attempt at discovering the importance of infrasegmental properties of clusters, which can turn out to be core characteristics motivating unusual sequences of consonants. Such properties can be expressed in terms of phonological features. As I will argue in Chap. 6, only a subset of such features underlies the very basic structure of clusters, syllables and words, and possibly brings us closer to inferring *elementary particles.*

Let me return to the discussion on the complexity of Polish phonotactics. From the descriptive perspective, Polish violates the SSG. The Government Phonology perceptive is that long clusters are well structured in terms of sonority when split into sub-constituents. The two approaches provide different conclusions on Polish phonology. Disregarding which interpretation the reader subscribes to, a new fact has emerged: the place of articulation is key to the understanding of at least some aspects of Polish phonotactics. How exactly POA distances are interpreted in the mind of the speaker or realized in articulation, or what specific place features are referred to (e.g. anterior, coronal, labial, etc.) remains unclear. Or which aspects of sonority (e.g. obstruency, stridency) play a role in intuitive judgement? Therefore, Chap. 5 addresses these questions on the basis of articulatory data, which allows for a more detailed analysis of phonological features.

4.7 Conclusions

The goal of the chapter was to investigate the psychological reality of three factors which contribute to the processing of phonotactics: existence, well-formedness in terms of sonority, and the place of articulation distance. Two reaction time experiments were conduced, and two types of data were collected: response latencies and accuracy rates. The results of the experiments are largely comparable for word-initial and word-final consonant clusters.

First, it is demonstrated the processing of word-edge phonotactics in native speakers of Polish is primarily affected by place of articulation distances. Response latencies are the longest for clusters characterized by medial distances and the shortest for clusters which display the largest POA distance. Large distances are represented by labial and dorsal articulation. That is, the combinations of bilabial and velar segments in clusters such as /pk bw xm mk/ involve the least cognitive effort for Polish speakers. As regards correctness rates, they are influenced by the principle of sonority and clusters' existence. In other words, intuitive judgements rely on the distinction between well-formed (sonority-obeying) and ill-formed (sonority-violating) clusters as well as between existent (attested in Polish) and non-existent (hypothetical) clusters.

The results of the experiments contribute to the ongoing discussion on phonotactic processing, and shed light on the relevance of phonological factors beyond the principle of sonority. The literature overview presented in the introductory part of the chapter reports on numerous studies that have attempted to disentangle the relationship between phonotactic well-formedness and existence in online processing. The results of the present reaction time experiments, further supported by empirically-based feature rankings in Chap. 3, reveal a gap between what phonological theory actually accounts for, and what is yet to be discovered. If the perception of labial, coronal and dorsal segments as well as their combinations has an impact on cognitive effort involved, are there any other place-related features which play a role in the processing of phonotactics? And, by the same token, could sonority be studied in different and possibly more accurate terms, tailored for a particular phonological system? Whether features such as consonance, stridency or continuancy affect phonotactic processing requires large-scale research, and making use of different methodologies. Generally, what we have seen so far is that place- and manner-related features play a different role in Polish phonotactics depending on word positions and language domains such as the lexicon and online processing. In order to gain insights into forces which motivate cluster structure in the articulatory domain, the following chapter focuses on the analysis of casual speech data.

References

Amadeus Pro software. (HairerSoft, Kenilworth, UK; version 2.1, 1523; *User reference guide for v1.4*, Hairer 2009). Online access: https://www.hairersoft.com/manual.pdf.

Baayen, H., D.J. Douglas, and M.B. Douglas. 2008. Mixed-effects modeling with crossed random effects for subjects and items. *Journal of Memory and Language* 59 (4): 390–412.

Baayen, H. (to appear). *Analyzing linguistic data: A practical introduction to statistics using R*, 2nd ed. Cambridge: Cambridge University Press.

Bentin, S., L.Y. Deouell, and N. Soroker. 1999. Selective visual streaming in face recognition: Evidence from developmental prosopagnosia. *NeuroReport* 10 (4): 823–827.

Berent, I., M.L. Bennett, V. Deshpande, J. Epstein, H. Pan, R.T. Seethamraju, E. Stern, and X. Zhao. 2014. Language universals engage Broca's Area. *PLoS ONE* 9 (4): 1–10.

Berent, I., D. Steriade, T. Lennertz, and V. Vaknin. 2007. What we know about what we have never heard: Evidence for perceptual illusions. *Cognition* 104 (3): 591–630.

Berent, I., V. Vaknin, and J. Shimron. 2004. Does a theory of language need a grammar? Evidence from Hebrew root structure. *Brain and Language* 90 (1–3): 170–182.

Bertinetto, P. M., S. Scheuer, K. Dziubalska-Kołaczyk, and M. Agonigi. 2007. Intersegmental cohension and syllable division in Polish. In *Proceedings of the 16th international congress of phonetic sciences, Saarbrücken,* 6–10 Aug 2007, eds. J. Trouvain, and W. J. Barry, 1953–1956. Saarbruecken: University of Saarbruecken.

Bethin, C.Y. 1992. *Polish syllables: The role of prosody in phonology and morphology.* Colombus, OH: Slavica Publishers.

Bethin, C.Y. 2006. *Slavic prosody: Language change and phonological theory* [Cambridge studies in linguistic 86]. Cambridge: Cambridge University Press.

Cetnarowska, B., and M. Żygis. 2004. Syllabification across a prefix-stem boundary in Polish: The role of semantic compositionality. *Zeitschrift für Slawistik* 49: 42–60.

Cetnarowska, B., and M. Żygis. 2007. Phonetic syllabification and morphological parsability: The case of prefixed words in Polish. In *Challenging tasks for psycholinguistics in the New Century*, ed. J. Arabski, 149–163. Katowice: Uniwersytet Śląski.

Chambers, J.K., and P. Trudgill. 1998. *Dialectology*, 2nd ed. Cambridge: Cambridge University Press.

Chomsky, N., and M. Halle. 1968. *The Sound Pattern of English*. New York: Harper and Row.

Clements, G.N. 1985. The geometry of phonological features. *Phonology Yearbook* 2: 225–252.

Clements, G. N. 1990. The role of the sonority cycle in core syllabification. In *Papers in laboratory phonology. 1: Between the grammar and physics of speech*, eds. J. Kingston, and M.E. Beckman, 283–333. Cambridge: Cambridge University Press.

Coleman, J.S. 1996. Declarative syllabification in Tashlhit Berber. In *Current trends in phonology: Models and methods* 1, eds. J. Durand, and B. Laks, 177–218. Salford: European Studies Research Institute, University of Salford.

Coleman, J., and J. Pierrehumbert. 1997. Stochastic phonological grammars and acceptability. In *Computational phonology. Third meeting of the ACL special interest group in computational phonology: Proceedings of the workshop*, ed. J. Coleman, 49–56. Somerset: Association for Computational Linguistics.

Cyran, E., and E. Gussmann. 1999. Consonantal clusters and governing relations: Polish initial consonant sequences. In *The syllable: Views and facts*, eds. H. van der Hulst, and A.N. Ritter, 219–249. Berlin: Mouton de Gruyter.

Daland, R., M. Garellek, B. Hayes, and J. White. 2011. Explaining sonority projection effects. *Phonology* 28 (2): 197–234.

Długosz-Kurczabowa, K., and S. Dubisz. 2006. *Gramatyka historyczna języka polskiego*. Warszawa: Wydawnictwa Uniwesytetu Warszawskiego.

Domahs, U., W. Kehrein, J. Knaus, R. Wiese, and M. Schlesewsky. 2009. Event-related potentials reflecting the processing of phonological constraint violations. *Language and Speech* 52 (4): 415–435.

Donegan, P., and D. Stampe. 2009. Hypotheses of Natural Phonology. *Poznań Studies in Contemporary Linguistics* 45 (1): 1–31.

Dziubalska-Kołaczyk, K. 2014. Explaining phonotactics using NAD. *Language Sciences* 46 (A): 6–17.

E-Prime software. (E-Prime 2.0 Psychology Software Tools, Inc., Pittsburgh, PA, USA, Schneider et al. 2012).

Ernestus, M., and A. Cutler. 2015. BALDEY: A database of auditory lexical decisions. *The Quarterly Journal of Experimental Psychology* 68 (8): 1469–1488.

Fasiolo, M., Y. Goude, R. Nedellec, and S.N. Wood. 2017. *Fast calibrated additive quantile regression*. Manuscript. Bristol: University of Bristol.

Feng, Ch., T. Chen, H. He, N. Lu, Y. Lu, X.M. Tu, and H. Wang. 2014. Log-transformation and its implications for data analysis. *Shanghai Archives of Psychiatry* 26 (2): 105–109.

Flemming, E.S. 2002. *Auditory representations in phonology*. London, New York: Routledge.

Flemming, E.S. 2004. Contrast and perceptual distinctiveness. In *Phonetically-based phonology*, eds. B. Hayes, R. Kirchner, and D. Steriade, 232–276. Cambridge: Cambridge University Press.

Friederici, A.D. 2002. Towards a neural basis of auditory sentence processing. *Trends in Cognitive Sciences* 6 (2): 78–84.

Frisch, S.A. 2004. Language processing and segmental OCP effects. In *Phonetically-based phonology*, eds. B. Hayes, R. Kirchner, and D. Steriade, 346–371. Cambridge: Cambridge University Press.

Frisch, S.A., and B. Zawaydeh. 2001. The psychological reality of OCP-Place in Arabic. *Language* 77: 91–106.

Frisch, S.A., N.R. Large, and D.B. Pisoni. 2000. Perception of wordlikeness: Effects of segment probability and length on the processing of nonce words. *Journal of Memory and Language* 42 (4): 481–496.
Frisch, S.A., J.B. Pierrehumbert, and M.B. Broe. 2004. Similarity avoidance and the OCP. *Natural Language and Linguistic Theory* 22: 179–228.
Gibbon, D. 2014. *Visualisation of distances in language quality spaces: DistGraph, an online teaching tool for language typology data mining*. Bielefeld: U Bielefeld. Online access: http://wwwhomes.uni-bielefeld.de/gibbon/DistGraph/.
Gibbon, D. 2016. Legacy language atlas data mining: Mapping Kru languages. In *Proceedings of the international conference on language resources and evaluation, Portorož*, 23–28 May 2016, eds. N. Calzolari, K. Choukri, T. Declerck, S. Goggi, M. Grobelnik, B. Maegaard, J. Mariani, H. Mazo, A. Moreno, J. Odijk, and S. Piperidis, 3235–3242 Paris: ELRA.
Goldsmith, J.A. 1990. *Autosegmental and metrical phonology*. Oxford: Blackwell.
Gordon, M. 2016. *Phonological typology*. Oxford: Oxford University Press.
Greenberg, J.H. 1978. Some generalizations concerning initial and final consonant clusters. In *Universals of human language*, eds. J.H. Greenberg, C.A. Ferguson, and E.A. Moravcsik, 243–279. Stanford. CA: Stanford University Press.
Gussmann, E. 1991. Polish syllable structure: A hypothesis and its problems. In *Words are physicians for an ailing mind*, eds. M. Grochowski, and D. Weiss, 207–213. München: Sagner.
Gussmann, E. 1992. Resyllabification and delinking: The case of Polish voicing. *Linguistic Inquiry* 23 (1): 29–56.
Gussmann, E. 2007. *The phonology of Polish*. Oxford: Oxford University Press.
Hairer, M. 2009. *Amadeus Pro. User reference guide for v1.4*. Online access: https://www.hairersoft.com/manual.pdf.
Hall, T.A. 1997. *The Phonology of coronals* [Current issues in linguistic theory 149]. Amsterdam: John Benjamins.
Harris, J.W. 1983. *Syllable structure and stress in Spanish: A nonlinear analysis*. Cambridge, MA: The MIT Press.
Hayes, B. 2011. Interpreting sonority-projection experiments: The role of phonotactic modeling. In *Proceedings of the 17th international congress of phonetic sciences, Hong Kong*, 17–21 Aug 2011, eds. W.S. Lee, and E. Zee, 835–838. Hong Kong: City University of Hong Kong.
Hayes, B., and J. White. 2013. Phonological naturalness and phonotactic learning. *Linguistic Inquiry* 44 (1): 45–75.
Heeringa, W. J. 2004. *Measuring dialect pronunciation differences using Levenshtein distance*. Ph.D. diss., Groningen: University of Groningen.
Itô, J. 1986. *Syllable theory in prosodic phonology*. Ph.D diss., Amherst: University of Massachusetts.
Jarosz, G. 2017. Defying the stimulus: Acquisition of complex onsets in Polish. *Phonology* 34 (2): 269–298.
Jarosz, G., and A. Rysling. 2017. Sonority sequencing in Polish: The combined roles of prior bias and experience. In *Proceedings of the annual meetings on phonology*, 2016, eds. K. Jesney, C. O'Hara, C. Smith, R. Walker, 1–12. USC.
Jassem, W. 2003. Polish. *Journal of the International Phonetic Association: Illustrations of the IPA* 33 (1): 103–107.
Kawahara, S. 2016. *Psycholinguistic methodology in phonological research*. Oxford Bibliography Online. https://doi.org/10.1093/obo/9780199772810-0021.
Kawasaki, H. 1982. *An acoustical basis for universal constraints on sound sequences*, Ph.D. diss., Berkeley: University of California.
Klemensiewicz, Z., T. Lehr-Spławiński, and S. Urbańczyk (eds.). 1981. *Gramatyka historyczna języka polskiego*, 4th ed. Warszawa: Państwowe Wydawnictwo Naukowe.
Koenker, R. 2010. *Quantile regression*. Cambridge: Cambridge University Press.
Koenker, R., and G. Jr. Bassett. 1978. Regression quantiles. *Econometrica* 46 (1): 33–50.
Kohler, K. 1990. German. *Journal of the International Phonetic Association: Illustrations of the IPA* 20 (1): 48–50.

Leben, W. R. 1973. *Suprasegmental phonology*. Ph.D. diss., Cambridge, MA: The MIT Press.

Łubowicz, A. 2007. Paradigmatic contrast in Polish. *Journal of Slavic Linguistics* 15 (2): 229–262.

Łubowicz, A. 2012. *The phonology of contrast*. London: Equinox.

Łubowicz, A. 2016. Contrast preservation in Polish Palatalization. *Glossa: A Journal of General Linguistics* 1 (21): 1–27.

Łukaszewicz, B. 2006. Extrasyllabicity, transparency and prosodic constituency in the acquisition of Polish. *Lingua* 116: 1–30.

Łukaszewicz, B. 2007. Reduction in syllable onsets in the acquisition of Polish: Deletion, coalescence, metathesis and gemination. *Journal of Child Language* 34: 53–82.

Łukaszewicz, B. 2010. *Phonological acquisition in Optimality Theory. Towards an integrated comprehension-production Grammar*. Warszawa: Uniwersytet Warszawski.

Marinis, T. 2003. Psycholinguistic techniques in second language acquisition research. *Second Language Research* 19 (2): 144–161.

McCarthy, J.J. 1986. OCP effects: Gemination and antigemmination. *Linguistic Inquiry* 17: 207–263.

McCarthy, J.J. 1988. Feature geometry and dependency: A review. *Phonetica* 43: 84–108.

Mester, R. A. 1986. *Studies in tier structure*. Ph.D. diss., Amherst, MA: The MIT Press.

Miller, G.A., and P. Nicely. 1995. An analysis of perceptual confusions among some English consonants. *Journal of the Acoustical Society of America* 27 (2): 338–352.

Moreton, E. 2002. Structural constraints in the perception of English stop-sonorant clusters. *Cognition* 84 (1): 55–71.

Moreton, E., and J. Pater. 2012a. Structure and substance in artificial-phonology learning, Part I: Structure. *Linguistics and Language Compass* 6 (11): 686–701.

Moreton, E., and J. Pater. 2012b. Structure and substance in artificial-phonology learning, Part II: Substance. *Linguistics and Language Compass* 6 (11): 702–718.

Myers, S., and J. Padgett. 2014. Domain generalisation in artificial language learning. *Phonology* 31 (3): 399–433.

Ohala, J.J., and H. Kawasaki-Fukumori. 1997. Alternatives to the sonority hierarchy for explaining segmental sequential constraints. In *Language and its ecology: essays in memory of Einar Haugen* [Trends in linguistics. Studies and monographs 100], eds. S. Eliasson, and E. H. Jahr, 343–365. Berlin: Mouton de Gruyter.

Orzechowska, P., J. Mołczanow, and M. Jankowski. 2018. Struktura sylaby a akcent wyrazowy w języku rosyjskim. *Studia et Documenta Slavica* 1–2 (5–6): 79–91.

Orzechowska, P., J. Mołczanow, and M. Jankowski. 2019. Prosodically-conditioned syllables structure in English. *Research in Language* 17 (1): 1–12.

Padgett, J. 2001. Contrast dispersion and Russian palatalization. In *The role of speech perception in phonology*, eds. E. Hume, and K. Johnson, 187–218. San Diego: Academic Press.

Padgett, J. 2003. The emergence of contrastive palatalization in Russian. In *Optimality Theory and language change* [Studies in natural language and linguistic theory 56], ed. D.E. Holt, 307–335. Dordrecht: Springer.

Paradis, C., and J.-F. Prunet. 1991. *The special status of coronals: Internal and external evidence*. San Diego: Academic Press.

Parker, S. 2012. Sonority distance vs. sonority dispersion—A typological survey. In *The sonority controversy*, ed. S. Parker, 101–166. Berlin: Walter de Gruyter.

Pham, H., and H. Baayen. 2015. Vietnamese compounds show an anti-frequency effect in visual lexical decision. *Language, Cognition and Neuroscience* 30 (9): 1077–1095.

Pitt, M. 1998. Phonological processes and the perception of phonotactically illegal consonant clusters. *Perception and Psychophysics* 60 (6): 941–951.

R Development Core Team. 2013. *R: A language and environment for statistical computing. R foundation for statistical computing*. Vienna, Austria. Online access: http://www.R-project.org/.

Rice, K. 2007. Markedness in phonology. In *The Cambridge handbook of phonology*, ed. P. de Lacy, 89–97. Cambridge: Cambridge University Press.

Rochoń, M. 2000. *Optimality in complexity: The case of Polish consonant clusters* [Studia grammatica 48]. Berlin: Akademie Verlag.
Rodriguez, R.N., and Y. Yao. 2017. Five things you should know about quantile regression. In *Proceedings of the SAS global forum 2017 conference, Orlando,* 2–5 Apr 2017. Cary, NC: SAS Institute Inc.
Rubach, J. 2016. Polish yers: Representation and analysis. *Journal of Linguistics* 52: 421–466.
Rubach, J., and G. Booji. 1990a. Syllable structure assignment in Polish. *Phonology* 7: 121–158.
Rubach, J., and G. Booji. 1990b. Edge of constituent effects in Polish. *Natural Language & Linguistic Theory* 8 (3): 427–463.
Schneider, W., A. Eschman, and A. Zuccolotto. 2012. *E-Prime reference guide*. Pittsburgh: Psychology Software Tools, Inc.
Schwartz, G. 2013. A representational parameter for onsetless syllables. *Journal of Linguistics* 49 (3): 613–646.
Selkirk, E.O. 1984. On the major class features and syllable theory. In *Language Sound Structure*, eds. M. Aronoff, and R.T. Oehrle, 107–136. Cambridge, MA: The MIT Press.
Shademan, S. 2006. Is phonotactic knowledge grammatical knowledge? In *Proceedings of the 25th west coast conference on formal linguistics, Seattle*, 28–30 Apr 2006, eds. D. Baumer, D. Montero, and M. Scanlon, 371–379. Somerville, MA: Cascadilla Proceedings Project.
Sommerstein, A.H. 1974. On phonotactically motivated rules. *Journal of Linguistics* 10 (1): 71–94.
Steriade, D. 1982. *Greek prosodies and the nature of syllabification*. Ph.D. diss., Cambridge, MA: The MIT Press.
Steriade, D. 1993. Closure, release, and nasal contour. In *Nasals, nasalization, and the velum*, ed. M. Huffman and R. Krakow, 401–470. San Diego, CA: Academic Press.
Szpyra, J. 1992. Ghost segments in nonlinear phonology: Polish yers. *Language* 68 (2): 277–312.
Szpyra, J. 1995. *Three tiers in Polish and English phonology*. Lublin: Wydawnictwo Uniwersytetu Marii Curie-Skłodowskiej.
Szpyra-Kozłowska, J. 1998. The sonority scale and phonetic syllabification in Polish. *Biuletyn Polskiego Towarzystwa Językoznawczego* 54: 63–82.
Szpyra-Kozłowska, J. 2000. On some misconceptions concerning phonetic syllabifications in Polish. *Folia Linguistica Anglica* 2: 159–173.
Tamasi, K., and I. Berent. 2015. Sensitivity to phonological universals: The case of stops and fricatives. *Journal of Psycholinguistic Research* 44 (4): 359–381.
Ulbrich, C., P. Alday, J. Knaus, P. Orzechowska, and R. Wiese. 2016. The role of phonotactic principles in language processing. *Language, Cognition and Neuroscience* 31 (5): 662–682.
Vitevitch, M.S., and P.A. Luce. 1999. Probabilistic phonotactics and neighborhood activation in spoken word recognition. *Journal of Memory and Language* 40 (3): 374–408.
Vitevitch, M.S., E.T. Auer, P.A. Luce, and D.B. Pisoni. 1999. Phonotactics, neighborhood activation, and lexical access for spoken words. *Brain and Language* 68 (1–2): 306–311.
Wagner, M., M. Brett, V.L. Shafer, and M. Steinschneider. 2012. The phonotactic influence on the perception of a consonant cluster /pt/ by native English and native Polish listeners: A behavioral and event related potential (ERP) study. *Brain and Language* 123: 30–41.
Walczak, B. 1999. *Zarys Dziejów Języka Polskiego*. Wrocław: Wydawictwo Uniwersytetu Wrocławskiego.
Westbrook, A., and T.S. Braver. 2015. Cognitive effort: A neuroeconomic approach. *Cognitive, Affective and Behavioral Neuroscience* 15 (2): 395–415.
Wiese, R. 1996. *The phonology of German*. Oxford: Clarendon Press.
Wiese, R., P. Orzechowska, P. Alday, and C. Ulbrich. 2017. Structural principles or frequency of use? An ERP experiment on the learnability of Polish consonant clusters. *Frontiers in Psychology—Auditory Cognitive Neuroscience* 7: 2005.
Wood, S. 2018. *Package 'mgcv'. Mixed GAM computation vehicle with automatic smoothness estimation*. Online access: https://cran.r-project.org/web/packages/mgcv/mgcv.pdf.
Yip, M. 1988. The Obligatory Contour Principle and phonological rules: A loss of identity. *Linguistic Inquiry* 19 (1): 65–100.

Zydorowicz, P., and P. Orzechowska. 2016. The study of Polish phonotactics: Measures of phonotactic preferability. *Studies in Polish Linguistics* 11 (3): 97–136.

Zydorowicz, P., P. Orzechowska, M. Jankowski, K. Dziubalska-Kołaczyk, P. Wierzchoń, and D. Pietrala. 2016. *Phonotactics and morphonotactics of Polish and English: Description, tools and applications*. Poznań: Wydawnictwo Naukowe UAM.

Chapter 5
Phonological Processes in Phonotactics: Evidence from Casual Speech

We need to investigate casual speech to truly understand language production, processing and the mental lexicon.
(Benjamin Tucker and Mirjam Ernestus 2016)

5.1 Introduction

The core theme of this chapter is the study of casual speech processes in native speakers of Polish. Emphasis is placed on processes which are held accountable in word-initial and word-final consonant clusters such as deletion, substitution or insertion. A distinction is drawn between target forms of clusters, which reflect the pronunciation of a word in isolation, and casual speech forms of clusters, which are found in the speech sound continuum, where pauses signalling word and phrase boundaries tend to be omitted. The investigation of target and modified forms aims at identifying phonological (subsegmental and suprasegmental) and non-phonological factors which contribute to cluster modification, on the one hand, and which determine the choice of a process type, on the other. The results of the analysis are threefold. First, initial and final phonotactics display different modification preferences. Initial cluster modification is primarily triggered by lexical frequency, while final cluster modification is induced by phonological properties of consonants forming clusters: stridency of C1, quality of a vowel neighbouring on a cluster, a number of coronals in a cluster and a continuant in absolute word-final position. Second, the selection of a process type is primarily related to stridency in initial clusters, and continuance in final clusters. Third, initial position, being more salient, supports a greater variety and severeness of cluster modifications.

P. Orzechowska, *Complexity in Polish Phonotactics*, Prosody, Phonology and Phonetics, https://doi.org/10.1007/978-981-13-7299-5_5

5.2 State of the Art

Psycholinguistic questions, which have been pursued in the literature, are mainly focused on speech produced and processed in a supervised style. This style is substantially different from speech produced in unmonitored settings, especially during casual conversations. Since casual or conversational speech diverges substantially from what speakers are exposed to in laboratory settings, it offers insights not only into the linguistic strategies that underlie communication, but also into the mental lexicon. This point was raised by Tucker and Ernestus (2016). The authors argue that cognitive processes can be truly understood when more unmonitored types of speech are studied in psycholinguistic research, and that casual or spontaneous speech provide a testing ground for linguistic models, theories and hypotheses. Therefore, in order to gain further insights into the phonotactic behaviour of native speakers of Polish, this chapter discusses the articulation of consonant clusters in spontaneous conversations.

The focal theme of this chapter is the study the phonetic forms in word-initial and word-final consonant clusters in casual speech. Emphasis is placed on phonostylistic processes which affect sequences of consonants such as deletion, substitution or insertion. The analysis addresses three major questions.

(1) Which subsegmental properties of consonant clusters motivate cluster modification?
(2) What is the role of phonological and non-phonological factors in cluster modification?
(3) And, finally, which properties trigger the selection of a process type?

The careful reader should have noticed that the scope of the analysis to follow is broader than that in the previous chapters. Casual speech is non-careful, unmonitored, unscripted and reduced. It reflects the preferences of speakers and properties of lexical items. Therefore, the modelling of phonotactics in casual speech requires accounting for supra-segmental and non-phonological criteria.

The discussion on casual speech phenomena first necessitates a terminological clarification. A distinction needs to be between target forms and casual speech forms. The term *target form* refers to the realization of a sequence of consonants which is a phonetic variant produced in careful speech or in an isolated word, also called a citation form. In the present analysis, a cluster target matches the norm of Modern Polish (Karaś and Madejowa 1977; Madejowa 1987, 1990, 1993; Mizerski 2005; Witaszek-Samborska 1986). To the contrary, the term *casual speech form* is used to refer to the realization of a consonant cluster in the continuum of speech sounds, where pauses signalling word and phrase boundaries are omitted. Typically, such a form diverges from normative pronunciation by being modified or reduced. It must be noted that a casual speech does not imply a pronunciation mistake, although it can be one (Shockey 2003). Under the view that phonetic variants should be treated as normal pronunciation variants, the term *modification* or *reduction* is not related strictly to a process type such as lenition but to the divergence from a citation form.

In other words, a type of cluster reduction is a measure of phonetic distance between a cluster target, which is taken as a reference point, and its modified variant.

The notion of *casual speech* is rather ambiguous. So far I have used the term interchangeably with spontaneous speech, conversational speech, non-careful speech, unmonitored speech, or reduced speech, in opposition to, among others, formal speech, careful speech, monitored speech (for overviews and discussions see Llisterri 1992; Shockey 1974, 2003; Tucker and Ernestus 2016; Kul 2018) in the present analysis, casual speech is treated as an umbrella term for articulation which reflects every-day speech in displaying all the aforementioned characteristics. Although the greatest mismatch occurs between the casual and careful extreme, there is a continuum between a citation form and a casual form (Ernestus et al. 2015; Labov 1972; Tucker 2007; Wagner et al. 2015). For instance, Labov (1972) proposes a scale, in which the arrangement of styles is based on a single criterion of attention. One extreme of the scale is represented by a "reading style" which is characterized by pronouncing isolated words and minimal pairs. The other extreme of the scale is occupied by "spontaneous speech", which is excited and emotionally charged as the constraints of a formal situation are overridden. In Labov's (1972) account, spontaneous speech is kept separate from casual speech. In a similar vein, Tucker (2007) proposes a nine-point continuum of styles, whose extremes are occupied by unnatural speech which is computer generated, and natural speech which is defined in terms of "spontaneous conversation between close friends on a familiar topic with a lot of background knowledge and animated affect and with no microphone or observer present" (Tucker 2007: 20).

Disregarding the definition and interpretation of casual speech, linguists agree that it has a phonetic basis. This fact is explained in Zwicky (1972):

> We cannot rule out any pair of segments as impossible morphophonemic alternants; morphophonemics often includes remnants of linguistic history. The alternation [i]-[æ] in sing-sang is unexpected, but not devastating to linguistic theory. Casual speech processes, on the other hand, seem to be constrained to be phonetically natural. In their extreme case they can be explained as the inevitable result of increasing speed of speech: the articulators simply cannot achieve their targets in the time available. (Zwicky 1987: 608)

The literature on the topic has successfully differentiated between target and casual speech forms based on a variety of factors such as phonetic context, morphological complexity, speech rate, frequency, gender as well as age (among others, Brown 1977; Kerswill 1987; Lodge 1984; Shockey 1974, 2003). As for phonotactics, consonant deletion, consonant and vowel insertion, place assimilation, and reciprocal assimilation (i.e. yod coalescence) have been studied. A large body of sociophonetic research has focused on English casual speech, and processes such as glottalization, 'th'-fronting, 'h' dropping and, most typically, /t d/ deletion in British English (Tagliamonte and Temple 2005), Standard American English (Guy 1980; Kul 2018), and in different dialects and varieties, such as Cambridge English (Kerswill 1985), Mancunian English (Baranowski and Turton 2015), African American English (Fasold 1972; Labov et al. 1968; Wolfram 1969), Chicano English (Santa Ana 1991, 1996) or Jamaican English (Patrick 1999).

In Polish, casual speech has been discussed mainly in prescriptive terms in Dunaj (1985), Dukiewicz and Sawicka (1995), Karaś and Madejowa (1977), Madejowa (1993), Mizerski (2005) and Nagórko (2006). Theoretical analyses of phonostylistic processes have been proposed in a generative account of Rubach (1981), in an Optimality Theory account of Rochoń (2000) and in a Natural Phonology account of Dziubalska-Kołaczyk (1990). Production in Polish has been studied in terms of gestural coordination (Hermes et al. 2017; Mücke et al. 2010) and types of phonostylistic processes in casual speech in adults (Gonet and Trochymiuk 2007; Jaskuła 2014, 2018; Kaźmierski 2016). Processes affecting specifically consonant clusters have been studied mainly in the domain of first and second language acquisition.

Dziubalska-Kołaczyk and Zielińska (2011), and Dziubalska-Kołaczyk and Zydorowicz (2014) analysed correct and incorrect renditions of Polish phonotactic and morphonotactic clusters in word-initial, word-medial and word-final positions by native speakers of CV languages. Strategies of cluster modification were also investigated in Polish children with developing phonologies in Milewski (2005) and Szreder (2013). Łukaszewicz (2006, 2007, 2010) showed that processes such as deletion and coalescence prevail in word initial onsets, while metathesis and gemination are preferred in word-medial position. Predictions made by the *Sonority Sequencing Generalization* and *Net Auditory Distance* (Chap. 2, Sect. 2.4) were tested on the example of sC clusters in Yavaş and Marecka (2014), and Marecka and Dziubalska-Kołaczyk (2014), respectively. The studies showed that in spite of their marked structure (i.e. ill-formed in terms of the SSG, or dispreferred in terms of NAD), /s/-initial clusters are generally preferred in L1 phonotactics, and tend to be produced correctly. A broader perspective on the most marked clusters in term of NAD was provided in Zydorowicz and Dziubalska-Kołaczyk (2017). The authors demonstrated that children's performance is significantly worse on the most dispreferred clusters compared to the remaining clusters. Similarly in casual speech, highly marked clusters have higher modification rates, particularly in word-final position.

The analysis pursued in this chapter address two broad themes which have been discussed in the subject literature. First, an attempt is made at identifying factors that trigger cluster modification. Second, insights are provided into factors which influence the selection of a specific process type. The way in which the present analysis diverges from the aforementioned accounts consists in seeking a feature-based motivation for cluster modification. For instance, the role of coronality, stridency, anteriorness or continuance in cluster reduction has not been studied in Polish, let alone the competition into which the features possibly enter. I am not aware of any contributions which would investigate these or related features in the selection of a casual speech process (e.g. consonant deletion or substitution, vowel insertion) in Polish speakers. The analysis to follow is based on a wide array of phonological features. The sonority profile of clusters is also discussed; however, the SSG, as a generalizing principle is not a factor in the statistical analysis. Factors which underlie cluster modification are inferred from the observation of the data, and offer new insights into the *positional weight of phonological features* in articulatory deviations in Polish. Note that production studies which have investigated the importance of phonological features have been concerned with languages other than Polish.

5.3 Phonological Features in Articulation

A battery of studies has been devoted to the role of phonological features in perception, native and foreign language production and disorders (see Singh 1976; Pajak and Levy 2014 and references cited therein). A response to some of my considerations regarding Polish is provided in Yavaş et al. (2008) and Yavaş (2013a, b, 2014). The studies on the acquisition of phonotactics in Croatian, Dutch, English, Hebrew, Norwegian and Polish children demonstrated that sC reduction varies across the languages, and is not related to the sonority profile of clusters per se, but to the continuancy of the second consonant. In the Germanic languages (Dutch, English, Norwegian), the accuracy in the production of C1C2 clusters was correlated with the [±continuant] status of C2. That is, the rates for correct renditions were always higher in /s/ + [+continuant] targets (i.e. /sl sw/) than in /s/ + [−continuant] targets (i.e. /s/ + stop and /s/ + nasal). No such correlation was observed in Hebrew, Croatian, and Polish, where clusters ending in a non-continuant segment were either equal or more successfully rendered than /s/ + [+continuant] clusters. Yavaş (2013a) attributes the differences in production to cluster inventories of the languages. Hebrew, Croatian, and Polish are rich in consonant clusters (including sC). Therefore, the child raised in the ambience of such a language tends to produce the sonority-disobeying sequences more frequently, which, in turn, results in their greater automaticity and accuracy.

Before, I proceed with the analysis of word-edge clusters in casual speech, Sect. 5.4 focuses on the presentation of phonetic and phonological correlates which have been considered to affect pronunciation choices of speakers.

5.4 Factors Influencing Consonant Modification

Casual speech forms display a wide range of deviations from their cited equivalents. In the most extreme cases, segments and whole syllables can be omitted. The range to which produced variants can vary cannot be described in terms of a simple pattern, which is illustrated in detail in Sect. 5.5.3.3 in initials, and Sect. 5.5.4.3 in finals. Factors which influence different realizations of word target are presented in Table 5.1.

It must be borne in mind that Shockey's (2003) account summarizes factors which were identified in casual speech in English. In this chapter, it will be demonstrated that some of the processes hold in Polish. The question that arises at this point refers to correlates of speech styles. Llisterri (1992) provides an overview of phonetic and phonological correlates based on 24 conference presentations on "Phonetics and Phonology of Speaking Styles" at ESCA in Barcelona (1991). A summary of Llisterri's (1992) account is given in Table 5.2. Style correlates are subsumed under three groups: segmental, suprasegmental and phonological processes. Segmental and suprasegmental features pertain to the domain of phonetics, while processes refer to the domain of phonology. Llisterri (1992) reports that

Table 5.1 Factors affecting reduction in casual speech

	Low reduction	High reduction
(a) Frequency	Infrequent	Frequent
(b) Discourse		
Focus	Focal	Non- or defocal
Prescription	Prescriptive	Unnoticed
Medium	Scripted	Unscripted
(c) Rate	Slow	Fast
(d) Function in larger linguistic units		
Stress	Stressed	Unstressed
Place in word	Beginning	End
Place in syllable	Beginning	End
Part of speech	Content	Function (Short frequent)
(e) Phonetic/phonological		
Environment	Non-cluster	Cluster
Place of articulation	Non-alveolar	Alveolar
	Non-ð	ð
Incredibly vulnerable: [t], [ð], [ə]		
Moderately vulnerable: [n], [d], [l], [z]		
Practically invulnerable: [f], [m], [ʃ], [ʧ], [ʤ]		
(f) Morphological		
	Gerund polymorphemic	Present participle monomorphemic

Shockey (2003: 15)

segmental correlates tend to be investigated in terms of acoustic, rather than articulatory, properties (particularly vowel formants). Suprasegmental parameters, in turn, involve duration, F0, pauses, speaking rate as well as voice quality. Among these cues are temporal acoustic properties (duration and pausing) constitute good determinants of speech styles. As far as phonological correlates are concerned, they tend to focus on assimilation and elision.

Overall, the majority of contributions on the topic have investigated speech styles at the level of suprasegmental features. In the following, I discuss possible types of cluster modification in Polish from the perspective of phonological processes. The main process types involve deletion and substitution. The divergence from a target is determined on the basis of a phonetic norm for Modern Polish. Table 5.3 presents possible realization variants for initial and final consonant clusters according to the literary language norm reported in Madejowa (1993). The column labelled as ‘Grapheme’ and ‘Phonetic norm’ list all combinations of segments in the written language which are realized as clusters as well as correct and acceptable pronunciation variants. Preferred variants are given as first. The ‘Comments’ column provides additional information related to the preferability and frequency of use of each variant. Word-initial and word-final clusters are listed in the upper part and lower part of the table, respectively. Palatalized variants are marked with a diacritic [^{j}] as in, e.g. [k^{j} g^{j}].

Table 5.2 Phonetic and phonological correlates of speaking styles

Segmental correlates
Formant values: vowels/transitions *Vowel reduction* *Articulatory correlates*: jaw height/tongue displacement/articulatory paths *Coarticulation*
Suprasegmental correlates
Duration: phonemes or allophones/syllables/words/paragraphs/utterances (with or without pauses) *Fundamental frequency*, pitch: average, median, maximum/range (standard deviation)/register (mean)/final and non final slope/gradient/contour, pitch patterns *Pauses*: total duration/number/duration of voiced pauses/duration of silent pauses/pause time between sentences/pause time within sentences/no. of tone units/no. of syllables per tone unit *Speaking rate* *Voice quality*
Phonological processes
Assimilation: palatalisation/nasalisation *Deletion or elision*: phonemes or allophones/syllables *Gemination* *Stress*

Llisterri (1992: 8ff.)

Table 5.3 Normative rules of Modern Polish pronunciation for consonant clusters

Grapheme	Phonetic norm	Example	Comment
Initial clusters			
<trz>	[ʧʃ], [tʃ]	trzeć ‘to rub’	[ʧ]—pronunciation mistake
<drz>	[ʤʒ], [dʒ]	drzewo ‘tree’	[ʤ]—incorrect
<scz>	[ʃʧ], [sʧ]	sczerniać ‘to blacken’	Both variants are correct
<zdz(i)>	[ʑʥ], [z,ʥ]	zdzielić ‘to hit’	Both variants are correct
<zrz, zż>	[ʒʒ], [zʒ]	zrzucać ‘to throw about’	Both variants are correct
<ł> in CłV	[Cw]	błogosławić ‘to bless’	Other variants (esp. [w] weakening or deletion)—incorrect
<tw, sw, kw, chw, czw, krw, trw>	[tf], [sf], [kf], [xf], [ʧf], [krf], [trf], (rarely [tv], [sv], [kv], [xv], [ʧv], [krv],[trv])	trwoga ‘fear’	A voiced realization of the allophone [v] or [v^j] is a rare and disappearing variant, heard in the oldest generation from Poznań
<strz>	[ʃʧʃ], [stʃ], [sʧʃ]	strzecha ‘thatched roof’	[ʃʧ] or [sʧ], which have a regional nature, or [ʃ] which is a result of articulatory carelessness—glaring pronunciation mistakes
<zdrz>	[ʒʤʒ], [zʤ], [zʤʒ]	zdrzemnąć ‘to doze off’	Regional variants [ʒʤ] and [zʤ]—incorrect

(continued)

Table 5.3 (continued)

Grapheme	Phonetic norm	Example	Comment
<wsk, wsp, wst>	[fsk], [fsp], [fst]	wskazać 'to point'	Reduced variants [sp], [st] and [sk]—incorrect
<trzm(i), trzp(i), trzc (i)>	[ʧm], [tʃm], [ʧʃm],[ʧp], [tʃp], [ʧʃp], [ʧʲtɕ], [tʃʲtɕ], [ʧʃʲtɕ]	trzmiel 'beatle'	All the variants are correct
<drzw(i)>	[ʤvʲ], [dʒvʲ], [ʤʒvʲ]	drzwi 'door'	[ʤv]—the most frequent realization; [dʒv], [ʤʒv]—less frequent
<eN, aN> before a fricative	[ɛ], [ɛN], [ɔ], [ɔN]	sens 'sense'	1. A nasal homorganic with a fricative—[ɛ], [ɔ] variants are given priority 2. Otherwise, [ɛN] and [ɔN]—preferred
<pi, bi, fi, wi, mi> before a V	[pʲj], [bʲj], [fʲj], [vʲj], [mʲj], [pʲ], [bʲ], [fʲ], [vʲ], [mʲ]	pieniądze 'money'	Both the asynchronous and synchronous pronunciation variants are correct
<ki, gi> before a V	[kʲ], [gʲ], [kj], [gj]	kiedy 'when'	The hard (regional) pronunciation of <ki, gi> before [e] is incorrect
final clusters			
<trz>	[ʧ], [ʧʃ], [tʃ]	patrz! 'to look' (imp)	[ʧʃ], [tʃ]—rarer and unnatural
<ng, nk>	[ŋg], [ŋk]	bank 'bank'	[nk]—incorrect
<ł> in Cł#	[C], [Cw] Possible clusters: [dw]—[tw] [gw]—[kw] [zw]—[sw], [rw]	1. pomógł 'to help' (3rd sg past masc) 2. pomysł 'idea'	1. In the preterite: [C] and [Cw]—correct, [C]—more frequent than a voiceless cluster [Cw] 2. In nouns: voiceless [Cw]; total reduction of [w]—incorrect
<ść>	[ɕtɕ]	wolność 'freedom'	Simplified pronunciation as in [vɔlnɔɕ]—mistake
<szcz>	[ʃʧ]	deszcz 'rain'	Omission of the final [ʧ]—careless and incorrect
<zd, st>	[st]	zajazd 'inn'	Omission of [t] (frequent in casual speech)—incorrect
<zm, śl, źń, śń>	[sm], [ɕl], [ɕɲ]	pomyśl! 'to think' (imp)	Variants with a loss of the sonorant—incorrect
<strz>	[ʃʧ], [sʧ], [stʃ], [ʃʧʃ]	baletmistrz 'ballet master'	[ʃʧ] and [sʧ]—favoured, [stʃ] and [ʃʧʃ]—correct
<ą, ę>	[ow̃], [ew̃]	kęs 'bite'	Realization only before hard fricatives /s z ʃ ʒ/
	[oj], [ej]	gęś 'goose'	Realization after a hard/soft C and before soft fricatives /ɕ ʑ/

Madejowa (1993: 20ff)

Madejowa (1993) lists several pronunciation possibilities for a single cluster type. The discrepancy between correct and incorrect forms can be illustrated on the example of final clusters ending in <ł>, i.e. [Cw]. In the preterite form of verbs, both [Cw] and [C] are acceptable. For instance, clusters in *szed+ł* 'to go' (3rd sg past masc) and *umar+ł* 'to die' (3rd sg past masc) can be pronounced either as sequences [tw rw] or a single consonant [t r]. Although both variants are considered to be correct, the deletion of the final glide is more common in speakers of Polish. The same cluster type is expected to be pronounced in its full form when occurring in nouns, as in *przemysł* [pʃemɨsw] 'industry' and *pomysł* [pomɨsw] 'idea'. This observation suggests that the acceptability of a form also depends on part of speech. Pronunciation variants given by Madejowa (1993) will constitute a major reference point for the classification of consonant clusters that match and mismatch cluster targets.

5.5 The Study

5.5.1 Methodology

The data collected for the purpose of the present analysis was extracted from the electronic version of a dictionary *Słownik Wariantywności Fonetycznej Współczesnej Polszczyzny* [The Dictionary of Phonetic Variation in Contemporary Polish] by Madelska (2005). The author recorded spontaneous speech interactions of students at Adam Mickiewicz University in Poznań. Most of the participants came from the Greater Poland region. Students' output was transcribed by several phonetically-trained transcribers. Variability in pronunciation was documented in the form of a phonetic dictionary, which lists 8,607 word forms and their pronunciation variants. Additionally, for each variant, Madelska (2005) provides token frequencies indicating how many times a variant was used by subjects and its corresponding place in a frequency-based ranking. Lists of transcribed words containing initial and final clusters were compiled in an excel file, along with their usage frequencies given in the dictionary. The data was tagged with respect to the following criteria: morphological composition of a consonant cluster (phonotactic vs. morphonotactic), cluster status (target vs. modified) and the type of a process type applied, whenever possible. Section 5.5.2 presents the results of the analysis.

5.5.2 Results

In the following sections, the results of the analysis for initial and final clusters are presented. Two types of results are discussed. First, I provide an overview of citation forms of clusters, which are here referred to as targets. An ideal (citation) form of a cluster typically occurs in slow, careful and monitored speech, in particular when a word is pronounced in isolation. A target is expected to meet the phonetic norm of Modern Polish, as defined by, inter alia, Karaś and Madejowa (1977), Madejowa (1993) and Dunaj (2006). These accounts provide a reference point for the classification of clusters as matching the normative pronunciation or not. The analysis starts with the presentation of word-initial clusters, followed by word-final clusters. For each word position, two types of data are discussed.

First, in Sects. 5.5.3.1 and 5.5.4.1, I analyse all dictionary words containing initial and final clusters in terms of their normative (or expected) pronunciation. This count makes it possible to estimate which words are most common in language use. For instance, one of the most frequently used cluster types is /pʃ/ in *przykład* /pʃɨkwat/ 'example'. These cluster targets are contrasted with modified cluster renditions in casual speech. Therefore, the second type of counts presented in Sects. 5.5.3.2 and 5.5.4.2 refers to different types of cluster modification. Casual speech forms arise due to processes such as deletion, insertion or substitution. For instance, target cluster /pʃ/ in *przykład* is either preserved as [pʃ] or modified to [ʃ], [fʃ] and [pʃk] as in [ʃɨkwa], [fʃɨkwat] or [pʃkat]. The same cluster can be realized differently depending on a word. For example, /pʃ/ can surface phonetically as [əpʃ], [pʧ] or [pʃn] in *przykładać* [əpʃɨkwadatɕ] 'to bust', *przeczytałem* [pʧɨtaem] 'to read' (1st sg past masc) and *przynajmniej* [pʃnajmɲej] 'at least'. The counts based on casual speech forms provide insights into the factors which underlie cluster modification.

It must be noted that Madelska's (2005) dictionary lists words extracted from spontaneous conversations, where co-articulatory and phonostylistic processes apply at word boundaries. Since the dictionary provides only lists of words, not much is known about the phonetic context preceding and following targets. The phonological feature which is most sensitive to the boundary phenomena is voicing, which was illustrated on the example of final devoicing and voice assimilation in Chap. 1, Sect. 1.5.1. Therefore, to avoid bias, [±voice] is disregarded in the analysis to follow. Given the structure of the dictionary data, it is impossible to determine: (a) which of the voice-related cluster modifications result from the voicing profile of the surrounding segments, (b) which modifications constitute preferred pronunciation variants and (c) which modifications can be attributed to idiosyncratic preferences of speakers. Initial sequences such as /br fj sfj fzdw/ in *prawda* 'truth', *wiek* 'age', *związany* 'connected' and *wzdłuż* 'alongside' are considered to be produced according to the phonetic norm, although their citation forms are /pravda/, /vjek/, /zvjowzanɨ/ and /vzdwuʃ/, in line with the voice assimilation rule. Similar examples are found word-finally. Although word-final obstruent voicing is banned in Polish, voiced terminal obstruents are listed in the dictionary in items such as *błąd* [bwond] 'mistake', *czymś* [ʧɨmʑ] 'something', *fakt* [fagd] 'fact'. Since the voicing characteristics of clusters are due to coarticulation, which cannot be controlled in the data, clusters are not analysed in terms of voicing. Therefore, all types of voicing are considered to match the target form.

5.5.3 *Word-Initial Phonotactics*

5.5.3.1 Cluster Targets in Citation Forms

This section aims at providing an overview of the data in terms of cluster targets, disregarding their phonetic variants given in the dictionary. I summarize the results obtained for the classification of words with initial clusters according to their size (i.e. CC, CCC, CCCC) and morphological composition (i.e. phonotactic vs. morphonotactic). These results provide a general quantitative summary of cluster types which are found in natural conversations. The presentation of the results starts with cluster size. All initial cluster targets, along with their word and token frequencies, are tabulated in Appendix L.

Table 5.4 lists the number (labelled 'No') of initial cluster types, words starting with clusters as well as their repetitions (labelled 'Word tokens') depending on the number of constituent consonants. CC, CCC and CCCC refer to two-, three- and four-member sequences. Percentages (labelled '%') are calculated for the total of targets in each set, i.e. 187 types, 3,437 words containing initial clusters and 10,162 word tokens.

The most common pattern with respect to size is CC. 65% of cluster types are represented by two-member sequences. The prevalence of CCs is also observable among words and word tokens, where CCs represent 88% of words and 92% of their repetitions. It must be emphasized that the percentage share of longer clusters drops substantially, particularly in word tokens.

Table 5.5 presents an overview of the classification of initial clusters with respect to morphological complexity. Phonotactic clusters prevail in the dataset. 80% of words and 88% of their tokens start with phonologically-motivated clusters. Among all available cluster types, 65% are phonotactic and 35% are morphonotactic. Some types can be found in both contexts. For instance, /ft sx skr/ are phonotactic in *wtorek* 'Tuesday', *schemat* 'scheme', *skromny* 'modest', and morphonotactic in *w+tajemniczony* 'initiated', *s+charakteryzować* 'to characterize' and *s+krót* 'shortcut'. Such cluster types are subsumed under both groups, which results in the sum equal to 212.

Table 5.4 The distribution of initial targets in terms of cluster types, words and word tokens depending on cluster size

Size	Cluster types		Words		Word tokens	
	No	%	No	%	No	%
CC	122	65	3,015	88	9,339	92
CCC	58	31	391	11	742	7
CCCC	7	4	31	1	81	1
Total	187	100	3,437	100	10,162	100

Table 5.5 The distribution of initial targets in terms of types, words and word tokens depending on morphological complexity

Size	Cluster types		Words		Word tokens	
	No	%	No	%	No	%
Phon	137	65	2,753	80	8,908	88
Morph	75	35	684	20	1,254	12
Total	212	100	3,437	100	1,0162	100

At this point, a distinction must be drawn between clusters which are produced according to their target norm and clusters which are subject to modification. Section 5.5.3.2 provides a systematic comparison between correct and incorrect renditions of clusters.

5.5.3.2 Cluster Modification in Casual Speech Forms

The discussion of the production data starts with the presentation of a whole range of phonetic variants which were identified in casual speech. Table 5.6 lists all types of realizations of CC, CCC and CCCC targets presented in Table 5.4. Percentages are calculated separately for all attested realizations (N = 282), words in which they occur word-initially (N = 3,437) and word repetitions (N = 10,162). Bear in mind that the table reports on general modification possibilities identified in the production data, disregarding the change within each size group.

A variety of phonetic variants has arisen from three size types among cluster targets (CC, CCC, CCCC) to eight types in casual forms. On the one hand, faithful renditions of citation forms involve CC, CCC and CCCC sequences. For example, all instances of /dv sk ɕmj/ in *dwa* 'two', *skutek* 'effect', *śmieszny* 'funny' are

Table 5.6 Phonetic realizations of initial CC, CCC and CCCC targets in terms of cluster size

Realized size	Cluster type realization		Word realization		Word token realization	
	No	%	No	%	No	%
Ø	4	1	17	0	60	1
VCC	23	8	34	1	34	0
VCCC	2	1	4	0	5	0
C	22	8	153	4	522	5
CC	144	51	2,824	82	8,724	86
CCC	76	27	380	11	748	7
CCCC	10	4	24	1	68	1
CCCCC	1	0	1	0	1	0
Total	282	100	3,437	100	10,162	100

produced according to their phonetic norm. On the other hand, the cluster targets are modified in several ways shown in 46.

46. Types of modification of initial clusters

(46.a) deletion of a single consonant
chłopak /xwopak/ 'boy' → [xopak]
(46.b) deletion of a sequence of consonants
właśnie /vwaɕɲe/ 'just' → [aɕɲe]
(46.c) insertion of a prothetic vowel
ktoś /ktoɕ/ 'somebody' → [əktoɕ]
(46.d) insertion of a medial vowel
zresztą /zreʃtõw̃/ 'besides' → [zerʃtõw̃]
(46.e) syllable merge
wszystko /fʃɪstko/ 'everything' → [fʃstko]

The examples of (46.a) through (46.d) lead to cluster simplification. The only example of an increase in complexity resulting from vowel deletion is found in (46.e). Target and modified renditions of initial cluster types are listed in Appendix M.

As can be seen in Table 5.6, the preferred phonetic variants of cluster targets are the following: CC > CCC > C, VCC (where '>' means 'more common than'). That is, two-member sequences are favoured among cluster types. CC is also a dominant realization pattern across words and word tokens suggesting that CCs are generally the most favoured variants in production. CCCs are the second most common realization pattern although there is a large drop between CC and CCC realizations in words and tokens. Modifications of clusters resulting in a single consonant C and vowel-initial sequences VCC(C) are even less common. This overview provides no information on cluster targets, only on the variants which arise due to casual speech processes. I shall now look closer into the differences between target and modified realizations.

Table 5.7 shows the division into matching and mismatching cluster targets with respect to their size. Percentages are calculated for the total of words (N = 3,437) and word tokens (N = 10,162) containing initial clusters.

As can be seen, the vast majority of words (91%) feature initial clusters which match the target phonetic norm. Also, matching renditions of word tokens amount to 92%. As regards cluster types, apart from a straightforward classification into matched and mismatched, some sequences of consonants can have both realizations. For example, /vj fsp vzgl/ always match the targets in *wiele* 'a lot', *wspaniały* 'wonderful', *względem* 'regard' (instr sg), and are always modified in *wiadomo* /vjadomo/ 'it is known' → [vadomo], *wspólnota* /fspulnota/ 'community' → [spulnota] and *względu* /vzglendu/ 'regard' (gen sg) → [zzendu].

Apart from size, morphological complexity is considered to be as a possible factor affecting cluster modification. Table 5.8 shows the proportion of matched and mismatched words with initial clusters (N = 3,437) and their tokens (N = 10,162). As it turns out, the vast majority of clusters in words are produced

Table 5.7 Matched and mismatched realizations of initial types, words and word tokens in terms of cluster size

Target size	Words				Word tokens			
	Match		Mismatch		Match		Mismatch	
	No	%	No	%	No	%	No	%
CC	2,762	80	253	7	8,608	85	731	7
CCC	351	10	40	1	695	7	47	0
CCCC	18	1	13	0	43	0	38	0
Total	3,131	91	306	9	9,346	92	816	8

according to their target norm. Only 9% of observed words feature a mispronounced cluster, which corresponds to 8% of all word tokens. The results suggest that the presence of a morphological boundary does not affect cluster change. Phonotactic clusters and morphonotactic clusters are reduced in 7 and 2% of words, respectively. This proportion is comparable to word tokens, where reduced clusters amount to 7 and 1% of word repetitions.

Further subdivisions of the data can be proposed. In order to observe how casual speech forms are related to cluster size and morphological complexity, I compare the realization of matched and mismatched renditions of phonotactic and morphonotactic clusters of varying size. Table 5.9 juxtaposes the results for cluster types produced according to the phonetic norm (N_{word} = 3,131, N_{token} = 9,346). Table 5.10 presents the results for types which diverge from the target form (N_{word} = 306, N_{token} = 816). Percentages are calculated for each dataset: word types and wprd tokens.

The results show that targets are largely produced according to their phonetic norm. As regards phonotactic clusters, the proportion between 2,499 words that matched the target, and 254 words which diverged from the phonetic norm amount to 10:1. The proportion is higher for morphonotactic clusters, i.e. 12:1. This suggests that the modification rate in morphologically-motivated clusters is lower. This observation can be attributed to the fact that there is a tendency to preserve grammatical information coded in a morphologically-motivated cluster.

Table 5.8 Matched and mismatched realizations of initial types, words and word tokens in terms of morphological complexity

Motiv.	Words				Word tokens			
	Match		Mismatch		Match		Mismatch	
	No	%	No	%	No	%	No	%
Phon	2,499	73	254	7	8,196	81	712	7
Morph	632	18	52	2	1150	11	104	1
Total	3,131	91	306	9	9,346	92	816	8

Table 5.9 Matched realizations of initial targets in terms of cluster size and morphological composition

Size	Words				Word tokens			
	Phon		Morph		Phon		Morph	
	No	%	No	%	No	%	No	%
CC	2,342	75	420	13	7,838	84	770	8
CCC	156	5	195	6	357	4	338	4
CCCC	1	0	17	1	1	0	42	0
Total	2,499	80	632	20	8,196	88	1,150	12

Table 5.10 Mismatched realizations of initial targets in terms of cluster size and morphological composition

Size	Words				Word tokens			
	Phon		Morph		Phon		Morph	
	No	%	No	%	No	%	No	%
CC	230	75	23	8	684	84	47	6
CCC	23	8	17	6	26	3	21	3
CCCC	1	0	12	4	2	0	36	4
Total	254	83	52	17	712	87	104	13

5.5.3.3 Phonological Processes in Casual Speech Forms

Deletion

One of the most common processes applied in natural speech is *deletion* (or omission). The process refers to the shortening of a cluster by omitting at least one consonant. Table 5.11 presents all initial cluster targets (labelled 'Target form') which underwent deletion. For each cluster type, all casual speech forms resulting from deletion are listed in the column 'Modified form'. The table provides an example of a word in which the process applied, as well as the transcription of a mismatched pronunciation form. A type of deletion is given in the column 'Deletion type' by stating the deleted segments, where C1, C2, C3 refer to the first, second or the third consonant in a sequence. Depending on the size of a cluster target, a single consonant (C), a sequence of consonants (CC, CCC) or the whole cluster (−) can be omitted. Whenever possible, the qualitative change is commented on.

A visual inspection of the deletion types among CC clusters reveals two clear patterns. First in obstruent + sonorant clusters (OS), a sonorant tends to be omitted. In the majority of OS sequences, deletion is motivated by an increase in the manner of articulation distances, which can be equated with an increase in sonority (labelled 'OS: max SSG'). For instance, /dl kw pj/ targets entail the omission of the lateral

Table 5.11 Types of deletion in initial modified clusters

Size	Target form	Modif. form	Example	Modif. transcription	Del. type	Comment
2	dl	l	dlatego	latego	C1	*OS: min SSG
2	dr	d	drugiej	dugʲjej	C2	OS: max SSG
2	dw	d	długo	dugo	C2	OS: max SSG
2	fʃ	ʃ	wszystko	ʃɨsko	C1	OO: C1 del
2	ft	t	wtedy	tedɨ	C1	OO: C1 del
2	fʧ	ʧ	wczoraj	ʧoraj	C1	OO: C1 del
2	gd	d	gdybym	dɨ̃w̃	C1	OO: C1 del
2	gʥ	ʥ	gdzie	ʥē	C1	OO: C1 del
2	gm	m	gmachem	mahem	C1	*OS: min SSG
2	gw	g	głosy	gosɨ	C2	OS: max SSG
2	xf	f	chwilą	fʲilõw̃	C1	OO: C1 del
2	xʨ	ʨ	chciałabym	ʨaabɨm	C1	OO: C1 del
2	xw	x	chłopak	xopak	C2	OS: max SSG
2	kɕ	ɕ	książeczek	ɕõw̃ʒeʧek	C1	OO: C1 del
2	kj	k	kiedy	kʲedɨ	C2	OS: max SSG
2	kt	k t	których którym	kurɨx turɨm:	C2 C1	*OO: C2 del OO: C1 del
2	kw	k	kłopoty	kopotɨ	C2	OS: max SSG
2	mn	m	mną	mõw̃	C2	
2	mɲ	m ɲ	mnie mniej	mʲi ɲej	C2 C1	
2	pj	p	pięć	pʲiɲʥ	C2	OS: max SSG
2	pr	p r –	prostu prostu prostu	postu rostu stu	C2 C1 cluster	OS: max SSG *OS: min SSG –
2	pʃ	p ʃ	przyjdzie przykład	pɨjʥe ʃɨkwa	C2 C1	*OO: C2 del OO: C1 del
2	sf	s(s)	swoim	s:sojim	C2	*OO: C2 del
2	st	s(s) s	stara stąd	s:sara son	C2 C2	*OO: C2 del *OO: C2 del
2	sw	s	słuchać	suxaʨ	C2	OS: max SSG
2	ʃk	ʃ	szkole	ʃole	C2	*OO: C2 del
2	ʃl	ʃ	szliśmy	ʃʲiɕmɨ	C1	OS: max SSG
2	tr	t	troszeczkę	toʃeʧke	C2	OS: max SSG
2	ʧw	ʧ	człowiek	ʧoek	C2	OS: max SSG
2	tw	t	tłumaczył	tumaʧɨw	C2	OS: max SSG
2	vj	v j –	więc wiem wiesz	vents jem eʃ	C2 C1 cluster	OS: max SSG *OS: min SSG –
2	vw	v w –	właśnie właśnie właśnie	vaɕɲje waɕɲe aɕɲe	C2 C1 cluster	OS: max SSG *OS: min SSG –
2	zd	z(z)	zdążyłem	z:zõw̃ʒɨwem	C2	*OO: C2 del

(continued)

Table 5.11 (continued)

Size	Target form	Modif. form	Example	Modif. transcription	Del. type	Comment
2	zn	n z nʧ	znaczy znaczy znaczy	naʃɨ zaʧɨ nʧɨ	C1 C2 cluster	*OS: min SSG OS: max SSG –
2	zr	z –	zresztą zresztą	zeʃʧõw̃ ʃom	C2 cluster	OS: max SSG –
2	ʑʥ	ʑ(ʑ)	zdziwiona	ʑʑivʲjona	C2	*OO: C2 del
3	ɕfj	ɕj	świadomy	ɕjadomɨ	C2	
3	fɕr	ɕr	wśród	ɕrud^{n}	C1	
3	fsp	sp	wspaniale	spaɲale	C1	
3	fst	st	wstaje	staje	C1	
3	skw	sk	składają	skadajõw̃	C3	
3	str	sr s(s)r tr st	strajku strajku strajku strasznie	srajku sːsrajku trajku starʃɲe	C2 C2 C1 C3	
3	vzl	zl	wzlot	zlot	C1	
3	zdj	zj	zdjęcia	zjeɲʨa	C2	
3	zvj	sj zj	związane związku	sʲjõw̃zane zj̃õw̃sku	C2 C2	
3	zvr	z	zwracają	zaʦajõw̃	C2C3	
4	fstr	str	wstręt	strendː	C1	
4	stfj	sfj	stwierdziła	sfʲjerʥiwa	C2	
4	vzgl	zgl zl z vzl sgl z(z)	względem względu względem względu względów względu	zglendem zlendu zendem vzlendu sglenduf zːzendu	C1 C1C4 C1C3C4 C3 C1 C1C3C4	

and the glides. The emergent obstruent + vowel structure displays larger articulatory and perceptual contrast than a sequence of a sonorant and a vowel. In some targets, deletion does not ensure the maximization of contrast. This type of deletion results in minimizing the manner distance between adjacent segments (labelled '*OS: min SSG'), e.g. in the reduction of /gm/ to /m/. Some C1C2 clusters display both options, e.g. /pr vj vw zn/ are reduced to both C1 or C2. The latter variant violates three principles relating to sonority distances.

The *Sonority Dispersion Principle* of Clements' (1990) ranks sequences of initial consonants in demisyllables, and posits equal distance transitions between adjacent pairs of clusters, namely C1 – 2 and C2 – V in initial CCs. As a consequence, an obstruent + liquid combination is the most natural, followed by an obstruent + glide combination. Similarly, the *Optimal Sonority Distance Principle* by Dziubalska-Kołaczyk (2001) predicts neither maximum nor minimum distances but their optimal distribution in a successful sequence of segments. A different prediction is made by the *Minimal Sonority Distance Principle* (Selkirk 1984; Steriade 1982), which posits minimal (one-step or two-step) sonority differences between consonants. In spite of some variation, Polish speakers seem to favour an increase in manner contrast between a consonant and a vowel. Out of 24 OS realizations, the distance is enlarged in 67% of cases (16 instances of OS: max SSG vs. 6 instances of *OS: min SSG).

The second type of deletion refers to obstruent + obstruent (OO) sequences. This group of clusters does not display a sonority-motivated pattern. That is, there are C1C2 realizations which involve the deletion of either the first consonant (labelled 'OO: C1 del') as in /ft gd xf/, or the the second consonant (labelled 'OO: C2 del') as in /sf zd ʑdʑ/. A lack of a phonologically-motivated pattern in reduction can be possibly accounted for by the sonority hierarchy of Rubach and Booij (1990a, b), which requires no sonority differential between obstruents in Polish. As a result, plosives, fricatives and affricates are subsumed under a single class, resulting in the following 5-point scale: obstruents < nasals < liquids < glides < vowels. The phonological consequences of such an analysis are discussed in Chap. 2, Sect. 2.4.1.

If articulatory distances in terms of sonority do not play a role in Polish, it should be the case that both slots of a C1C2 cluster, i.e. C1 and C2, create a potential and fully-fledged context for deletion. The data in Table 5.11 suggest that speakers admit the reduction of both segments to a similar degree. Out of 18 realizations of OO clusters, the first consonant (C1) is omitted in 56% of cases (10 instances of OO: C1 del vs. 8 instances of OO: C2 del). A closer inspection of the data, however, reveals a frequency-based reduction pattern.

Whenever targets have only one realization, there is a strong preference for the deletion of C1. For instance, /ft gd kɕ xf/ are always pronounced as [t d ɕ f] followed by a vowel. In turn, cluster types which admit two or more pronunciation forms have high token frequency. Targets /kt/ and /pʃ/ are reduced to both [k] and [t] as well as [p] and [ʃ], or are deleted altogether. Both clusters are among the five most frequent types found in written corpora. For example, Tables 1.9 and 1.10 in Chap. 1 show that /kt/ and /pʃ/ occupy the top of the frequency lists in scientific texts and in artistic prose (Dobrogowska 1992). High type and token frequencies of the clusters were also reported in Zydorowicz et al. (2016), and Orzechowska and Zydorowicz (2019), who analysed dictionary and corpus data. A similar observation holds for SO sequences. Targets /vj/ and /pr/, found at the very top of the aforementioned frequency lists, admit three pronunciation forms.

It can be concluded that frequency is a potentially relevant factor which influences cluster simplification. Disregarding a type of deletion, words with mispronounced initial clusters are likely not to inhibit communication provided they are frequent. Also, the most severe modification of a cluster resulting in its total deletion, is permitted only in common words. No generalizations can be formulated for sonorant + sonorant clusters, as the data contain only two examples of this type. Whether the reduction of /mn/ and /mɲ/ to [m] follows a particular pattern cannot be stated at this point. Finally, as regards three-member and four-member sequences, they are typically reduced to CC. However, given the variety of reduction patterns observed, no further generalizations can be inferred from the data.

Substitution

Another strategy employed in casual speech is *substitution*. The process consists in replacing a segment with another one, disregarding their phonetic similarity. In word-initial targets, substitution affects only one consonant in a sequence, which means that a part of a cluster target is preserved. Table 5.12 presents all targets which underwent substitution in natural conversational style. The last column, labelled 'Substitution type', specifies the replaced segment. C1, C2, and C3 refer to the first, second, and third consonant forming a cluster.

Table 5.12 Types of substitution in initial modified clusters

Size	Target form	Modif.form	Example	Modif. transcription	Subst. type
2	ɕɲ	ɕj	śniadaniu	ɕjadaɲu	C2
2	ʥv	zv	dzwonił	zvoɲiw	C1
2	ftɕ	ɕtɕ	wcinali	ɕtɕinalʲi	C1
2	gr	ɣr	gramatyka	ɣramat'ɨka	C1
2	xtɕ	ɕtɕ xɕ	chciał chciałem	ɕtɕaw xɕawem	C1 C2
2	xw	ɣw	chłopaków	ɣwopakuf	C1
2	kt	xt	ktoś	xtoʑ	C1
2	mɲ	mj	mnie	mje	C2
2	pr	fr	proszę	froʃe	C1
2	pʃ	pʧ fʃ (ʃ)ʃ	przeczytałem przy przyjechałam	pʧɨtaem fʃɨʃ: ʃɨjexaam	C2 C1 C1
2	sf	ʦf	swoich	ʦfojix	C1
2	st	ʦt sʦ	startowałam sto	ʦtartovawam sʦo	C1 C2
2	ʃt	ʃʧ	sztuka	ʃʧuka	C2
2	tɕf	tɕɕ	ćwiczenia	tɕɕiʧeɲa	C2
2	ʧt	ʃt	cztery	ʃterɨ	C1
2	vj	ɣj	wiadomo	ɣʲjadomo	C1
2	zd	zʥ	zdecydować	zʥeʦɨdovatɕ	C2
3	ɕfj	ɕvj tɕfj	świat świętami	ɕvʲjad tɕfʲjentamʲi	C2 C1
3	trf	trv	trwa	trva	C3
3	zvj	ʥvj	zwiejemy	ʥvʲjejemɨ	C1

Table 5.13 Consonant fusion in initial modified clusters

Size	Target form	Modif. form	Example	Modif. transcription	Subst. type
2	tʃ	ʧ ʧʃ	trzy trzeba	ʧɨ ʧʃa	fusion fusion
3	dʒv	ʤv	drzwi	ʤvʲi	fusion
4	dʒvj	ʤvj	drzwiach	ʤvʲjah	fusion
3	stʃ	ʃʧ	strzelali	ʃʧelalʲi	subst + fusion
3	stʃ	ʃʧ	strzelić	ʃʧelʲiʨ	subst + fusion

As can be seen, substitution involves changes in terms of the place and manner of articulation but no clear patterns emerge. Some types of reduction are motivated by an increase in phonetic similarity. For instance, /fʨ xʨ/ are modified to [ɕʨ], and /ʨf/ is modified to [ʨɕ]. These casual speech forms exhibit place assimilation in that the emergent consonant [ɕ] is articulated in the alveolo-palatal region, similarly to the neighbouring [ʨ]. As for the manner of articulation, it is ensured that the differential in sonority is present. This tendency can be illustrated on the example of obstruent plateaus such as /kt sf zvj ɕfj/, which are modified to [xt ʦf ʣvj ʨfj], respectively, ensuring a sonority distance. However, the data is too scarce to formulate a generalization.

Fusion is regarded as a specific type of substitution. The process consists in combining two consonants into one segment, which bears phonetic similarity to both target constituents. Fusion is represented by three cluster types, which are listed in Table 5.13. Additionally, the table includes two words in which a combination of fusion (/t/ + /ʃ/ → [ʧ]) and substitution (/s/ → [ʃ]) co-occur, leading to a two-member cluster [ʃʧ].

As can be observed, the sequences of plosives /t d/ followed by fricatives /ʃ ʒ/ are combined to form complex segments [ʧ ʤ]. According to the phonetic norm in Madejowa (1993), this articulation is considered a common pronunciation mistake.

Other Processes

Among other spontaneous speech processes applied in initial phonotactics, three types of vowel-related modifications can be distinguished: prothetic vowel insertion, vowel split and syllable merge. Vowel insertion and vowel split lead to cluster simplification, while syllable merge results in producing a more complex cluster compared to the target one.

Vowel insertion (labelled 'V insert') consists in inserting a prothetic vowel. The process changes word-initial types such as /dl kr st/ into word-medial clusters [ədl əkr əst]. Similarly, *vowel split* (labelled 'V split') involves an insertion of a vowel between two consonants forming a cluster, which splits a cluster target into two adjacent syllables. Only two instances of this process are found in the data. Clusters in words *tradycyjnej* /tradɨtsɨjnej/ 'traditional' (gen sg fem) and *zresztą* /zreʃtõw̃/ 'after all' are pronounced as [təradɨtsɨjnej] and [zerʃtõw̃]. The last process type is represented by a *syllable merge* (labelled 'syll merge'), i.e. a merge of two neighbouring syllables resulting from the deletion of a heterosyllabic vowel. The merge results in combining all or some consonants in the first and the second syllable into a single cluster as in *wszystko* /fʃɨstko/ 'everything' → [fʃstko], *studentom* /studentom/ 'students' (dat pl) → [stdentom]. The data are summarized in Table 5.14. As before, cluster targets and their phonetic realizations are provided in the columns '|Target form' and 'Modified form', respectively. A type of a vowel-related process is indicated in the right-most column. In order to be able to observe different types of structures generated by vowel-related processes, speakers' pronunciation variant are presented after an arrow.

Table 5.14 Vowel-related processes in initial modified targets

Size	Target form	Modif.form	Example	Modif. transcription	Vowel-related process type
2	dl	Vdl	dla	ɘdla	V insert → VCC
2	dr	Vdr	drugiej	ɘdrugʲjej	V insert → VCC
2	fʃ	Vfʃ	wszystkiego	ɘfʃɨstkʲjego	V insert → VCC
2	fʧ	Vfʧ	wczoraj	ɘfʧoraj	V insert → VCC
2	xw	Vxw	chłopiec	ɘhwopʲjeʦ	V insert → VCC
2	kj	Vkj	kiedy	ɘkʲjedɨ	V insert → VCC
2	kr	Vkr	króla	ɘkrula	V insert → VCC
2	kt	Vkt	ktoś	ɘktoɕ	V insert → VCC
2	mj	Vmj	mieszkam	ɘmʲjeʃkam	V insert → VCC
2	pj	Vpj	pierwszej	ɘpʲjerʃej	V insert → VCC
2	pl	Vpl	plakaty	ɘplakatɨ	V insert → VCC
2	pr	Vpr	prostu	ɘprostu	V insert → VCC
2	pʃ	Vpʃ	przebrać	ɘpʃebraʨ	V insert → VCC
2	sp	Vsp	spektakl	ɘspektagl	V insert → VCC
2	st	Vst	starać	ɘstaraʨ	V insert → VCC
2	ʃk	Vʃk	szkole	ɘʃkole	V insert → VCC
2	tr	Vtr t	troszeczkę tradycyjnej	ɘtroʃeʧke tɘradɨʦɨjnej	V insert → VCC V split → CVC
2	ʧf	Vʧf	czwartej	ɘʧfartej	V insert → VCC
2	vj	Vvj	wiesz	ɘvʲjeʃ	V insert → VCC
2	vw	Vvw	właśnie	ɘvwaɕɲe	V insert → VCC
2	zd	Vzd	zdarzyło	ɘzdaʒɨwo	V insert → VCC
2	zn	Vzn	znawcy	ɘznafʦɨ	V insert → VCC
2	zr	z	zresztą	zerʃtõw̃	V split → CVCC
2	zw	Vzw	złożyłam	ɘzwoʒɨwam	V insert → VCC
3	spʃ	Vspʃ	sprzątałyśmy	ɘspʃontawɨʑmɨ	V insert → VCC
3	str	Vstr	strajk	ɘstrajk	V insert → VCC
2	fʃ	sʃs fʃstk fʃʦ fʃsk	wszyscy wszystko wszyscy wszystko	fʃsɨ fʃstko fʃsʦɨ fʃsko	syll merge → CCC syll merge → CCCCC syll merge → CCCC syll merge → CCCC
2	pʃ	pʃʧ pʃpr	przeczytała przeprowadzone	pʃʧɨtawa pʃprovaʣone	syll merge → CCC syll merge → CCCC

(continued)

Table 5.14 (continued)

Size	Target form	Modif.form	Example	Modif. transcription	Vowel-related process type
		pʃk	przykład	pʃkat	syll merge → CCC
		pʃn	przynajmniej	pʃnajmʲij	syll merge → CCC
		pʃɲ	przyniosła	pʃɲoswa	syll merge → CCC
		pʃp	przypada	pʃpada	syll merge → CCC
		pʃs	przysypane	pʃsɨpane	syll merge → CCC
		pʃkw	przykład	pʃkwa	syll merge → CCCC
2	st	std	studentom	s̩tdentom	syll merge → CCC
2	zd	zʦ	zdecydowałam	z̩ʦɨdovaam	syll merge → CC
2	zn	nʧ	znaczy	n̩ʧɨ	syll merge → CC

Table 5.14 shows that no well-defined pattern of modification can be observed for cluster targets. In particular, the strategy of syllable merge seems to involve random modifications. On the one hand, four-member and five-member clusters [fʃstk fʃsʦ fʃsk pʃpr pʃkw] in *wszystko* 'everything', *wszyscy* 'everybody', *przeprowadzone* 'to perform' (pret) and *przykład* 'example' arise from CC targets. On the other hand, the complexity of an emergent cluster stems from an additional omission of a cluster member in *zdecydowałam* [z̩ʦɨdovaam] 'to decide' (1st sg past fem) ← /zdeʦɨdovawam/ and *znaczy* [n̩ʧɨ] 'to mean' (3rd sg) ← /znaʧɨ/. What is more, there seems to be no sonority-motivated behaviour in modification. The majority of clusters which are simplified due to vowel insertion are SSG-obeying according to the detailed sonority scales of Foley (1972) and Goldsmith (1990). Obstruent-only clusters are also viewed as well-formed according to the general hierarchy proposed by Rubach and Booij (1990a, b).

The idea put forward in this book is that there is a force, which motivates cluster modification beyond well-formedness conditions. A principle such as sonority overshadows the role of phonological features in phonotactics. Although some sonority-related modifications have been observed in the production of initial clusters, the sections to follow aim at discovering subtle (particularly subsegmental) properties which affect the choices of native speakers.

5.5.3.4 Statistical Modelling of Articulatory Data

As was already mentioned, the majority of clusters in the dictionary are produced according to their targets. Only 9% of initial clusters diverge from the phonetic norm of Modern Polish. Although the proportion of matching and non-matching renditions of clusters amounts to 9:1, it would be interesting to identify the motivation behind cluster modification. In this section, seeking featural patterns which govern deletion, substitution or vowel-related processes involves statistical methods.

In order to distinguish between the role of variables in cluster modification, a hierarchical optimal discriminant analysis was selected. This method is considered to be adequate for the present study as it predicts the value of a categorical dependent variable based on a dataset composed of both categorical and continuous (numeric) variables. In contrast to the analysis of variance (ANOVA) and regression, the method does not express the dependent variable in terms of a linear combination of predictors.

The algorithm used in the present analysis is based on the *Classification and Regression Trees* (henceforth CART, for an overview see Loh 2011). This explanatory technique makes a set of predictions on the relevance of individual variables and generates non-parametric trees, which start with observations (given as branches) and end with conclusions on observations (given in tree leaves). A learned binary tree makes it possible to sort data into different classes. The classification is possible on the assumption that there exists a measurement on which the observations differ. That is, the partitioning of the input data is based on variables which yield maximum predictive accuracy. A tree is composed of a root (decision) node which is split into two daughter nodes based on one variable (also referred to as a split condition). The procedure is repeated for each daughter node of the tree. In other words, with each binary split, the data is further subcategorized leading to a hierarchical tree-like system. The procedure ends at a terminal (or leaf) node which represents the output data that can be no longer divided.

The ultimate goal of the CART procedure is to generate a simple tree structure. As a result, given a large set of predictors, only few of them can surface as node splitters in a tree. It must be emphasized that this does not mean that other predictors are of lesser importance or that they do not predict the dependent variable at all. A contribution of a variable to the classification is not determined only by primary splits which are presented at each node in a tree but also by cumulative contribution of a variable to the whole tree. A variable can thus be a highly important predictor in the whole learning process even if it is not listed in the tree. The tree, in turn, captures those variables which are relevant at a given node. Therefore, the results presented in the analysis are twofold.

First, I construct classification trees with a view to identifying factors which are most likely to be used in the decision making process. In other words, a prediction is made on a variable which splits the data best at each consecutive node. This method is used to determine: (1) criteria which motivate native speakers' selection of a target form or a modified form, and (2) criteria which make speakers decide on the selection of a process type. These results are taken as a prime source for discovering phonological features which motivate phonotactics at the level of production. In such a way, it is possible to arrive at feature weight, and preferred feature-based organization of consonant clusters in—what will be referred here as—articulatory or spoken phonotactics. Second, I provide the CART variable importance measure, which gives an importance score for each variable independent of a tree visualization. The ranking of scores reflects the cumulative importance of a variable for the splitting procedure, and is therefore used as supplementary information in the analysis. In the domain of articulation, importance scores are taken to reflect properties which are generally considered by speakers as potentially triggering the preservation of a cluster target or its modification.

The analysis was performed using *Statistica* (ver. 13.1). The best split condition is found on the basis of the *Gini index*, which measures how well the data is split into two classes. The size of a tree is determined with a direct stopping rule FACT set at a default. Since no a priori prediction is made regarding the importance of the variables, all of them are considered to be equally probable (a priori probability estimates = equal). The first tree was run on all dictionary words containing initial and final clusters. Matched and mismatched realizations, labelled as *target* and *modified* respectively, were entered into the model as a dependent variable. In the second tree, only modified realizations of cluster targets were taken into consideration, where types of processes served as a dependent variable coded as consonant deletion (C del), cluster deletion (cluster del), substitution of a single consonant (C subst), vowel insertion (V insert) or syllable merge (syll merge). Other process types exemplified by several words were subsumed under one group referred to as 'Other'. 23 independent variables were tested.

The decision on the selection of predictors was motivated by factors generally employed in the study on phonostylistics (e.g. Shockey 2003) and by the analyses conducted in Chaps. 3 and 4 of this book. Although the primary goal of the statistical modelling in this chapter is to investigate a feature-based motivation for articulatory phonotactics, casual speech is influenced by a number of factors beyond the phonological properties of consonant clusters. Generally, there is less control over data coming from spontaneous conversations as idiosyncratic properties of words and speakers' preferences come into play. Therefore, the scope of the statistical analysis embraces not only the phonological structure of clusters but also suprasegmental, morphological and lexical characteristics of words (see Shockey 2003). The set of predictors does not account for speaker variability and speech tempo (Shockey 2003) due to the written form of the data and lack of assignment of word forms to individual speakers in Madelska (2005).

The first set of predictors was drawn from the analysis of parameters presented in Chap. 3. 18 parameters pertaining to the place of articulation, manner of articulation and size were selected. Emphasis was placed on the parameters which have shown to be contrastive in the previous analyses. The place parameters involve: POA distances (P4), directionality (P5), POA type cluster-initially and cluster-finally (P11, P12), number of labials / coronals / dorsals in a cluster (P6-P8), anteriorness cluster-initially and cluster-finally (P9, P10). The manner parameters are represented by: MOA distances (P13), articulatory opening (P14), MOA type cluster-initially and cluster-finally (P22, P23), continuancy cluster-initially and cluster-finally (P18, P19), stridency cluster-initially and cluster-finally (P20, P21). Since the vast majority of clusters are compositional and avoid the repetition of segments, the complexity dimension is represented by only one parameter, namely cluster size (P1). No voice parameters are taken into account.

Apart from the feature-based variables, I employ other phonological predictors which are not strictly related to consonant clusters. First, in line with the sonority hierarchies which distinguish between vowels of different height, a type of a vowel neighbouring on a consonant (i.e. /a e i o u ɨ/) is taken into consideration. What is more, there is a body of research on the relationship between phonotactic complexity and stress placement. As a response to studies of Kelly (2004) and Ryan (2014), Orzechowska et al. (2018, 2019) investigated Russian and English onset clusters in relation to the stressed position in a word, and demonstrated that the propensity for a complex cluster increases with an increasing distance from the stressed position. Polish, in contrast to Russian and English, has penultimate stress with several exceptions. That is, the distance of a word-initial cluster from a stressed syllable changes depending on the length of a word. If an accented syllable attracts heavier phonotactics, the modification rate in initial clusters can be affected by their proximity to a stressed position.

Frequency has also been considered to be a factor influencing cluster modification (Bybee 2003; Shockey 2003). Two types of frequency counts are included in the analysis as independent variables: usage frequency and text corpus frequency. The first frequency type reflects the number of occurrences of a word featuring a cluster variant. This frequency count is extracted from the dictionary of phonetic variants in Madelska (2005). Text frequency, in turn, is represented by token frequencies of words containing target clusters, which was compiled from a corpus of the *Rzeczpospolita* newspaper reported in Zydorowicz et al. (2016) (for a detailed description see Sect. 1.6.1).

The last predictor is related to the morphological composition of consonant clusters. In line with Dressler and Dziubalska-Kołaczyk (2006), a distinction is made between phonotactic and morphonotactic clusters. In Chap. 2, it was demonstrated that approaches based on well-formedness conditions tend to classify morphologically-motivated clusters as ill-formed or dispreferred. A more marked status of such sequences results from the intervention of morphological operations which cannot be always repaired by phonology. Therefore, morphology is considered to be a potential factor influencing modification rates.

It must be noted that apart from the factors under consideration, casual speech forms are related to speech rate, formality of a situation and individual variation. The data in the phonetic dictionary makes it impossible to put the variables to statistical testing.

Factors Affecting Target and Modified Forms

The first tree generated for the purpose of the present analysis is aimed at revealing factors which play a decisive role in producing a target form or a modified form of a cluster. Figure 5.1 presents a decision tree for initial clusters. Starting from the top node, text corpus frequency offers the best split for the data. The split condition indicates that initial clusters in words with frequency lower than 3,138.5 (corpus freq <= 3,138.5) tend to be produced according to their target norm. In turn, initial clusters in words with frequency higher than the threshold are most likely to be modified. This split separates 2,745 (80%) clusters produced faithfully to their target norm from 691 (20%) modified clusters. The result of the first split can thus be rephrased in the following manner: there is a large probability for an initial cluster to diverge from a target form in words with mid and high token frequencies.

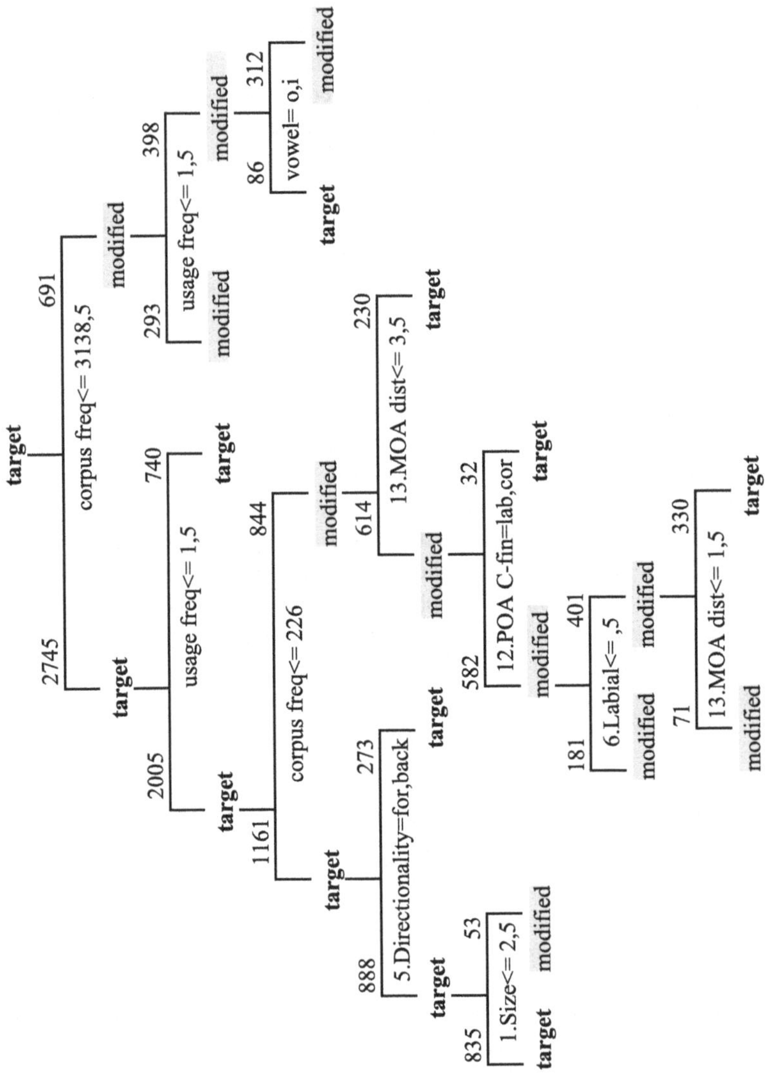

Fig. 5.1 A classification tree for target or modified production of initial clusters

The concept of high frequency is relative. The casual speech data in Madelska's (2005) dictionary contain words, whose text corpus frequencies range from 0 (e.g. *dialektologia* /djalektologja/ 'dialectology', *fiołka* 'violet' (gen sg)) to 146,173 occurrences of *dla* /dla/ 'for' and 177,921 occurrences of *przez* /pʃez/ 'through, via'. The frequency of the third word found at the top of the corpus list, namely *które* /kture/ 'which' (nom pl fem), drops substantially to 72,121. Given the disproportions in the frequency counts between words, the cut-off point equal to 3,138.5 would suggest that the split involves low frequency lexical items. However, note that as much as 30% of the production data have corpus frequency $\leq$ 100, and that the top-most frequency band is occupied by only several words. Similar disproportions have been observed in other dictionary- and corpus-based studies on Polish phonotactics. Let me refer to the most recent contribution by Orzechowska and Zydorowicz (2019), who discuss the relationship between logarithmic frequencies of cluster types and tokens, and phonotactic markedness. Logarithmic frequencies established for tokens are calculated on the basis of the text corpus, which is employed in the present study.

Orzechowska and Zydorowicz (2019) demonstrate a way of managing extremes in type and token frequencies of Polish consonant clusters in word initial and final position. The frequencies are characterized by a long tail of low frequency words and only several high frequency words. Since token frequencies of words containing initial clusters range from 0 to 432,972 occurrences in the text corpus, the authors propose a logarithmic transformation (using the GZipf equation) and devise a 7-point log scale, following the Likert scale. The scaled frequencies make the study material more manageable and comparable across languages (Polish vs. English) and different resources (dictionary vs. corpus). Frequencies grouped under 1 are rare, while frequencies grouped under 7 are the most frequent ones. In this log scale, the frequency of 3,138.5 is subsumed under log freq = 4, which corresponds to a mid frequency band. Therefore, for the purpose of the present analysis, we can safely assume that speakers' propensity of modifying an initial cluster is greater in high frequency words.

Moving rightwards in the tree, the next step of the decision making process is based on usage frequency, i.e. the frequency of words in casual speech. This variable distinguishes between 239 modified words with the frequency lower than or equal to 1.5 (usage freq <= 1.5) and 398 modified words with the frequency ranging from 1.5 to 258. Since at this node the data is not partitioned sufficiently (42% vs. 58%), further splitting conditions are sought. Vowel quality shows to be the next relevant splitter. Initial clusters followed by /o/ and /i/ are most likely to be pronounced according to their target norm, while the presence of /a e u ɨ/ leads to cluster modification. The transition from the decision node to the leaf node can be summarized in the following way: initial clusters in words with medial and high (> 3,138.5) text frequencies will be *most probably* modified. However, if additionally their usage frequency is higher than 1.5 and the cluster is followed by /o/ or /i/, the probability of cluster modification *increases substantially*.

The same analytic procedure applied to the left-most branches of the tree makes it possible to define subtle differences between groups of words with target and modified clusters. That is, each set of observations found in a terminal indivisible node can be specified by means of a unique composition of phonological and frequency factors determined by all the splitting conditions that lead from the root to this leaf. For reasons of clarity of presentation, I shall not investigate each node individually, but provide a general synopsis of the variables which provide the most accurate splits.

As can be observed in Fig. 5.1, frequency counts (in particular corpus frequency) constitutes the major driving force for modification of initial clusters, followed by phonetic and phonological properties such as directionality, cluster size, MOA distance and POA cluster-finally. The tree suggests several decision paths for producing target and modified forms. First of all, cluster targets are rendered primarily in low frequency words (in terms of text and usage), which additionally: (1) start with CC clusters involving either forward or backward articulation (i.e. unidirectional), or (2) display mixed articulatory gestures (i.e. movement towards the front and rear part of the mouth cavity). These paths are most clear as they involve only nodes labelled as cluster 'targets'. Another path also leads leftwards of the root node. Namely, cluster targets are achieved in low frequency words which additionally: (1) display medial and large manner distances (>3.5), or (2) display small MOA distances and have a dorsal consonant in prevocalic position. This means that clusters containing a labial or a coronal segment cluster-finally tend to be modified.

When one pursues to recreate the paths which determine cluster modification, the following observations can be made. First, modifications occur in words with mid and high text corpus frequencies. Further modification is triggered by usage frequency lower than 1.5, or higher than 1.5 when the cluster is followed by vowels other than /o i/. It must be borne in mind that larger trees contain more nodes. As a consequence, a greater number of variables is used as splitters. The present analysis focuses on the description of a three up to four levels.

Table 5.15 presents a ranking of importance scores for each variable. Each predictor is assigned a score, ranging from 0 to 100. The higher the value, the greater the importance of a variable, and the greater its splitting potential in a tree. Variables with a score = 0 play no role in the classification of the data. It must be emphasized that scores reflect the cumulative importance of a variable in a decision tree.

The interpretation of the estimates of importance is straightforward. Table 5.15 shows the following ranking of predictors: corpus frequency (100) > MOA distance (87) > size (73) > coronal C, stridency in C1 (70) (where '>' denotes 'more important than'). The results partially correspond with the tree in Fig. 5.1. Token frequency in the corpus offers the best split for the data. The manner of articulation distances also have strong predictive power. The number of coronals and the presence of [±strident] consonants in C1 are equally important. Stridency, ranked fourth, does not show in the tree, which suggests that the variable might be the second best splitting condition at various nodes.

Table 5.15 Estimates of predictor importance (scores) for initial target and modified clusters (0 = the lowest importance, 100 = the highest importance)

Rank	Variables	Scores	Rank	Variables	Scores
1	(text) corpus freq	100	11	6. Labial C	29
2	13. MOA dist	87	12	10. Ant C-fin	26
3	1. Size	73	13	18. Cont C1	22
4	20. Strid C1	70	14	no of syllables	21
	7.Coronal C	70	15	19. Cont C-fin	18
5	4. POA dist	66	16	21. Strid C-fin	17
6	vowel	60	17	9. Ant C1	16
	5. Directionality	60		8. Dorsal C	16
7	14. Opening	52	18	23. MOA C-fin	13
8	12. POA C-fin	49	19	phon/morph	7
9	usage freq	45	20	22. MOA C1	5
10	11. POA C1	30			

Factors Affecting Process Types

A tentative analysis of the production data in Sect. 5.5.3.3 demonstrated that modifications are affected by phonological factors such as the place and manner of articulation, and non-phonological factors such as frequency. It was suggested that deletion is motivated by token frequencies, while substitution by phonetic similarity between consonants. Let me now look closer into the role that different variables play in the selection of a specific process. The phonetic realization of /pʃ/ can serve as an example.

47. Casual speech realizations of word-initial /pʃ/

(47.a) deletion: [pɨjʥe], [ʃɨkwa]
(47.b) substitution: [pʧɨtaem], [fʃɨʃː], [ʃɨjexaam]
(47.c) vowel insertion: [ɘpʃebraʨ]
(47.d) syllable merge: [pʃʧɨtawa], [pʃprovaʥone], [pʃkat], [pʃnajmʲij], [pʃɲoswa], [pʃpada], [pʃsɨpane], [pʃkwa]

As shown in 47, /pʃ/ occurs in words of varying in length and token frequency, and is followed by different vowels. The question is whether the selection of a process type is motivated by any of the factors under investigation, and if yes, which one. In order to answer the question and verify the tentative findings related to the weight of phonological features in articulation, another classification tree for words containing exclusively modified clusters was generated. Process types were entered into the model as a dependent variable: deletion of a consonant (C del), total deletion of a cluster (cluster del), substitution of a consonant (C subst), vowel insertion (V insert, classified together with vowel split) and syllable merge. Note that processes which were identified in several words only were subsumed under the category labelled 'Other'. This group contains examples of fusion and

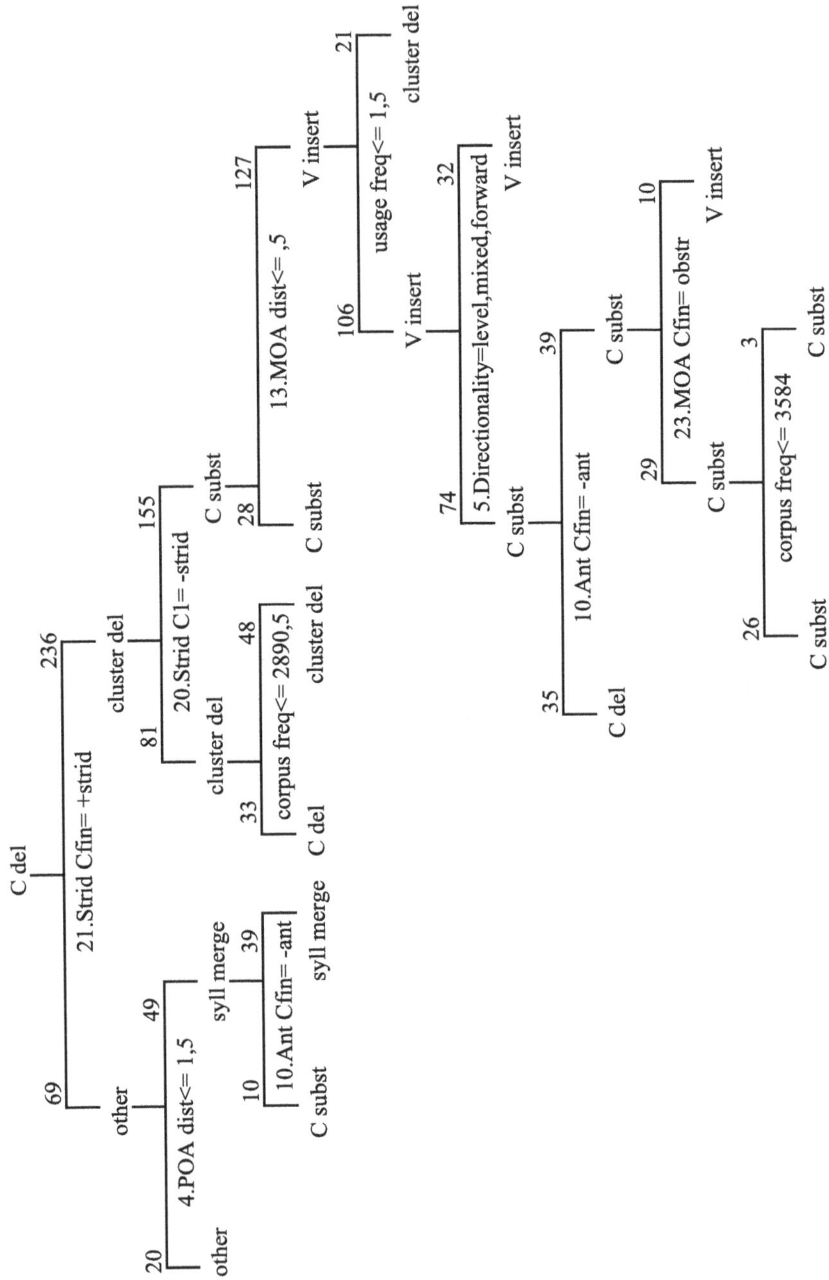

Fig. 5.2 A classification tree for process types in initial clusters

substitution + fusion listed in Table 5.13. The analysis was run on words containing initial modified clusters only (N = 306).

The tree in Fig. 5.2 shows that stridency plays a key role in the selection of a modification strategy. [+strident] consonants, i.e. /s z ʦ ʣ ʃ ʒ ʧ ʤ ɕ ʑ ʨ ʥ/, found in the prevocalic position create a context for the application of marginal processes (labelled 'Other') and syllable merge. Note that the latter process type is defined by a single path in the tree. Heterosyllabic consonants as in CCVC, CCVCC and CCVCCC are combined into a single cluster when the target has the POA distance larger than 1.5, and when cluster-final position is occupied by a [+strident, −anterior] consonant. This pattern suggests that initial clusters ending in /s z ʦ ʣ/ are likely to be merged with other consonants in the following syllable.

More common processes are also motivated by stridency. As can be observed, cluster targets starting with a [−strident] segment are most likely to be deleted, while the presence of the remaining consonants in C1 is highly likely to trigger substitution. At this level of the tree, the next splitting criterion constitutes corpus frequency. In other words, the whole cluster can be deleted only when the word has mid or high frequency in the text (corpus freq <= 2,890.5). A frequency range lower than the threshold allows for the deletion of a single consonant. This criterion ensures that a severe change in a cluster target resulting in its total omission does not hinder communication when a word is frequent. In turn, the right branch of this node shows that substitution is most likely to occur when the MOA distance is very small (MOA dist <= 0.5). This variable corresponds with the sonority differential (cf. Parker 2012). Therefore, in plateau clusters a segment is replaced with another one.

Table 5.16 presents the results of the analysis for the CART variable importance. Generally, the scores are higher than in Table 5.15, which suggests that the variables play a greater role in the decision-making process. That is, more factors seem to motivate the selection of a modification strategy than the decision regarding the production of a target form or a casual speech form. The top of the ranking embraces the following predictors: MOA dist (100) > MOA C-fin (99) > POA dist

Table 5.16 Estimates of predictor importance (scores) for process types in initial modified clusters (0 = the lowest importance, 100 = the highest importance)

Rank	Variables	Scores	Rank	Variables	Scores
1	13. MOA dist	100	11	6. Labial	72
2	23. MOA C-fin	99	12	20. Strid C1	70
3	4. POA dist	97	13	19. Cont C-fin	67
4	vowel	93	14	usage freq	54
5	14. Opening	92	15	18. Cont C1	53
	(text) corpus freq	92	16	size	51
6	5. Directionality	90	17	no of syllables	46
7	9. Ant C1	87	18	phon/morph	40
	10. Ant C-fin	87		12. POA C-fin	40
8	7. Coronal	86	19	22. MOA C1	33
9	21. Strid C-fin	84	20	8. Dorsal	24
10	11. POA C1	75			

(97) > vowel (93) > (text) corpus freq / articulatory opening (92). Generally, the MOA (or sonority) distance is a strong predictor for the whole tree. The second factor is the manner of articulation of the prevocalic consonant, which lends further support to the MOA distances. What is more, in their selection of a process type, native speakers of Polish consider the POA distances, vowels following a cluster as well as corpus frequencies to be relevant factors. The number of dorsals in a clusters has the lowest contribution to the model.

5.5.4 *Word-Final Phonotactics*

5.5.4.1 Cluster Targets in Citation Forms

This section summarizes the results for word-final cluster targets. First, I present the subdivisions of the data according to their size (i.e. CC vs. CCC vs. CCCC), and morphological composition (i.e. phonotactic vs. morphonotactic). Table 5.17 presents expected final targets ranging in size from CC to CCCC. Percentages are calculated for 46 cluster types, 482 words containing final clusters, and 1,655 word tokens. Two-member clusters constitute the most common pattern in terms of size. 80% of cluster types, 93% of words and 96% of word tokens are represented by CCs. Although the results are comparable to the word-initial position, the preference for CC is stronger word finally. All final cluster targets along with their word and token frequencies are given in Appendix N.

An overview of the morphological complexity of final targets is presented in Table 5.18. As can be seen, clusters are represented by phonotactic and morphonotactic types in 59 and 41%, respectively. Seven types are subsumed under both classes as they can have both realizations. That is, /j̃ɕtɕ ɲtɕ ŋk nt sk st sw ɕtɕ/ are phonologically-motivated in words such as *pięść* 'fist', *pięć* 'five', *pociąg* 'train', *prezent* 'gift', *kiosk* 'kiosk', *jest* 'there is', *pomysł* 'idea', *ilość* 'amount'. They are the product of morphological operations in *usiąś* + *ć* 'to sit down', *ciągną* +*ć* 'to pull', *rąk* 'hand' (gen pl), *zwierząt* 'animal' (gen pl), *schronisk* 'shelter' (gen pl), *ust* 'mouth' (gen pl), *zawióz+ł* 'drive' (3rd sg past masc) and *iś+ć* 'to go'.

Let me now inspect the phonetic realizations of cluster targets. Section 5.5.4.2 provides an overview of matched and mismatched renditions of cluster types.

Table 5.17 The distribution of final targets in terms of cluster types, words and word tokens depending on cluster size

Size	Cluster types		Words		Word tokens	
	No	%	No	%	No	%
CC	37	80	447	93	1,593	96
CCC	9	20	35	7	62	4
Total	46	100	482	100	1,655	100

Table 5.18 The distribution of final targets in terms of types, words and word tokens depending on morphological complexity

Size	Cluster types		Words		Word tokens	
	No	%	No	%	No	%
Phon	32	59	356	74	1,412	85
Morph	22	41	126	26	243	15
Total	54	100	482	100	1,655	100

5.5.4.2 Cluster Modification in Casual Speech Forms

Spontaneous speech features a wide range of phonetic forms. Table 5.19 presents the inventory of all realization possibilities representing CC and CCC targets found in the data (see Table 5.17). Percentages are calculated for cluster types (N = 97), words in which they occur (N = 781) and word repetitions (N = 1,697).

Target forms composed of two and three consonants are phonetically realized as C, CC, CCC or are deleted altogether (∅). Some of these realizations are identical to a cluster target, while others are the result of a modification. For instance, 37 final CC targets presented in Table 5.17 are phonetically realized in terms of 59 different CC sequences. All words ending in cluster types such as /kl rs w̃s/ in *spektakl* 'play', *kurs* 'course', *sens* 'sense' are articulated according to their phonetic norm, while other types are modified. For example, CC targets /ɕtɕ nt ɲtɕ/ are modified by consonant deletion, insertion or substitution, which results in the shortening or prolonging the cluster or in changing its quality, respectively (e.g. *kłaść* /kwaɕtɕ/ 'to put down' → [kwaɕ], *procent* /protsent/ 'percent' → [protsents], *wziąć* /vʑoɲtɕ/ 'to take' → [vʑõj̃ɕ]).

Generally, Table 5.19 shows that word-final cluster targets tend to be realized as a single consonant and CC. Words ending in two-member clusters prevail in casual speech, although word tokens ending in C are equally common (47%). What is more, words ending in three-member clusters and open syllables are largely disfavoured. Compared to word-initial position, the word final context admits fewer and simpler pronunciation variants, which points to its greater instability. In order to observe the extent to which final targets were produced faithfully to the phonetic norm,

Table 5.19 Phonetic realizations of final CC, CCC, CCCC targets in terms of cluster size

Realized size	Cluster type realization		Word realization		Word token realization	
	No	%	No	%	No	%
∅	5	5	7	1	22	1
C	20	21	159	20	803	47
CC	59	61	582	75	797	47
CCC	13	13	33	4	75	4
Total	97	100	781	100	1,697	100

Table 5.20 Matched and mismatched realizations of final types, words and word tokens in terms of cluster size

Target size	Words				Word tokens			
	Match		Mismatch		Match		Mismatch	
	No	%	No	%	No	%	No	%
CC	272	56	175	36	751	45	842	51
CCC	17	4	18	4	24	1	38	2
Total	289	60	193	40	775	47	880	53

Table 5.20 presents their matched and mismatched renditions. Matching realizations correspond with the accurate production of cluster targets as if in isolation, while mismatched realizations signal a cluster modification. Percentages are calculated for words (N = 482) and word tokens (N = 1,655) containing final clusters.

Table 5.20 shows that normative renditions of final clusters are identified in 60% of words, which corresponds to 47% of word tokens. This result diverges substantially from the results obtained in word-initial position. As was demonstrated earlier, more than 90% of initial clusters in words and word tokens are produced according to their target form. This observation suggests that cluster modification is more likely to occur word-finally. As far as cluster types are concerned, they have a three-fold realization. Some types are always produced as their targets. Other types are always modified. The third group of clusters can have both realizations. For instance, matching and non-matching renditions of /ɕtɕ/ and /ɲtɕ/ are found in words such as *większość* 'majority' [vʲjeŋkʃoɕtɕ]/[vʲjeŋkʃoɕ] and *pięc* 'five' [pʲjeɲtɕ] / [pʲjẽj͂ʑ]. Target and modified realizations of final cluster types are listed in Appendix O.

An additional criterion investigated in the present analysis constitutes morphological complexity. Table 5.21 shows the modification rate of final phonotactic and morphonotactic clusters in all words featuring final clusters (N = 482) and their tokens (N = 1,655). Similarly to the results obtained for size, clusters are produced according to their target norm in 60% of words and 47% of tokens. Words with final phonologically-motivated and morphologically-motivated clusters are preserved more often than not. The only exception constitute word tokens ending in phonotactic clusters, which undergo modification.

On the basis of Tables 5.20 and 5.21, further subdivisions of the data can be proposed. Tables 5.22 and 5.23 present the relationship between cluster size and

Table 5.21 Matched and mismatched realizations of final types, words and word tokens in terms of morphological complexity

Motiv.	Words				Word tokens			
	Match		Mismatch		Match		Mismatch	
	No	%	No	%	No	%	No	%
Phon	209	43	147	30	628	38	784	47
Morph	80	17	46	10	147	9	96	6
Total	289	60	193	40	775	47	880	53

Table 5.22 Matched realizations of final targets in terms of cluster size and morphological composition

Size	Words				Word tokens			
	Phon		Morph		Phon		Morph	
	No	%	No	%	No	%	No	%
CC	198	69	74	26	614	79	137	18
CCC	11	4	6	2	14	2	10	1
Total	209	72	80	28	628	81	147	19

Table 5.23 Mismatched realizations of final targets in terms of cluster size and morphological composition

Size	Words				Word tokens			
	Phon		Morph		Phon		Morph	
	No	%	No	%	No	%	No	%
CC	141	73	34	18	770	88	72	8
CCC	6	3	12	6	14	2	24	3
Total	147	76	46	24	784	89	96	11

morphological complexity in casual speech forms. Separate counts are provided for matched and mismatched clusters in words and word tokens. In both datasets, percentages are calculated for each subgroup: 289 words and 775 word tokens in Table 5.22, and 193 words and 880 word tokens in Table 5.23.

The results demonstrate the realization of phonotactic and morphonotactic clusters depending on cluster size. The data point to an increased participation of morphologically-motivated clusters in word-final position, compared the initial position. Also, the proportion between mismatched and matched renditions is larger word-finally. The right word-edge is less salient than word-initial position, which is likely to result in cluster mispronunciation or deletion.

5.5.4.3 Phonological Processes in Casual Speech Forms

Deletion

The process of deletion refers to the omission of a consonant, which results in the shortening of a cluster. Table 5.24 presents all word-final targets which underwent deletion. For each cluster type, all casual speech forms resulting from deletion are listed in the column ‘Modified form’. The table provides examples of word to which the process applied as well as the transcription of the pronunciation forms which diverge from the literary phonetic norm. The column ‘Deletion type’ indicates the segment in a sequence which was omitted. C1, C2 and ‘cluster’ refer to the deletion of first consonant, the second consonant or of the whole sequence. The final column provides a comment on the produced form.

Table 5.24 Types of deletion in final modified clusters

Size	Target form	Modif. form	Example	Modif. transcription	Del. type	Comment
2	ɕtɕ	ɕ	iść	iɕ	C2	OO: C2 del
		ʑ	dość	doʑ	C2	OO: C2 del
		–	zjeść	zʲje	cluster	–
2	xɕ	ɕ	jakichś	jakʲiɕ	C1	OO: C1 del
		ɣ	jakichś	jakʲiɣ	C2	OO: C2 del
		ʑ	jakichś	jakʲiʑ	C1	OO: C1 del
2	jɕ	ɕ	jakiejś	jakʲjeɕ	C1	SO: max SSG
		ʑ	jakiejś	jakʲjeʑ	C1	SO: max SSG
2	jk	j	strajk	straj	C2	*SO: min SSG
		–	strajk	stra	cluster	–
2	kt	g	fakt	fag	C2	OO: C2 del
		k	nikt	ɲik	C2	OO: C2 del
		–	kontakt	konta	cluster	–
2	kw	k	mógł	muk	C2	OS: + SSG
		g	mógł	mug	C2	OS: + SSG
2	mp	m	wstęp	fstem	C2	*SO: min SSG
2	nt	n	błąd	bwon	C2	*SO: min SSG
		ɲ	skąd	skoɲ	C2	*SO: min SSG
2	ŋk	ŋ	ciąg	tɕoŋʲ	C2	*SO: min SSG
2	rf	r	najpierw	najpʲjer	C2	*SO: min SSG
2	rt	r	sport	spor	C2	*SO: min SSG
2	rw	r	umarł	umar	C2	SS
2	sk	z	schronisk	shroɲiz	C2	OO: C2 del
2	sm	z	mechanizm	mehaɲiz	C2	OS: + SSG
		s	mesjanizm	mesʲjaɲis	C2	OS: + SSG
2	st	s	jest	jes	C2	OO: C2 del
		z	jest	jez	C2	OO: C2 del
		–	jest	je	cluster	–
2	sw	s	znalazł	znalas	C2	OS: + SSG
		z	pomysł	pomɨzʲ	C2	OS: + SSG
2	tw	w	wpadł	fpaw̥	C1	*OS: − SSG
		t	zjadł	zʲjat	C2	OS: + SSG
		d	wypadł	vɨpad	C2	OS: + SSG
		–	doszedł	doʃe	cluster	–
3	jɕtɕ	jʑ	wejść	vejʑ	C3	
		jɕ	dojść	dojɕ	C3	
3	kst	ks	tekst	teks	C3	
3	str	s	semestr	semes	C2C3	
3	w̃sw	w̃s	wklęsł	fklẽw̃s	C3	

Several types of deletion can be distinguished depending on the structure of clusters. In obstruent + obstruent (OO) sequences, the first or the second consonant can be omitted (labelled 'OO: C1 del', 'OO: C2 del'), although C2 tends to be targeted. The only cluster which displays a two-fold variation is /xɕ/, which is reduced either to /ɣ/ or to /ɕ/. Another type of deletion refers to sonorant + obstruent (OS) clusters. In the majority of SO sequences, deletion is motivated by a decrease in the sonority distance (labelled '*SO: min SSG'). Out of 9 sonorant + obstruent realizations, 7 (78%) exhibit an omission of the obstruent, e.g. /mp/ → [m] in *wstęp* 'introduction', /jk/ → [j] in *strajk* 'strike' and /rf/ → [r] in *najpierw* 'first'. The resulting vowel + sonorant sequence word-finally has a smaller sonority distance than a vowel + obstruent sequence would have. Note that the reverse pattern was found in word-initial position, where the manner distance between a consonant and a vowel was maximized.

The last pattern presented in Table 5.24 embraces sequences composed of an obstruent and a sonorant such as /kw tw sm/. The clusters involve a severe violation of the SSG. In the majority of cases (8 out of 9), Polish speakers simplify the clusters by deleting the sonorant (labelled 'OS: + SSG') and produce a sonority-based sequence. In contrast to the remaining deletion types, speakers preserve a consonant which leads to a larger sonority distance. This strategy might be attributed to the fact that the majority of sonorant-final clusters are morphologically motivated. With the exception of *pomysł* 'idea' and *mechanism* 'mechanism', final /w/ is a past marker (3rd sg masc). Normative pronunciation of final clusters in past verbs such as *szed+ł* 'to go' admits three correct variants, namely [dw], [tw] and [t].

Substitution

Another process type employed in casual speech involves substitution. The process entails the replacement of one consonant with another disregarding their phonetic similarity. As I demonstrated in section "Substitution", word-initially substitution affects only one consonant in a cluster. In word-final position, modifications are more severe as they affect two consonants or the whole cluster. Table 5.25 lists all cluster targets which underwent substitution in casual speech. The indication of the change is provided in the column 'Substitution type'. As before, C1 and C2 denote the substitution of the first and the second consonant in a sequence, respectively. Instances of a modification of the whole cluster are indicated as well.

As can be seen, the majority of targets, with the exception of /ɕtɕ fts st/, have a sonorant + obstruent structure or an obstruent + obstruent structure. The results reveal an interesting pattern of substitution. In SO clusters, the post-vocalic nasal tends to be replaced by a glide /j w/. The modification results in a sonority-obeying profile, where the sonority distance between the vowel and the sonorant is minimized. The same strategy of reducing the MOA distance has been observed in deletion word-finally. Since substitution preserves the number of consonants forming cluster targets, smaller distances between a vowel and a sonorant result in

Table 5.25 Types of substitution in final modified clusters

Size	Target form	Modif. form	Example	Modif. transcription	Subst. type
2	ɕʨ	jʑ	cześć	ʧẽj̃ʑ	cluster
2	fʦ	vz	szewc	ʃevz	C2
2	j̃ɕ	w̃ɕ w̃ʑ	jakąś jakąś	jakõw̃ɕ jakõw̃ʑ	C1 C1
2	mɕ	jɕ jʑ	jakimś kimś	jakʲĩj̃ɕ kʲĩj̃ʑ	C1 C1
2	ns	w̃s w̃z	dystans anons	dɨstãw̃s: anõw̃z	C1 C1
2	nʦ	w̃s w̃z	więc więc	vʲjẽw̃s jẽw̃z	cluster cluster
2	ɲʨ	jʥ jʑ jɕ	dziesięć pięć wziąć	ʥeɕẽj̃ʥ pʲjẽj̃ʑ vʑõj̃ɕ	C1 cluster cluster
2	st	sʦ	jest	jesʦ	C2
3	ntʃ	nʧʃ	zewnątrz	zevnonʧʃ	C2

larger distances between adjacent consonants. The observations made with respect to word-final clusters are based on a smaller data sample compared to word-initial position. Whether the sonority-based patterns identified in the previous sections really hold in the production of final clusters, and whether there are additional factors triggering the articulatory behaviour of speakers is subject to statistical testing.

In the sections to follow, I present a decision algorithm for two types of data. The first classification tree in section "Factors Affecting Target and Modified Forms" Identifies factors which predict the likelihood of producing a target form or a casual speech form. The second tree in Section "Factors Affecting Process Types" serves to identify variables, which distinguish between different types of phonological processes: consonant deletion (C del), cluster deletion (cluster del), substitution of a single consonant (C subst), substitution of the whole cluster (cluster subst), consonant insertion (C insert). Other process types exemplified by several words were classified as 'Other'. 23 predictors presented in Sect. 5.5.3.4 were entered into the model. Default settings for the CART procedure were selected in order to provide the most comparable analysis between initial and final clusters.

Factors Affecting Target and Modified Forms

This section focuses on the presentation of a classification tree which reveals the motivation underlying cluster modification in word-final phonotactics. Figure 5.3 presents the results of the analysis. The most accurate splitting condition is stridency. The variable teases apart 310 (64%) target renditions of clusters from 172

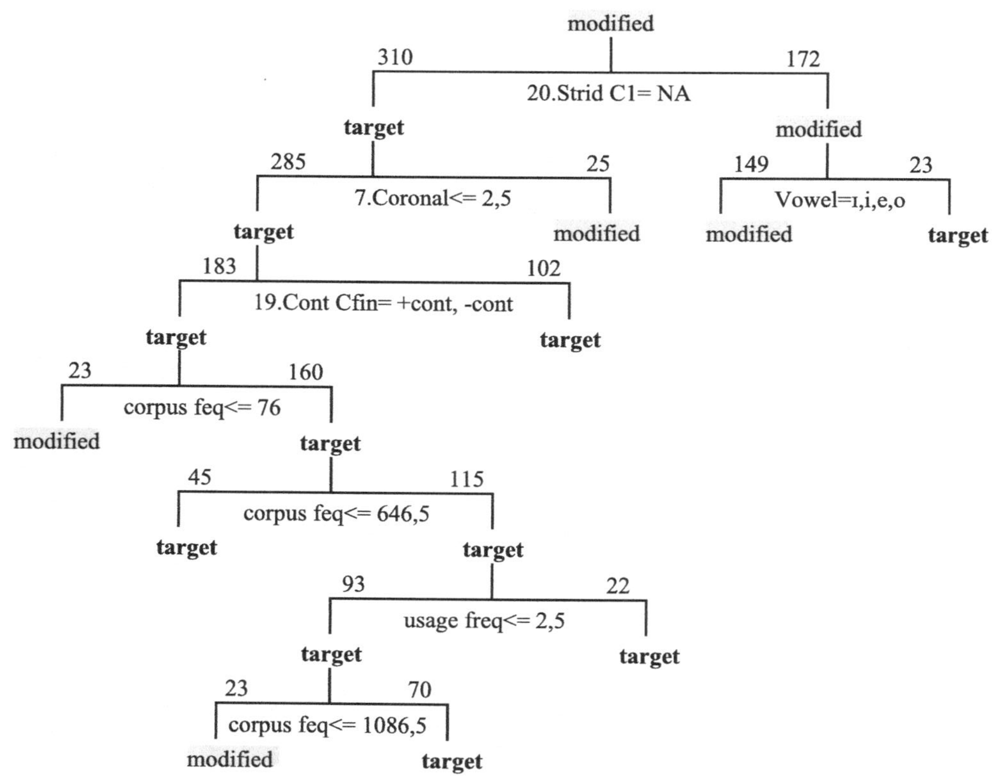

Fig. 5.3 A classification tree for target or modified production of final clusters

(36%) modified forms. This feature, together with vowel quality, create the most straightforward path leading to cluster modification in the tree. That is, the presence of coronal fricatives and affricates in post-vocalic position is highly likely to lead to cluster modification, especially when the prevocalic vowel is represented by /i ɨ e o/. In turn, if a cluster target starts with other consonants, namely a plosive or a sonorant (labelled '20.Strid = NA'), the cluster is most likely to be articulated in its full form.

It must be noted that the propensity for modifying clusters which start with coronal fricatives and affricates reflects the feature weight specification for final phonotactics proposed in 42. Recall that the study of lexical statistics in Chap. 3 has demonstrated that a preferred final clusters should start with a plosive or a sonorant (i.e. *NA strident C). In other words, the group of consonants to which the feature [±strident] can be allocated are disfavoured in the lexicon. The specification is restated in 48.

48. Feature weight specification for final phonotactics

C1	x	C2
*NA strident		[-voice]
*dorsal		*dorsal

Overall, the articulatory behaviour of native speakers of Polish reflects the specification for a preferred final cluster in the lexicon. No conclusions can be drawn on voicing as the feature is not considered in the present analysis.

Further splits in the tree are performed on the basis of coronality and continuancy. Among glides, liquids, nasals and plosives, a cluster which contains more than two coronals is most likely to undergo modification. This variable is extremely precise as it distinguishes between 25 (8%) modified renditions and 285 (92%) target renditions. The latter group is further split on the basis of continuancy. The presence of an affricate (i.e. [±continuant]) guarantees the normative articulation, while the presence of [+continuant] or [−continuant] segments leads to further partitioning. As we can see, in contrast to word-initial position, frequency seems to play a secondary role in the decision learning.

The cumulative role of the variables in the classification procedure is indicated by a ranking of importance scores in Table 5.26. According to this measure, (text) corpus frequency (100) followed by MOA distances (85) and continuancy in C1 (70) are the strongest predictors for the whole tree. The first two variables in the ranking comply with the importance scores generated for word-initial clusters.

The scores in Table 5.26 correspond with the classification tree only partially. Note that (text) corpus frequency splits clusters only at lower levels of the tree. This variable's first rank in terms of importance indicates that frequency can generally serve as the second best splitting condition at all nodes of the tree. Phonological features, in particular the absence of [+strident] and [−strident] segments in C1, constitute the prime force motivating mismatched articulation.

Table 5.26 Estimates of predictor importance (scores) for final target and modified clusters (0 = the lowest importance, 100 = the highest importance)

Rank	Variables	Scores	Rank	Variables	Scores
1	(text) corpus freq	100	12	10. Ant C-fin	40
2	13. MOA dist	85	13	22. MOA C1	38
3	18. Cont C1	70	14	9. Ant C1	37
4	vowel	62	15	21. Strid C-fin	36
5	7. Coronal	61	16	12. POA C-fin	32
6	19. Cont C-fin	54		1. size	32
	Usage freq	54	17	14. Opening	31
7	20. Strid C1	53	18	no_of_syll	27
8	4. POA dist	50	19	11. POA C1	19
9	23. MOA C-fin	47	20	phon/morph	11
10	5. Directionality	46	21	8. Dorsal	10
11	6. Labial	45			

Factors Affecting Process Types

In order to find out which predictors determine the selection of a process type, another classification tree is designed. Figure 5.4 shows a decisions tree with splitting conditions for processes subsumed under several types, namely insertion (insert), deletion (del) and substitution (subst) of a consonant or a cluster. As can be observed, the first splits in the tree rely on the subsegmental properties of consonants rather than on suprasegmental features, morphology or frequency.

The first binary division distinguishes between the substitution of one consonant (C subst) and the substitution of a cluster (cluster subst). This split is motivated by the phonological feature of continuancy of the cluster-final consonant. Namely, the presence of affricates, marked as [±continuant], triggers the replacement of all consonants in a sequence. In turn, when the cluster-final slot is occupied by any other segment, only one consonant is replaced. Another condition relevant for the decision learning is continuancy of C1. The [−continuant] specification in post-vocalic position is likely to lead to an insertion of an additional consonant, while the presence of [+continuant] cluster-initially leads to deletion. Note that this criterion has high accuracy. The right branch of the tree shows the following. In the group of clusters which end with segments other than affricates, stridency of C-fin provides another split. Clusters which end with a [+strident] consonant are likely to undergo substitution. All other segments word-finally are likely to lead to cluster deletion. Finally, POA distances also show to be an important predictor in the selection of a process type.

As far as importance scores are concerned, Table 5.27 presents the ranking of predictors: directionality and POA distances (100) > MOA C1 (98) > (text) corpus freq / MOA distance (97). We can observe that variables get higher scores compared to initial position, which suggests that a wider range of factors influences the splits. Out of several features visualized in the tree, rank 1 is allocated to POA

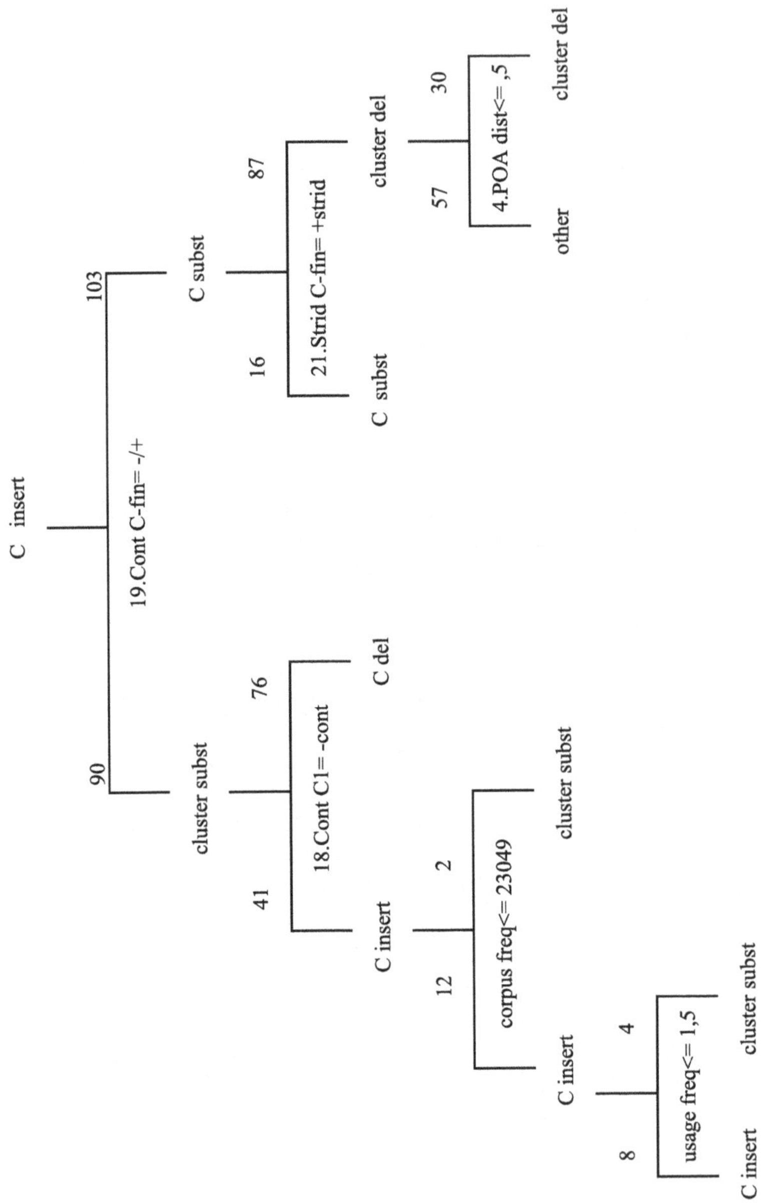

Fig. 5.4 A classification tree for process types in final clusters

Table 5.27 Estimates of predictor importance (scores) for process types in final modified targets (0 = the lowest importance, 100 = the highest importance)

Rank	Variables	Scores	Rank	Variables	Scores
1	5. Directionality	100	11	14. Opening	69
	4. POA dist	100	12	10. Ant C-fin	68
2	22. MOA C1	98	13	usage freq	65
3	(text) corpus freq	97	14	20. Strid C1	62
	13. MOA dist	97		23. MOA C-fin	62
4	19. Cont C-fin	93	15	12. POA C-fin	57
5	21. Strid C-fin	88	16	no_of_syll	56
6	9. Ant C1	87	17	8. Dorsal	45
7	vowel	85	18	phon/morph	44
8	18. Cont C1	78	19	6. Labial	41
9	7. Coronal	73	20	Size	21
10	11. POA C1	71			

distances. The highest rank is also occupied by directionality. Thus, the two criteria are considered to be crucial predictors for the whole tree.

The analyses pursued in this chapter have demonstrated that the phonotactic behaviour of Polish speakers is motivated by different predictors depending on word position. In particular, frequency and subsegmental properties underlie the modification rate and modification type.

5.6 Discussion

This chapter has demonstrated that linguistic behaviour of Polish speakers is motivated by a set of criteria specific to word-initial and word-final position. From a wide range of phonological and non-phonological factors, which have been considered to influence cluster modification, word frequency and selected phonological features have shown to be critical. More specifically, in word-initial position, cluster modification is mainly due to frequency. In word-final position, the phonological feature of stridency of the first consonant (C1) plays a decisive role in matched and mismatched renditions of cluster targets.

As regards frequency, we have seen in Fig. 5.1 that text corpus frequency is the main factor affecting cluster modification, followed by usage frequency. The relationship between logarithmically transformed type / token frequencies in the text corpus and well-formedness of cluster types was investigated in Orzechowska and Zydorowicz (2019). It must be noted that the frequencies used in the present study are raw numbers which reflect the number of repetitions of words with initial and final clusters in the text corpus and in natural conversations. The question is whether logarithmic frequencies would influence the results in any way. For instance, it would be interesting to test whether the modification rate of clusters is affected by frequencies type, token, log freq (for a similar proposal in German see Wiese and Orzechowska submitted). Since a series of studies would be required to answer the question, we leave the discussion for the future. However, for the interested reader, lists of log transformed token frequencies from the dictionary of Madelska (2005) along with the modification rate expressed in percentages are provided in Appendix P.

As regards the selection of a process type (e.g. deletion, substitution, insertion), phonological features come to the forefront as factors in the decision making process. In word-initial clusters, stridency plays a crucial role in consonant deletion. The presence of a [+strident] segment cluster-finally leads to different processes. A clearer pattern of consonant deletion can be observed in clusters, in which the prevocalic slot is occupied by a non-strident segment (i.e. [−strident] and *NA strident). This process is further strengthened by the presence of a [−strident] segment in C1. In word-final position, substitution is triggered by continuancy of the cluster-final consonant. The presence of affricates (i.e. [± continuant]) in absolute word-final position (C-fin) motivates the substitution of the whole cluster disregarding its length, while the presence of [−continuant] and [+continuant] consonants in the same position triggers the substitution of one consonant only. The process of single segment substitution is further supported by [+strident] consonants cluster-finally.

These observations suggest that there is one dominant feature which governs the rate and type of cluster modification in Polish phonotactics, on the one hand, and that there are other position-specific features which are critical to modification, on the other. Stridency plays a crucial role in Polish phonotactics disregarding word position. In general, words in which [−strident] and [+strident] consonants define word margins, and in which a non-strident consonant is found prevocalically tend to be modified. In other words, coronal fricatives and affricates are dispreferred word-finally, while plosives and sonorants are dispreferred word initially. The production data provide additional support in favour of the *positional weight of phonological features*. However, the general picture which emerges from the analysis is by no means complete. Although the statistical modelling makes use of a wide array of predictors, casual speech is also influenced by speech rate, voice quality, pauses and stress (Llisterri 1992; Shockey 2003), which could not have been included into the analysis due to the type of the data under scrutiny. Nevertheless, an analogous analysis conducted for word-initial and word-final clusters has revealed new feature-based patterns, which are favoured and disfavoured in terms of articulation. The importance of stridency and continuancy in cluster modification gets further support from preferences related to sonority distances.

I have demonstrated that deletion reveals different sonority-based preferences. In word initial position, deletion in OS clusters tends to affect a sonorant. In consequence, the realization of a cluster target is obstruent + vowel, which implies larger contrast. In terms of articulation, such a combination involves a constriction in the vowel tract followed by free and unconstrained air flow for a vowel. This contrast, however, is not favoured in word-final position. The analysis of final SO clusters shows that an obstruent tends to be omitted. The resulting vowel + sonorant sequence is characterized by a smaller sonority distance. In other words, in sequences such as /pra/ in *praca* 'work' and /arp/ in *karp* 'carp fish', a preferred articulatory modification is towards /pa/ word-initially and /ar/ word finally. A similar pattern was observed in substitution. Word-finally, postvocalic nasals in nasal + obstruent sequences tend to be replaced by a glide: either /j/ or /w/. This modification results in minimizing the manner of articulation distances between a vowel and a following consonant.

The results of the present analysis complement the observations made by Yavaş (2013a, b), who investigated the role of the sonority distance in the acquisition of sC targets cross-linguistically. Yavaş (2013a, b) observes that correct and incorrect renditions of /s/-initial clusters in Polish children are not attributed to the sonority distance. The results of the present analysis show that the manner distances do affect cluster modification in adults and across cluster types. It might be the case that the discrepancy in the results is due to the population studied (children vs. adults) or the selection of clusters under investigation (sC vs. all initials). Further studies would be required to be able to account for the differences. However, on a more general note the present results lend support to the hypothesis of Clements (1990), who argued for a steady but sharp sonority rise in onsets, and a mild fall in codas in English. The same pattern is observed in Polish.

Moreover, I have shown that Polish speakers display a low modification rate in both initial and final phonotactics; however, modification is more common word-finally. This difference is attributed to the salience of the initial position. Faithful renditions of cluster targets also prevail among phonotactic and morphonotactic sequences, which suggests that the morphological composition of clusters does not have a major impact on production. The only exception constitute phonotactic clusters in word tokens, which are subject to modification more often than not.

5.7 Conclusions

The goal of this chapter was to discover phonological and non-phonological factors which trigger modification of consonant clusters in casual speech in native speakers of Polish. Emphasis was placed on phonological processes which are held accountable in phonotactics, in particular consonant and cluster deletion, consonant substitution, insertion of a prothetic vowel or vowel deletion resulting in syllable merge. The study of target forms, which correspond with phonetic norms of Modern Polish, and modified forms made it possible to identify factors which contribute to cluster modification, on the one hand, and which underlie the choice of a process type, on the other. The results of the analysis are threefold. First, initial and final phonotactics display different modification preferences. Initial cluster modification is primarily triggered by lexical frequency, while final cluster modification is induced by subsegmental properties of consonants forming clusters such as stridency of C1, vowel quality, the number of coronals in a sequence and the presence of a continuant consonant at cluster offset. Second, the selection of a process type is primarily related to stridency in initial clusters, and stridency and continuancy in final clusters. Third, initial position, being more salient, supports a greater variety and severeness of cluster modifications.

References

Baranowski, M., and D. Turton. 2015. Researching Northern Englishes. In *Researching Northern English* [Varietes of English around the World 55], ed. R. Hickey, 293–316. Amsterdam, Philadelphia: John Benjamins.

Brown, G. 1977. *Listening to spoken English*. London: Longman.

Bybee, J. 2003. *Phonology and language use*. Cambridge: Cambridge University Press.

Clements, G.N. 1990. The role of the sonority cycle in core syllabification. In *Papers in laboratory phonology vol. 1: Between the grammar and physics of speech*, eds. J. Kingston, and M.E. Beckman, 283–333. Cambridge: Cambridge University Press.

Dobrogowska, K. 1992. Word initial and word final consonant clusters in Polish popular science texts and in artistic prose. *Studia Phonetica Posnaniensia* 3: 47–121.

Dressler, W.U., and K. Dziubalska-Kołaczyk. 2006. Proposing morphonotactics. *Wiener Linguistische Gazette* 73: 1–19.

Dukiewicz, L., and I. Sawicka. 1995. *Gramatyka współczesnego języka polskiego: Fonetyka i fonologia*. Kraków: Instytut Języka Polskiego PAN.

Dunaj, B. 1985. *Grupy spółgłoskowe współczesnej polszczyzny mówionej (w języku mieszkańców Krakowa)*. Kraków: Uniwersytet Jagielloński.

Dunaj, B. 2006. Zasady poprawnej wymowy polskiej. *Język Polski* 86: 161–172.

Dziubalska-Kołaczyk, K. 1990. Phonostylistics and second language acquisition. *Papers and Studies in Contrastive Linguistics* 25: 71–83.

Dziubalska-Kołaczyk, K. 2001. Phonotactic constraints are preferences. In *Constraints and preferences*, ed. K. Dziubalska-Kołaczyk, 69–100. Berlin: Mouton de Gruyter.

Dziubalska-Kołaczyk, K., and D. Zielińska. 2011. Universal phonotactic and morphonotactic preferences in second language acquisition. In *Achievements and perspectives in SLA of speech: New Sounds 2010*, eds. K. Dziubalska-Kołaczyk, M. Wrembel, and M. Kul, 53–63. Frankfurt am Main: Peter Lang Verlag.

Dziubalska-Kołaczyk, K., and P. Zydorowicz. 2014. The production of high-frequency clusters by native and non-native users of Polish. *Concordia Working Papers in Applied Linguistics* 5: 130–144.

Ernestus, M., I. Hanique, and E. Verboom. 2015. The effect of speech situation on the occurrence of reduced word pronunciation variants. *Journal of Phonetics* 48: 60–75.

Fasold, R.W. 1972. *Tense marking in black English: A linguistic and social analysis*. Arlington: Center for Applied Linguistics.

Foley, J. 1972. Rule precursors and phonological change by meta-rule. In *Linguistic change and generative theory*, eds. R. Stockwell, and R. Macauley, 96–100. Bloomington: Indiana University Press.

Goldsmith, J.A. 1990. *Autosegmental and metrical phonology*. Oxford: Blackwell.

Gonet, W., and A. Trochymiuk. 2007. Typologia procesów fonologicznych opracowana na podstawie materiału zawartego w bazie danych COPERNICUS 1304-BEBEL PL. In *Język, interakcja, zaburzenia mowy. Metodologia badań*, eds. A. Domagała, and T. Woźniak, 185–211. Lublin: Wydawnictwo Uniwersytetu Marii Curie-Skłodowskiej.

Guy, G.R. 1980. Variation in the group and the individual: The case of final stop deletion. In *Locating language in time and space*, ed. W. Labov, 1–36. New York: Academic Press.

Hermes, A., D. Mücke, and B. Auris. 2017. The variability of syllable patterns in Tashlhiyt Berber and Polish. *Journal of Phonetics* 64: 127–144.

Jaskuła, K. 2014. Intervocalic elision of labials in Polish. In *Crossing phonetics-phonology lines*, eds. E. Cyran, and J. Szpyra-Kozłowska, 63–74. Newcastle upon Tyne: Cambridge Scholars Publishing.

Jaskuła, K. 2018. Uwagi o elizji spółgłosek wargowych we współczesnej polszczyźnie mediów. *LingVaria* 1 (25): 65–77.

Karaś, M., and M. Madejowa. 1977. *Słownik wymowy polskiej*. Warszawa: Państwowe Wydawnictwo Naukowe.

Kaźmierski, K. 2016. The reduction of intervocalic /w/ in Polish. In *Phonology, its faces and interfaces*, eds. J. Szpyra-Kozłowska, and E. Cyran, 201–218. Frankfurt am Main: Peter Lang.
Kelly, M.H. 2004. Word onset patterns and lexical stress in English. *Journal of Memory and Language* 50: 231–244.
Kerswill, P. 1985. A sociophonetic study of connected speech processes in Cambridge English: An outline and some results. In *Cambridge papers in phonetics and experimental linguistics*, ed. F. J. Nolan, 1–39. Cambridge: Cambridge University Press.
Kerswill, P. 1987. Levels of linguistic variation in Durham. *Journal of Linguistics* 23 (1): 25–49.
Kul, M. 2018. *Quantification and modeling of selected consonantal processes of casual speech in American English*. Poznań: Wydawnictwo Naukowe UAM.
Labov, W., P. Cohen, C. Robins, and J. Lewis. 1968. A study of the nonstandard English of Negro and Puerto Rican speakers of New York City. *Cooperative Research Report, no. 3288*. Washington, DC: U.S. Office of Education.
Labov, W. 1972. *Sociolinguistic patterns*. Philadelphia: University of Pennsylvania Press.
Llisterri, J. 1992. Speaking styles in speech research. In *ELSNET/ESCA/SALT workshop on integrating speech and natural language, Dublin,* 15–17 July 1992.
Lodge, K. 1984. *Studies in the phonology of colloquial English*. London: Croom Helm.
Loh, W.-Y. 2011. Classification and regression trees. *WIREs Data Minimin and Knowledge Discovery* 1 (1): 14–23.
Łukaszewicz, B. 2006. Extrasyllabicity, transparency and prosodic constituency in the acquisition of Polish. *Lingua* 116: 1–30.
Łukaszewicz, B. 2007. Reduction in syllable onsets in the acquisition of Polish: Deletion, coalescence, metathesis and gemination. *Journal of Child Language* 34: 53–82.
Łukaszewicz, B. 2010. *Phonological acquisition in optimality theory. Towards an integrated comprehension-production grammar*. Warszawa: Uniwersytet Warszawski.
Madejowa, M. 1987. Współczesna polska norma językowa w zakresie wymowy samogłosek nosowych. *Studia Phonetica Posnaniensa* 1: 31–56.
Madejowa, M. 1990. Modern Polish linguistic norm with special reference to the pronunciation of consonants. *Studia Phonetica Posnaniensa* 2: 69–105.
Madejowa, M. 1993. Normative rules of modern Polish pronunciation. *Studia Phonetica Posnaniensa* 4: 19–30.
Madelska, L. 2005. *Słownik wariantywności fonetycznej współczesnej polszczyzny*. Kraków: Collegium Collumbinum.
Marecka, M., and K. Dziubalska-Kołaczyk. 2014. Evaluating models of phonotactic constraints on the basis of sC cluster acquisition data. *Language Sciences* 46 (A): 37–47.
Milewski, S. 2005. Grupy spółgłoskowe w języku mówionym dzieci przedszkolnych. *Logopeda* 1: 5–32.
Mizerski, W. ed. 2005. *Język polski. Encyklopedia w tabelach*. Warszawa: Adamantan.
Mücke, D., J. Sieczkowska, H. Niemann, M. Grice, and G. Dogil. 2010. Sonority profiles, gestural coordination and phonological licensing: Obstruent-sonorant clusters in Polish. *LabPhon conference,* January 23 2015 (poster).
Nagórko, A. 2006. *Zarys gramatyki polskiej*. Warszawa: Państwowe Wydawnictwo Naukowe.
Orzechowska, P., J. Mołczanow, and M. Jankowski. 2018. Struktura sylaby a akcent wyrazowy w języku rosyjskim. *Studia et Documenta Slavica* 1–2 (5–6): 79–91.
Orzechowska, P., J. Mołczanow, and M. Jankowski. 2019. Prosodically-conditioned syllables structure in English. *Research in Language* 17 (1): 1–12.
Orzechowska, P., and P. Zydorowicz. 2019. Frequency effects and markedness in phonotactics. *Poznań Studies in Contemporary Linguistics* 55(1): 157–179.
Pajak, B., and R. Levy. 2014. The role of abstraction in non-native speech perception. *Journal of Phonetics* 46: 147–160.
Parker, S. 2012. Sonority distance vs. sonority dispersion—A typological survey. In *The sonority controversy*, ed. S. Parker, 101–166. Berlin: Walter de Gruyter.
Patrick, P. 1999. *Urban Jamaican Creole: Variation in the Mesolect*. Amsterdam: Benjamins.

Rochoń, M. 2000. *Optimality in complexity: The case of Polish consonant clusters* [*Studia Grammatica* 48]. Berlin: Akademie Verlag.
Rubach, J. 1981. Contrastive phonostylistics. In *Theoretical issues in contrastive linguistics* [Current issues in linguistic theory 12], ed. J. Fisiak, 263–272. Amsterdam: John Benjamins.
Rubach, J., and G. Booij. 1990a. Syllable structure sssignment in Polish. *Phonology* 7: 121–158.
Rubach, J., and G. Booij. 1990b. Edge of constituent effects in Polish. *Natural Language and Linguistic Theory* 8 (3): 427–463.
Ryan, K.M. 2014. Onsets contribute to syllable weight: Statistical evidence from stressed meter. *Language* 90 (2): 309–341.
Santa Ana, O. 1991. *Phonetic simplification processes in the English of the barrio: A cross-generational sociolinguistic study of the Chicanos of Los Angeles*. PhD diss., Philadelphia: University of Pennsylvania.
Santa Ana, O. 1996. Sonority and syllable structure in Chicano English. *Language Variation and Change* 8: 63–91.
Selkirk, E.O. 1984. On the major class features and syllable theory. In *Language sound structure*, eds. M. Aronoff, and R.T. Oehrle, 107–136. Cambridge, MA: The MIT Press.
Shockey, L. 1974. Phonetic and phonological properties of connected speech. *Ohio State Working Papers in Linguistics* 17: 1–143.
Shockey, L. 2003. *Sound patterns of spoken English*. Oxford: Blackwell Publishing.
Singh, S. 1976. *Distinctive features: Theory and validation*. Baltimore: University Park Press.
Statistica software. Data analysis software system, version 13.1.
Steriade, D. 1982. *Greek prosodies and the nature of syllabification*. PhD diss., Cambridge, MA: The MIT Press.
Szreder, M. 2013. The acquisition of consonant clusters in Polish: A case study. In *The emergence of phonology: Whole-word approaches and cross-linguistic evidence*, eds. M. Vihman, and T. Keren-Portnoy, 343–361. Cambridge: Cambridge University Press.
Tagliamonte, S., and R. Temple. 2005. New perspectives on an ol' variable: (t, d) in British English. *Language Variation and Change* 17: 281–302.
Tucker, B. V. 2007. *Spoken word recognition of the reduced American English flap*. Ph.D diss., Tucson: University of Arizona.
Tucker, B., and M. Ernestus. 2016. Why we need to investigate casual speech to truly understand language production, processing and the mental lexicon. In *The mental lexicon, vol. 11. New questions for the next decade*, eds. G. Jarema, G. Libben, and V. Kuperman, 375–400. Amsterdam: John Benjamins.
Wagner, P., J. Trouvain, and F. Zimmerer. 2015. In defense of stylistic diversity in speech research. *Journal of Phonetics* 48: 1–12.
Wiese, R., and P. Orzechowska. submitted. Structure and usage do not explain each other: An analysis of German word-initial clusters.
Witaszek-Samborska, M. 1986. Mowa poznańskiej inteligencji. In *Mowa mieszkańców Poznania*, eds. M. Gruchmanowa, M. Witaszek-Samborska, and M. Żak-Święcicka, 29–87. Poznań: Wydawnictwo Poznańskie.
Wolfram, W. 1969. *A linguistic description of Detroit negro speech*. Washington, DC: Center for Applied Linguistics.
Yavaş, M. 2013a. What explains the reductions in /s/-clusters: Sonority or [continuant]? *Clinical Linguistics and Phonetics* 27: 394–403.
Yavaş, M. 2013b. Acquisition of #sC clusters: universal grammar versus language- specific grammar. *Letras de Hoje* 48: 355–361.
Yavaş, M. 2014. What guides children's acquisition of #sC clusters: a cross-linguistic account. In *Perspectives on phonological theory and acquisition. In honor of Daniel A. Dinnsen* [Language acquisition and language disorders 56], eds. A. Farris-Trimble, and J.A. Barlow, 115–131. Amsterdam, Philadelphia: John Benjamins.
Yavaş, M., and M. Marecka. 2014. Acquisition of Polish #sC clusters in typically-developing children and children with phonological disorders. *International Journal of Speech-Language Pathology* 16 (2): 132–141.

Yavaş, M., A. Ben-David, E. Gerrits, K.E. Kristoffersen, and H.G. Simonsen. 2008. Sonority and cross-linguistic acquisition of initial s-clusters. *Clinical Linguistics and Phonetics* 22 (6): 421–441.

Zwicky, A.M. 1972. On casual speech. In *Papers from the eighth regional meeting of the Chicago Linguistic Society, Chicago,* 14–16 April 1972, eds. P.M. Paranteau, J.N. Levi, and G.C. Phares, 607–615. Chicago: Chicago Linguistic Society.

Zydorowicz, P., and K. Dziubalska-Kołaczyk. 2017. The dynamics of marked consonant clusters in Polish. In *Proceedings of the international symposium on monolingual and bilingual speech, Chania,* 4–7 September 2017, ed. E. Babatsouli, 318–324. Chania: Institute of Monolingual and Bilingual Speech.

Zydorowicz, P., P. Orzechowska, M. Jankowski, K. Dziubalska-Kołaczyk, P. Wierzchoń, and D. Pietrala. 2016. *Phonotactics and morphonotactics of Polish and English: Description, tools and applications*. Poznań: Wydawnictwo Naukowe UAM.

Chapter 6
Quo Vadimus? Towards an Elementary Particle in Phonology

Where is then the difference between the universe and the tiniest constituent? There is no difference.
After all, even if the summation process goes on and on endlessly, the smallest part remains divisible interminably.
(Titus Lucretius Carus Ancient Roman poet, philosopher, 99–55 BC translation after Harald Fritzsch)

In physics, *elementary particles* are the tiniest indivisible constituents of all matter. They have no substructure, and are therefore considered to be the basic building blocks of the universe. The idea of such basic particles was known already to ancient philosophers, whose works foresaw the principles of modern particle physics. For instance, Lucretius was preoccupied with the laws governing the universe. He believed in the existence of invisible elements which cannot exist alone but which are deeply rooted in a larger coherent structure. More importantly, he believed that these elements are tied together by their *simplicity*. Although centuries have passed, the need to understand the nature of observable phenomena has not faded away. All the questions asked in Chaps. 1, 2, 3, 4 and 5 stemmed from the linguistic need to understand the most basic principles which underlie the static distribution patterns of consonants in Polish words.

This volume was an attempt at accounting for word-initial and word-final phonotactics and morphonotactics in terms of phonological features. Consonant clusters have been studied from the perspective of lexical statistics, processing and production. Although the generalizations presented in this chapter are a comprehensive summary of the research results, they are barely a starting point for further, more oriented explorations. Already now, at the outset of my considerations, it is clear that an adequate formulation of the idea of weight of phonological features, let alone elements smaller than features, their representation and interaction will be possible only when cross-linguistic and methodologically-diverse data have been analysed. The selection of subsegmental properties, and methods employed in discovering their arrangement in clusters suggested in the book is by no means

P. Orzechowska, *Complexity in Polish Phonotactics*, Prosody, Phonology and Phonetics, https://doi.org/10.1007/978-981-13-7299-5_6

exhaustive. Although the very concept of elementary particles defining a phonological system or a group of systems is a proposal, I hope to have shown that weighted features, as a type of such elements, are a part of Polish phonology, and can find their place in phonological typology.

Central to the discussion on elementary particles is the notion of feature weight as well as absolute constraints and graded preferences. Weight stands for the importance of a feature, which is expressed in terms of numerical rankings. Constraints and preferences serve to formalize the relations between such weighted features. These concepts are used to describe an approach to Polish phonology, in which a large set of features is explored, and in which clusters are not classified according to well-formedness conditions. Elementary particles as such are an attempt at naming phenomena which—I conjure—exist in a language, but whose existence has not been explicitly addressed in phonological theory.

The empirical chapters do not provide clear evidence in favour of the existence of particles, but they lend support to the general idea of positional weight of phonological features, and to the validity of *featuretactics,* which arises from a set of such particles. Below, I provide the main points of the approach proposed in this volume using the wording supplied by phonological theory, and the current state of knowledge about languages, and Language with a capital L, viewed as a general construct serving communication. The principal ideas presented in the book are summarized in several points.

49. Summary of the proposal

(49.a) Cluster inventories are regulated by *inviolable constraints* and *graded preferences.* Constraints and preferences determine dependency relations between segments and ensuing structure of syllables and words.

(49.b) Phonotactic constraints and preferences arise from *positionally weighted phonological features.*

(49.c) Phonological features vary in weight, which reflects their importance in different linguistic domains such as the structure of the lexicon, processing and production.

(49.d) Weighted phonological features are positional, which means that feature weight is allocated to a position in a word and a position in a cluster.

In the following sections, I provide a synopsis of the findings obtained in Chap. 3 through Chap. 5, and define clusters in terms of rankings of weighted features and preferences.

6.1 Relative Importance of Phonological Features

Let me start with the discussion on the nature of constraints and preferences. In Chap. 2, I presented theory-specific approaches to phonotactic generalizations, which make use of either notion. I argue that constraints and preferences, although ontologically different, can be reconciled into a unified model. This idea is reflected in the scale of phonotactic preferability, which was proposed in Chap. 2 to classify generalizations of different strength. The scale is restated in 50.

50 Scale of phonotactic preferability

(50.a) prerequisites
(50.b) strong preferences
(50.c) weak preferences

The three-level hierarchy encompasses both absolute constraints and graded preferences. *Perquisites* are viewed as mandatory building blocks in phonotactics. They are statements on constraints, which in general phonological theory distinguish between admissible structures and unattested structures in a language. Phonotactic prerequisites are easy to define on the example of Germanic systems, in which all initial clusters start with an obstruent. Therefore, for languages such English and German, a prerequisite would state that C1 in word-initial clusters is unconditionally occupied by a plosive, a fricative or an affricate. *Preferences*, in turn, specify types of available obstruents that are favoured: Continuant or non-continuant? Strident or non-strident? Labial or coronal? These preferences vary in strength. Some preferences specify a larger majority of consonant clusters, while others define the structure of a smaller majority of clusters. That is, preferences which apply as strong or weak default determine subtle characteristics of sequences of consonants in a given phonological system, and in a given word position. The preferability scale in 50 provides a necessary background for formulating featural preferences in Polish phonotactics for lexical, cognitive and articulatory phonotactics.

6.1.1 Lexical Phonotactics

The term *lexical phonotactics* is used to refer to the structure of cluster types which are found in a representative list of Polish words, or in a dictionary. Basic sub-segmental properties defining a preferred cluster structure can be proposed on the basis of percentage-based and PCA-based rankings in Chap. 3. The observations for initial and final clusters are summarized in 51.

In initial clusters, C1 and C-fin refer to the left-most (first) and right-most (last, prevocalic) consonant in a sequence. In final clusters, the specification refers to two-member clusters (C1 × C2) as CCs were shown to be preferred word-finally. In this position, C1 stands for the postvocalic segment, and C2 stands for absolute final position in a word. The features are ordered according to their importance. Numerical values from 1 to 4 indicate a decrease in weight of a feature. Features given in grey-shaded slots are not present in the statistical rankings.

51 Feature weight in lexical phonotactics

(51.a) initial position:

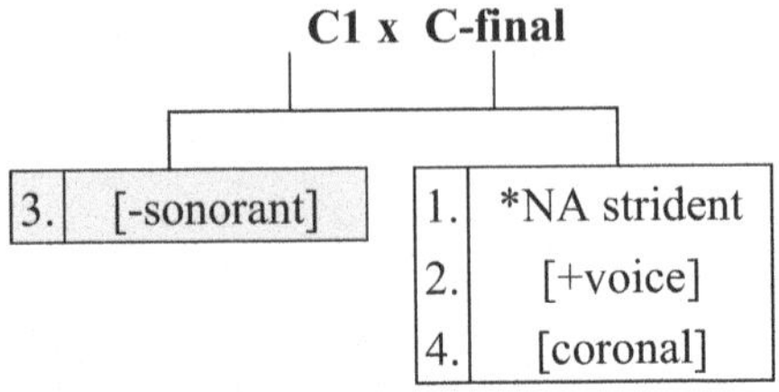

(51.b) final position:

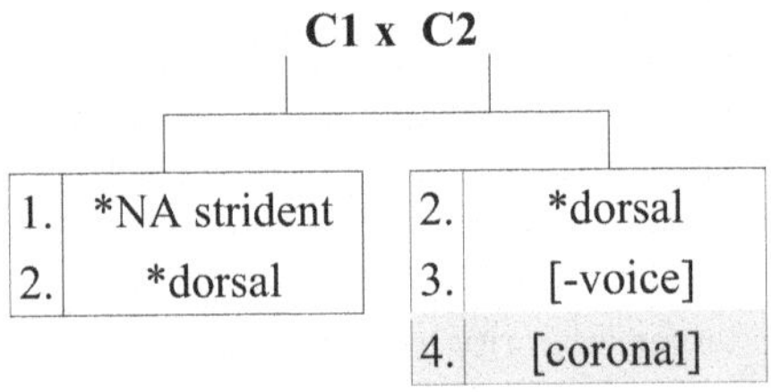

The specifications show that *NA strident is the most important feature defining initial and final cluster inventories. Bear in mind that *NA strident refers to consonants, to which feature [±strident] does not apply. In other words, plosives and sonorants are favoured in prevocalic and postvocalic position. The remaining features have lower weight, and therefore lead to weaker preferences.

As regards initial clusters, the second strongest preference states that a voiced segment is favoured before a vowel. The third preference requires the presence of an obstruent cluster-initially. Finally, there is a preference for a coronal consonants before a vowel. Preferences inferred for word-final position are largely comparable. Stridency, dorsality and voice have the greatest discriminatory power. Plosives and sonorants are favoured in postvocalic position, while dorsals (*dorsal) are generally disfavoured as cluster constituents. The status of [-sonorant] in initial phonotactics and [coronal] in final phonotactics is dubious. The features function as defaults in percentage-based rankings, but they do not explain the variability in the data at the statistical level.

Initial and final word positions differ in terms of a preference for voicing: a voiced segment is favoured before a vowel, while a voiceless one in absolute word-final position. The comparison of (51.a) and (51.b) suggests that although the manner of articulation (defined by *NA strident) is the prime force which motivates cluster structure, the place of articulation is a particularly relevant building block of right-edge phonotactics. Preference 2 limits the occurrence of dorsals in a cluster, while Preference 4 (possibly) requires a coronal consonant cluster-finally.

Table 6.1 Lexical phonotactics: initial preferred clusters according to (51.a), where C1 = obstruent, C-final = voiced coronal plosive / sonorant

CC	CCC	CCCC
bj, bl, br, ɕl, ɕɲ, ɕr, dj, dl, dn, dɲ, dr, fj, fl, fr, gd, gj, gl, gn, gɲ, gr, kj, kl, kn, kɲ, kr, pj, pl, pn, pɲ, pr, sj, sl, sn, sr, ʃl, ʃn, ʃr, tj, tl, tn, tɲ, tr, ʦl, ʦn, vd, vj, vl, vn, vɲ, vr, xj, xl, xr, zd, zn, zr, ʑl, ʑr, ʒd, ʒl, ʒɲ, ʒr	brd, brn, brɲ, bzd, bʒd, ɕfj, ɕmj, ɕpj, dmj, drj, dvj, fkl, fkr, grd, gvd, gvj, kfj, kln, klɲ, kmj, kpj, krj, krn, prj, pxl, skj, skl, skn, skr, smr, spj, spr, stj, str, sʦj, sxl, sxn, sxɲ, ʃkj, ʃkl, ʃkr, ʃpj, ʃpr, ʃtr, ʨfj, ʨmj, tfj, tkl, tkn, tkɲ, trj, ʦfj, ʦkl, ʦkɲ, ʧkɲ, tʃn, txn, txɲ, vbr, vzn, vzr, vʒd, xfj, xmj, zbr, zdj, zdr, zgj, zgl, zgr, zmj, zvj, ʥvj, sfj	bʒmj, drvj, dʒvj, gʒbj, gʒmj, pstr, skfj, ʃtfj, tkfj, tʃmj, tʃpj, vzdr

Table 6.2 Lexical phonotactics: final preferred clusters according to (51.a), where C1 = labial / coronal plosive / sonorant, C-final = voiceless coronal C

CC
j̃ɕ, js, jt, jʦ, jʧ, ls, lʃ, lt, lʦ, ms, mʃ, nʃ, nt, nʦ, nʧ, ɲtɕ, ɲʦ, pl, pɲ, pr, ps, pʃ, pt, rɕ, rf, rs, rʃ, rt, rtɕ, rʦ, rʧ, tf, tl, tr, ws, w̃s, wʃ, w̃ʃ, wt, wtɕ, wʧ

Polish initial and final clusters which meet the specifications in (51.a) and (51.b) are provided in Tables 6.1 and 6.2, respectively. The lists are compiled on the basis of phonotactic clusters.

These cluster types are preferred in the lexicon. Note that the list of initials encompasses sequences ranging from CC to CCCC since (51.a) does not delimit the number of consonants in a cluster. This results from the nature of the proposed parameters, none of which refers to medial segments in CCCs and CCCCs. With each additional parameter included in the analysis, the specification of clusters would be more precise, and their number would be delimited. For instance, including new place parameters such as [±round], [±high], [±back], [±low], [±distributed], and investigating their distribution cluster-medially would yield more degrees of preferability, and eventually lead to a minimum cluster.

Apart from gradient preferences, the preferability scale in 50 accounts for inviolable constraints. The data suggest that only one[1] obligatory pattern can be established in Polish. Namely, final clusters display the property of 'identity avoidance', which is expressed in 52.

[1]A pattern referring to final morphonotactic clusters refers to only one 5-member sequence, and therefore cannot be treated as a generalization.

52 Prerequisites in lexical phonotactics

Identical segments must not recur in final phonotactic clusters.

Word-initial phonotactics is not governed by any inviolable constraints. Initial position, being the most salient one in a word, is liberal in phonotactic terms: it supports not only a greater variety of cluster types (N = 458) but also types of more varied phonological make-up. Final phonotactics shows to be more constrained.

6.1.2 Cognitive Phonotactics

The experiments in Chap. 4 provide insights into the psycholinguistic reality of two phonological factors which can have an influence on the processing of phonotactics: place of articulation distances and sonority. Key to online processing is the size of perceptual contrast determined by place distances. Initial and final consonant clusters are processed according to the same pattern, whereby larger distances (distance = 5, 6) are processed faster than medial distances (distance = 2, 3, 4). Results obtained for small distances, in particular distance equal to zero, are considered to be referential. Therefore, the specification of feature weight for cognitive phonotactics is based only on large distances.

The design of Exp 1 and Exp 2 makes it possible to infer tentative feature weight in *cognitive phonotactics*. In Chap. 3, I have included place parameters accounting for labiality, coronality, dorsality and anteriorness, and demonstrated that coronal consonants are favoured in initial and final phonotactics. Large-scale experimentation would be required to determine the weight of these features and their rankings in online processing. Also, future investigation should have a broader scope, and investigate the role of other place features in processing.

It must be noted that the results for latency responses provide a large simplification of preferences that hold for the processing of the place of articulation. In spite of this fact, they unambiguously point to the importance of the combination of labial and dorsal segments. Representations in 53 account for two-member clusters in both initial and final position. Since the ordering of features is unclear, the specifications should be read either as labial + dorsal or dorsal + labial. Among labials, [±continuant] distinguishes bilabial non-continuant stops /p b m/ from labio-dental continuant fricatives /f v/. Feature [dorsal] embraces consonantal velar /k g x ŋ/, while [coronal] refers to non-consonantal /j/. Both preferences given in I and IIa, b facilitate processing, although I is more favoured.

53 Feature weight in cognitive phonotactics

(53.a) Preference I:

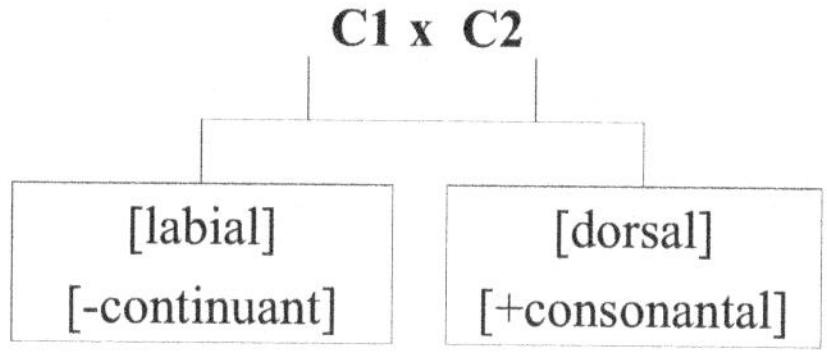

(53.b) Preference II a:

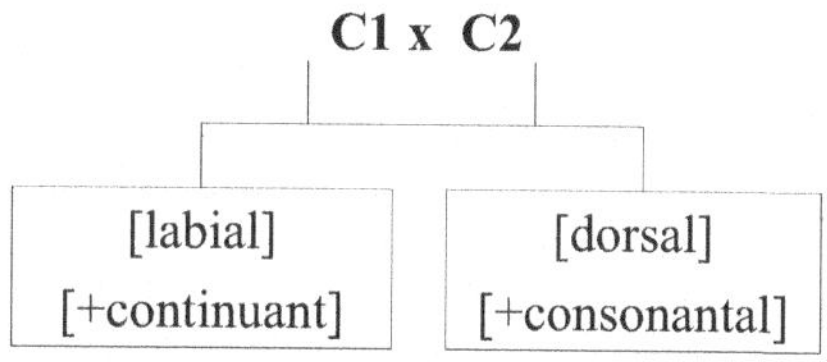

(53.c) Preference II b:

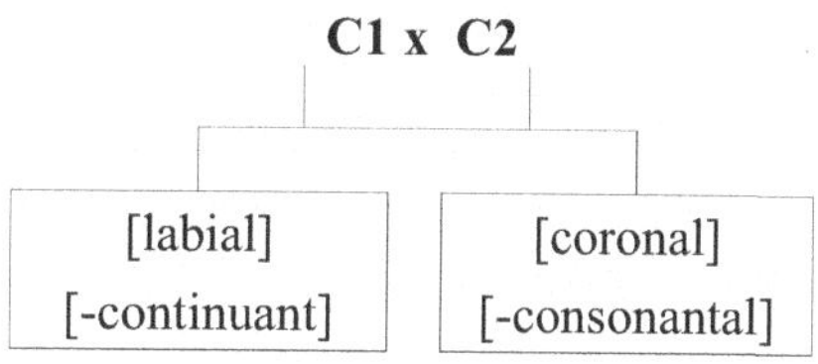

The specifications given above describe clusters, whose processing involves the least cognitive effort. The largest distance = 6 is represented by the combination of bilabial and velar consonants, in either order. Sequences of consonants which follow the specification in (53.a) in Polish are represented by initials /gb gm kp km px xm mx/ and finals /km hm/. Additionally, as shown in (53.b) and (53.c), slightly weaker preferences involve a POA distance equal to 5. This distance is represented by the combination of labio-dental and velar segments as well as by the combination of bilabial and palatal segments. (53.b) characterizes Polish initials /bj pj mj gv kf xf fk fx vg/, and final /jm fk kf/. The lists do not include labio-velar /w/. It is unclear how to the glide should be classified with respect to distance as it involves both labial and velar articulation.

It must be borne in mind that the division of clusters into those that exhibit small or large distances is conventional. POA distances are here treated in terms of an interval scale, although the distance of one is not identical for all the consecutive place points in the vocal tract. That is, examples of distance = 1 (e.g. between bilabial and labio-dental, alveolar and alveolo-palatal, palatal and velar segments) are not directly comparable due to the asymmetry of the oral cavity, not to mention the labial area. Therefore, the measure of POA distances largely reflects the size of the articulatory trajectory, in particular the path that the tongue has to cover on the way from one consonant to another. Large distances thus correspond with a wide movement from, say, the bilabial to velar regions, while small distances hold between consonants which are found close to each other in the articulatory space. The preference for large distances in both word positions complies with the principle of the clarity of perception (Donegan and Stampe 2009). Larger contrasts are listener friendly as they facilitate perception.

The preferences for lexical and cognitive phonotactics differ with respect to the place dimension. In Sect. 6.1.1, I have identified a preference for coronality in both word positions. The presence of a coronal consonant in a cluster increases the probability of a small distance between adjacent segments. First, the coronal articulation is represented by a great variety of phonetic places of articulation increasing the incidence of their co-occurrence. Second, coronal consonants are central: any combination with either a labial segment or a dorsal segment is smaller than a combination of extreme places in the mouth cavity such as labial + dorsal, or the reverse. To the contrary, an instantiation of extreme articulatory types, represented by bilabial + velar or velar + bilabial sequences, is shown to be favoured in online processing. Although coronal consonants are universally unmarked (Hall 1997; Paradis and Prunet 1991), cognitive phonotactics requires at least sufficient perceptual contrast. These conflicting forces are strengthened when the articulatory data is taken into consideration.

6.1.3 Articulatory Phonotactics

The study on casual speech described in Chap. 5 provides insights into the preferred featural organization of phonotactics in language as it is spoken. The term *articulatory phonotactics* is here used to refer to the phonetic realization of clusters when they are spoken in casual conversations. The analysis based on classification trees teases apart the properties of consonant clusters which contribute to the preservation of cluster targets or to their modification. Given that casual speech processes are triggered by the principle of the ease of articulation, phonological features which trigger cluster modification should be viewed as more demanding, difficult, unnatural for the articulation, and therefore prone to deletion, substitution or vowel insertion. In turn, phonological features which are preserved are seen as favoured. Such features can be derived from clusters produced faithfully to their targets.

The specification in 54 presents a preferred structure of consonant clusters in articulatory terms. That is, clusters following (54.a) and (54.b) tend to be pronounced according to the phonetic norm of Modern Polish. Note that the specification for initial phonotactics disregards non-phonological factors such as frequency, which has been identified as the most important variable leading to cluster preservation. The ordering of features is based on splitting conditions which lead to cluster targets. The higher the feature is located in the tree, the greater its importance.

54 Feature weight in articulatory phonotactics

(54.a) initial position:
Preference I: uniform directionality (forward or backward)
Preference II: CC size

(54.b) final position:

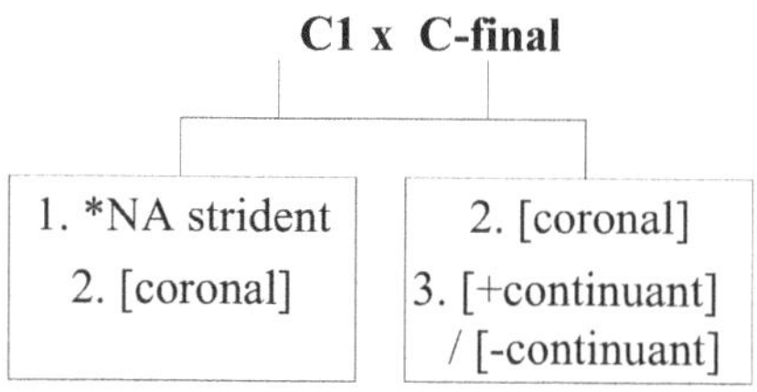

As regards word-initial position, directionality refers to the movement of the tongue. A forward gesture proceeds towards a more fronted region (such as velar → alveolar / dental / bilabial), while a backward gesture involves a movement towards a rear part of the oral cavity (e.g. dental → alveolar / palatal). This preference is a reflex of the POA distances identified in cognitive phonotactics. What is more, as discussed in Chap. 5, clusters are produced as their targets when they are composed of two consonants (i.e. size ≤ 2.5). These preferences suggest that clusters longer than CC, whose production involves mixed articulatory movement or no movement at all, tend to be modified. Such sequences are exemplified by /spr mgw ɕmj/. As regards word-final position, three features underlie preferred clusters. First, there is a preference for the C1 slot to be occupied by plosives or sonorants (i.e. *NA strident), especially those articulated with the front part of the tongue. Moreover, preferred final clusters do not end with affricates (i.e. [+continuant] / [−continuant] specification).

Word-initial and word-final clusters which follow the preferred specification in Polish are provided in Tables 6.3 and 6.4, respectively. The clusters tend to be preserved in casual speech. As before, the lists are compiled on the basis of phonotactic clusters.

(54.a) and (54.b) also imply a dispreferred feature setting which leads to cluster modification. For instance, the probability for cluster modification increases when constituent consonants are labials and dorsals, or when affricates occur word-finally. If casual speech is motivated by ease of articulation, coronals as the most preferred segments due to their central articulation. To the contrary, the more extreme places of articulation such as labial and dorsal, especially when combined, are disfavoured and trigger reduction. In a similar vein, affricates are disfavoured due to their complex articulation.

Table 6.3 Articulatory phonotactics: initial preferred clusters according to (54.a), which are CCs produced with unidirectional movement of the tongue

CC
bj, bl, br, bw, bz, bʑ, bʒ, ɕf, ɕl, ɕm, ɕp, ɕr, db, dj, dm, dɲ, dr, dv, ʥb, ʥv, ʥg, ʥv, dʒ, ʤv, fɕ, fj, fl, fr, fʃ, ft, fʧ, gb, gd, gʥ, gj, gl, gm, gn, gɲ, gr, gv, gw, gz, gʑ, gʒ, kɕ, kf, kj, kl, km, kn, kɲ, kp, kr, ks, kʃ, kt, kʨ, kʦ, kw, lj, lʒ, mj, ml, mn, mɲ, mr, mʃ, mʦ, mw, mʒ, pɕ, pj, pl, pn, pɲ, pr, ps, pʃ, pt, pʨ, pw, px, rd, rʥ, rj, rt, rv, sf, sj, sk, sm, sp, sr, sx, ʃf, ʃk, ʃl, ʃm, ʃn, ʃp, ʃt, ʨf, ʨm, ʨp, tf, tj, tk, tɲ, tr, ʦf, ʦm, tʃ, ʧf, ʧk, ʧm, ʧt, ʧʨ, ʧx, tʧ, tx, vd, vʥ, vʥ, vj, vl, vn, vɲ, vr, vz, vʑ, vʒ, wg, wk, xf, xj, xl, xm, xr, xʃ, xt, xʨ, xʦ, xw, zb, zg, zm, zr, zv, ʑl, ʑr, ʒb, ʒd, ʒg, ʒl, ʒm, ʒɲ, ʒv

Table 6.4 Articulatory phonotactics: final preferred clusters according to (54.b), where C1 = plosive/sonorant, C-final = all segments but affricates, across the cluster = two coronals

CC	CCC
j̃ɕ, jl, jn, js, jt, ls, lʃ, lt, nr, ns, nʃ, nt, rɕ, rn, rɲ, rs, rʃ, rt, tl, tr	j̃sk, kst, lft, lsk, rsk, wnt, wst, w̃ʃt, w̃ʃʧ

Generally, I have demonstrated that Polish phonotactics is motivated by a set of feature-based patterns specific to different linguistic domains (the lexicon, processing and articulation) as well as to different positions in a word (initial and final) and in a cluster (C1 and C-fin). As a consequence, for each domain different types of minimal and preferred clusters, syllables or words can be proposed. Out of a wide array of consonantal properties employed in the analyses in Chap. 1, 2, 3, 4 and 5, only several show to play a crucial role in Polish phonotactics.

6.2 Phonological Typology

The concept of feature weight was originally introduced in Orzechowska (2016) to account for the cross-linguistic variability in phonotactics. If consonant clusters are avoided in the languages of the world, what motivates their existence and phonological make-up? The analyses targetting individual phonological features, as presented in this book, provide new insights into intrinsic properties of clusters only in Polish. However, the nature of the modelling gives a reason to believe that a systematic comparison of typologically different systems in terms of such infrasegmental and intersegmental properties would bring us closer to the understanding of phonotactics and more general phonological phenomena.

The idea that there exist tiny subsegmental properties which underlie phonological systems is at this point a speculation. Large scale cross-linguistic research involving different methodologies and genetically distant language families would be required to discover minimum elements, which are shared by all languages or language families. Nevertheless, the results of preliminary analyses discussed in Orzechowska (2018) as well as Orzechowska and Ridouane (2018) show complex trajectories between the distribution of phonological features in segments and the structure of consonant clusters. The Principal Component Analysis (see Chap. 3) based on representative lists

Table 6.5 Weight of manner and voice parameters in cluster types cross-linguistically

Rank	Parameters	P1–P8	%
English initial clusters			
1	Number of obstruents	P2	42
2	Manner cluster-finally	P4	28
3	Voice cluster-finally	P7	20
German initial clusters			
1	Cluster length	P1	36
2	Voice cluster-finally	P7	30
3	Number of obstruents	P2	18
Polish initial clusters			
1	Voice agreement	P8	47
2	Voice cluster-finally	P7	29
Russian initial clusters			
1	Voice cluster-finally	P7	26
2	Manner cluster-initially	P3	21
3	Number of obstruents	P2	20
4	Voice agreement	P8	17
Tashlhiyt Berber vowelles verbal roots			
1	S/O contrast word-initially	P2	47
2	Cluster length	P1	22
3	Manner word-initially	P3	16

Orzechowska (2018: 1002), Orzechowska and Ridouane (2018: 540)

of clusters in Slavic languages (Polish, Russian), Germanic languages (English, German) and Tashlhiyt Berber languages reveals tactic patterns of infrasegmental properties specific to individual languages and language families. In all the languages, I have investigated two dimensions which are viewed as exponents of sonority, namely the manner of articulation and voicing. I analysed eight parameters (labelled 'P1–P8') such as cluster size, sonorant / obstruent contrast at cluster or word edges, S/O proportion and voicing characteristics. Table 6.5 provides a synopsis of findings. Statistical weight of parameters is indicated by means of ranks.

The first general observation is that all the languages differ in terms of the ranking of dimensions. That is, the top-most rank is occupied by voicing in Slavic languages, manner-related parameters in German and Berber, or cluster size in English. Second, the importance of parameters varies in each language. For instance, the voicing specification of the prevocalic consonant is an important component of phonotactics in Slavic and Germanic languages, in opposition to Berber. What is more, this feature is particularly important in Slavic languages, in which voice agreement is favoured across all cluster constituents. Also, the distinction between sonorants and obstruents, expressed by the manner of articulation parameter, has an explanatory power only in Berber. Finally, the column '%' indicates a degree, to which a parameter explains the variability in the data. For instance, voice agreement has a predictive power in 47% of initials in Polish and only in 17% of initials in Russian.

Overall, the results—although limited to several parameters only—show that the lexicon in each language operates on a subset of two to four parameters. The differences in the phonological make-up of clusters and the phonotactic potential of the languages are associated with different weight of parameters (P1–P8). 58 English, 54 German, 460 Polish, 327 Russian word-initial clusters and 436 vowelless verbal roots in Tashlhiyt Berber are motivated by a ranked language-specific set of phonological properties. This finding is particularly important for approaches based on well-formedness conditions.

Given its long-standing history and contribution to phonological theory, the role of sonority as a principal driving force for a wide range of phonological phenomena cannot be denied. However, as it turns out, languages are sensitive to different aspects of sonority, be it voicing, sonorant / obstruent contrast or manner distances between adjacent consonants. The S/O distinction corresponds with the undisputed juncture which is captured by all sonority hierarchies, while distances reflect the number of classes found on a scale. Note that the parameters in Table 6.5 disregard the place of articulation dimension. Therefore, another vexing question is related not only to the contribution of specific manner and laryngal features to language-specific sonority hierarchies, but also to place features.

I have demonstrated that, inter alia, (non-)stridency and continuancy play a substantial role in articulation in Polish. In production, the processes of deletion and substitution lead to an increase in the C—V distances and a decrease in the V—C distances, which is partially supported by the psycholinguistic data. Therefore, I conjure that the reformulation of the sonority hierarchy in more fine-grained terms can be critical for the classification of Polish clusters. This goal can be reached by replacing generalizing classes of segments with features or smaller entities. For instance, a sonority scale which subsumes plosives, affricates and fricatives under a single class of obstruents does not account for some casual speech processes such as modifications disfavouring affricates in cluster final position and word-finally. In order to propose a feature-based scale, more research is needed, especially in the domain of syllabification. Given the findings of the analyses in this book, we must acknowledge a possibility that different scales hold for initial and final phonotactics, in line with Clements's (1990) predictions.

My future research will pursue analyses involving a richer set of parameters, phonotactically complex languages and varied methodologies, with a view to discovering the role of the manner, place and laryngeal dimensions in the formation, processing, production and perception of clusters. The main theme of my investigation will be focused on further explorations of tactic patterns of features, elements or smaller properties. I suspect that some of such properties are shared by all languages, while others are specific to a language family or a single language. Some properties are atomic, i.e. imperative for the emergence and preservation of clusters, while others are favoured to different degrees. A study which is exploratory allows for a meticulous analysis of segments forming clusters and larger linguistic units such as syllables and words. Such investigation carries the potential for revealing the structure which is otherwise overshadowed by generalizing principles and researchers' theoretical inclinations.

Naturally, the question is where this quest leads to, and what such basic elements are. They can be, for example, melodic primes or even smaller composite parts of primes. Are they articulatory gestures, half-gestures or approximations? Are they related to directions of articulatory movement or do they correspond to acoustic properties such as intensity? Or maybe they can be expressed in terms of simple mathematical equations or logical implications? The results of the analyses presented in this book have revealed that different features are favoured in different linguistic domains, different positions in a word and even in a cluster. However, it can be the case that true elementary particles hold for all domains (e.g. perception, production), all populations (e.g. healthy, aphasic) and account for the structure of linguistic units outside of phonology (i.e. also morphology and syntax).

Finding a path to the elementary design of phonological systems, languages and Language is a challenge. At this stage, the pursuit of such elementary particles is an attempt at defining something that has never been proven, and something that can be supported only by solid and large-scale research. It is unclear what properties of segments and clusters should be looked into or what tools and methodologies should be applied. Let me speak with the words of a renown anthropologist, Jack Goody (1996): "Terminology that researchers have at their disposal makes it impossible to provide correct answers to questions posed" [translation mine]. In spite of such terminological limitations, it is imperative to search for heretofore undiscovered sources of known and well-defined phenomena. In this book, I have tried to show that the search of the properties motivating the structure of consonant clusters can start at the subsegmental level, as if from scratch. A systematic study of consonant clusters by means of exploratory methods can shed light on whether elementary particles have their well-established place in phonology.

References

Clements, G. N. 1990. The role of the sonority cycle in core syllabification. In *Papers in laboratory phonology vol.* 1: *Between the grammar and physics of speech*, eds. J. Kingston, and M. E. Beckman, 283–333. Cambridge: Cambridge University Press.

Donegan, P.J., and D. Stampe. 2009. Hypotheses of Natural Phonology. *Poznań Studies in Contemporary Linguistics* 45 (1): 1–31.

Goody, J. 1996. *L'homme, l'écriture et la mort. Entretiens avec Pierre-Emmanuel Dauzat*. Paris: Les Belles Lettres.

Hall, T.A. 1997. *The phonology of coronals* [Current issues in linguistic theory 149]. Amsterdam: John Benjamins.

Orzechowska, P. 2016. In search of phonotactic preferences. *Yearbook of the Poznań Linguistic Meeting* 2: 167–193.

Orzechowska, P. 2018. Exponents of sonority in Slavic and Germanic languages. In *Proceedings of the 9th international conference on speech prosody, Poznań*, 13–16 June 2018, eds. Klessa, K., J. Bachan, A. Wagner, M. Karpiński, and D. Śledziński, 999–1003. Poznań: Adam Mickiewicz University.

Orzechowska, P., and R. Ridouane. 2018. The structure of vowelless verbal roots in Tashlhiyt Berber. In *Proceedings of the 9th international conference on speech prosody, Poznań,* 13–16 June 2018, eds. K. Klessa, J. Bachan, A. Wagner, M. Karpiński, and D. Śledziński, 537–541. Poznań: Adam Mickiewicz University.

Paradis, C., and J.-F. Prunet. 1991. *The special status of coronals: Internal and external evidence.* San Diego: Academic Press.

Chapter 7
Conclusions

The goal of this book was to offer a new approach to the study of Polish phonotactics and morphonotactics. The motivation for proposing the volume was to understand phonetic, phonological and morphological characteristics of word-initial and word-final consonant clusters, and to discover mechanisms which underlie their formation, processing and articulation. Traditionally, phonotactics has been analysed from the perspective of universals, generalizations and well-formedness conditions. The principle of sonority has largely monopolized research on consonant clusters over the past century, in spite of challenges it has been confronted with in cluster-rich systems. This gap provides an excellent testing ground for exploratory analyses which seek the motivation for the phonological structure of clusters disregarding whether they are considered to be well-formed or ill-formed.

Sequences of consonants in Polish are probably among the most remarkable ones the Reader has encountered in their linguistic explorations. With this volume, I hope to have shown that hundreds of “unusually long”, “odd-looking”, sonority-violating and morphologically-complex clusters can be viewed as well-structured in terms of the established weights of phonological features and ensuring preferences. An in-depth analysis of clusters makes it possible to discover tactic patterns of phonological features which have not been identified so far. In a language, features differ in importance, which is expressed in terms of numerical weights, rankings and specifications of preferability. The relative importance of features reflects the degree to which they are exploited in phonotactics. The empirical chapters of the book have shown that features display different weights depending on a position in a word, on a position in a cluster, and on a domain of language.

This type of an analysis is captured by the term *featuretactics*, which describes the featural organization of segments forming clusters. The same set of phonological features pertaining to place, manner and voice is universally available to all the languages in the world. However, languages differ in terms of weights allocated

P. Orzechowska, *Complexity in Polish Phonotactics*, Prosody, Phonology and Phonetics, https://doi.org/10.1007/978-981-13-7299-5_7

to these features. For instance, given features X Y Z, some languages make use of feature X in the construction of consonant clusters, while others require a well-defined distribution of Y and Z, resulting in a unique ordering of consonants in strings. The data presented in this book reveal that feature weight relates not only to the structure of the lexicon (Chap. 3), but also to language processing, i.e. to response latencies (Chap. 4) and to modifications in casual speech (Chap. 5).

We have seen that absolute constraints and fine-grained preferences arise from feature weight. A close inspection of the featural organization of consonants within clusters suggests that broad categories of place, manner and voice are exploited differently in phonotactics. In general, at the level of lexical statistics, features pertaining to the manner of articulation play a greater role in the construction of initial clusters, while the place of articulation is a more important building block of final phonotactics. Voicing is relevant at both word edges. At the level of cognitive phonotactics, the place of articulation features outweigh the manner features (i.e. sonority) in both word positions, while in articulatory phonotactics, both place and manner features are relevant. What is more, weights of features lead to positional constraints and preferences. Such preferences are different for initial and final clusters in the lexicon and in articulation. Only at the cognitive level, coherent results have been obtained whereby the same principle of the place of articulation distances, or the combinations of labial and dorsal consonants, facilitates online processing at both word edges.

This method can be viewed as an alternative to sonority. It describes a different fragment of phonotactic reality by accounting for the structure of sequences which sonority does not apply to. The principle of sonority has been defined mainly in terms of the manner of articulation and voicing. The proposed parameters are a convenient way of decomposing sonority into constituent parameters. The findings suggest that sonority, in its present form, can be too general to accurately account for cluster-related phenomena in Polish. It is a matter of speculation that providing a more fine-grained scale which accounts for voicing and place features would be more accurate. The current state of knowledge on the topic is too limited: the role of the place of articulation in Polish phonotactics has not been sufficiently explored. What is more, a different set of predictors could have been exploited in the empirical studies. In order to be able to determine accurately the role of individual phonetic and phonological features in clustering in Polish and cross-linguistically, a series of well-designed experiments is required. This ambitious and large-scale enterprise will be pursued as a part of another project, whose foundations have been presented in this volume.

Appendix A

Classification of all word-initial phonotactic clusters (N = 336) by three sonority scales (ordered according to cluster size and alphabetically): 5-point scale (Rubach and Booij 1990a, b), 6-point scale (Foley 1972), 7-point scale (Goldsmith 1990).

no	cl	son	5	6	7	no	cl	son	5	6	7	no	cl	son	5	6	7
2	bj	OS	+	+	+	2	ʃp	OO	+	–	–	3	kln	OSS	–	–	–
2	bl	OS	+	+	+	2	ʃr	OS	+	+	+	3	klɲ	OSS	–	–	–
2	br	OS	+	+	+	2	ʃt	OO	+	–	–	3	klv	OSO	–	–	–
2	bw	OS	+	+	+	2	ʃʧ	OO	+	–	–	3	kmj	OSS	+	+	+
2	bz	OO	+	+	+	2	ʃw	OS	+	+	+	3	kpj	OOS	+	+	+
2	bʑ	OO	+	+	+	2	ʨf	OO	+	+	+	3	krj	OSS	+	+	+
2	bʒ	OO	+	+	+	2	ʨm	OS	+	+	+	3	krn	OSS	–	–	–
2	ɕf	OO	+	=	=	2	ʨp	OO	+	=	–	3	krt	OSO	–	–	–
2	ɕl	OS	+	+	+	2	tf	OO	+	+	+	3	kʃt	OOO	+	–	–
2	ɕm	OS	+	+	+	2	tj	OS	+	+	+	3	kʃʧ	OOO	+	–	–
2	ɕɲ	OS	+	+	+	2	tk	OO	+	=	=	3	lɕɲ	SOS	–	–	–
2	ɕp	OO	+	–	–	2	tl	OS	+	+	+	3	lgn	SOS	–	–	–
2	ɕr	OS	+	+	+	2	tn	OS	+	+	+	3	lgɲ	SOS	–	–	–
2	ɕʨ	OO	+	–	–	2	tɲ	OS	+	+	+	3	mɕʨ	SOO	–	–	–
2	db	OO	+	=	=	2	tr	OS	+	+	+	3	mdl	SOS	–	–	–
2	dj	OS	+	+	+	2	ts	OO	+	+	+	3	mdw	SOS	–	–	–
2	dl	OS	+	+	+	2	ʦf	OO	+	+	+	3	mgj	SOS	–	–	–
2	dm	OS	+	+	+	2	ʦl	OS	+	+	+	3	mgl	SOS	–	–	–
2	dn	OS	+	+	+	2	ʦm	OS	+	+	+	3	mgɲ	SOS	–	–	–
2	dɲ	OS	+	+	+	2	ʦn	OS	+	+	+	3	mgw	SOS	–	–	–
2	dr	OS	+	+	+	2	ʦw	OS	+	+	+	3	mkn	SOS	–	–	–
2	dv	OO	+	+	+	2	tʃ	OO	+	+	+	3	mkɲ	SOS	–	–	–
2	dw	OS	+	+	+	2	ʧf	OO	+	+	+	3	mst	SOO	–	–	–

(continued)

P. Orzechowska, *Complexity in Polish Phonotactics*, Prosody, Phonology and Phonetics, https://doi.org/10.1007/978-981-13-7299-5

(continued)

no	cl	son	5	6	7	no	cl	son	5	6	7	no	cl	son	5	6	7
2	ʣb	OO	+	=	−	2	ʧk	OO	+	=	−	3	mʃʧ	SOO	−	−	−
2	ʣv	OO	+	+	+	2	ʧm	OS	+	+	+	3	plv	OSO	−	−	−
2	ʥg	OO	+	=	−	2	ʧt	OO	+	=	−	3	prj	OSS	+	+	+
2	ʥv	OO	+	+	+	2	ʧʨ	OO	+	=	=	3	psk	OOO	+	−	−
2	dʒ	OO	+	+	+	2	ʧʧ	OO	+	=	=	3	pʃt	OOO	+	−	−
2	dʒdʒ	OO	+	=	=	2	ʧw	OS	+	+	+	3	pʃʧ	OOO	+	−	−
2	fɕ	OO	+	=	=	2	ʧx	OO	+	+	+	3	pxl	OOS	+	+	+
2	fj	OS	+	+	+	2	tʧ	OO	+	=	+	3	pxw	OOS	+	+	+
2	fl	OS	+	+	+	2	tw	OS	+	+	+	3	rvj	SOS	−	−	−
2	fr.	OS	+	+	+	2	tx	OO	+	+	+	3	rʒn	SOS	−	−	−
2	fʃ	OO	+	=	=	2	vd	OO	+	−	−	3	rʒɲ	SOS	−	−	−
2	ft	OO	+	−	−	2	vʣ	OO	+	−	−	3	sfj	OOS	+	+	+
2	fʧ	OO	+	−	−	2	vʥ	OO	+	−	−	3	skf	OOO	+	−	−
2	gb	OO	+	=	=	2	vj	OS	+	+	+	3	skj	OOS	+	−	−
2	gd	OO	+	=	=	2	vl	OS	+	+	+	3	skl	OOS	+	−	−
2	gʥ	OO	+	=	+	2	vn	OS	+	+	+	3	skn	OOS	+	−	−
2	gj	OS	+	+	+	2	vɲ	OS	+	+	+	3	skr	OOS	+	−	−
2	gl	OS	+	+	+	2	vr	OS	+	+	+	3	skʃ	OOO	+	−	−
2	gm	OS	+	+	+	2	vw	OS	+	+	+	3	smr	OSS	+	+	+
2	gn	OS	+	+	+	2	vz	OO	+	=	=	3	spj	OOS	+	−	−
2	gɲ	OS	+	+	+	2	vʑ	OO	+	=	=	3	spr	OOS	+	−	−
2	gr	OS	+	+	+	2	vʒ	OO	+	=	=	3	spʃ	OOO	+	−	−
2	gv	OO	+	+	+	2	wg	SO	−	−	−	3	stj	OOS	+	−	−
2	gw	OS	+	+	+	2	wk	SO	−	−	−	3	str	OOS	+	−	−
2	gz	OO	+	+	+	2	wz	SO	−	−	−	3	stʦj	OOS	+	−	−
2	gʑ	OO	+	+	+	2	wʑ	SO	−	−	−	3	stʃ	OOO	+	−	−
2	gʒ	OO	+	+	+	2	wʒ	SO	−	−	−	3	sxl	OOS	+	+	+
2	kɕ	OO	+	+	+	2	xf	OO	+	=	=	3	sxn	OOS	+	+	+
2	kf	OO	+	+	+	2	xj	OS	+	+	+	3	sxɲ	OOS	+	+	+
2	kj	OS	+	+	+	2	xl	OS	+	+	+	3	ʃkf	OOO	+	−	−
2	kl	OS	+	+	+	2	xm	OS	+	+	+	3	ʃkj	OOS	+	−	−
2	km	OS	+	+	+	2	xr	OS	+	+	+	3	ʃkl	OOS	+	−	−
2	kn	OS	+	+	+	2	xʃ	OO	+	=	=	3	ʃkr	OOS	+	−	−
2	kɲ	OS	+	+	+	2	xt	OO	+	−	−	3	ʃkw	OOS	+	−	−
2	kp	OO	+	=	=	2	xʨ	OO	+	−	−	3	ʃpj	OOS	+	−	−
2	kr	OS	+	+	+	2	xʦ	OO	+	−	−	3	ʃpr	OOS	+	−	−
2	ks	OO	+	+	+	2	xw	OS	+	+	+	3	ʃtr	OOS	+	−	−
2	kʃ	OO	+	+	+	2	zb	OO	+	−	−	3	ʃʧf	OOO	+	−	−
2	kt	OO	+	=	=	2	zd	OO	+	−	−	3	ʨfj	OOS	+	+	+
2	kʨ	OO	+	=	+	2	zg	OO	+	−	−	3	ʨmj	OSS	+	+	+
2	kʦ	OO	+	=	+	2	zm	OS	+	+	+	3	tfj	OOS	+	+	+
2	kw	OS	+	+	+	2	zn	OS	+	+	+	3	tkf	OOO	+	+	+

(continued)

(continued)

no	cl	son	5	6	7	no	cl	son	5	6	7	no	cl	son	5	6	7
2	lj	SS	+	+	+	2	zr	OS	+	+	+	3	tkl	OOS	+	+	+
2	lʒ	SO	–	–	–	2	zv	OO	+	=	=	3	tkn	OOS	+	+	+
2	mj	SS	+	+	+	2	zw	OS	+	+	+	3	tkɲ	OOS	+	+	+
2	ml	SS	+	+	+	2	zz	OO	+	=	=	3	trf	OSO	–	–	–
2	mn	SS	=	=	=	2	zʥ	OO	+	–	–	3	trj	OSS	+	+	+
2	mɲ	SS	=	=	=	2	ʑl	OS	+	+	+	3	ʦfj	OOS	+	+	+
2	mr	SS	+	+	+	2	ʑr	OS	+	+	+	3	ʦkl	OOS	+	+	–
2	mʃ	SO	–	–	–	2	ʒb	OO	+	–	–	3	ʦkɲ	OOS	+	+	–
2	mʦ	SO	–	–	–	2	ʒd	OO	+	–	–	3	ʧkɲ	OOS	+	+	–
2	mw	SS	+	+	+	2	ʒg	OO	+	–	–	3	tʃn	OOS	+	+	+
2	mʒ	SO	–	–	–	2	ʒl	OS	+	+	+	3	tʃʨ	OOO	+	–	–
2	pɕ	OO	+	+	+	2	ʒm	OS	+	+	+	3	txn	OOS	+	+	+
2	pj	OS	+	+	+	2	ʒɲ	OS	+	+	+	3	txɲ	OOS	+	+	+
2	pl	OS	+	+	+	2	ʒr	OS	+	+	+	3	vbr	OOS	+	–	–
2	pn	OS	+	+	+	2	ʒv	OO	+	=	=	3	vzn	OOS	+	+	+
2	pɲ	OS	+	+	+	2	ʒw	OS	+	+	+	3	vzr	OOS	+	+	+
2	pr	OS	+	+	+	3	brd	OSO	–	–	–	3	vʒd	OOO	+	–	–
2	ps	OO	+	+	+	3	brʥ	OSO	–	–	–	3	xfj	OOS	+	+	+
2	pʃ	OO	+	+	+	3	brn	OSS	–	–	–	3	xmj	OSS	+	+	+
2	pt	OO	+	=	=	3	brɲ	OSS	–	–	–	3	xʃʨ	OOO	+	–	–
2	pʨ	OO	+	=	+	3	bzd	OOO	+	–	–	3	xʃʧ	OOO	+	–	–
2	pw	OS	+	+	+	3	bzʥ	OOO	+	–	–	3	zbr	OOS	+	–	–
2	px	OO	+	+	+	3	bʒd	OOO	+	–	–	3	zdj	OOS	+	–	–
2	rd	SO	–	–	–	3	bʒm	OOS	+	+	+	3	zdr	OOS	+	–	–
2	rʥ	SO	–	–	–	3	ɕfj	OOS	+	+	+	3	zgj	OOS	+	–	–
2	rj	SS	+	+	+	3	ɕmj	OSS	+	+	+	3	zgl	OOS	+	–	–
2	rt	SO	–	–	–	3	ɕpj	OOS	+	–	–	3	zgr	OOS	+	–	–
2	rv	SO	–	–	–	3	dmj	OSS	+	+	+	3	zgʒ	OOO	+	–	–
2	rʒ	SO	–	–	–	3	drg	OSO	–	–	–	3	zmj	OSS	+	+	+
2	sf	OO	+	=	=	3	drj	OSS	+	+	+	3	zvj	OOS	+	+	+
2	sj	OS	+	+	+	3	drv	OSO	–	–	–	3	zvw	OOS	+	+	+
2	sk	OO	+	–	–	3	drʒ	OSO	–	–	–	3	zʥb	OOO	+	–	–
2	sl	OS	+	+	+	3	dvj	OOS	+	+	+	4	bʒmj	OOSS	+	+	+
2	sm	OS	+	+	+	3	ʥvj	OOS	+	+	+	4	drvj	OSOS	–	–	–
2	sn	OS	+	+	+	3	dʒv	OOO	+	+	+	4	dʒvj	OOOS	+	+	+
2	sp	OO	+	–	–	3	fɕʨ	OOO	+	–	–	4	gʒbj	OOOS	+	–	–
2	sr	OS	+	+	+	3	fkl	OOS	+	–	–	4	gʒmj	OOSS	+	+	+
2	ss	OO	+	=	=	3	fkr	OOS	+	–	–	4	pstr	OOOS	+	–	–
2	st	OO	+	–	–	3	fkʃ	OOO	+	–	–	4	skfj	OOOS	+	–	–
2	sʦ	OO	+	–	–	3	fsp	OOO	+	–	–	4	skrf	OOSO	–	–	–
2	sw	OS	+	+	+	3	fst	OOO	+	–	–	4	ʃtfj	OOOS	+	–	–
2	sx	OO	+	=	=	3	fʃʧ	OOO	+	–	–	4	tkfj	OOOS	+	+	+

(continued)

(continued)

no	cl	son	5	6	7	no	cl	son	5	6	7	no	cl	son	5	6	7
2	ʃf	OO	+	=	=	3	grd	OSO	−	−	−	4	tʃmj	OOSS	+	+	+
2	ʃk	OO	+	−	−	3	gvd	OOO	+	−	−	4	tʃpj	OOOS	+	−	−
2	ʃl	OS	+	+	+	3	gvj	OOS	+	+	+	4	vzdr	OOOS	+	−	−
2	ʃm	OS	+	+	+	3	gʒm	OOS	+	+	+	4	zʥbl	OOOS	+	−	−
2	ʃn	OS	+	+	+	3	kfj	OOS	+	+	+	4	zʥbw	OOOS	+	−	−

'+' refers to SSG-obeying, '−' refers to SSG-violating, '=' refers to plateau

References

Foley, J. 1972. Rule precursors and phonological change by meta-rule. In *Linguistic change and generative theory*, eds. R. Stockwell, and R. Macauley, 96–100. Bloomington: Indiana

Goldsmith, J.A. 1990. *Autosegmental and metrical phonology*. Oxford: Blackwell.

Rubach, J., and G. Booij. 1990a. Syllable structure assignment in Polish. *Phonology* 7: 121–158.

Rubach, J., and G. Booij. 1990b. Edge of constituent effects in Polish. *Natural Language and Linguistic Theory* 8 (3): 427–463.

Appendix B

Classification of all word-final phonotactic clusters (N = 131) by three sonority scales (ordered according to cluster size and alphabetically): 5-point scale (Rubach and Booij 1990a, b), 6-point scale (Foley 1972), 7-point scale (Goldsmith 1990).

no	cl	son	5	6	7	no	cl	son	5	6	7	no	cl	son	5	6	7
2	ɕl	OS	–	–	–	2	nʦ	SO	+	+	+	2	wp	SO	+	+	+
2	ɕɲ	OS	–	–	–	2	nʧ	SO	+	+	+	2	wr	SS	+	+	+
2	ɕʨ	OO	+	+	+	2	ɲʨ	SO	+	+	+	2	w̃s	SO	+	+	+
2	fk	OO	+	+	+	2	ɲʦ	SO	+	+	+	2	ws	SO	+	+	+
2	fl	OS	–	–	–	2	ŋk	SO	+	+	+	2	w̃ʃ	SO	+	+	+
2	fn	OS	–	–	–	2	pl	OS	–	–	–	2	wʃ	SO	+	+	+
2	fr	OS	–	–	–	2	pɲ	OS	–	–	–	2	wt	SO	+	+	+
2	ft	OO	+	+	+	2	pr	OS	–	–	–	2	wʨ	SO	+	+	+
2	fʦ	OO	+	+	+	2	ps	OO	+	–	–	2	wʧ	SO	+	+	+
2	ȷ̂ɕ	SO	+	+	+	2	pʃ	OO	+	–	–	2	w̃x	SO	+	+	+
2	jf	SO	+	+	+	2	pt	OO	+	=	=	2	wx	SO	+	+	+
2	jk	SO	+	+	+	2	rɕ	SO	+	+	+	2	xʃ	OO	+	=	=
2	jl	SS	+	+	+	2	rf	SO	+	+	+	2	xt	OO	+	+	+
2	jm	SS	+	+	+	2	rk	SO	+	+	+	3	ȷ̂ɕʨ	SOO	+	+	+
2	jn	SS	+	+	+	2	rm	SS	+	+	+	3	jnt	SSO	+	+	+
2	js	SO	+	+	+	2	rn	SS	+	+	+	3	ȷ̂sk	SOO	+	+	+
2	jt	SO	+	+	+	2	rɲ	SS	+	+	+	3	jst	SOO	+	+	+
2	jʦ	SO	+	+	+	2	rp	SO	+	+	+	3	kst	OOO	–	–	–
2	jʧ	SO	+	+	+	2	rs	SO	+	+	+	3	lɕɲ	SOS	–	–	–
2	jx	SO	+	+	+	2	rʃ	SO	+	+	+	3	lft	SOO	+	+	+
2	kl	OS	–	–	–	2	rt	SO	+	+	+	3	lsk	SOO	+	+	+
2	kr	OS	–	–	–	2	rʨ	SO	+	+	+	3	ltr	SOS	–	–	–

(continued)

P. Orzechowska, *Complexity in Polish Phonotactics*, Prosody, Phonology and Phonetics, https://doi.org/10.1007/978-981-13-7299-5

(continued)

no	cl	son	5	6	7	no	cl	son	5	6	7	no	cl	son	5	6	7
2	ks	OO	+	−	−	2	rʦ	SO	+	+	+	3	mpl	SOS	−	−	−
2	kt	OO	+	=	=	2	rʧ	SO	+	+	+	3	mpr	SOS	−	−	−
2	kx	OO	+	−	−	2	rx	SO	+	+	+	3	mpt	SOO	+	+	+
2	lf	SO	+	+	+	2	sk	OO	+	+	+	3	ntr	SOS	−	−	−
2	lk	SO	+	+	+	2	sm	OS	−	−	−	3	ntʃ	SOO	−	−	−
2	lm	SS	+	+	+	2	st	OO	+	+	+	3	ŋkr	SOS	−	−	−
2	lp	SO	+	+	+	2	sw	OS	−	−	−	3	ŋks	SOO	−	−	−
2	ls	SO	+	+	+	2	ʃp	OO	+	+	+	3	ŋkt	SOO	+	+	+
2	lʃ	SO	+	+	+	2	ʃt	OO	+	+	+	3	psk	OOO	+	−	−
2	lt	SO	+	+	+	2	ʃʧ	OO	+	+	+	3	rɕʨ	SOO	+	+	+
2	lʦ	SO	+	+	+	2	ʃx	OO	+	=	=	3	rsk	SOO	+	+	+
2	lx	SO	+	+	+	2	tf	OO	+	−	−	3	rʃt	SOO	+	+	+
2	mf	SO	+	+	+	2	tl	OS	−	−	−	3	rʃʧ	SOO	+	+	+
2	mn	SS	=	=	=	2	tm	OS	−	−	−	3	stm	OOS	−	−	−
2	mp	SO	+	+	+	2	tr	OS	−	−	−	3	str	OOS	−	−	−
2	ms	SO	+	+	+	2	ʦk	OO	+	=	+	3	stʃ	OOO	−	−	−
2	mʃ	SO	+	+	+	2	tw	OS	−	−	−	3	wnt	SSO	+	+	+
2	nf	SO	+	+	+	2	wf	SO	+	+	+	3	wst	SOO	+	+	+
2	nr	SS	−	−	−	2	wk	SO	+	+	+	3	w̃ʃt	SOO	+	+	+
2	ns	SO	+	+	+	2	wl	SS	+	+	+	3	w̃ʃʧ	SOO	+	+	+
2	nʃ	SO	+	+	+	2	wm	SS	+	+	+	3	xtr	OOS	−	−	−
2	nt	SO	+	+	+	2	wn	SS	+	+	+						

'+' refers to SSG-obeying, '−' refers to SSG-violating, '=' refers to plateau

References

Foley, J. 1972. Rule precursors and phonological change by meta-rule. In *Linguistic change and generative theory*, eds. R. Stockwell, and R. Macauley, 96–100. Bloomington: Indiana

Goldsmith, J.A. 1990. *Autosegmental and metrical phonology*. Oxford: Blackwell.

Rubach, J., and G. Booij. 1990a. Syllable structure sssignment in Polish. *Phonology* 7: 121–158.

Rubach, J., and G. Booij. 1990b. Edge of constituent effects in Polish. *Natural Language and Linguistic Theory* 8 (3): 427–463.

Appendix C

Classification of all word-initial phonotactic clusters (N = 321) in terms of NAD. The NAD product is given in the column 'NAD'.

no	cl	NAD	Pref.	no	cl	NAD	Pref.	no	cl	NAD	Pref.
2	bj	5	+	2	ʃf	−4.2	−	3	fkr	2.7	+
2	bl	2	+	2	ʃk	−3.8	−	3	fkʃ	−1.8	−
2	br	3.3	+	2	ʃl	0.3	+	3	fsp	−1.25	−
2	bw	4.25	+	2	ʃm	0.3	+	3	fst	−2.25	−
2	bz	−3	−	2	ʃn	−0.7	−	3	fʃʧ	−2.65	−
2	bʑ	−2.4	−	2	ʃp	−3.7	−	3	grd	−1.3	−
2	bʒ	−2.7	−	2	ʃr	1	+	3	gvd	−3	−
2	ɕf	−3.9	−	2	ʃt	−4.7	−	3	gvj	2.75	+
2	ɕl	0.6	+	2	ʃʧ	−5	−	3	gʒm	0.7	+
2	ɕm	0.6	+	2	ʃw	2.05	+	3	kfj	2.75	+
2	ɕɲ	−1	−	2	ʨf	−3.4	−	3	kln	−3.5	−
2	ɕp	−3.4	−	2	ʨm	1.1	+	3	klɲ	−2.9	−
2	ɕr	1.3	+	2	ʨp	−3.9	−	3	klv	−2	−
2	ɕʨ	−5	−	2	tf	−3.5	−	3	kmj	0	−
2	db	−5	−	2	tj	4	+	3	kpj	4.5	+
2	dj	4	+	2	tk	−4.5	−	3	krj	−2.15	−
2	dl	1	+	2	tl	1	+	3	krn	−2.8	−
2	dm	1	+	2	tn	0	+	3	krt	−1.3	−
2	dn	0	+	2	tɲ	0.6	+	3	kʃt	−2.8	−
2	dɲ	0.6	+	2	tr	2.3	+	3	kʃʧ	−3.35	−
2	dr	2.3	+	2	ts	−4	−	3	lɕɲ	−1.05	−
2	dv	−3.5	−	2	ʦf	−4	−	3	lgn	0.5	−
2	dw	3.25	+	2	ʦl	0.5	+	3	lgɲ	−0.1	−

(continued)

P. Orzechowska, *Complexity in Polish Phonotactics*, Prosody, Phonology and Phonetics, https://doi.org/10.1007/978-981-13-7299-5

(continued)

no	cl	NAD	Pref.	no	cl	NAD	Pref.	no	cl	NAD	Pref.
2	ʣb	−4.5	−	2	ʦm	0.5	+	3	mɕtɕ	−4.05	−
2	ʣv	−4	−	2	ʦn	−0.5	−	3	mdl	0.25	−
2	ʥg	−4.6	−	2	ʦw	2.75	+	3	mdw	2	+
2	ʥv	−3.4	−	2	tʃ	−3.7	−	3	mgj	1.5	−
2	dʒ	−3.7	−	2	ʧf	−3.7	−	3	mgl	1	−
2	ʤʤ	−5.5	−	2	ʧk	−4.3	−	3	mgɲ	−0.35	−
2	fɕ	−3.9	−	2	ʧm	0.8	+	3	mgw	2.25	+
2	fj	3.5	+	2	ʧt	−5.2	−	3	mkn	0.25	−
2	fl	0.5	+	2	ʧtɕ	−5.2	−	3	mkɲ	−0.35	−
2	fr.	1.8	+	2	ʧʧ	−5.5	−	3	mst	−3.5	−
2	fʃ	−4.2	−	2	ʧw	2.55	+	3	mʃʧ	−3.9	−
2	ft	−4.5	−	2	ʧx	−3.3	−	3	plv	−1.75	−
2	fʧ	−4.2	−	2	tʧ	−4.7	−	3	prj	−2.2	−
2	gb	−3.5	−	2	tw	3.25	+	3	psk	−1.5	−
2	gd	−4.5	−	2	tx	−2.5	−	3	pʃt	−2.85	−
2	gʥ	−4.1	−	2	vd	−4.5	−	3	pʃʧ	−3.4	−
2	gj	3.5	+	2	vʣ	−4.5	−	3	pxl	1	+
2	gl	2.5	+	2	vʥ	−3.9	−	3	pxw	2.25	+
2	gm	2.5	+	2	vj	3.5	+	3	rvj	2.35	+
2	gn	1.5	+	2	vl	0.5	+	3	rʒn	−0.7	−
2	gɲ	0.9	+	2	vn	−0.5	−	3	rʒɲ	−0.7	−
2	gr	3.2	+	2	vɲ	0.1	+	3	sfj	4	+
2	gv	−2	−	2	vr	1.8	+	3	skf	−0.75	−
2	gw	4.25	+	2	vw	2.75	+	3	skj	3	+
2	gz	−2.5	−	2	vz	−4.5	−	3	skl	2.5	+
2	gʑ	−3.1	−	2	vʑ	−3.9	−	3	skn	1.75	+
2	gʒ	−2.8	−	2	vʒ	−4.2	−	3	skr	2.95	+
2	kɕ	−3.1	−	2	wg	−0.25	−	3	skʃ	−1.55	−
2	kf	−2	−	2	wk	−0.25	−	3	smr	−0.2	−
2	kj	3.5	+	2	wz	−1.25	−	3	spj	4.75	+
2	kl	2.5	+	2	wʑ	−1.15	−	3	spr	3.3	+
2	km	2.5	+	2	wʒ	−1.45	−	3	spʃ	−1.2	−
2	kn	1.5	+	2	xf	−3	−	3	stj	4.25	+
2	kɲ	0.9	+	2	xj	2.5	+	3	str	2.8	+
2	kp	−3.5	−	2	xl	1.5	+	3	sʦj	4	+
2	kr	3.2	+	2	xm	1.5	+	3	stʃ	−1.7	−
2	ks	−2.5	−	2	xr	2.2	+	3	sxl	2	+
2	kʃ	−2.8	−	2	xʃ	−3.8	−	3	sxn	1.25	+
2	kt	−4.5	−	2	xt	−3.5	−	3	sxɲ	0.65	−
2	ktɕ	−4.1	−	2	xtɕ	−4.1	−	3	ʃkf	−0.6	−

(continued)

(continued)

no	cl	NAD	Pref.	no	cl	NAD	Pref.	no	cl	NAD	Pref.
2	kʦ	−3.5	−	2	xʦ	−3.5	−	3	ʃkj	3.15	+
2	kw	4.25	+	2	xw	3.25	+	3	ʃkl	2.65	+
2	lj	0.5	+	2	zb	−4	−	3	ʃkr	3.1	+
2	lʒ	−2.2	−	2	zd	−5	−	3	ʃkw	3.9	+
2	mj	2	+	2	zg	−3.5	−	3	ʃpj	4.6	+
2	ml	−1	−	2	zm	0	+	3	ʃpr	3.15	+
2	mn	−2	−	2	zn	−1	−	3	ʃtr	2.65	+
2	mɲ	−1.4	−	2	zr	1.3	+	3	ʃʧf	−1.45	−
2	mr	0.3	+	2	zv	−4.5	−	3	ʨfj	3.45	+
2	mʃ	−1.7	−	2	zw	2.25	+	3	ʨmj	0.7	−
2	mʦ	−2	−	2	zz	−5	−	3	tfj	3.5	+
2	mw	1.25	+	2	ʑʥ	−5	−	3	tkf	−0.25	−
2	mʒ	−1.7	−	2	ʑl	0.6	+	3	tkl	3	+
2	pɕ	−2.4	−	2	ʑr	1.3	+	3	tkn	2.25	+
2	pj	5	+	2	ʒb	−3.7	−	3	tkɲ	1.65	+
2	pl	2	+	2	ʒd	−4.7	−	3	trf	−0.85	−
2	pn	1	+	2	ʒg	−3.8	−	3	trj	−1.7	−
2	pɲ	1.6	+	2	ʒl	0.3	+	3	ʦfj	3.75	+
2	pr	3.3	+	2	ʒm	0.3	+	3	ʦkl	2.75	+
2	ps	−3	−	2	ʒɲ	−0.7	−	3	ʦkɲ	1.4	+
2	pʃ	−2.7	−	2	ʒr	1	+	3	ʧkɲ	1.55	+
2	pt	−5	−	2	ʒv	−4.2	−	3	tʃn	0.15	−
2	pʨ	−3.4	−	2	ʒw	2.05	+	3	tʃʨ	−2.6	−
2	pw	4.25	+	2	brd	−1.35	−	3	txn	0.75	+
2	px	−1.5	−	3	brʥ	−1.6	−	3	txɲ	0.15	−
2	rd	−1.7	−	3	brn	−2.85	−	3	vbr	3.55	+
2	rʣ	−1.7	−	3	brɲ	−2.85	−	3	vzn	0.25	−
2	rj	−0.3	−	3	bzd	−3	−	3	vzr	2.05	+
2	rt	−1.7	−	3	bʑʥ	−3.55	−	3	vʒd	−2.1	−
2	rv	−1.2	−	3	bʒd	−2.85	−	3	xfj	3.25	+
2	rʒ	−2	−	3	bʒm	0.65	+	3	xmj	0.5	−
2	sf	−4.5	−	3	ɕfj	3.7	+	3	xʃʨ	−2.55	−
2	sj	3	+	3	ɕmj	0.95	−	3	xʃʧ	−2.85	−
2	sk	−3.5	−	3	ɕpj	4.45	+	3	zbr	3.3	+
2	sl	0	+	3	dmj	0.75	−	3	zdj	4.25	+
2	sm	0	+	3	drg	0.05	−	3	zdr	2.8	+
2	sn	−1	−	3	drj	−1.7	−	3	zgj	3	+
2	sp	−4	−	3	drv	−0.85	−	3	zgl	2.5	+
2	sr	1.3	+	3	drʒ	−1.65	−	3	zgr	2.95	+
2	ss	−5	−	3	dvj	3.5	+	3	zgʒ	−1.55	−

(continued)

(continued)

no	cl	NAD	Pref.	no	cl	NAD	Pref.	no	cl	NAD	Pref.
2	st	−5	−	3	ʥvj	3.45	+	3	zmj	1.25	+
2	sts	−5	−	3	dʒv	−2.35	−	3	zvj	4	+
2	sw	2.25	+	3	fɕʨ	−2.8	−	3	zvw	3.25	+
2	sx	−3.5	−	3	fkl	2.25	+	3	zʥb	−1.15	−

'+' refers to preferred clusters, '−' refers to dispreferred clusters

Appendix D

Classification of all word-initial morphonotactic clusters (N = 172) in terms of NAD. The NAD product is given in the column 'NAD'.

no	cl	NAD	Pref.	no	cl	NAD	Pref.	no	cl	NAD	Pref.
2	bz	5	–	2	zv	5	–	3	sxj	1.5	+
2	ɕtɕ	5.5	–	2	zw	1.5	+	3	sxl	2.5	+
2	dɲ	3	+	2	zz	5	–	3	sxr	2	+
2	fɕ	5	–	2	zʑ	5	–	3	sxʃ	5	–
2	fk	6	–	2	zʒ	5	–	3	sxw	1.5	+
2	fp	6	–	3	brv	5	–	3	ʃfj	1.5	+
2	fs	5	–	3	ʥgn	3	+	3	ʧkn	3	+
2	fʃ	5	–	3	ʥgɲ	3	+	3	vbj	1.5	+
2	ft	6	–	3	fɕl	2.5	+	3	vdm	3	+
2	fʨ	5.5	–	3	fɕr	2	+	3	vdr	2	+
2	fʦ	5.5	–	3	fkr	2	+	3	vgj	1.5	+
2	fʧ	5.5	–	3	fkw	1.5	+	3	vgl	2.5	+
2	fx	5	–	3	fpj	1.5	+	3	vgɲ	3	+
2	ln	3	–	3	fpl	2.5	+	3	vgr	2	+
2	lɲ	3	–	3	fpr	2	+	3	vgw	1.5	+
2	lv	5	–	3	fpʃ	5	–	3	vgʒ	5	–
2	mx	5	–	3	fpw	1.5	+	3	vmj	1.5	+
2	pɕ	5	–	3	fsk	6	–	3	vvj	1.5	+
2	pɲ	3	+	3	fsp	6	–	3	vzb	6	–
2	ps	5	–	3	fsʃ	5	–	3	vzd	6	–
2	sɕ	5	–	3	fst	6	–	3	vzg	6	–
2	sf	5	–	3	fsw	1.5	+	3	vzl	2.5	+
2	sk	6	–	3	fsx	5	–	3	vzm	3	+

(continued)

P. Orzechowska, *Complexity in Polish Phonotactics*, Prosody, Phonology and Phonetics, https://doi.org/10.1007/978-981-13-7299-5

(continued)

no	cl	NAD	Pref.	no	cl	NAD	Pref.	no	cl	NAD	Pref.
2	sn	3	–	3	fʃʧ	5.5	–	3	vzn	3	–
2	sp	6	–	3	ftr	2	+	3	vzɲ	3	–
2	ss	5	–	3	ftʃ	5	–	3	vzr	2	+
2	sʃ	5	–	3	ftw	1.5	+	3	vzv	5	–
2	st	6	–	3	fxw	1.5	+	3	wbj	1.5	+
2	sʦ	5.5	–	3	krf	5	–	3	xʃt	6	–
2	sʧ	5.5	–	3	lvj	1.5	+	3	zbj	1.5	+
2	sx	5	–	3	pwʨ	5.5	–	3	zbl	2.5	+
2	ʃf	5	–	3	pxn	3	–	3	zbr	2	+
2	vb	6	–	3	pxɲ	3	–	3	zbw	1.5	+
2	vd	6	–	3	sfl	2.5	+	3	zbʑ	5	–
2	vʥ	5.5	–	3	sfr	2	+	3	zbʒ	5	–
2	vg	6	–	3	skf	5	–	3	zdj	1.5	+
2	vj	1.5	+	3	skj	1.5	+	3	zdm	3	+
2	vl	2.5	+	3	skl	2.5	+	3	zdr	2	+
2	vm	3	–	3	skn	3	+	3	zdv	5	–
2	vn	3	–	3	skr	2	+	3	zdw	1.5	+
2	vɲ	3	+	3	sks	5	–	3	zʥv	5	–
2	vr	2	+	3	skʃ	5	–	3	zdʒ	5	–
2	vv	5	–	3	skw	1.5	+	3	zgj	1.5	+
2	vw	1.5	+	3	spɕ	5	–	3	zgn	3	+
2	vz	5	–	3	spj	1.5	+	3	zgɲ	3	+
2	vʒ	5	–	3	spl	2.5	+	3	zgr	2	+
2	wb	6	–	3	spr	2	+	3	zgv	5	–
2	zb	6	–	3	spʃ	5	–	3	zgw	1.5	+
2	zd	6	–	3	spw	1.5	+	3	zgʒ	5	–
2	zʥ	5.5	–	3	sst	6	–	3	zmj	1.5	+
2	zg	6	–	3	stf	5	–	3	zmɲ	3	–
2	zj	1.5	+	3	stl	2.5	+	3	zmr	2	–
2	zl	2.5	+	3	str	2	+	3	zmw	1.5	–
2	zm	3	+	3	stʃ	5	–	3	zvj	1.5	+
2	zn	3	–	3	stw	1.5	+	3	zvl	2.5	+
2	zɲ	3	–	3	stx	5	–	3	zvr	2	+
2	zr	2	+	3	sxf	5	–	3	zvw	1.5	+
								3	ʒgn	3	+

'+' refers to preferred clusters, '–' refers to dispreferred clusters

Appendix E

Classification of all word-final phonotactic clusters (N = 131) in terms of NAD. The NAD product is given in the column 'NAD'.

no	cl	NAD	Pref.	no	cl	NAD	Pref.	no	cl	NAD	Pref.
2	ɕl	−1.9	−	2	nʦ	−0.5	−	2	wp	4.25	+
2	ɕɲ	−3	−	2	nʧ	−0.2	−	2	wr	−0.95	−
2	ɕʨ	−4.5	−	2	ɲʨ	−0.5	−	2	w̃s	3.25	+
2	fk	−2	−	2	ɲʦ	0.1	+	2	ws	2.25	+
2	fl	−2	−	2	ŋk	0	+	2	w̃ʃ	3.05	+
2	fn	−2.5	−	2	pl	−1.5	−	2	wʃ	2.05	+
2	fr	−1.2	−	2	pɲ	−1.4	−	2	wt	3.25	+
2	ft	−3.5	−	2	pr	−0.7	−	2	wʨ	2.85	+
2	fʦ	−4	−	2	ps	−4	−	2	wʧ	2.55	+
2	j̃ɕ	3.4	+	2	pʃ	−3.7	−	2	w̃x	3.25	+
2	jf	3.5	+	2	pt	−5	−	2	wx	3.25	+
2	jk	3.5	+	2	rɕ	1.3	+	2	xʃ	−3.8	−
2	jl	0.5	+	2	rf	1.8	+	2	xt	−2.5	−
2	jm	2	+	2	rk	3.2	+	3	ĵɕʨ	3.65	+
2	jn	1	+	2	rm	0.3	+	3	jnt	0.25	−
2	js	3	+	2	rn	−0.7	−	3	j̃sk	3.25	+
2	jt	4	+	2	rɲ	−0.7	−	3	jst	3.25	+
2	jʦ	3.5	+	2	rp	3.3	+	3	kst	−1	−
2	jʧ	3.2	+	2	rs	1.3	+	3	lɕɲ	0.85	+
2	jx	2.5	+	2	rʃ	1	+	3	lft	1	+
2	kl	−1	−	2	rt	2.3	+	3	lsk	0	−
2	kr	−0.8	−	2	rʨ	1.8	+	3	ltr	0.1	−
2	ks	−3.5	−	2	rʦ	1.8	+	3	mpl	−0.75	−

(continued)

P. Orzechowska, *Complexity in Polish Phonotactics*, Prosody, Phonology and Phonetics, https://doi.org/10.1007/978-981-13-7299-5

(continued)

no	cl	NAD	Pref.	no	cl	NAD	Pref.	no	cl	NAD	Pref.
2	kt	−4.5	−	2	rʧ	1.5	+	3	mpr	−1.15	−
2	kx	−5	−	2	rx	2.2	+	3	mpt	1	+
2	lf	0.5	+	2	sk	−2.5	−	3	ntr	−0.65	−
2	lk	2.5	+	2	sm	−2	−	3	ntʃ	0.85	+
2	lm	−1	−	2	st	−4	−	3	ŋkr	−1.1	−
2	lp	2	+	2	sw	−1.25	−	3	ŋks	0.25	+
2	ls	0	+	2	ʃp	−2.7	−	3	ŋkt	0.75	+
2	lʃ	0.3	+	2	ʃt	−3.7	−	3	psk	−2.25	−
2	lt	1	+	2	ʃʧ	−4.5	−	3	rɕʨ	2.05	+
2	lʦ	0.5	+	2	ʃx	−3.8	−	3	rsk	1.05	+
2	lx	1.5	+	2	tf	−4.5	−	3	rʃt	1.35	+
2	mf	−0.5	−	2	tl	−2.5	−	3	rʃʧ	1.75	+
2	mn	−2	−	2	tm	−2	−	3	stm	−3.5	−
2	mp	0	+	2	tr	−1.7	−	3	str	−3.65	−
2	ms	0	+	2	ʦk	−3.5	−	3	stʃ	−2.15	−
2	mʃ	0.3	+	2	tw	−1.25	−	3	wnt	−0.5	−
2	nf	−0.5	−	2	wf	2.75	+	3	wst	2.5	+
2	nr	−1.7	−	2	wk	4.25	+	3	w̃ʃt	2.9	+
2	ns	−1	−	2	wl	−0.25	−	3	w̃ʃʧ	3.3	+
2	nʃ	−0.7	−	2	wm	1.25	+	3	xtr	−2.15	−
2	nt	0	+	2	wn	0.25	+				

'+' refers to preferred clusters, '−' refers to dispreferred clusters

Appendix F

Classification of all word-final morphonotactic clusters (N = 97) in terms of NAD. The NAD product is given in the column 'NAD'.

no	cl	NAD	Pref.	no	cl	NAD	Pref.	no	cl	NAD	Pref.
2	ɕl	−1.9	–	2	ɲʨ	−0.5	–	2	tm	−2	–
2	ɕm	−1.4	–	2	ɲʧ	−0.2	–	2	tr	−1.7	–
2	ɕp	−2.4	–	2	ŋk	0	+	2	tʃ	−4.7	–
2	ɕʨ	−4.5	–	2	pr	−0.7	–	2	ʧp	−3.7	–
2	fr	−1.2	–	2	ps	−4	–	2	ʧt	−4.7	–
2	ft	−3.5	–	2	pt	−5	–	2	tw	−1.25	–
2	fʨ	−3.4	–	2	pʧ	−4.2	–	2	wn	0.25	+
2	fʦ	−4	–	2	rf	1.8	+	2	wp	4.25	+
2	jɕ	2.4	+	2	rk	3.2	+	2	w̃s	3.25	+
2	jm	2	+	2	rm	0.3	+	2	w̃ʃ	3.05	+
2	jt	4	+	2	rn	−0.7	–	2	wt	3.25	+
2	jʨ	2.9	+	2	rɲ	−0.7	–	2	xɕ	−4.1	–
2	jʦ	3.5	+	2	rp	3.3	+	2	xm	−0.5	–
2	jx	2.5	+	2	rs	1.3	+	2	xt	−2.5	–
2	kf	−3	–	2	rʃ	1	+	3	jɕʨ	2.9	+
2	km	−0.5	–	2	rt	2.3	+	3	j̃ɕʨ	3.65	+
2	kr	−0.8	–	2	rʨ	1.8	+	3	jsk	2.5	+
2	kt	−4.5	–	2	rʦ	1.8	+	3	jsʦ	3.5	+
2	kw	−0.25	–	2	rʧ	1.5	+	3	lsk	0	–
2	lf	0.5	+	2	rw	−1.45	–	3	mst	1	+
2	lk	2.5	+	2	sf	−4.5	–	3	ntf	0.75	+
2	lm	−1	–	2	sk	−2.5	–	3	ntr	−0.65	–
2	lɲ	−1.4	–	2	sm	−2	–	3	ntʃ	0.85	+

(continued)

P. Orzechowska, *Complexity in Polish Phonotactics*, Prosody, Phonology and Phonetics, https://doi.org/10.1007/978-981-13-7299-5

(continued)

no	cl	NAD	Pref.	no	cl	NAD	Pref.	no	cl	NAD	Pref.
2	lp	2	+	2	sn	−3	–	3	psk	−2.25	–
2	ls	0	+	2	sp	−3	–	3	rst	1.8	+
2	lt	1	+	2	st	−4	–	3	rʃʧ	1.75	+
2	lʧ	0.8	+	2	sw	−1.25	–	3	rtf	2.55	+
2	mɕ	0.6	+	2	ʃp	−2.7	–	3	stf	−2.25	–
2	mn	−2	–	2	ʃt	−3.7	–	3	str	−3.65	–
2	mp	0	+	2	ʃʧ	−4.5	–	3	ʃtr	−3.35	–
2	nt	0	+	2	tf	−4.5	–	3	ʦtf	−3	–
2	nʦ	−0.5	–	2	tl	−2.5	–	3	wnt	−0.5	–
2	nʧ	−0.2	–								

'+' refers to preferred clusters, '–' refers to dispreferred clusters

Appendix G

Stimuli used in Experiment 1: Nonce words containing initial CC clusters.

cl	POA	/es/	/ot/	/um/	cl	POA	/es/	/ot/	/um/
Non-existent well-formed words					*Existent well-formed words*				
pm	0	pmes	pmot	pmum	ɕɲ	0	ɕɲes	ɕɲot	ɕɲum
ʦs	0	ʦses	ʦsot	ʦsum	dl	0	dles	dlot	dlum
dʣ	0	dʣes	dʣot	dʣum	tl	0	tles	tlot	tlum
fm	1	fmes	fmot	fmum	ʣv	1	ʣves	ʣvot	ʣvum
ʥr	1	ʥres	ʥrot	ʥrum	tr	1	tres	trot	trum
nr	1	nres	nrot	nrum	vm	1	vmes	vmot	vmum
bʣ	2	bʣes	bʣot	bʣum	bz	2	bzes	bzot	bzum
ʨx	2	ʨxes	ʨxot	ʨxum	pn	2	pnes	pnot	pnum
ʥɲ	2	ʥɲes	ʥɲot	ʥɲum	dɲ	2	dɲes	dɲot	dɲum
ʤm	3	ʤmes	ʤmot	ʤmum	ʃm	3	ʃmes	ʃmot	ʃmum
kʧ	3	kʧes	kʧot	kʧum	lj	3	ljes	ljot	ljum
xʒ	3	xʒes	xʒot	xʒum	br	3	bres	brot	brum
xn	4	xnes	xnot	xnum	fj	4	fjes	fjot	fjum
ʦx	4	ʦxes	ʦxot	ʦxum	bʑ	4	bʑes	bʑot	bʑum
pʨ	4	pʨes	pʨot	pʨum	kl	4	kles	klot	klum
vŋ	5	vŋes	vŋot	vŋum	gv	5	gves	gvot	gvum
kv	5	kves	kvot	kvum	pj	5	pjas	pjot	pjum
gf	5	gfes	gfot	gfum	kf	5	kfes	kfet	kfum
bŋ	6	bŋes	bŋot	bŋum	gm	6	gmes	gmot	gmum
bx	6	bxes	bxot	bxum	px	6	pxes	pxot	pxum
pŋ	6	pŋes	pŋot	pŋum	xm	6	xmes	xmot	xmum

(continued)

P. Orzechowska, *Complexity in Polish Phonotactics*, Prosody, Phonology and Phonetics, https://doi.org/10.1007/978-981-13-7299-5

(continued)

cl	POA	/es/	/ot/	/um/	cl	POA	/es/	/ot/	/um/
Non-existent ill-formed words					*Existent ill-formed words*				
mp	0	mpes	mpot	mpum	ʑʥ	0	ʑʥes	ʑʥot	ʑʥum
xk	0	xkes	xkot	xkum	ln	0	lnes	lnot	lnum
rʃ	0	rʃes	rʃot	rʃum	ɕʨ	0	ɕʨes	ɕʨot	ɕʨum
mf	1	mfes	mfot	mfum	ʧt	1	ʧtes	ʧtot	ʧtum
rd	1	rdes	rdot	rdum	rt	1	rtes	rtot	rtum
rʑ	1	rʑes	rʑot	rʑum	lv	1	lves	lvot	lvum
ʦʨ	2	ʦʨes	ʦʨot	ʦʨum	pt	2	ptes	ptot	ptum
mz	2	mzes	mzot	mzum	lɲ	2	lɲes	lɲot	lɲum
ʦp	2	ʦpes	ʦpot	ʦpum	zʥ	2	zʥes	zʥot	zʥum
mʤ	3	mʤes	mʤot	mʤum	mʒ	3	mʒes	mʒot	mʒum
xʧ	3	xʧes	xʧot	xʧum	ʃp	3	ʃpes	ʃpot	ʃpum
nk	3	nkes	nkot	nkum	fʨ	3	fʨes	fʨot	fʨum
nx	4	nxes	nxot	nxum	xt	4	xtes	xtot	xtum
ʣg	4	ʣges	ʣgot	ʣgum	ɕp	4	ɕpes	ɕpot	ɕpum
lk	4	lkes	lkot	lkum	sk	4	skes	skot	skum
vx	5	vxes	vxot	vxum	xf	5	xfes	xfot	xfum
jm	5	jmes	jmot	jmum	vg	5	vges	vgot	vgum
ŋv	5	ŋves	ŋvot	ŋvum	fk	5	fkes	fkot	fkum
pk	6	pkes	pkot	pkum	kp	6	kpes	kpot	kpum
bg	6	bges	bgot	bgum	gb	6	gbes	gbot	gbum
xp	6	xpes	xpot	xpum	mx	6	mxes	mxot	mxum

Appendix H

Stimuli used in Experiment 2: Nonce words containing final CC clusters.

CC	POA	/ge/	/fa/	/no/	CC	POA	/ge/	/fa/	/no/
Non-existent well-formed words					*Existent well-formed words*				
ŋx	0	geŋx	faŋx	noŋx	ɕtɕ	0	geɕtɕ	faɕtɕ	noɕtɕ
sts	0	gests	fasts	nosts	ʃʧ	0	geʃʧ	faʃʧ	noʃʧ
xk	0	gexk	faxk	noxk	ɲtɕ	0	geɲtɕ	faɲtɕ	noɲtɕ
fp	1	gefp	fafp	nofp	ʃt	1	geʃt	faʃt	noʃt
sʧ	1	gesʧ	fasʧ	nosʧ	rs	1	gars	fers	nors
ʃʦ	1	geʃʦ	faʃʦ	noʃʦ	ʧt	1	geʧt	faʧt	noʧt
fʧ	2	gefʧ	fafʧ	nofʧ	sp	2	gesp	fasp	nosp
np	2	genp	fanp	nonp	lm	2	gelm	falm	nolm
ŋʧ	3	geŋʧ	faŋʧ	noŋʧ	js	3	gejs	fajs	nojs
rŋ	3	gerŋ	farŋ	norŋ	rk	3	gerk	fark	nork
ʃk	3	geʃk	faʃk	noʃk	mʃ	3	gemʃ	famʃ	nomʃ
ʧk	3	geʧk	faʧk	noʧk	ftɕ	3	geftɕ	faftɕ	noftɕ
xʧ	3	gexʧ	faxʧ	noxʧ	ʧp	3	geʧp	faʧp	noʧp
lŋ	4	gelŋ	falŋ	nolŋ	lk	4	gelk	falk	nolk
nk	4	genk	fank	nonk	sk	4	gesk	fask	nosk
nx	4	genx	fanx	nonx	mɕ	4	gemɕ	famɕ	nomɕ
ŋʦ	4	geŋʦ	faŋʦ	noŋʦ	ɕp	4	geɕp	faɕp	noɕp
ŋf	5	geŋf	faŋf	noŋf	jm	5	gejm	fajm	nojm
mk	6	gemk	famk	nomk	fk	5	gefk	fafk	nofk
ŋp	6	geŋp	faŋp	noŋp	jp	5	gejp	fajp	nojp
xp	6	gexp	faxp	noxp	mx	6	gemx	famx	nomx

(continued)

P. Orzechowska, *Complexity in Polish Phonotactics*, Prosody, Phonology and Phonetics, https://doi.org/10.1007/978-981-13-7299-5

(continued)

CC	POA	/ge/	/fa/	/no/	CC	POA	/ge/	/fa/	/no/
Non-existent ill-formed words					*Existent ill-formed words*				
sʃ	1	gesʃ	fasʃ	nosʃ	kx	0	gekx	fakx	nokx
ʦf	1	geʦf	faʦf	noʦf	tf	1	getf	fatf	notf
ʦʃ	1	geʦʃ	faʦʃ	noʦʃ	fn	1	gefn	fafn	nofn
ʧs	1	geʧs	faʧs	noʧs	nr	1	genr	fanr	nonr
ʧʦ	1	geʧʦ	faʧʦ	noʧʦ	tr	1	gatr	fetr	notr
fʃ	2	gefʃ	fafʃ	nofʃ	fr	2	gefr	fafr	nofr
pʦ	2	gepʦ	fapʦ	nopʦ	ps	2	geps	faps	nops
ʃf	2	geʃf	faʃf	noʃf	pt	2	gept	fapt	nopt
tp	2	getp	fatp	notp	mn	2	gemn	famn	nomn
ʧf	2	geʧf	faʧf	noʧf	ɕl	2	geɕl	faɕl	noɕl
kʃ	3	gekʃ	fakʃ	nokʃ	xʃ	3	gexʃ	faxʃ	noxʃ
kʧ	3	gekʧ	fakʧ	nokʧ	pʧ	3	gepʧ	fapʧ	nopʧ
ʧx	3	geʧx	faʧx	noʧx	ʃx	3	geʃx	faʃx	noʃx
tk	4	getk	fatk	notk	kl	4	gekl	fakl	nokl
ʦx	4	geʦx	faʦx	noʦx	pʨ	4	gepʨ	fapʨ	nopʨ
tx	4	getx	fatx	notx	pɲ	4	gepɲ	fapɲ	nopɲ
fx	5	gefx	fafx	nofx	kf	5	gakf	fokf	nekf
xf	5	gexf	faxf	noxf	kf	5	gekf	fakf	nokf
kp	6	gekp	fakp	nokp	xm/km	6	gakm	foxm	nekm
pk	6	gepk	fapk	nopk	xm	6	gexm	faxm	noxm
px	6	gepx	fapx	nopx	km	6	gekm	fakm	nokm

Appendix I

The results of the *Principal Component Analysis* for initial and final clusters: importance of components and PCA loadings. Parts 1–8 refer to each set of clusters.

'SD' refers to Standard Deviation, 'P.Var.' refers to Proportion of Variance, 'C. Prop' refers to Cumulative Proportion.

Part 1. Initial phonotactic clusters: importance of components

	Comp.1	Comp.2	Comp.3	Comp.4	Comp.5	Comp.6	Comp.7
SD	0.353580	0.288204	0.260953	0.2285708	0.207404	0.1935021	0.1839182
P.Var.	0.200098	0.132944	0.108991	0.0836199	0.068850	0.0599293	0.0541399
C.Prop.	0.200098	0.333043	0.442034	0.5256547	0.594505	0.6544344	0.7085743

	Comp.8	Comp.9	Comp.10	Comp.11	Comp.12	Comp.13
SD	0.16922412	0.14945023	0.12795453	0.12533802	0.11925867	0.11721898
P.Var.	0.04583452	0.03574879	0.02620472	0.02514397	0.02276397	0.02199197
C.Prop.	0.7544088	0.7901576	0.8163624	0.8415063	0.8642703	0.8862623

	Comp.14	Comp.15	Comp.16	Comp.17	Comp.18	Comp.19
SD	0.10846330	0.10292390	0.09467212	0.08995835	0.08473629	0.08053698
P.Var.	0.01882928	0.01695511	0.01434539	0.01295243	0.01149230	0.01038147
C.Prop.	0.9050915	0.9220467	0.9363920	0.9493445	0.9608368	0.9712182

	Comp.20	Comp.21	Comp.22	Comp.23	Comp.24	Comp.25
SD	0.0747342	0.06623754	0.06023685	0.0423672	0.03877057	0.02628084
P.Var.	0.0089393	0.00702225	0.00580754	0.0028729	0.00240587	0.00110546
C.Prop.	0.9801576	0.98717991	0.99298746	0.9958604	0.99826629	0.99937176

P. Orzechowska, *Complexity in Polish Phonotactics*, Prosody, Phonology and Phonetics, https://doi.org/10.1007/978-981-13-7299-5

	Comp.26
SD	0.019811935
P.Var.	0.000628234
C.Prop.	1.000000000

Part 2. Initial phonotactic clusters: PCA loadings

	Comp.1	Comp.2	Comp.3	Comp.4	Comp.5	Comp.6	Comp.7	Comp.8	Comp.9	Comp.10
V1	−0.137	0.114	−0.070	0.255	−0.167	0.016	−0.033	0.115	−0.153	−0.075
V2	−0.163	0.554	−0.316	0.636	−0.036	−0.083	−0.118	−0.146	0.043	0.158
V3	0.045	−0.002	0.043	0.012	−0.026	−0.013	−0.138	0.072	−0.157	−0.225
V4	0.003	−0.008	0.040	0.011	0.007	0.007	0.002	0.007	0.014	−0.099
V5	0.033	−0.030	0.053	−0.009	0.053	−0.026	−0.095	0.008	0.019	−0.070
V6	−0.033	0.019	−0.077	0.018	−0.033	−0.078	0.033	0.001	−0.014	−0.122
V7	−0.055	0.021	−0.128	0.022	−0.070	0.047	0.069	0.052	−0.177	−0.182
V8	−0.013	0.013	−0.062	0.188	0.082	0.114	0.524	−0.100	−0.128	−0.290
V9	0.008	0.006	−0.049	−0.064	−0.045	−0.027	−0.070	−0.018	−0.094	0.550
V10	0.068	−0.075	−0.277	−0.027	0.017	0.032	0.013	−0.040	0.024	0.015
V11	0.028	0.089	0.155	0.013	−0.079	0.032	0.706	−0.228	−0.160	0.176
V12	0.220	−0.231	−0.818	−0.140	0.197	0.010	0.098	−0.103	0.024	−0.033
V13	0.007	0.014	−0.045	−0.061	−0.017	0.023	0.044	0.076	−0.226	−0.098
V14	0.205	0.203	−0.046	0.011	0.148	−0.054	−0.062	0.501	−0.579	−0.172
V15	0.067	0.190	0.008	−0.088	−0.144	−0.082	0.145	0.074	0.380	−0.180
V16	0.035	0.097	−0.029	−0.177	0.080	0.119	0.038	−0.064	−0.275	0.47
V17	−0.386	−0.089	−0.249	−0.179	−0.716	0.173	0.053	0.246	−0.064	0.060
V18	0.013	−0.056	−0.073	0.021	0.037	0.029	−0.165	0.031	0.073	0.116
V19	0.054	0.060	0.008	0.052	0.241	−0.133	0.088	0.135	0.092	0.016
V20	0.027	−0.100	0.084	0.070	−0.006	−0.076	0.057	0.150	−0.223	0.251
V21	0.564	0.022	0.080	0.116	−0.358	0.409	−0.234	−0.428	−0.174	−0.108
V22	0.009	0.688	−0.052	−0.536	0.102	0.272	−0.005	0.014	0.118	−0.060
V23	0.171	0.014	0.002	0.019	−0.014	0.017	0.003	0.035	−0.055	0.014
V24	0.000	0.071	−0.012	−0.085	−0.028	−0.142	−0.024	−0.093	−0.066	−0.010
V25	0.449	−0.010	0.006	0.231	−0.103	0.267	0.191	0.564	0.375	0.200
V26	−0.379	−0.144	0.041	0.156	0.369	0.745	−0.051	0.050	0.008	−0.059

Part 3. Initial morphonotactic clusters: importance of components

	Comp.1	Comp.2	Comp.3	Comp.4	Comp.5	Comp.6	Comp.7
SD	0.353580	0.288204	0.260953	0.2285708	0.207404	0.1935021	0.1839182
P.Var.	0.200098	0.132944	0.108991	0.0836199	0.068850	0.0599293	0.0541399
C.Prop.	0.200098	0.333043	0.442034	0.5256547	0.594505	0.6544344	0.7085743

	Comp.8	Comp.9	Comp.10	Comp.11	Comp.12	Comp.13
SD	0.1692241	0.1494502	0.1279545	0.1253380	0.1192586	0.1172189
P.Var.	0.0458345	0.0357487	0.0262047	0.0251439	0.0227639	0.0219919
C.Prop.	0.7544088	0.7901576	0.8163624	0.8415063	0.8642703	0.8862623

	Comp.14	Comp.15	Comp.16	Comp.17	Comp.18	Comp.19
SD	0.1084633	0.1029239	0.0946721	0.0899583	0.0847362	0.0805369
P.Var.	0.0188292	0.0169551	0.0143453	0.0129524	0.0114923	0.0103814
C.Prop.	0.9050915	0.9220467	0.9363920	0.9493445	0.9608368	0.9712182

	Comp.20	Comp.21	Comp.22	Comp.23	Comp.24	Comp.25
SD	0.0747342	0.06623754	0.06023685	0.0423672	0.03877057	0.02628084
P.Var.	0.0089393	0.00702225	0.00580754	0.0028729	0.00240587	0.00110546
C.Prop.	0.9801576	0.98717991	0.99298746	0.9958604	0.99826629	0.99937176

	Comp.26
SD	0.0198119354
P.Var.	0.0006282348
C.Prop.	1.0000000000

Part 4. Initial morphonotactic clusters: PCA loadings

	Comp.1	Comp.2	Comp.3	Comp.4	Comp.5	Comp.6	Comp.7	Comp.8	Comp.9	Comp.10
V1	−0.137	0.114	−0.070	0.255	−0.167	0.016	−0.033	0.115	−0.153	−0.075
V2	−0.163	0.554	−0.316	0.636	−0.036	−0.083	−0.118	−0.146	0.043	0.158
V3	0.045	−0.002	0.043	0.012	−0.026	−0.013	−0.138	0.072	−0.157	−0.225
V4	0.003	−0.008	0.040	0.011	0.007	0.007	0.002	0.007	0.014	−0.099
V5	0.033	−0.030	0.053	−0.009	0.053	−0.026	−0.095	0.008	0.019	−0.070
V6	−0.033	0.019	−0.077	0.018	−0.033	−0.078	0.033	0.001	−0.014	−0.122
V7	−0.055	0.021	−0.128	−0.022	−0.070	0.047	0.069	0.052	−0.177	−0.182
V8	−0.013	0.013	−0.062	0.188	0.082	0.114	0.524	−0.100	−0.128	−0.290
V9	0.008	0.006	−0.049	−0.064	0.045	0.027	−0.070	−0.018	−0.094	0.550
V10	0.068	−0.075	−0.277	−0.027	0.017	0.032	0.013	−0.040	0.024	0.015
V11	0.028	0.089	0.155	0.013	−0.079	0.032	0.706	−0.228	−0.160	0.176
V12	0.220	−0.231	−0.818	−0.140	0.197	0.010	0.098	−0.103	0.024	−0.033
V13	0.007	0.014	−0.045	−0.061	−0.017	0.023	0.044	0.076	−0.226	−0.098
V14	0.205	0.203	−0.046	0.011	0.148	−0.054	−0.062	0.501	−0.579	−0.172
V15	0.067	0.190	0.008	−0.088	−0.144	−0.082	0.145	0.074	0.380	−0.180
V16	0.035	0.097	−0.029	−0.177	0.080	0.119	0.038	−0.064	−0.275	0.476

(continued)

(continued)

	Comp.1	Comp.2	Comp.3	Comp.4	Comp.5	Comp.6	Comp.7	Comp.8	Comp.9	Comp.10
V17	−0.386	−0.089	−0.249	−0.179	−0.716	0.173	0.053	0.246	−0.064	0.060
V18	0.013	−0.056	−0.073	0.021	0.037	0.029	−0.165	0.031	0.073	0.116
V19	0.054	0.060	0.008	0.052	0.241	−0.133	0.088	0.135	0.092	0.016
V20	0.027	−0.100	0.084	0.070	−0.006	−0.076	0.057	0.150	−0.223	0.251
V21	0.564	0.022	0.080	0.116	−0.358	0.409	−0.234	−0.428	−0.174	−0.108
V22	0.009	0.688	−0.052	−0.536	0.102	0.272	−0.005	0.014	0.118	−0.060
V23	0.171	0.014	0.002	0.019	−0.014	0.017	0.003	0.035	−0.055	0.014
V24	0.000	0.071	−0.012	−0.085	−0.028	−0.142	−0.024	−0.093	−0.066	−0.01
V25	0.449	−0.010	0.006	0.231	−0.103	0.267	0.191	0.564	0.375	0.200
V26	−0.379	−0.144	0.041	0.156	0.369	0.745	−0.051	0.050	0.008	−0.059

Part 5. Final phonotactic clusters: importance of components

	Comp.1	Comp.2	Comp.3	Comp.4	Comp.5	Comp.6	Comp.7
SD	0.077598	0.335438	0.307156	0.291184	0.2514556	0.230899	0.200320
P.Var.	0.212225	0.143619	0.120422	0.108224	0.0807068	0.068051	0.051219
C.Prop.	0.212225	0.355844	0.476267	0.584491	0.6651986	0.733249	0.784469

	Comp.8	Comp.9	Comp.10	Comp.11	Comp.12	Comp.13
SD	0.176642	0.158254	0.1339657	0.1280264	0.1188895	0.115229
P.Var.	0.039826	0.031966	0.0229073	0.0209212	0.0180416	0.016947
C.Prop.	0.824296	0.856263	0.8791706	0.9000918	0.9181334	0.935081

	Comp.14	Comp.15	Comp.16	Comp.17	Comp.18	Comp.19
SD	0.1046623	0.1004021	0.08643639	0.07445535	0.06545584	0.05754667
P.Var.	0.0139819	0.0128669	0.00953632	0.00707586	0.00546870	0.00422696
C.Prop.	0.9490632	0.9619301	0.97146646	0.97854233	0.98401104	0.98823800

	Comp.20	Comp.21	Comp.22	Comp.23	Comp.24	Comp.25
SD	0.056667396	0.048881222	0.040963899	0.031905200	0.030305162	0
P.Var.	0.004098778	0.003049805	0.002141857	0.001299304	0.001172252	0
C.Prop.	0.992336782	0.995386586	0.997528443	0.998827748	1.000000000	1

	Comp.26
SD	0
P.Var.	0
C.Prop.	1

Part 6. Final phonotactic clusters: PCA loadings

	Comp.1	Comp.2	Comp.3	Comp.4	Comp.5	Comp.6	Comp.7	Comp.8	Comp.9	Comp.10
V1	0.025	0.012	0.346	−0.454	−0.199	−0.580	−0.019	−0.092	0.044	0.102
V2	−0.009	−0.017	0.005	−0.087	−0.082	−0.129	0.007	0.031	−0.157	−0.338
V3										
V4	0.022	−0.048	−0.011	−0.016	0.064	0.030	0.053	0.077	0.060	−0.170
V5	−0.032	0.012	0.017	0.045	0.052	−0.044	−0.054	0.100	0.042	−0.288
V6	−0.029	0.031	−0.109	−0.010	−0.105	0.030	−0.357	−0.328	0.453	0.178
V7	−0.050	−0.042	0.043	−0.071	−0.033	−0.247	−0.014	−0.147	−0.063	0.021
V8	0.121	−0.487	−0.074	−0.538	0.353	0.139	0.113	0.306	−0.198	0.099
V9	0.023	0.009	0.018	−0.077	0.116	0.081	−0.204	−0.088	0.014	−0.024
V10	−0.064	−0.261	−0.337	0.041	−0.293	−0.147	0.014	−0.101	−0.216	−0.267
V11	0.124	−0.035	0.071	−0.264	0.273	0.280	−0.321	−0.159	0.246	0.068
V12	−0.071	−0.452	−0.557	−0.084	−0.264	−0.091	−0.066	−0.091	0.207	0.135
V13	0.010	0.038	−0.038	−0.010	−0.029	0.136	−0.132	0.071	−0.036	−0.045
V14	0.472	0.068	0.122	−0.237	−0.426	0.263	−0.058	−0.232	−0.294	0.086
V15	0.239	0.274	−0.291	−0.220	0.313	−0.186	0.335	−0.461	0.075	−0.258
V16	−0.260	0.083	−0.085	−0.090	0.247	−0.100	−0.635	−0.141	−0.425	−0.187
V17	0.043	−0.029	−0.061	0.052	−0.159	0.011	−0.097	0.070	−0.041	−0.233
V18	0.029	−0.008	0.055	−0.083	−0.085	0.168	0.164	−0.017	0.196	−0.083
V19	−0.061	−0.012	0.105	0.136	0.030	0.016	0.119	−0.149	−0.257	0.061
V20	0.509	−0.132	−0.068	0.388	0.272	−0.458	−0.165	0.126	−0.053	0.325
V21	−0.145	−0.186	0.049	0.156	0.062	0.162	0.178	−0.503	−0.372	0.357
V22	0.370	−0.079	−0.017	0.113	0.028	0.070	−0.056	−0.083	−0.002	−0.252
V23	0.204	0.311	−0.184	−0.105	−0.306	0.064	−0.186	0.292	−0.180	0.203
V24	0.370	−0.079	−0.017	0.113	0.028	0.070	−0.056	−0.083	−0.002	−0.252
V25	−0.053	0.483	−0.495	−0.164	0.116	−0.014	0.132	0.115	−0.116	0.225
V26	−0.051	0.006	0.139	−0.161	−0.070	−0.192	−0.001	−0.010	0.041	0.008

Part 7. Final morphonotactic clusters: importance of components

	Comp.1	Comp.2	Comp.3	Comp.4	Comp.5	Comp.6	Comp.7
SD	0.4077598	0.335438	0.307156	0.291184	0.2514556	0.230899	0.2003202
P.Var.	0.212225	0.143619	0.120422	0.108224	0.0807068	0.068051	0.051219
C.Prop.	0.212225	0.355844	0.476267	0.584491	0.6651986	0.733249	0.7844695

	Comp.8	Comp.9	Comp.10	Comp.11	Comp.12	Comp.13
SD	0.1766421	0.1582543	0.13396577	0.12802642	0.11888956	0.11522922
P.Var.	0.0398269	0.0319668	0.02290739	0.02092123	0.01804161	0.01694779
C.Prop.	0.8242964	0.8562632	0.87917062	0.90009185	0.91813346	0.93508125

	Comp.14	Comp.15	Comp.16	Comp.17	Comp.18	Comp.19
SD	0.10466232	0.10040217	0.086436393	0.074455357	0.065455848	0.057546671
P.Var.	0.01398198	0.01286691	0.009536328	0.007075869	0.005468709	0.00422696
C.Prop.	0.9490632	0.9619301	0.97146646	0.97854233	0.98401104	0.98823800

	Comp.20	Comp.21	Comp.22	Comp.23	Comp.24	Comp.25
SD	0.056667396	0.048881222	0.040963899	0.031905200	0.030305162	0
P.Var.	0.004098778	0.003049805	0.002141857	0.001299304	0.001172252	0
C.Prop.	0.992336782	0.995386586	0.997528443	0.998827748	1.000000000	1

	Comp.26
SD	0
P.Var.	0
C.Prop.	1

Part 8. Final morphonotactic clusters: PCA loadings

	Comp.1	Comp.2	Comp.3	Comp.4	Comp.5	Comp.6	Comp.7	Comp.8	Comp.9	Comp.10
V1	0.025	0.012	0.346	−0.454	−0.199	−0.580	−0.019	−0.092	0.044	0.102
V2	−0.009	−0.017	0.005	−0.087	−0.082	−0.129	0.007	0.031	−0.157	−0.338
V3										
V4	0.022	−0.048	−0.011	−0.016	0.064	0.030	0.053	0.077	0.060	−0.170
V5	−0.032	0.012	0.017	0.045	0.052	−0.044	−0.054	0.100	0.042	−0.288
V6	−0.029	0.031	−0.109	−0.010	−0.105	0.030	−0.357	−0.328	0.453	0.178
V7	−0.050	−0.042	0.043	−0.071	−0.033	−0.247	−0.014	−0.147	−0.063	0.021
V8	0.121	−0.487	−0.074	−0.538	0.353	0.139	0.113	0.306	−0.198	0.099
V9	0.023	0.009	0.018	−0.077	0.116	0.081	−0.204	−0.088	0.014	−0.024
V10	−0.064	−0.261	−0.337	0.041	−0.293	−0.147	0.014	−0.101	−0.216	−0.267
V11	0.124	−0.035	0.071	−0.264	0.273	0.280	−0.321	−0.159	0.246	0.068
V12	−0.071	−0.452	−0.557	−0.084	−0.264	−0.091	−0.066	−0.091	0.207	0.135
V13	0.010	0.038	−0.038	−0.010	−0.029	0.136	−0.132	0.071	−0.036	−0.045
V14	0.472	0.068	0.122	−0.237	−0.426	0.263	−0.058	−0.232	−0.294	0.086
V15	0.239	0.274	−0.291	−0.220	0.313	−0.186	0.335	−0.461	0.075	−0.258
V16	−0.260	0.083	−0.085	−0.090	0.247	−0.100	−0.635	−0.141	−0.425	−0.187
V17	0.043	−0.029	−0.061	0.052	−0.159	0.011	−0.097	0.070	−0.041	−0.233
V18	0.029	−0.008	0.055	−0.083	−0.085	0.168	0.164	−0.017	0.196	−0.083
V19	−0.061	−0.012	0.105	0.136	0.030	0.016	0.119	−0.149	−0.257	0.061
V20	0.509	−0.132	−0.068	0.388	0.272	−0.458	−0.165	0.126	−0.053	0.325
V21	−0.145	−0.186	0.049	0.156	0.062	0.162	0.178	−0.503	−0.372	0.357
V22	0.370	−0.079	−0.017	0.113	0.028	0.070	−0.056	−0.083	−0.002	−0.252
V23	0.204	0.311	−0.184	−0.105	−0.306	0.064	−0.186	0.292	−0.180	0.203
V24	0.370	−0.079	−0.017	0.113	0.028	0.070	−0.056	−0.083	−0.002	−0.252
V25	−0.053	0.483	−0.495	−0.164	0.116	−0.014	0.132	0.115	−0.116	0.225
V26	−0.051	0.006	0.139	−0.161	−0.070	−0.192	−0.001	−0.010	0.041	0.008

Appendix J

The results of quantile regression for fixed factors in Experiment 1. Quantiles 0.1–0.9 corresponds to each decile of reaction times.

0.1	Estimate Std.	Error	z value	Pr(>|z|)
(Intercept)	0.0809	0.0010	77.5059	0.0000
ExistenceEX	−0.0003	0.0015	−0.2227	0.8237
SonorityWF	0.0000	0.0005	−0.0018	0.9985
ExistenceEX:SonorityWF	0.0003	0.0006	0.4738	0.6356

0.2	Estimate Std.	Error	z value	Pr(>|z|)
(Intercept)	0.0850	0.0011	77.6723	0.0000
ExistenceEX	−0.0007	0.0015	−0.4384	0.6611
SonorityWF	0.0001	0.0004	0.2927	0.7698
ExistenceEX:SonorityWF	0.0006	0.0006	0.9498	0.3422

0.3	Estimate Std.	Error	z value	Pr(>|z|)
(Intercept)	0.0882	0.0011	78.4672	0.0000
ExistenceEX	−0.0007	0.0016	−0.4190	0.6752
SonorityWF	−0.0002	0.0004	−0.4361	0.6628
ExistenceEX:SonorityWF	0.0010	0.0006	1.5811	0.1139

P. Orzechowska, *Complexity in Polish Phonotactics*, Prosody, Phonology and Phonetics, https://doi.org/10.1007/978-981-13-7299-5

0.4	Estimate Std.	Error	z value	Pr(>|z|)
(Intercept)	0.0906	0.0011	80.7157	0.0000
ExistenceEX	−0.0007	0.0016	−0.4633	0.6432
SonorityWF	−0.0001	0.0004	−0.1509	0.8801
ExistenceEX:SonorityWF	0.0012	0.0006	1.9352	0.0530

0.5	Estimate Std.	Error	z value	Pr(>|z|)
(Intercept)	0.0927	0.0011	83.2207	0.0000
ExistenceEX	−0.0006	0.0016	−0.3710	0.7106
SonorityWF	0.0002	0.0004	0.4287	0.6681
ExistenceEX:SonorityWF	0.0010	0.0006	1.7246	0.0846

0.6	Estimate Std.	Error	z value	Pr(>|z|)
(Intercept)	0.0947	0.0011	86.0652	0.0000
ExistenceEX	−0.0003	0.0015	−0.2114	0.8326
SonorityWF	0.0003	0.0004	0.6695	0.5032
ExistenceEX:SonorityWF	0.0008	0.0006	1.4074	0.1593

0.7	Estimate Std.	Error	z value	Pr(>|z|)
(Intercept)	0.0968	0.0011	88.4107	0.0000
ExistenceEX	−0.0002	0.0015	−0.1479	0.8825
SonorityWF	0.0001	0.0004	0.3422	0.7322
ExistenceEX:SonorityWF	0.0010	0.0006	1.7590	0.0786

0.8	Estimate Std.	Error	z value	Pr(>|z|)
(Intercept)	0.0991	0.0011	90.0005	0.0000
ExistenceEX	0.0000	0.0015	0.0010	0.9992
SonorityWF	0.0001	0.0004	0.1914	0.8482
ExistenceEX:SonorityWF	0.0009	0.0005	1.6542	0.0981

0.9	Estimate Std.	Error	z value	Pr(>|z|)
(Intercept)	0.1020	0.0011	92.0427	0.0000
ExistenceEX	0.0004	0.0016	0.2808	0.7789
SonorityWF	0.0002	0.0004	0.5697	0.5689
ExistenceEX:SonorityWF	0.0005	0.0005	0.9562	0.3390

Appendix K

The results of the quantile regression for fixed factors in Experiment 2. Quantiles 0.1–0.9 corresponds to each decile of reaction times.

0.1	Estimate Std.	Error	z value	Pr(>|z|)
(Intercept)	0.4686	0.0019	240.5173	0.0000
ExistenceEX	0.0004	0.0027	0.1315	0.8954
SonorityWF	−0.0003	0.0007	−0.3791	0.7046
ExistenceEX:SonorityWF	0.0009	0.0010	0.9215	0.3568

0.2	Estimate Std.	Error	z value	Pr(>|z|)
(Intercept)	0.4751	0.0019	247.1497	0.0000
ExistenceEX	0.0009	0.0027	0.3319	0.7400
SonorityWF	−0.0007	0.0006	−1.1086	0.2676
ExistenceEX:SonorityWF	0.0011	0.0009	1.2477	0.2121

0.3	Estimate Std.	Error	z value	Pr(>|z|)
(Intercept)	0.4797	0.0019	253.1605	0.0000
ExistenceEX	0.0008	0.0027	0.2823	0.7777
SonorityWF	−0.0007	0.0006	−1.1173	0.2639
ExistenceEX:SonorityWF	0.0015	0.0009	1.6489	0.0992

P. Orzechowska, *Complexity in Polish Phonotactics*, Prosody, Phonology and Phonetics, https://doi.org/10.1007/978-981-13-7299-5

0.4	Estimate Std.	Error	z value	Pr(>|z|)
(Intercept)	0.4829	0.0019	258.8765	0.0000
ExistenceEX	0.0011	0.0026	0.4006	0.6887
SonorityWF	−0.0003	0.0006	−0.4456	0.6559
ExistenceEX:SonorityWF	0.0014	0.0008	1.6621	0.0965

0.5	Estimate Std.	Error	z value	Pr(>|z|)
(Intercept)	0.4857	0.0019	260.3564	0.0000
ExistenceEX	0.0015	0.0026	0.5651	0.5720
SonorityWF	0.0000	0.0006	−0.0839	0.9331
ExistenceEX:SonorityWF	0.0012	0.0008	1.4645	0.1431

0.6	Estimate Std.	Error	z value	Pr(>|z|)
(Intercept)	0.4883	0.0019	260.1808	0.0000
ExistenceEX	0.0018	0.0027	0.6665	0.5051
SonorityWF	0.0000	0.0006	0.0661	0.9473
ExistenceEX:SonorityWF	0.0013	0.0008	1.6295	0.1032

0.7	Estimate Std.	Error	z value	Pr(>|z|)
(Intercept)	0.4910	0.0019	255.0082	0.0000
ExistenceEX	0.0018	0.0027	0.6522	0.5142
SonorityWF	0.0001	0.0006	0.2343	0.8148
ExistenceEX:SonorityWF	0.0015	0.0008	1.8312	0.0671

0.8	Estimate Std.	Error	z value	Pr(>|z|)
(Intercept)	0.4940	0.0020	245.9315	0.0000
ExistenceEX	0.0018	0.0028	0.6356	0.5251
SonorityWF	0.0003	0.0006	0.4564	0.6481
ExistenceEX:SonorityWF	0.0016	0.0008	1.8363	0.0663

0.9	Estimate Std.	Error	z value	Pr(>|z|)
(Intercept)	0.4981	0.0021	236.3385	0.0000
ExistenceEX	0.0018	0.0030	0.6165	0.5375
SonorityWF	0.0003	0.0006	0.4150	0.6782
ExistenceEX:SonorityWF	0.0019	0.0009	2.1121	0.0347

Appendix L

Citation forms of initial clusters in Madelska's (2005) dictionary. Cluster types 'cl' are ordered according to size. 'W' and 'WT' refer to word types starting with a cluster and word tokens.

no	cl	W	WT	no	cl	W	WT	no	cl	W	WT	no	cl	W	WT
2	bj	25	29	2	xw	22	39	2	ʧw	18	75	3	fsp	38	63
2	bl	13	18	2	kɕ	18	42	2	tw	6	7	3	fst	23	29
2	br	38	69	2	kf	5	11	2	vʥ	1	1	3	ftr	1	1
2	bw	7	7	2	kj	32	116	2	vj	148	777	3	gvj	6	6
2	bʑ	1	1	2	kl	22	98	2	vl	3	3	3	kfj	1	2
2	bʒ	2	2	2	kr	48	56	2	vm	1	1	3	krf	1	1
2	ɕf	1	2	2	kʃ	7	10	2	vn	1	1	3	kʃt	1	1
2	ɕl	6	6	2	kt	36	310	2	vɲ	5	7	3	mɕʨ	1	1
2	ɕɲ	4	5	2	kw	17	31	2	vr	38	83	3	sxr	6	9
2	ɕp	7	19	2	mj	105	485	2	vw	49	526	3	sxʃ	1	1
2	ɕr	25	59	2	ml	1	1	2	vz	2	2	3	skj	2	3
2	ɕʨ	11	16	2	mn	7	27	2	vʑ	10	20	3	skl	5	7
2	dj	3	3	2	mɲ	14	229	2	vʒ	6	20	3	skr	10	11
2	dl	6	187	2	mʃ	3	7	2	wb	1	1	3	skw	8	8
2	dm	1	1	2	mw	15	20	2	zb	10	13	3	spj	1	1
2	dɲ	10	62	2	mʒ	1	1	2	zd	87	166	3	spr	28	90
2	dr	28	102	2	px	1	1	2	zg	25	34	3	spʃ	12	14
2	dv	30	143	2	pj	94	246	2	zj	9	9	3	spw	1	2
2	dw	11	25	2	pl	28	45	2	zl	2	2	3	stf	2	3
2	ʥv	7	9	2	pr	186	714	2	zm	12	21	3	str	61	191
2	fɕ	5	14	2	ps	14	18	2	zn	76	376	3	stʃ	2	2
2	fx	9	16	2	pʃ	467	937	2	zɲ	7	11	3	ʃkl	1	2
2	fj	4	4	2	pw	21	28	2	zr	62	159	3	ʃkw	2	2

(continued)

P. Orzechowska, *Complexity in Polish Phonotactics*, Prosody, Phonology and Phonetics, https://doi.org/10.1007/978-981-13-7299-5

(continued)

no	cl	W	WT	no	cl	W	WT	no	cl	W	WT	no	cl	W	WT
2	fk	3	3	2	sf	31	93	2	zv	30	39	3	tfj	7	8
2	fp	14	26	2	sx	6	7	2	zw	19	30	3	trf	10	13
2	fr	11	14	2	sk	49	62	2	zʒ	1	1	3	vbr	1	1
2	fʃ	34	310	2	sm	7	9	2	ʑʥ	6	7	3	vzl	1	1
2	ft	6	77	2	sn	1	1	2	ʑl	2	15	3	vzr	3	3
2	ftɕ	6	7	2	sp	117	246	3	bzd	1	2	3	zbj	10	12
2	fʦ	1	10	2	st	175	348	3	bʒd	1	1	3	zdj	3	6
2	fʧ	11	36	2	sʦ	7	17	3	ɕfj	24	39	3	zdr	5	7
2	gd	10	37	2	sw	66	107	3	ɕmj	14	24	3	zgɲ	1	1
2	gʥ	9	74	2	ʃf	1	1	3	ɕpj	7	8	3	zgr	3	6
2	gj	1	1	2	ʃk	22	130	3	drʒ	1	1	3	zgw	4	4
2	gm	3	3	2	ʃl	3	4	3	dvj	2	28	3	zgʒ	1	1
2	gɲ	1	1	2	ʃp	5	23	3	dʒv	1	2	3	zmj	21	44
2	gr	62	129	2	ʃt	4	4	3	fɕr	5	6	3	zvj	17	30
2	gv	8	11	2	ʃʧ	16	46	3	fɕtɕ	1	1	3	zvr	8	8
2	gw	35	62	2	ʃw	3	13	3	fkl	2	2	3	zvw	1	6
2	gʒ	7	8	2	tɕf	6	13	3	fkr	4	4	4	bʒmj	1	1
2	xf	13	44	2	tf	13	16	3	fkw	1	1	4	dʒvj	1	2
2	xl	2	2	2	tl	1	1	3	fpj	2	2	4	fstr	2	2
2	xm	1	1	2	tr	77	279	3	fpl	1	1	4	fstʃ	2	2
2	xr	2	2	2	ʦw	3	3	3	fpr	3	3	4	stfj	9	25
2	xʃ	2	2	2	tʃ	47	138	3	fpw	8	13	4	vzdw	1	1
2	xtɕ	24	104	2	ʧf	15	47	3	fsx	1	1	4	vzgl	15	48
2	xʦ	4	33	2	ʧt	15	56	3	fsk	2	2				

Reference

Madelska, L. 2005. *Słownik Wariantywności Fonetycznej Współczesnej Polszczyzny*. Kraków: Collegium Collumbinum.

Appendix M

Matched ('yes' = target) and mismatched ('no' = modified) realizations of initial cluster targets in Madelska's (2005) dictionary.

size	cl	word		word tok.		size	cl	word		word tok.	
		no	yes	no	yes			no	yes	no	yes
2	bj		25		29	2	ʧw	4	14	4	71
2	bl		13		18	2	tw	1	5	1	6
2	br		38		69	2	vʥ		1		1
2	bw		7		7	2	vj	30	118	123	654
2	bʑ		1		1	2	vl		3		3
2	bʒ		2		2	2	vm		1		1
2	ɕf		1		2	2	vn		1		1
2	ɕl		6		6	2	vɲ		5		7
2	ɕɲ	1	3	1	4	2	vr		38		83
2	ɕp		7		19	2	vw	16	33	102	424
2	ɕr		25		59	2	vz		2		2
2	ɕʨ		11		16	2	vʑ		10		20
2	dj		3		3	2	vʒ		6		20
2	dl	3	3	15	172	2	wb		1		1
2	dm		1		1	2	zb		10		13
2	dɲ		10		62	2	zd	7	80	7	159
2	dr	2	26	2	100	2	zg		25		34
2	dv		30		143	2	zj		9		9
2	dw	2	9	2	23	2	zl		2		2
2	ʥv	1	6	1	8	2	zm		12		21
2	fɕ		5		14	2	zn	8	68	83	293
2	fh		9		16	2	zɲ		7		11
2	fj		4		4	2	zr	10	52	34	125

(continued)

P. Orzechowska, *Complexity in Polish Phonotactics*, Prosody, Phonology and Phonetics, https://doi.org/10.1007/978-981-13-7299-5

(continued)

size	cl	word		word tok.		size	cl	word		word tok.	
		no	yes	no	yes			no	yes	no	yes
2	fk		3		3	2	zv		30		39
2	fp		14		26	2	zw	1	18	1	29
2	fr		11		14	2	zʒ		1		1
2	fʃ	8	26	16	294	2	ʑʥ	1	5	1	6
2	ft	1	5	3	74	2	ʑl		2		15
2	fʨ	1	5	1	6	3	bzd		1		2
2	fʦ		1		10	3	bʒd		1		1
2	fʧ	2	9	2	34	3	ɕfj	3	21	3	36
2	gd	1	9	1	36	3	ɕmj		14		24
2	gʥ	5	4	28	46	3	ɕpj		7		8
2	gj		1		1	3	drʒ		1		1
2	gm	1	2	1	2	3	dvj		2		28
2	gɲ		1		1	3	dʒv	1		2	
2	gr	1	61	1	128	3	fɕr	1	4	1	5
2	gv		8		11	3	fɕʨ		1		1
2	gw	7	28	12	50	3	fkl		2		2
2	gʒ		7		8	3	fkr		4		4
2	hf	3	10	3	41	3	fkw		1		1
2	hl		2		2	3	fpj		2		2
2	hm		1		1	3	fpl		1		1
2	hr		2		2	3	fpr		3		3
2	hʃ		2		2	3	fpw		8		13
2	hʨ	3	21	3	101	3	fsh		1		1
2	hʦ		4		33	3	fsk		2		2
2	hw	4	18	4	35	3	fsp	12	26	17	46
2	kɕ	1	17	1	41	3	fst	2	21	2	27
2	kf		5		11	3	ftr		1		1
2	kj	2	30	2	114	3	gvj		6		6
2	kl		22		98	3	kfj		1		2
2	kr	1	47	1	55	3	krf		1		1
2	kʃ		7		10	3	kʃt		1		1
2	kt	15	21	36	274	3	mɕʨ		1		1
2	kw	1	16	1	30	3	shr		6		9
2	mj	1	104	1	484	3	shʃ		1		1
2	ml		1		1	3	skj		2		3
2	mn	1	6	1	26	3	skl		5		7
2	mɲ	9	5	74	155	3	skr		10		11
2	mʃ		3		7	3	skw	1	7	1	7
2	mw		15		20	3	spj		1		1

(continued)

(continued)

size	cl	word		word tok.		size	cl	word		word tok.	
		no	yes	no	yes			no	yes	no	yes
2	mʒ		1		1	3	spr		28		90
2	ph		1		1	3	spʃ	1	11	1	13
2	pj	5	89	5	241	3	spw		1		2
2	pl	1	27	1	44	3	stf		2		3
2	pr	6	180	10	704	3	str	9	52	10	181
2	ps		14		18	3	stʃ	2		2	
2	pʃ	28	439	44	893	3	ʃkl		1		2
2	pw		21		28	3	ʃkw		2		2
2	sf	2	29	2	91	3	tfj		7		8
2	sh		6		7	3	trf	2	8	2	11
2	sk		49		62	3	vbr		1		1
2	sm		7		9	3	vzl	1		1	
2	sn		1		1	3	vzr		3		3
2	sp	3	114	3	243	3	zbj		10		12
2	st	12	163	12	336	3	zdj	1	2	1	5
2	sʦ		7		17	3	zdr		5		7
2	sw	14	52	21	86	3	zgɲ		1		1
2	ʃf		1		1	3	zgr		3		6
2	ʃk	2	20	2	128	3	zgw		4		4
2	ʃl	1	2	2	2	3	zgʒ		1		1
2	ʃp		5		23	3	zmj		21		44
2	ʃt	1	3	1	3	3	zvj	3	14	3	27
2	ʃʧ		16		46	3	zvr	1	7	1	7
2	ʃw		3		13	3	zvw		1		6
2	ʨf	1	5	1	12	4	bʒmj		1		1
2	tf		13		16	4	dʒvj	1		2	
2	tl		1		1	4	fstr	1	1	1	1
2	tr	3	74	3	276	4	fstʃ		2		2
2	ʦw		3		3	4	stfj	1	8	1	24
2	tʃ	17	30	53	85	4	vzdw		1		1
2	ʧf	1	14	1	46	4	vzgl	10	5	34	14
2	ʧt	1	14	1	55						

Reference

Madelska, L. 2005. *Słownik Wariantywności Fonetycznej Współczesnej Polszczyzny*. Kraków: Collegium Collumbinum.

Appendix N

Citation forms of final clusters in Madelska's (2005) dictionary. Cluster types 'cl' are ordered according to size. 'W' and 'WT' refer to word types starting with a cluster and word tokens.

no	cl	W	WT	no	cl	W	WT	no	cl	W	WT	no	cl	W	WT
2	ɕm	1	1	2	lm	2	15	2	rs	1	1	wt	1	1	
2	ɕp	1	1	2	mɕ	9	31	2	rt	10	11	jɕʨ	14	28	
2	ɕʨ	92	157	2	mp	5	6	2	rw	2	2	ĵɕʨ	5	18	
2	fʦ	1	1	2	ns	2	2	2	sk	2	2	jsʦ	1	1	
2	hɕ	5	17	2	nt	59	84	2	sm	9	9	kst	3	3	
2	jɕ	6	15	2	nʦ	53	181	2	st	50	789	ntʃ	5	5	
2	ĵɕ	6	18	2	ɲʨ	48	81	2	sw	7	7	ŋkt	2	2	
2	jk	5	26	2	ŋk	9	14	2	ʃʧ	1	1	str	3	3	
2	kl	3	7	2	ps	2	2	2	tr	3	10	ŵsk	1	1	
2	ks	6	12	2	pt	1	1	2	tʃ	1	1	ŵsw	1	1	
2	kt	16	35	2	rf	6	18	2	tw	14	16				
2	kw	3	8	2	rm	1	1	2	ŵs	4	9				

Reference

Madelska, L. 2005. *Słownik Wariantywności Fonetycznej Współczesnej Polszczyzny*. Kraków: Collegium Collumbinum.

P. Orzechowska, *Complexity in Polish Phonotactics*, Prosody, Phonology and Phonetics, https://doi.org/10.1007/978-981-13-7299-5

Appendix O

Matched ('yes' = target) and mismatched ('no' = modified) realizations of final cluster targets in Madelska's (2005) dictionary.

size	cl	word		word tok.		size	cl	word		word tok.	
		no	yes	no	yes			no	yes	no	yes
2	ɕm		1		1	2	rm		1		1
2	ɕp		1		1	2	rs		1		1
2	ɕʨ	62	30	109	48	2	rt	4	6	4	7
2	fʦ	1		1		2	rw		2		2
2	hɕ	4	1	16	1	2	sk	1	1	1	1
2	jɕ	3	3	4	11	2	sm	6	3	6	3
2	ĵɕ	2	4	8	10	2	st	32	18	600	189
2	jk	2	3	2	24	2	sw	2	5	2	5
2	kl		3		7	2	ʃʧ		1		1
2	ks		6		12	2	tr		3		10
2	kt	7	9	25	10	2	tʃ		1		1
2	kw		3		8	2	tw	4	10	4	12
2	lm		2		15	2	ŵs		4		9
2	mɕ	3	6	4	27	2	wt		1		1
2	mp	1	4	1	5	3	jɕʨ	9	5	19	9
2	ns	2		2		3	ĵɕʨ	4	1	14	4
2	nt	21	38	25	59	3	jsʦ		1		1
2	nʦ	2	51	3	178	3	kst	1	2	1	2
2	ɲʨ	12	36	19	62	3	ntʃ	2	3	2	3
2	ŋk	3	6	4	10	3	ŋkt		2		2
2	ps		2		2	3	str	1	2	1	2
2	pt		1		1	3	ŵsk		1		1
2	rf	1	5	2	16	3	ŵsw	1		1	

P. Orzechowska, *Complexity in Polish Phonotactics*, Prosody, Phonology and Phonetics, https://doi.org/10.1007/978-981-13-7299-5

Reference

Madelska, L. 2005. *Słownik Wariantywności Fonetycznej Współczesnej Polszczyzny*. Kraków: Collegium Collumbinum.

Appendix P

Logarithmically-transformed usage frequencies of initial clusters and their reduction rate (ordered in a decreasing order of log freq). The column 'WT' lists raw token frequencies of clusters in the dictionary of Madelska (2005). 'Log' provides the corresponding logarithmic frequencies (Log10), rounded to the nearest tens. The column '%' presents the rate of cluster modification, calculated for the total number of tokens for a given cluster.

cl	WT	Log	%	cl	WT	Log	%	cl	WT	Log	%
Word-initial clusters											
pʃ	937	2.97	5	fp	26	1.41	4	gm	3	0.48	33
vj	777	2.89	16	dw	25	1.40	0	dj	3	0.48	0
pr	714	2.85	1	stfj	25	1.40	8	fk	3	0.48	0
vw	526	2.72	19	ɕmj	24	1.38	4	ʦw	3	0.48	0
mj	485	2.69	0	ʃp	23	1.36	0	vl	3	0.48	0
zn	376	2.58	22	zm	21	1.32	0	fpr	3	0.48	0
st	348	2.54	3	mw	20	1.30	0	vzr	3	0.48	0
kt	310	2.49	12	vʑ	20	1.30	0	skj	3	0.48	0
fʃ	310	2.49	5	vʒ	20	1.30	0	stf	3	0.48	0
tr	279	2.45	1	ɕp	19	1.28	0	stʃ	2	0.30	100
pj	246	2.39	2	ps	18	1.26	0	dʒv	2	0.30	100
sp	246	2.39	1	bl	18	1.26	0	dʒvj	2	0.30	100
mɲ	229	2.36	32	sts	17	1.23	0	fstr	2	0.30	50
str	191	2.28	5	tf	16	1.20	0	bʒ	2	0.30	0
dl	187	2.27	8	ɕʨ	16	1.20	0	xl	2	0.30	0
zd	166	2.22	4	fx	16	1.20	0	xr	2	0.30	0
zr	159	2.20	21	ʑl	15	1.18	0	xʃ	2	0.30	0
dv	143	2.16	0	spʃ	14	1.15	0	vz	2	0.30	0
tʃ	138	2.14	38	fr	14	1.15	7	zl	2	0.30	0

(continued)

P. Orzechowska, *Complexity in Polish Phonotactics*, Prosody, Phonology and Phonetics, https://doi.org/10.1007/978-981-13-7299-5

(continued)

cl	WT	Log	%	cl	WT	Log	%	cl	WT	Log	%
ʃk	130	2.11	2	fɕ	14	1.15	0	fkl	2	0.30	0
gr	129	2.11	1	trf	13	1.11	0	fpj	2	0.30	0
kj	116	2.06	2	ʨf	13	1.11	15	fsk	2	0.30	0
sw	107	2.03	20	zb	13	1.11	8	ʃkw	2	0.30	0
xʨ	104	2.02	3	fpw	13	1.11	0	fstʃ	2	0.30	0
dr	102	2.01	2	ʃw	13	1.11	0	ɕf	2	0.30	0
kl	98	1.99	0	zbj	12	1.08	0	bzd	2	0.30	0
sf	93	1.97	2	skr	11	1.04	0	kfj	2	0.30	0
spr	90	1.95	0	gv	11	1.04	0	spw	2	0.30	0
vr	83	1.92	0	zɲ	11	1.04	0	ʃkl	2	0.30	0
ft	77	1.89	4	kf	11	1.04	0	vzl	1	0.00	100
ʧw	75	1.88	5	kʃ	10	1.00	0	bʑ	1	0.00	0
gʥ	74	1.87	38	fʦ	10	1.00	0	dm	1	0.00	0
br	69	1.84	0	ʣv	9	0.95	0	gj	1	0.00	0
fsp	63	1.80	27	zj	9	0.95	11	gɲ	1	0.00	0
gw	62	1.79	19	sm	9	0.95	0	xm	1	0.00	0
sk	62	1.79	0	sxr	9	0.95	0	ml	1	0.00	0
dɲ	62	1.79	0	skw	8	0.90	0	mʒ	1	0.00	0
ɕr	59	1.77	0	zvr	8	0.90	13	px	1	0.00	0
kr	56	1.75	2	gʒ	8	0.90	13	sn	1	0.00	0
ʧt	56	1.75	2	ɕpj	8	0.90	0	ʃf	1	0.00	0
vzgl	48	1.68	71	tfj	8	0.90	0	tl	1	0.00	0
ʧf	47	1.67	2	fʨ	7	0.85	0	vʥ	1	0.00	0
ʃʧ	46	1.66	0	tw	7	0.85	14	vm	1	0.00	0
pl	45	1.65	2	ʑʥ	7	0.85	14	vn	1	0.00	0
xf	44	1.64	7	bw	7	0.85	14	wb	1	0.00	0
zmj	44	1.64	0	sx	7	0.85	0	zʒ	1	0.00	0
kɕ	42	1.62	2	vɲ	7	0.85	0	bʒd	1	0.00	0
xw	39	1.59	10	skl	7	0.85	0	drʒ	1	0.00	0
ɕfj	39	1.59	8	zdr	7	0.85	0	fɕʨ	1	0.00	0
zv	39	1.59	0	mʃ	7	0.85	0	fkw	1	0.00	0
gd	37	1.57	3	fɕr	6	0.78	0	fpl	1	0.00	0
fʧ	36	1.56	6	zdj	6	0.78	17	fsx	1	0.00	0
zg	34	1.53	0	ɕl	6	0.78	17	ftr	1	0.00	0
xʦ	33	1.52	0	gvj	6	0.78	0	krf	1	0.00	0
kw	31	1.49	3	zgr	6	0.78	0	kʃt	1	0.00	0
zvj	30	1.48	10	zvw	6	0.78	0	mɕʨ	1	0.00	0
zw	30	1.48	3	ɕɲ	5	0.70	0	sxʃ	1	0.00	0
fst	29	1.46	7	ʃl	4	0.60	20	spj	1	0.00	0
bj	29	1.46	0	ʃt	4	0.60	50	vbr	1	0.00	0

(continued)

(continued)

cl	WT	Log	%	cl	WT	Log	%	cl	WT	Log	%
pw	28	1.45	0	fj	4	0.60	25	zgɲ	1	0.00	0
dvj	28	1.45	0	fkr	4	0.60	0	zgʒ	1	0.00	0
mn	27	1.43	0	zgw	4	0.60	0	bʒmj	1	0.00	0
								vzdw	1	0.00	0
Word-final clusters											
st	789	2.90	76	ŋk	14	1.15	29	ps	2	0.30	0
nʦ	181	2.26	2	ks	12	1.08	0	rw	2	0.30	0
ɕʨ	157	2.20	69	rt	11	1.04	36	fʦ	1	0.00	100
nt	84	1.92	30	tr	10	1.00	0	ŵsw	1	0.00	100
ɲʨ	81	1.91	23	sm	9	0.95	67	ɕm	1	0.00	0
kt	35	1.54	71	ŵs	9	0.95	0	ɕp	1	0.00	0
mɕ	31	1.49	13	kw	8	0.90	0	jsʦ	1	0.00	0
jɕʨ	28	1.45	68	sw	7	0.85	29	pt	1	0.00	0
jk	26	1.41	8	kl	7	0.85	0	rm	1	0.00	0
ĵɕʨ	18	1.26	78	mp	6	0.78	17	rs	1	0.00	0
ĵɕ	18	1.26	44	ntʃ	5	0.70	40	ʃʧ	1	0.00	0
rf	18	1.26	11	kst	3	0.48	33	tʃ	1	0.00	0
xɕ	17	1.23	94	str	3	0.48	33	ŵsk	1	0.00	0
tw	16	1.20	25	ns	2	0.30	100	wt	1	0.00	0
jɕ	15	1.18	27	sk	2	0.30	50				
lm	15	1.18	0	ŋkt	2	0.30	0				

Reference

Madelska, L. 2005. *Słownik Wariantywności Fonetycznej Współczesnej Polszczyzny*. Kraków: Collegium Collumbinum.

The manufacturer's authorised representative in the EU is Springer Nature Customer Service Centre GmbH, Europaplatz 3, 69115 Heidelberg, Germany. If you have any concerns regarding our products, please contact ProductSafety@springernature.com

Printed and bound by CPI Group (UK) Ltd, Croydon, CR0 4YY
25/09/2026
02222900-0016